A

NEW LOOK

AT

Old Words

STREET SLANG FROM THE

1600s TO THE 1800s

Designed and Edited by

Catherine Thrush

Based on

A DICTIONARY OF MODERN SLANG, CANT, AND VULGAR WORDS

by

John Camden Hotten

ISBN: 978-0-9914788-3-5

CONTENTS

Contents

Contents

Contents

Contents

INTRODUCTION

Broadly speaking, the short words are the best, and the old words best of all.
Winston Churchill

When I first came across a book titled *The Dictionary of Nautical, University, Gypsy and Other Vulgar Tongues: A Guide to Language on the 18th and 19th Century Streets of London*, I thought; Oh my God! This is exactly what I need!

At the time, I was writing a historical fiction pirate novel set in the early 1700s and I was looking for colorful and authentic language to salt the dialog of my pirate crew.

The book was perfect. Not only was it about history, it *was* history. It was a reprint of a book written in 1860 by John Camden Hotten called *A Dictionary of Modern Slang, Cant and Vulgar Words*. I ordered it on the spot and waited impatiently for it to arrive. When it did finally appear, I read the introduction and the entire -A- section with excited interest.

However, when I sat down to write with the book next to me, a problem arose. To use a dictionary, one must know the word one wants to look up. I knew the definition, not the word. For example, I wanted a colorful name for a black eye. The only way to find what I wanted would be to read the entire book.

Undaunted, I embarked upon a nine-month project to categorize all the words so I could find them quickly and easily when and if I should need them. Recently it occurred to me this might be a useful resource for other writers, and fun for any lexicographers, linguists, or lovers of old words. So after some *elbow grease*, here it is.

Please be aware of what this book is *not*. It is not an exhaustive piece of historical research. I simply reorganized the work of Mr. Hotten. Anything he got wrong, I did too. It was sometimes difficult to tell what was a typo and what was truly representative of the times. Some of the spellings he used look unusual to modern readers, like Hindoo, Gipsey, and Shakespere. I kept his spellings since I thought they might be of interest to logophiles, or to someone trying to represent the period accurately. I've also kept much of Hotten's unorthodox punctuation; except in cases where I thought it would confusing or distracting to modern readers.

There are a number of entries that are not politically correct. I've kept them because this book is meant to present the words and ideas of the past—and in the hopes that by recognizing old mistaken ideas we will not be doomed to repeat them.

In the body of the text you will often see Hotten's notation "&c." which I take to mean "and company" or etcetera. Hotten also makes personal references occasionally, such as "But this I conceive to be an error." The intrusions are Hotten's not mine. Any additions I've made (outside of the chapter introductions) are for the purpose of clarification and are marked in brackets.

The organization process was subjective; to say the least. I had to make a lot of decisions on what should be included where. I aimed for being inclusive rather than exclusive, in the hopes of making finding the right word as easy and natural as possible. As a result, many words are in more than one place. The term "**Culling** or **Culing:** stealing from the carriages on racecourses," for example is under **Work & Professions: Professions-** Drivers as well as under **Crime & Punishment: Criminals and Crimes-** Gamblers- *Horse and Other Racing* and under **Crime & Punishment: Criminals and Crimes-** Thieves- *Thieving.* Even some categories are in more than one place, for example, *Horse Racing and Other Races"* is under both **Crime & Punishment** and **Entertainment.**

Many words have more than one definition. I've include all the definitions except in two cases. The words **Cut** and **Take** each had over a dozen meanings listed, which took up half a page or more each time they were included. For brevity's sake, on those two words I listed only the relevant meanings along with a note to see the full definition in the Index at the back of this book.

A quick note on the difference between *Cant* and *slang.* Cant was a secret language, originally developed by Gypsies and thieves to communicate in front of the uninitiated without being understood. It was very like code. In fact, vagabonds and beggars developed a symbolic code that they scratched onto buildings and fences to let others of their kind know what sort of treatment they received at a certain place. Cant, therefore, is ancient and slow to change. Slang, in contrast, is always modern, always changing with fashion and taste. Slang demonstrates that a person is "in," or current with pop culture or identifies the speaker as part of a group—something to keep in mind when choosing which words to use.

I'd also like to mention that there are a few words that I didn't have a place for or that I didn't understand well enough to place – even after reading the definition. So rather than stick such words *nilly-willy* into inappropriate categories, I have a spot for them at the end of the book in a section titled, Words I don't Understand. I'm happy to say it's a very small section.

Over the process of organizing this book I've come to love these words. Some are lyrical, a few are frightening, many are funny, and all of them give us a glimpse into life – both the good aspects and the bad – from the 1600 to the 1800s. I hope you enjoy them as much as I do.

Catherine Thrush
December 3, 2015

 # How to Use this book

If you're a writer like me, looking for just the right historic slang word, then the table of contents is your first friend. I've tried to be as granular as I could and group things in a logical manner.

In the body of the text, I've included wayfinding in the left header of each set of pages. Wayfinding identifies precisely where you are at the top of the left-hand page.

The first wayfinding phrase – **<u>bold and underlined</u>** - is the chapter or main category that you are currently in. Each chapter is set apart with an illustration, a couple paragraphs of commentary and a few of my favorite words from that chapter. The second phrase in the wayfinding - **in bold** - tells you which section of that chapter you are in. In the text, these would be the section headings in decorative boxes. The third -

plain text - phrase in the wayfinding is the sub-section, which in the text will have the double underline with the flourish. And the occasional fourth word or phrase in the wayfinding, -*in italics* - will be the sub-sub-section indicated in the text by a simple underline with a single chevron. So if you open the book at random you should be able to immediately tell exactly where you are.

At the beginning of each chapter I've also included a short table of contents.

Good luck on your search for the perfect word!

Slictionary

If you're done working and want to have some fun, then the book will be useful once again. Fictionary is a simple word game that can be played with a dictionary, paper and pencils and a few friends. All that is required is some imagination and a love of words. Slictionary is the same game played with this book of slang.

Number of Players: 4 and up.

Goal: To win the highest number of points in a predetermined number of rounds.

To Begin: A game lasts three rounds. A round concludes once each player has had a turn choosing the word and reading answers aloud.

To decide who goes first, each player in turn closes their eyes, opens *A New Look at Old Words* and puts a finger on a page at random. The player whose finger lands on the word that comes first in alphabetical order becomes the "chooser."

Order of Play:

- The "chooser" picks a word from *A New Look at Old Words*, announces and spells it to the other players. The word should be one that either no other player knows or that has a slang meaning that no other player knows. If a word has more than one definition, the chooser decides which one to use. The chooser writes it on one of the answer forms.

- Each player writes a crafty and credible definition of the word, initials it, and submits it to the chooser.
- The chooser collects and shuffles the definitions, including their own, which is the correct one. As definitions are handed in, the chooser should check them over to ensure that they can read the handwriting. Stumbling over or misreading a definition is usually a sign that it is not the correct one—unless the chooser is trying to bluff.
- Once all definitions are collected, the chooser reads them aloud, once. On the second reading, each other player votes for the definition he/she believes is correct. The chooser does not vote.
- Players earn two points for voting for the correct definition, and one point for each vote cast for the definition they wrote. The chooser earns three points if no one selects the correct definition.
- Play proceeds with *A New Look at Old Words* going to the player on the right, who starts a new turn. A full circuit of the players constitutes a round.

Strategy: A player may vote for their own definition, although they do not get points for doing so. (This can encourage other people to vote for that definition as well, and the player would get those points.) Players may decide beforehand whether lexicographic labels (e.g., *Old Cant, Saxon, Norfolk*, etc.) are to be included. *A New Look at Old Words* may be passed around first, to remind players of its characteristic style. Have fun!

IN MY HUMBLE OPINION

All slang is metaphor, and all metaphor is poetry.

Gilbert K. Chesterton

Complaining seems to be nothing new. There are nearly twice as many insults as compliments. Is it merely human nature to dwell on the negative? Were people in the past generally pessimistic? Or is it just that insults are so much more fun?

There can be social discomfort in a compliment. Complimenting can mean admitting that you're drawn to someone, which lets people see a bit of your soul.

Insults can be bandied about playfully like a shuttlecock or spewed with venom. A good-natured insult can be a compliment in disguise and a way to hide the giver's heart.

Then, as now, fools were not suffered lightly. There are more words for fools than for any other section in this category. It seems that what they did like, they loved. There are twice as many words for excellent as there are for good.

Editor's Faves:

BUFFLE HEAD: a stupid or obtuse person. —*Miege. German,* BUFFEL-HAUPT, buffalo-headed.

DIMBER DAMBER: very pretty; a clever rogue who excels his fellows; chief of a gang. *Old Cant* in the latter sense. —*English Rogue.*

KILKENNY CAT: a popular simile for a voracious or desperate animal or person, from the story of the two cats in that county, who are said to have fought and bitten each other until a small portion of the tail of one of them alone remained.

IN THIS CHAPTER

COMPLIMENTS

TO PRAISE

BLARNEY: flattery, exaggeration.—*Hibernicism.*

BUTTER or **BATTER:** praise or flattery. To **BUTTER**, to flatter, cajole.

CHI-IKE: a hurrah, a good word, or hearty praise.

CHUCKING A JOLLY: when a costermonger praises the inferior article his mate or partner is trying to sell.

CRACK-UP: to boast or praise.—*Ancient English.*

FILLIBRUSH: to flatter, praise ironically.

FLUMMERY: flattery, gammon, genteel nonsense.

JOLLY: a word of praise or favourable notice; "chuck Harry a **JOLLY**, Bill!" *i.e.,* go and praise up his goods or buy of him, and speak well of the article, that the crowd standing around his stall may think it a good opportunity to lay out their money. "Chuck a **JOLLY**," literally translated, is to throw a shout or a good word.

KOTOOING: misapplied flattery.—*Illustrated London News, 7th January, 1860.* Lord Bacon, however, used the word in a similar sense a century before.

PUFF: to blow up, swell with praise, was declared by a writer in the Weekly Register, as far back as 1732, to be illegitimate.

> "**PUFF** has become a *Cant* word, signifying the applause set forth by writers, &c. to increase the reputation and sale of a book, and is an excellent stratagem to excite the curiosity of gentle readers."

Lord Bacon, however, used the word in a similar sense a century before.

SALVE: praise, flattery, chaff.

SOAP: flattery.—*See* **SOFT-SOAP** *below.*

SOFT-SOAP or **SOFT-SAWDER:** flattery, ironical praise.

WIPE: to strike; "he fetcht me a WIPE over the knuckles," he struck me on the knuckles; "to WIPE a person down," to flatter or pacify a person; to WIPE off a score, to pay one's debts, in allusion to the slate or chalk methods of account keeping; "to WIPE a person's eye," to shoot game which he has missed—*Sporting term*; hence to gain an advantage by superior activity.

❧ GOOD and EXCELLENT (ALSO INTENSIFIERS)

A 1: first-rate, the very best; "she's a prime girl she is; she is A 1."—*Sam Slick*. The highest classification of ships at Lloyd's; common term in the United States, also at Liverpool and other English seaports. Another even more intensive form is:"first-class, letter A, No. 1."

ALL-THERE: in strict fashion, first-rate, "up to the mark." A vulgar person would speak of a spruce, showily-dressed female as being ALL-THERE. An artisan would use the same phrase to express the capabilities of a skillful fellow workman.

APPLE PIE ORDER: in exact or very nice order.

AWFUL: (or, with the Cockneys, ORFUL), a senseless expletive, used to intensify a description of anything good or bad; "what an AWFUL fine woman!" *i.e.*, how handsome or showy!

BANG: to excel or surpass; BANGING, great or thumping.

BANG-UP: first-rate.

BENE: good.—*Ancient Cant;* BENAR was the comparative.—*See* BONE *below. Latin.*

BOBBISH: very well, clever, spruce; "how are you doing?" "Oh! Pretty BOBBISH."

BONE: good, excellent. ◊, the vagabond's hieroglyphic for BONE, or good, chalked by them on houses and street corners, as a hint to succeeding beggars. *French,* BON.

CHEESE: anything good, first-rate in quality, genuine, pleasant, or advantageous, is termed THE CHEESE. *Mayhew* thinks CHEESE, in this sense, is from the *Saxon,* CEOSAN, to choose, and quotes *Chaucer,* who uses CHESE in the sense of choice. The *London Guide,* 1818, says it was from some young fellow translating "c'est une autre CHOSE" into

20

"that is another **CHEESE**." **CHEESE** is also *Gipsey* and *Hindoo*; and *Persian*, **CHIZ**, a thing. — *See* **STILTON** *page 22.*

CLIPPING: excellent, very good.

CRACK: first-rate, excellent; "a **CRACK HAND**," an adept; a "**CRACK** article," a good one. — *Old.*

CRUSHING: excellent, first-rate.

DON: a clever fellow, the opposite of a muff; a person of distinction in his line or walk. At the Universities, the Masters and Fellows are **THE DONS**. **DON** is also used as an adjective, "a **DON** hand at a knife and fork," *i.e.*, a first-rate feeder at a dinner table. — *Spanish.*

FIZZING: first-rate, very good, excellent; synonymous with **STUNNING**.

OUT AND OUT: prime, excellent, of the first quality. **OUT AND OUTER**, "one who is of an **OUT AND OUT** description," **UP** to anything. An ancient MS. has this couplet, which shows the antiquity of the phrase—

> "The Kyng was good alle aboute,
>   And she was wycked *oute and oute.*"

PINK: the *acmé* of perfection. — *Shakespere.*

PLUMMY: round, sleek, jolly, or fat; excellent, very good, first-rate.

REAM: good or genuine. From the *Old Cant*, **RUM**.

RIPPER: a first-rate man or article. — *Provincial.*

RIPPING: excellent, very good.

ROOTER: anything good or of a prime quality; "that *is* a **ROOTER**," *i.e.*, a first-rate one of the sort.

RUM: like its opposite, **QUEER**, was formerly a much used prefix signifying fine, good, gallant, or valuable, perhaps in some way connected with **ROME**. Now-a-days it means indifferent, bad, or questionable, and we often hear even persons in polite society use such a phrase as "what a **RUM** fellow he is, to be sure," in speaking of a man of singular habits or appearance. The term, from its frequent use, long since claimed a place in our dictionaries; but, with the exception of *Johnson*, who says "**RUM**, a *Cant* word for a clergyman(?)," no lexicographer has deigned to notice it.

"Thus RUMLY floor'ed, the kind Acestes ran.
And pitying, rais'd from earth the game old man.
—*Virgil's Æneid,* book v., Translation by Thomas Moore.

SCREAMING: first-rate, splendid. Believed to have been first used in the *Adelphi* play-bills; "a SCREAMING farce," one calculated to make the audience scream with laughter. Now a general expression.

SHIP-SHAPE: proper, in good order; sometimes the phrase is varied to "SHIP-SHAPE and *Bristol* fashion." — *Sea.*

SLAP-UP: first-rate, excellent, very good.

SPLENDIFEROUS: sumptuous, first-rate.

STILTON: "that's the STILTON," or "it is not the STILTON," *i.e.,* that is quite the thing or that is not quite the thing;—polite rendering of "that is not the CHEESE," —*See* CHEESE *page 20.*

STUNNER: a first-rate person or article.

STUNNING: first-rate, very good. "STUNNING pears," shouts the coster, "only eight a penny." — *Vide Athenæum,* 26th March, 1859. Sometimes amplified to STUNNING JOE BANKS! when the expression is supposed to be in its most intense form. JOE BANKS was a noted character in the last generation. He was the proprietor of a public-house in Dyott Street, Seven Dials, and afterwards, on the demolition of the Rookery, of another in Cranbourne-alley. His houses became well-known from their being the resort of the worst characters, at the same time that the strictest decorum was always maintained in them. JOE BANKS also acquired a remarkable notoriety by acting as a medium betwixt thieves and their victims. Upon the proper payment to Joe, a watch or a snuff box would at any time be restored to its lawful owner "no questions in any case being asked." The most daring depredators in London placed the fullest confidence in Joe, and it is believed (although the *Biographic Universelle* is quiet upon this point) that he never, in any instance, "sold" them. He was of the middle height, stout, and strongly made, and was always noted for a showy pin, and a remarkably STUNNING *neck-tie.* It was this peculiarity in the costume of Mr. Banks, coupled with those true and tried qualities as a friend, for which, as I have just remarked, he was famous, that led his customers to proclaim him as STUNNING JOE BANKS! The Marquis of Douro, Colonel Chatterley, and men of their stamp, were accustomed to resort to a private room at his house, when too late or too early to gain admittance to the clubs or more aristocratic establishments.

TIP-TOP: first-rate, of the best kind.

TO-RIGHTS: excellent, very well, or good.

TWIG: style, *à-la-mode;* "get your strummel faked in TWIG," *i.e.,* have your hair dressed in style; **PRIME TWIG,** in good order, and high spirits. — *Pugilistic*

GOOD-NATURED

BRICK: a "jolly good fellow;" "a regular **BRICK**," a staunch fellow.

> "I bonneted Whewell, when we gave the Rads their gruel,
> And taught them to eschew all their addresses to the Quean.
> If again they try it on, why to floor them I'll make one,
> Spite of Peeler or of Don, like a **BRICK** and a *Bean.*"
> — *The Jolly Bachelors, Cambridge,* 1810.

Said to be derived from an expression of Aristotle.

BUFFER: a familiar expression for a jolly acquaintance, probably from the *French*, **BOUFFARD,** a fool or clown; a "jolly old **BUFFER**," said of a good-humoured or liberal old man. In 1737, a **BUFFER** was a "rogue that killed good sound horses for the sake of their skins, by running a long wire into them." — *Bacchus and Venus.* The term was once applied to those who took false oaths for a consideration.

COXY-LOXY: good-tempered, drunk. — *Norfolk.*

JOLLY: a word of praise or favourable notice; "chuck Harry a **JOLLY,** Bill!" *i.e.,* go and praise up his goods or buy of him, and speak well of the article, that the crowd standing around his stall may think it a good opportunity to lay out their money. "Chuck a **JOLLY**," literally translated, is to throw a shout or a good word.

LUMMY: jolly, first-rate.

PICKLE: a miserable or comical position; "he is in a sad **PICKLE**," said of anyone who has fallen into the gutter or got besmeared. "A **PICKLE** herring," a comical fellow, a merry Andrew. — *Old.*

PLUMMY: round, sleek, jolly, or fat; excellent, very good, first-rate.

QUIZZICAL: jocose, humorous.

REAM-BLOAK: a good man.

SAD DOG: a merry fellow, a joker, a gay or "fast" man.

SQUARE: honest; "on the SQUARE," *i.e.*, fair and strictly honest; "to turn SQUARE," to reform, and get one's living in an honest manner. The opposite of CROSS.

SQUARE COVE: an honest man.

SWEET: loving or fond; "how SWEET he was upon the moll," *i.e.*, what marked attention he paid the girl.

TRUMP: a good fellow; "a regular TRUMP," a jolly or good natured person—in allusion to a TRUMP card; "TRUMPS may turn up," *i.e.*, fortune may yet favour me.

HIGH POSITION

BOSMAN: a farmer; "faking a BOSMAN on the main toby," robbing a farmer on the highway. **BOSS**, a master.—*American*. Both terms from the *Dutch*, BOSCH-MAN, one who lives in the woods; otherwise *Boshjeman* or *Bushman*.

COCK OF THE WALK: a master spirit, head of the party. Places where poultry are fed are called WALKS, and the barn-door cocks invariably fight for the supremacy till one has obtained it.

DAB or **DABSTER:** an expert person. Johnson says, "in low language, an artist."

DIMBER DAMBER: very pretty; a clever rogue who excels his fellows; chief of a gang. *Old Cant* in the latter sense. —*English Rogue*.

DON: a clever fellow, the opposite of a muff; a person of distinction in his line or walk. At the Universities, the Masters and Fellows are THE DONS. DON is also used as an adjective, "a DON hand at a knife and fork," *i.e.*, a first-rate feeder at a dinner table.—*Spanish*.

GOVERNOR: a father, a master or superior person, an elder; "which way, GUV'NER, to Cheapside?"

JAGGER: a gentleman.—*German*, JAGER, a sportsman.

NIBS: the master or chief person; a man with no means but high pretensions, a "shabby genteel."

NOB: a person of high position, a "swell," a *nob*leman—of which word it may be an abbreviation.—*See* SNOB *page 51.*

RAG SPLAWGER: a rich man.

RHINOCERAL: rich, wealthy, abounding in RHINO.

SWELL: a man of importance; a person with a showy, jaunty exterior; "a rank SWELL," a very "flashily" dressed person, a man who by excessive dress apes a higher position than he actually occupies. Anything is said to be SWELL or SWELLISH that looks showy, or is many-coloured, or is of a desirable quality. Dickens and Thackeray are termed great SWELLS in literature; so indeed are the first persons in the learned professions.

TOP-SAWYER: the principal of a party or profession. "A TOP-SAWYER signifies a man that is a master genius in any profession. It is a piece of *Norfolk* slang, and took its rise from Norfolk being a great timber county, where the *top* sawyers get double the wages of those beneath them."—*Randall's Diary,* 1820.

LARGE and FINE

BANG: to excel or surpass; BANGING, great or thumping.

BULGER: large; synonymous with BUSTER.

BUSTER: an extra size; "what a BUSTER," what a large one; "in for a BUSTER," determined on an extensive frolic or SPREE. *Scotch,* BUSTUOUS; *Icelandic,* BOSTRA.

HULKY: extra-sized.—*Shropshire.*

RAPPING: enormous: "a RAPPING big lie."

SPANKING: large, fine, or strong; e.g., a SPANKING pace, a SPANKING breeze, a SPANKING fellow.

SWINGING: large, huge.

THUMPING: large, fine, or strong.

THUNDERING: large, extra-sized.

WALLOPING: a beating or thrashing; sometimes in an adjective sense, as big or very large.

WAPPING or **WHOPPING:** of a large size, great.

WHACKING: large, fine, or strong.

NEAT and NEW

BRAN-NEW: quite new. Properly, *Brent*, **BRAND** or *Fire-new*, *i.e.*, fresh from the anvil.

DIMBER: neat or pretty.—*Worcestershire*, but *Old Cant*.

NATTY: pretty, neat, tidy.—*Old*.

SHIP-SHAPE: proper, in good order; sometimes the phrase is varied to "SHIP-SHAPE and *Bristol* fashion."—*Sea*.

SMUG: extremely neat, after the fashion, in order.

SPICK AND SPAN: applied to anything that is quite new and fresh. —*Hudibras*.

WHISTLE: "as clean as a WHISTLE," neatly or "SLICKLY done," as an American would say; "to WET ONE'S WHISTLE," to take a drink. This is a very old term. *Chaucer* says of the Miller of Trumpington's wife (*Canterbury Tales*, 4153):

> "So was hir joly WHISTAL well Y-WET;"

"to WHISTLE FOR ANYTHING," to stand small chance of getting it, from the nautical custom of *whistling* for a wind in a calm, which of course comes none the sooner for it.

PASSIONATE and BRAVE

BLOOD: a fast or high-mettled man. *Nearly obsolete* in the sense in which it was used in George the Fourth's time.

FANCY-BLOAK: a fancy or sporting man.

HACKLE: "to show HACKLE," to be willing to fight. **HACKLES** are the long feathers on the back of a cock's neck, which he erects when angry—hence the metaphor.

PLUCK'D-'UN: a stout or brave fellow; "he's a rare **PLUCK'D-'UN**," *i.e.,* dares face anything.

During the Crimean war, **PLUCKY**, signifying courageous, seemed likely to become a favourite term in May-Fair, even among the ladies. An eminent critic, however, who had been bred a butcher, having informed the fashionable world that in his native town the *sheep's head* always went with the **PLUCK**, the term has been gradually falling into discredit at the West End.

It has been said that a brave soldier is **PLUCKY** in attack, and **GAME** when wounded. Women are more **GAME** than **PLUCKY**.

SPITFIRE: a passionate person.

SPUNK: spirit, *fire*, courage, mettle.

> "In that snug room, where any man of SPUNK
> would find it a hard matter to get drunk."
> —*Peter Pindar*, i., 245

Common in *America*. For derivation see **SPUNKS** on page 308.

WOOL: courage, pluck; "you are not half-**WOOLLED**," term of reproach from one thief to another.

PERSONAL and PHYSICAL QUALITIES

RANDY: rampant, violent, warm, amorous. *North*, **RANDYBEGGAR**, a Gipsey tinker.

SKY-SCRAPER: a tall man; "are you cold up there, old **SKY-SCRAPER**?" Properly a sea term; the light sails which some adventurous skippers set above the royals in calm latitudes are termed **SKY-SCRAPERS** and **MOON-RAKERS**.

SPRY: Active, strong, manly.—*Americanism*.

TIGHT: close, stingy; hard up, short of cash; **TIGHT**, spruce, strong, active; "a **TIGHT** lad," a smart, active young fellow; **TIGHT**, drunk or nearly so; "**TIGHT**-laced," puritanical, over-precise. Money is said to be TIGHT when the public, from want of confidence in the aspect of affairs, are not inclined to speculate.

TONGUED: talkative; "to TONGUE a person," *i.e.,* talk him down.

WARM: rich or well-off.

 # SMART and SHARP

AWAKE or FLY: knowing, thoroughly understanding, not ignorant of. The phrase WIDE-AWAKE carries the same meaning in ordinary conversation.

BLADE: a man—in ancient times the term for a soldier; "knowing BLADE," a wide-awake, sharp, or cunning man.

BOBBISH: very well, clever, spruce; "how are you doing?" "Oh! Pretty BOBBISH."

CLOCK: "to know what's O'CLOCK," a definition of knowingness in general.—*See* TIME O'DAY *page 221.*

COCUM: advantage, luck, cunning, or sly, "to fight COCUM," to be wily and cautious.

CUTE: sharp, cunning. Abbreviation of ACUTE.

DIMBER DAMBER: very pretty; a clever rogue who excels his fellows; chief of a gang. *Old Cant* in the latter sense. —*English Rogue*

DON: a clever fellow, the opposite of a muff; a person of distinction in his line or walk. At the Universities, the Masters and Fellows are THE DONS. DON is also used as an adjective, "a DON hand at a knife and fork," *i.e.,* a first-rate feeder at a dinner table.—*Spanish.*

DUMMACKER: a knowing or acute person.

ELEPHANT: "to have SEEN THE ELEPHANT," to be "*up* to the latest move," or "*down* to the last new trick;" to be knowing, and not "green," &c. Possibly a metaphor taken from the travelling menageries, where the ELEPHANT is the *finale* of the exhibition. —Originally an *Americanism. Bartlett* gives conflicting examples. *General* now, however.

FILE: a deep or artful man, a jocose name for a cunning person. Originally a term for a pickpocket, when TO FILE was to cheat or rob.

FILE, an artful man, was used in the thirteenth and fourteenth centuries.

FLY: knowing, wide-awake, fully understanding another's meaning.

KNOWING: a slang term for sharpness, "KNOWING codger," or "a KNOWING blade," one who can take you in or cheat you, in any transaction you may have with him. It implies also deep cunning and foresight, and generally signifies dishonesty.

> "Who, on a spree with black-eyed Sal, his blowen,
> So swell, so prime, so nutty and so KNOWING."
> —*Don Juan*

LEARY: flash or knowing.

O'CLOCK or **A'CLOCK:** "like ONE O'CLOCK," a favourite comparison with the lower orders, implying briskness; "to know what O'CLOCK it is," to be wide-awake, sharp, and experienced.

RUMGUMPTION or **GUMPTION:** knowledge, capacity, capability, —hence, RUMGUMPTIOUS, knowing, wide-awake, forward, positive, pert, blunt.

SHAVER: a sharp fellow; "a young" or "old SHAVER," a boy or man. —*Sea.*

SLUM: gammon; "up to SLUM," wide-awake, knowing.

> "And this, without more SLUM, began,
> Over a flowing Pot-house can,
> To settle, without botheration,
> The rigs of this here tip-top nation"
> —*Jack Randall's Diary*, 1820

TIGHT: close, stingy; hard up, short of cash; TIGHT, spruce, strong, active; "a TIGHT lad," a smart, active young fellow; TIGHT, drunk or nearly so; "TIGHT-laced," puritanical, over-precise. Money is said to be TIGHT when the public, from want of confidence in the aspect of affairs, are not inclined to speculate.

TOOTH: "he has cut his eye TOOTH," *i.e.*, he is sharp enough or old enough, to be so; "up in the TOOTH," far advanced in age—said often of old maids. *Stable term* for aged horses which have lost the distinguishing mark in their teeth.

TRAP: "up to TRAP," knowing, wide-awake—synonymous with "up to SNUFF."

UP: "to be UP to a thing or two," to be knowing or understanding; "to put a man UP to a move," to teach him a trick; "it's all UP with him," *i.e.*, it is all over with him, often pronounced U.P., naming the two letters separately; "UP a tree." —*See* TREE *page 110.* "UP to TRAP," "UP to SNUFF," wide-awake, acquainted with the last new move; "UP to one's GOSSIP," to be a match for one who is trying to take you in; —"UP to SLUM," proficient in roguery, capable of committing a theft successfully.

WIDO: wide-awake, no fool.

 # WELL-DRESSED and GOOD-LOOKING

BUCK: a gay or smart man, cuckold.

CHEESY: fine or showy.

DASHING: showy, fast.

DIMBER: neat or pretty.—*Worcestershire*, but *Old Cant*.

DIMBER DAMBER: very pretty; a clever rogue who excels his fellows; chief of a gang. *Old Cant* in the latter sense. —*English Rogue.*

DOWN THE ROAD: stylish, showy, after the fashion.

FANCY-BLOAK: a fancy or sporting man.

FIG: "in full FIG," *i.e.*, full dress costume, "extensively got-up."

GORGER: a swell, a well-dressed, or *gorgeous* man—probably derived from that word.

NATTY: pretty, neat, tidy.—*Old.*

NINES: "dressed up to the NINES," in a showy or *recherché* manner.

NOBBY or **NOBBISH:** fine or showy; NOBBILY, showily.—*See* SNOB *for derivation on page 51.*

RIGGED: "well-RIGGED," well-dressed. *Old slang,* in use in 1736.—*See Bailey's Dictionary.* —*Sea.*

SCRUMPTIOUS: nice, particular, beautiful.

SPIFFY: spruce, well-dressed, *tout à la mode.*

SQUARE-RIGGED: well-dressed.—*Sea.*

SWELL: a man of importance; a person with a showy, jaunty exterior; "a rank SWELL," a very "flashily" dressed person, a man who by excessive dress apes a higher position than he actually occupies. Anything is said to be SWELL or SWELLISH that looks showy, or is many-coloured, or is of a desirable quality. Dickens and Thackeray are termed great SWELLS in literature; so indeed are the first persons in the learned professions.

SWELL or **SWELLISH:** anything showy, many-coloured or of a desirable quality.

SWELL HUNG IN CHAINS: said of a showy man in the habit of wearing much jewellery.

TIPTOPPER: a "swell," or dressy man, a "*Gorger.*"

TOFFICKY: dressy, showy.

TWIG: style, *à-la-mode*; "get your strummel faked in TWIG," *i.e.*, have your hair dressed in style; PRIME TWIG, in good order, and high spirits.—*Pugilistic.*

WOMEN

BREECHES: "to wear the BREECHES," said of a wife who usurps the husband's prerogative.

BURERK: a lady. *Grose* gives BURICK, a prostitute.

CHICKEN: a young girl.

FEELE: a daughter or child.—*Corrupted French.*

FLAME: a sweetheart.

FROW: a girl or wife. *German,* FRAU; *Dutch,* VROUW.

GIMCRACK: a bijou, a slim piece of mechanism. *Old slang* for "a spruce wench."—*N. Bailey.*

JOMER: a sweetheart or favourite girl.—*See* BLOWER *page 35.*

LUNAN: a girl.—*Gipsey.*

MOLL: a girl; nickname for Mary.—*Old Cant.*

MURERK: the mistress of the house.—*See* BURERK *page 31.*

MUSLIN: a woman or girl; "he picked up a bit of MUSLIN,"

PETTICOAT: a woman.

RACLAN: a married woman.—*Gipsey.*

RIB: a wife.—*North.*

RUMY: a good woman or girl.—*Gipsey slang.* In the regular *Gipsey* language, ROMI, a woman, a wife, is the feminine of RO, a man; and in the *Robber's Language* of Spain (partly *Gipsey,*) RUMI signifies a harlot.

SQUARE MOLL: an honest woman.

TOFFER: a well-dressed, "gay" woman.

# OTHER COMPLIMENTS

BREECHED or **TO HAVE THE BAGS OFF:** to have plenty of money; "to be well BREECHED," to be in good circumstances.

CHOCK-FULL: full till the scale comes down with a shock. *French,* CHOC. A correspondent suggests CHOKED-FULL.

FAT: rich, abundant, &c.; "a FAT lot;" "to cut it FAT," to exaggerate, to show off in an extensive or grand manner, to assume undue importance; "CUT UP FAT."—*See* CUT *page 479.* As a *Theatrical* term, a part with plenty of FAT in it, is one which affords the actor an opportunity of effective display.

GOLOPSHUS: splendid, delicious, luscious.—*Norwhich.*

JANNOCK: sociable, fair dealing.—*Norfolk.*

KIDDYISH: frolicsome, jovial.

> "Think on the KIDDYISH spree we had on such a day."
> —*Randall's Diary,* 1820.

SIMON PURE: "the real SIMON PURE," the genuine article. Those who have witnessed Mr. C. Mathews' performance in Mrs. Centlivre's admirable comedy of *A Bold Stroke for a Wife,* and the laughable coolness with which he, the *false* SIMON PURE, assuming the quaker dress and character of the REAL ONE, elbowed that worthy out of his expected entertainment, will at once perceive the origin of this phrase. — *See* act v., scene 1.

SMACK SMOOTH: even, level with the surface, quickly.

SQUARE: honest; "on the SQUARE," *i.e.*, fair and strictly honest; "to turn SQUARE," to reform, and get one's living in an honest manner. The opposite of CROSS.

TEETOTALLER: a total abstainer from alcoholic drinks.

THICK: intimate, familiar. *Scotch*, CHIEF; "the two are very CHIEF now," *i.e.*, friendly.

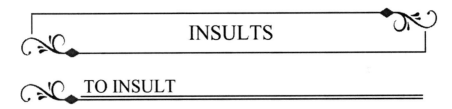

INSULTS

TO INSULT

CRAB: to offend or insult; to expose or defeat a robbery, to inform against.

FILLIBRUSH: to flatter, praise ironically.

FRUMP: to mock or insult. —*Beaumont and Fletcher.*

HOAX: to deceive or ridicule—*Grose* says was originally a *University Cant* word. Corruption of HOCUS, to cheat.

KOTOOING: misapplied flattery. —*Illustrated London News, 7th January, 1860.*

SIGHT: "to take a SIGHT at a person," a vulgar action employed by street boys to denote incredulity or contempt for authority, by placing the thumb against the nose and closing all the fingers except the little one, which is agitated in token of derision.—*See* WALKER *page 400.*

SLANG: to cheat, to abuse in foul language.

SOFT-SOAP or **SOFT-SAWDER:** flattery, ironical praise.

STUFF: to make false but plausible statements, to praise ironically, to make game of a person—literally, to STUFF or CRAM him with gammon or falsehood

BAD (ADJECTIVES, ALSO INTENSIFIERS)

AWFUL: (or, with the Cockneys, **ORFUL**), a senseless expletive, used to intensify a description of anything good or bad; "what an **AWFUL** fine woman!" *i.e.,* how handsome or showy!

BLACK-SHEEP: a "bad lot," "*mauvais sujet;*" also a workman who refuses to join in a strike.

DICKEY: bad, sorry, or foolish; food or lodging is pronounced **DICKEY** when of a poor description; "it's all **DICKEY** with him," *i.e.,* all over with him.

DOG-CHEAP or **DOG-FOOLISH:** very or singularly cheap, or foolish. Latham, in his *English Language,* says: "This has nothing to do with dogs. The first syllable is god = *good* transposed, and the second, the ch−p, is chapman, *merchant*: compare **EASTCHEAP**." *Old term.*

GALLOWS: very or exceedingly, a disgusting exclamation; "**GALLOWS** poor," very poor.

GAMMY: bad, unfavourable, poor-tempered. Those householders who are known enemies to the street folk and tramps are pronounced by them to be **GAMMY**. **GAMMY** sometimes means forged, as "**GAMMY MONEKER**," a forged signature; **GAMMY STUFF**, spurious medicine; **GAMMY LOWR**, counterfeit coin. *Hants,* **GAMY**, dirty. The hieroglyphic used by beggars and cadgers to intimate to those of the tribe coming after that things are not very favourable, is known as □, or **GAMMY**.

MULTEE KERTEVER: very bad. *—Italian,* **MOLTO CATTIVO**.

POTTY: indifferent, bad looking.

ROT: nonsense; anything bad, disagreeable, or useless.

ROUGH: bad; "**ROUGH** fish." bad or stinking fish.

RUM: like its opposite, **QUEER**, was formerly a much used prefix signifying fine, good, gallant, or valuable, perhaps in some way connected with **ROME**. Now-a-days it means indifferent, bad, or questionable, and we often hear even persons in polite society use such a phrase as "what a **RUM** fellow he is, to be sure," in speaking of a man of singular habits or appearance. The term, from its frequent use, long since claimed a place in our dictionaries; but, with the exception of *Johnson,* who says "**RUM**, a *Cant* word for a clergyman(?)," no lexicographer has deigned to notice it.

"Thus RUMLY floor'ed, the kind Acestes ran.
And pitying, rais'd from earth the game old man."
— *Virgil's Æneid*, book v., Translation by Thomas Moore.

CHILDREN

AREA-SNEAK: a boy thief who commits depredations upon kitchens and cellars.— *See* CROW *page 235.*

ARTICLE: a man or boy, derisive term.

BLOWER: a girl; a contemptuous name in opposition to JOMER.

BUZ-BLOAK: a pickpocket, who principally confines his attention to purses and loose cash. *Grose* gives BUZ-GLOAK (or CLOAK?), an *Ancient Cant* word. BUZ-NAPPER, a young pickpocket.

BYE-BLOW: a bastard child.

CHATTER BASKET: common term for a prattling child amongst nurses.

FAGOT: a term of opprobrium used by low people to children; "you little FAGOT, you!" FAGOT was originally a term of contempt for a dry, shriveled old woman, whose bones were like a bundle of sticks, only fit to burn. Compare the *French* expression for a heretic, *sentir le fagot.*

GRIFFIN: in India, a newly arrived cadet; general for an inexperienced youngster. "Fast" young men in London frequently term an umbrella a GRIFFIN.

LITTLE SNAKES-MAN: a little thief, who is generally passed through a small aperture to open any door to let in the rest of the gang.

MOLLISHER: a low girl or woman; generally a female cohabitating with a man, and jointly getting their living by thieving.

MOTT: a girl of indifferent character. Formerly *Mort. Dutch,* MOTT-KAST, a harlotry.

NIPPER: a small boy. *Old Cant* for a boy cut-purse.

SAUCEBOX: a mouth, also a pert young person.

VARMENT: "you young VARMENT, you!" you bad or naughty boy. Corruption of *vermin.*

COUNTRYMEN

CLOD-HOPPER: a country clown.

FLATTIES: rustic or uninitiated people.

HODGE: a countryman or provincial clown. I don't know that it has been elsewhere remarked, but most country districts in England have one or more families of the name of **HODGE**; indeed, **GILES** and **HODGE** appear to be the favourite hobnail nomenclature. Not in any way writing disrespectfully, was the slang word taken from Hog—with the *g* soft, which gives the *dg* pronunciation? In old canting dictionaries **HODGE** stands for a country clown; so, indeed, does **ROGER**, another favourite provincial name.—*Vide Bacchus and Venus.*

JOSKIN: a countryman.

LAND LUBBER: sea term for a landsman.—*See* **LOAFER** *page 62.*

SCOTCH FIDDLE: the itch; "to play the **SCOTCH FIDDLE,**" to work the index finger of the right hand like a fiddlestick between the index and middle finger of the left. This provokes a Scotchmen in the highest degree, it implying that he is afflicted with the itch.

SCOTCH GRAYS: lice. Our northern neighbours are calumniously reported, from their living on oatmeal, to be peculiarly liable to cutaneous eruptions and parasites.

SKIPPER-BIRDS or **KEYHOLE WHISTLERS:** persons who sleep in barns or outhouses in preference to lodging-houses.

SPLODGER: a lout, an awkward countryman.

WHOP-STRAW: *Cant* name for a countryman; *Johnny* **WHOPSTRAW,** in allusion to threshing.

YELLOW BELLY: a native of the Fens of Lincolnshire or the Isle of Ely, —in allusion to the frogs and a yellow-bellied eel caught there; they are also said to be *web-footed.*

YOKEL: a countryman.—*West.*

FOOLS and FOPS

BUFFLE HEAD: a stupid or obtuse person. —*Miege. German,* **BUFFEL-HAUPT**, buffalo-headed.

BUTTONS: "not to have all one's **BUTTONS**," to be deficient in intellect.

CAKE: a flat, a soft or doughy person, a fool.

CHUCKLE-HEAD: a fool.—*Devonshire.*

CRANKY: foolish, idiotic, ricketty, capricious, not confined to persons. *Ancient Cant,* **CRANKE**, simulated sickness. *German,* **KRANK**, sickly.

CUPBOARD-HEADED: an expressive designation for one whose head is both wooden and hollow.—*Norfolk.*

DANDY: a fop or fashionable nondescript. This word, in the sense of a fop, is of modern origin. *Egan* says it was first used in 1820, and *Bee* in 1816. *Johnson* does not mention it, although it is to be found in all late dictionaries. **DANDIES** wore stays, studied femininity, and tried to undo their manhood. Lord Petersham headed them. At the present day dandies of this stamp are fast disappearing. The feminine of **DANDY** was **DANDIZETTE**, but the term only lived for a short season.

DANDYPRAT: a funny little fellow, a mannikin; originally a half-farthing.

DEAD ALIVE: stupid, dull.

DUFFER: a hawker of "Brummagem" or sham jewelry; a sham of any kind; a fool or worthless person. **DUFFER** was formerly synonymous with **DUDDER**, and was a general term given to pedlars. It is mentioned in the *Frauds of London* (1760), as a word in frequent use in the last century to express cheats of all kinds. From the *German,* **DURFEN**, to want?

DUNDERHEAD: a blockhead.

FLAT: a fool, a silly or "soft" person, the opposite of **SHARP**. The term appears to be shortenings for "sharp-witted" and "flat-witted." "Oh! Messrs. Tyler, Donelson, and the rest, what **FLATS** you are."—*Times,* 5th September, 1847.

GAWKY: a lanky or awkward person; a fool. *Saxon,* **GEAC**; *Scotch,* **GOWK**.

GENT: a contraction of "gentleman," in more sense than one. A dressy, showy, foppish man, with a little mind, who vulgarizes the prevailing fashion.

GONNOF or **GUN:** a fool, a bungler, an amateur pickpocket. A correspondent thinks this may be a corruption of *gone off*, on the analogy of GO-ALONG; but the term is really as old as *Chaucer's* time. During Kett's rebellion in Norfolk, in the reign of Edward VI., a song was sung by the insurgents in which the term occurs:

> The country GNOFFES, Hob, Dick, and Hick,
> With clubbes and clouted shoou,
> Shall fill up Dussyn dale
> With slaughtered bodies soone.

GOOSECAP: a booby or noodle.—*Devonshire.*

GULPIN: a weak, credulous fellow.

HALF-BAKED: soft, doughy, half-witted, silly.

HALF FOOLISH: ridiculous; means often wholly foolish.

HALF-ROCKED: silly, half-witted. Compare HALF-BAKED above.

HORRID HORN: term of reproach amongst the street Irish, meaning a fool or half-witted fellow. From the *Erse* OMADHAUN, a brainless fellow. A correspondent suggests HERRIDAN, a miserable old woman.

JEMMY JESSAMY: a dandy.

LIGHTS: a "cake," a fool, a soft or "doughy" person.

LUBBER: a clown or fool.—*Ancient Cant,* LUBBARE.

MOLLYCODDLE: an effeminate man; one who caudles amongst the women or does their work.

MUFF: a silly or weak-minded person; MUFF has been defined to be "a soft thing that holds a lady's hand without squeezing it."

NATURAL: an idiot, a simpleton.

NINCOMPOOP: a fool, a hen-pecked husband, a "Jerry Sneak." Corruption of *non compos mentis.*

NIZZIE: a fool, a coxcomb. *Old Cant, vide Triumph, of Wit.*

PIGEON: a gullible or soft person. The *French* slang or *argot*, has the word PIGEON, dupe "PECHON, PECHON DE RUBY, apprenti gueux, enfant (sans doute dérobe)." The vagabonds and brigands of Spain also use the word in their *Germania* or *Robbers' Language*, PALOMO (pigeon), ignorant, simple.

ROCKED: "he's only HALF-ROCKED," *i.e.*, half-witted.

SAP or **SAPSCULL:** a poor green simpleton, with no heart for work.

SAWNEY: a simpleton.

SOFT: foolish, inexperienced. An old term for bank notes.

SOP: a soft or foolish man. Abbreviation of MILKSOP.

SPOON: synonymous with SPOONEY. A SPOON has been defined to be "a thing that touches a lady's lips without kissing them."

SPOONEY: a weak-minded and foolish person, effeminate or fond, "to be SPOONEY on a girl," to be foolishly attached to one.

TENPENCE TO THE SHILLING: a vulgar phrase denoting a deficiency in intellect.

UPPER STOREY or **UPPER LOFT:** a person's head; "his UPPER STOREY is unfurnished," *i.e.*, he does not know very much.

HOT-HEADED and BAD-TEMPERED

CRUSTY: ill-tempered, petulant, morose. —*Old.*

GASSY: liable to "flare up" at any offence.

KILKENNY CAT: a popular simile for a voracious or desperate animal or person, from the story of the two cats in that county, who are said to have fought and bitten each other until a small portion of the tail of one of them alone remained.

NASTY: ill-tempered, cross-grained.

OBSTROPOLOUS: Cockney corruption of obstreperous.

PUCKER: poor temper, difficulty, *deshabille*.

RACKETY: wild or noisy.

RATTLECAP: an unsteady, volatile person.

RUSTY: cross, ill-tempered, morose, one who cannot go through life like a person of easy and polished manners.

SHIRTY: ill-tempered or cross. When one person makes another in an ill humour he is said to have "got his **SHIRT** out."

SNAGGY: cross, crotchetty, malicious.

STREAKY: irritated, ill-tempered.

TOUCHY: peevish, irritable. *Johnson* terms it a low word.

WAXY: cross, ill-tempered.

WHITE LIVER'D or **LIVER-FACED:** cowardly, much afraid, very mean.

WILD: vexed, cross, passionate. In the United States the word *mad* is supplemented with a vulgar meaning similar to our Cockneyism, **WILD**; and to make a man **MAD** on the other side of the Atlantic is to vex him or "rile" his temper - not to render him a raving maniac or a fit subject for Bedlam.

INEXPERIENCED

BAKE: "he's only **HALF-BAKED**," *i.e.*, soft, inexperienced.

FLATTIES: rustic or uninitiated people.

GREEN: ignorant, not wide-awake, inexperienced.—*Shakespere*. "Do you see any **GREEN** in my eye?" ironical question in a dispute.

GREEN-HORN: a fresh, simple, or uninitiated person.

GRIFFIN: in India, a newly arrived cadet; general for an inexperienced youngster. "Fast" young men in London frequently term an umbrella a **GRIFFIN**.

RAW: uninitiated, a novice.—*Old*. Frequently a **JOHNNY RAW**.

SOFT: foolish, inexperienced. An old term for bank notes.

IRRITATING and BORING

BORE: a troublesome friend or acquaintance, a nuisance, anything which wearies or annoys. The *Gradus ad Cantabrigiam* suggests the derivation of **BORE** from the *Greek*, Bapos, a burden. *Shakespere* uses it, King Henry VIII., i.,

" — —at this instant
He **BORES** me with some trick."

Grose speaks of this word as being much in fashion about the year 1780-81, and states that it vanished of a sudden, without leaving a trace behind. Not so, burly Grose, the term is still in favour, and is as piquant and expressive as ever. Of the modern sense of the word **BORE**, the Prince Consort made an amusing and effective use in his masterly address to the British Association, at Aberdeen, September 14, 1859. He said (as reported by the *Times*):

> "I will not weary you by further examples, with which most of you are better acquainted than I am myself, but merely express my satisfaction that there should exist bodies of men who will bring the well-considered and understood wants of science before the public and the Government, who will even hand round the begging box, and expose themselves to refusal and rebuffs, to which all beggars are liable, with the certainty besides of being considered great **BORES**. Please to recollect that this species of "**BORE**" is a most useful animal, well adapted for the ends for which nature intended him. He alone, by constantly returning to the charge, and repeating the same truths and the same requests, succeeds in awakening attention to the cause which he advocates, and obtains that hearing which is granted him at last for self-protection as the minor evil compared to his importunity, but which is requisite to make his cause understood."

DUTCH UNCLE: a personage often introduced in conversation, but exceedingly difficult to describe; "I'll talk to him like a **DUTCH UNCLE!**" conveys the notion of anything but a desirable relation. —*Americanism.*

FOGEY or OLD FOGEY: a dullard, an old-fashioned or singular person. *Grose* says it is a nickname for an invalid soldier, from the *French*, **FOURGEAUX**, fierce or fiery, but it has lost this signification now. **FOGGER**, *old word* for a huckster or servant.

HUMBUG: an imposition or a person who imposes upon others. A very expressive but slang word, synonymous at one time with **HUM AND HAW**. Lexicographers have fought shy at adopting this word.

Richardson used it frequently to express the meaning of other words, but omits it in the alphabetical arrangement as unworthy of recognition! In the first edition of this work, 1785 was given as the earliest date at which the word could be found in a printed book. Since then I have traced HUMBUG half a century farther back, on the title-page of a singular old jest-book—"*The Universal Jester*; or a pocket companion for the Wits: being a choice collection of merry conceits, facetious drolleries, &c., clenchers, closers, closures, bon-mots, and HUMBUGS," by *Ferdinando Killigrew*. London, about 1735-40.

I have also ascertained that the famous Orator Henley was known to the mob as ORATOR HUMBUG. The fact may be learnt from an illustration in the exceedingly curious little collection of *Caricatures*, published in 1757, many of which were sketched by Lord Bolingbroke- Horace Walpole filling in the names and explanations. *Halliwell* describes HUMBUG as "a person who hums," and cites Dean Milles' MS., which was written about 1760. It has been stated that the word is a corruption of Hamburgh, from which town so many false bulletins and reports came during the war in the last century. "Oh, that is *Hamburgh* (or HUMBUG)," was the answer to any fresh piece of news which smacked of improbability. *Grose* mentions it in his Dictionary, 1785; and in a little printed squib, published in 1808, entitled *Bath Characters*, by *T. Goosequill*, HUMBUG is thus mentioned in a comical couplet on the title page:

> "Wee Three Bath Deities bee,
> HUMBUG, Foilie, and Varietee."

Gradually from this time the word began to assume a place in periodical literature, and in novels not written by squeamish or over-precise authors. In the preface to a flat, and, I fear, unprofitable poem, entitled, *The Reign of* HUMBUG, *a Satire*, 8vo., 1836, the author thus apologizes for the use of the word "I have used the term HUMBUG to designate this principle (wretched sophistry of life generally), considering that it is now adopted into our language as much as the words *dunce, jockey, cheat, swindler*, &c., which were formerly only colloquial terms." A correspondent, who in a late number of *Adersaria* ingeniously traced *bombast* to the inflated Doctor Paracelsus Bombast, considers that HUMBUG may, in like manner, be derived from *Homberg*, the distinguished chemist of the court of the Duke of Orleans, who, according to the following passage from Bishop

Berkeley's "Siris," was an ardent and successful seeker after the philosopher's stone!

> " § 194. —Of this there cannot be a better proof than the experiment of Monsieur Homberg, **Who made gold of Mercury by introducing light into its pores**, but at such trouble and expense, that, I suppose, nobody will try the experiment for profit. By this injunction of light and mercury, both bodies became fixed, and produced a third different to either, to wit, real gold. For the truth of which **Fact** I refer to the memoirs of the French Academy of Sciences." —*Berkeley's Works*, vol. ii., p. 366, (Wright's edition.)

The universal use of this term is remarkable; in California there is a town called *Humbug Flat*—a name which gives a significant hint of the acuteness of the first settler.

HUM-DRUM: tedious, tiresome, boring; "a society of gentleman who used to meet near the Charter house or at the King's Head, St. John's Street. They were characterised by less mystery and more pleasantry than the Freemasons." —*Bacchus and Venus*, 1737. In the *West*, a low cart.

PESKY: an intensive expression, implying annoyance; a PESKY, troublesome fellow. Corruption of PESTILENT?

SNOT: a term of reproach applied to persons by the vulgar when vexed or annoyed. In a Westminster school vocabulary for boys, published in the last century, the term is curiously applied. Its proper meaning is the glandular mucus discharged through the nose.

 MEAN and LOW

BLACKGUARD: a low or dirty fellow.

> "A *Cant* word amongst the vulgar, by which is implied a dirty fellow of the meanest kind. Dr. Johnson says, and he cites only the modern authority of Swift. But the introduction of this word into our language belongs not to the vulgar, and is more than a century prior to the time of Swift. Mr. Malone agrees with me in

exhibiting the two first of the following examples. The *black-guard* is evidently designed to imply a fit attendant on the devil. Mr. Gilford, however, in his late edition of Ben Johnson's works, assigns an origin of the name different from what the old examples which I have cited seem to countenance. It has been formed, he says, from those 'mean and dirty dependents, in great houses, who were selected to carry coals to the kitchen, halls, &c. To this smutty regiment, who attended the progresses, and rode in the carts with the pots and kettles, which, with every other article of furniture, were then moved from palace to palace, the people, in derision, gave the name of *black guards*; a term since become sufficiently familiar, and never properly explained.' —Ben Johnson, ii. 169, vii. 250" —*Todd's Johnson's Dictionary.*

BULLY: a braggart; but in the language of the streets, a man of the most degraded morals, who protects prostitutes, and lives off their miserable earnings.—*Shakespere*, Midsummer Night's Dream, iii. 1; iv. 2.

CAD or **CADGER** (from which it is shortened): a mean or vulgar fellow; a beggar; one who would rather live on other people than work for himself; a man trying to worm something out of another, either money or information. *Johnson* uses the word, and gives *huckster* as the meaning, but I never heard it used in this sense. CAGER or GAGER, the *Old Cant* term for a man. The exclusives in the Universities apply the term CAD to all non-members.

GAY: loose, dissipated; "GAY woman," a kept mistress or prostitute.

GUTTER BLOOD: a low or vulgar man.—*Scotch.*

JOHN THOMAS: generic for "flunkies," —footmen popularly represented with large calves and bushy whiskers.

KINCHIN COVE: a man who robs children; a little man.—*Ancient Cant.*

RAGAMUFFIN: a tattered vagabond, a tatterdemalion.

RAPSCALLION: a low tattered wretch.

RIP: a rake; "an old RIP," An old libertine or debauchee. Corruption of *Reprobate*. A person reading the letters R.I.P. (*Requiescat in Pace*) on the top of a tombstone as one word, said, soliloquizing, "Rip! Well, he *was* an old RIP, and no mistake." —*Cuthbert Bede.*

ROUGHS: coarse or vulgar men.

RUSTY GUTS: a blunt, rough, old fellow. Corruption of **RUSTICUS**.

SCAMP: a graceless fellow, a rascal; formerly the *Cant* term for plundering and thieving. A **ROYAL-SCAMP** was a highwayman, whilst a **FOOT-SCAMP** was an ordinary thief with nothing but his legs to trust to in case of an attempt at capture. Some have derived **SCAMP** from *qui ex campo exit*, viz., one who leaves the field, a deserter.

SCREW: a mean or stingy person.

SCURF: a mean fellow.

SHAKE: a prostitute, a disreputable man or woman.—*North*.

SHARP or **SHARPER:** a cunning cheat, a rogue—the opposite of **FLAT**.

SHICER: a mean man, a humbug, a "duffer,"—a person who is either worthless or will not work.

SWEEP: a low or shabby man.

TIN-POT: "he plays a **TIN-POT** game," *i.e.*, a low or shabby one. —*Billiards*.

TOOL: "a poor **TOOL**," a bad hand at anything.

WHITE LIVER'D or **LIVER-FACED:** cowardly, much afraid, very mean.

 ## MEN

ARTICLE: a man or boy, derisive term.

CODGER: an old man; "a rum old **CODGER**," a curious old fellow. **CODGER** is sometimes used synonymous with **CADGER**, and then signifies a person who gets his living in a questionable manner. **CAGER** or **GAGER**, was the *Old Cant* term for a man.

HEN-PECKED: said of one whose wife "wears the breeches."

JACK SPRAT: a diminutive boy or man.

NINCOMPOOP: a fool, a hen-pecked husband, a "Jerry Sneak." Corruption of *non compos mentis*.

SON OF A GUN: a contemptuous title for a man. In the army it is sometimes applied to an artilleryman.

STANGEY: a tailor; a person under petticoat government—derived from the custom of *"riding the* STANG," mentioned in Hudibras:

> "It is a custom used of course
> Where the grey mare is the better horse."

STICK: a derogatory expression for a person; "a rum" or "odd STICK," a curious man. More generally a "poor STICK." — *Provincial*

PHYSICAL QUALITIES

PEOPLE

BOSS-EYED: a person with one eye, or rather with one eye injured.

BUTTER-FINGERED: apt to let things fall.

CHATTY: a filthy person, one whose clothes are not free from vermin; **Chatty doss**, a lousy bed.

CHUBBY: round-faced, plump.

COCK-EYE: one that squints.

CODGER: an old man; "a rum old CODGER," a curious old fellow. CODGER is sometimes used synonymous with CADGER, and then signifies a person who gets his living in a questionable manner. CAGER or GAGER, was the *Old Cant* term for a man.

CONK: a nose; CONKY, having a projecting or remarkable nose. The Duke of Wellington was frequently termed "Old CONKY" in satirical papers and caricatures.

CRIBBAGE FACED: marked with the small pox, full of holes like a cribbage board.

CRUMMY: fat, plump. — *North.*

DANDYPRAT: a funny little fellow, a mannikin; originally a half-far thing.

DUMPY: short and stout.

FORTY GUTS: vulgar term for a fat man.

GAWKY: a lanky or awkward person; a fool. *Saxon*, GEAC; *Scotch*, GOWK.

GUMMY: thick, fat, generally applied to a woman's ankles or to a man whose flabby person betokens him a drunkard.

HOPPING GILES: a cripple. St. Ægidius or Giles, himself similarly afflicted, was their patron saint. The ancient lazar houses were dedicated to him.

HUMPTY DUMPTY: short and thick.

JACK SPRAT: a diminutive boy or man.

LORD: a humpbacked man. — *See* MY LORD *below.*

MY LORD: a nickname given to a hunchback.

NAMBY PAMBY: particular, over nice, effeminate. This, I think, was of Pope's invention, and first applied by him to the affected short-lined verses addressed by Ambrose Phillips to Lord Carteret's infant children. — *See Johnson's Life of Pope.*

OTTOMY: a thin man, a skeleton, a dwarf. Vulgar pronunciation of *Anatomy, Shakespere* has 'ATOMY.

PODGY: drunk; dumpy, short and fat.

SHAKY: said of a person of questionable health, integrity, or solvency; at the *University*, of one not likely to pass his examination.

SHRIMP: a diminutive person. — *Chaucer.*

SKY-SCRAPER: a tall man; "are you cold up there, old SKY-SCRAPER?" Properly a sea term; the light sails which some adventurous skippers set above the royals in calm latitudes are termed SKY-SCRAPERS and MOON-RAKERS.

SNAGGLE TEETH: uneven and unpleasant looking dental operators. — *West.* SNAGS (*Americanism*) ends of sunken drift-wood sticking out of the water, on which river steamers are often wrecked.

SQUABBY: flat, short, and thick.

SQUINNY-EYED: squinting. — *Shakespere.*

TRUCK-GUTTED: pot-bellied, corpulent. — *Sea.*

TWITCHETTY: nervous, fidgetty.

WHIPPER-SNAPPER: a waspish, diminutive person.

THINGS

ALL TO SMASH or GONE TO PIECES: bankrupt or smashed to pieces.—*Somersetshire.*

CLIGGY or CLIDGY: sticky.—*Anglo Saxon*, CLÆG, clay.—*See* CLAGGUM.

CRANKY: foolish, idiotic, ricketty, capricious, not confined to persons. *Ancient Cant*, CRANKE, simulated sickness. *German*, KRANK, sickly.

DICKEY: bad, sorry, or foolish; food or lodging is pronounced DICKEY when of a poor description; "it's all DICKEY with him," *i.e.*, all over with him.

FOXY: rank, tainted.—*Lincolnshire.*

GRUBBY: musty or old-fashioned.—*Devonshire.*

LOP-SIDED: uneven, one side larger than the other.—*Old.*

POKY: confined or cramped; "that corner is POKY and narrow."—*Times* article, 21ˢᵗ July, 1859.

RUGGY: fusty, frowsy.

SHACKLY: loose, rickety.—*Devonshire.*

SIXES AND SEVENS: articles in confusion are said to be all SIXES AND SEVENS. The Deity is mentioned in the Towneley Mysteries as He that "sett all on seven," *i.e.*, set or appointed everything in seven days. A similar phrase at this early date implies confusion and disorder, and from these, *Halliwell* thinks, has been derived the phrase "to be at SIXES AND SEVENS." A Scotch correspondent, however, states that the phrase probably came from the workshop, and that amongst needle makers when the points and eyes are "heads and tails" ("heeds and thraws"), or in confusion, they are said to be SIXES AND SEVENS, because those numbers are the sizes most generally used, and in the course of manufacture have frequently to be distinguished.

SLANTINGDICULAR: oblique, awry—as opposed to PERPENDICULAR.

SMITHERS or SMITHEREENS: "all to SMITHEREENS," all to smash. SMITHER, is a *Lincolnshire* word for a fragment.

SMUTTY: obscene—vulgar as applied to conversation.

TANNY or TEENY: little. *Gipsey*, TAWNO, little.

TOPSY-TURVY: the bottom upwards. *Grose* gives an ingenious etymology of this once *Cant* term, viz., "*top-side turf-ways,*"—turf being always laid the wrong side upwards.

TWO-HANDED: awkward.

VINNIED: mildewed or sour.—*Devonshire.*

SHABBY

CRANKY: foolish, idiotic, ricketty, capricious, not confined to persons. *Ancient Cant*, **CRANKE**, simulated sickness. *German*, **KRANK**, sickly.

DICKEY: bad, sorry, or foolish; food or lodging is pronounced **DICKEY** when of a poor description; "it's all **DICKEY** with him," *i.e.*, all over with him.

GUY: a fright, a dowdy, an ill-dressed person. Derived from the effigy of Guy Fawkes carried about by boys on Nov. 5.

NEEDY MIZZLER: a shabby person; a tramp who runs away without paying for his lodging.

NIBS: the master or chief person; a man with no means but high pretensions—a "shabby genteel."

ROWDY-DOW: low, vulgar; "not the **CHEESE**," or thing.

SCALY: shabby or mean. *Shakespere* uses **SCALD**, an old word of reproach.

SEEDY: worn out, poverty-stricken, used-up, shabby. Metaphorical expression from the appearance of flowers when off bloom and running to *seed*: hence said of one who wears clothes until they crack and become shabby; "how **SEEDY** he looks," said of any man whose clothes are worn threadbare, with greasy facings, and hat brightened up by perspiration and continual polishing and wetting. When a man's coat begins to look worn out and shabby he is said to look **SEEDY** and ready for *cutting*. This term has been "on the streets" for nearly two centuries, and latterly has found its way into most dictionaries. Formerly slang, it is now a recognised word, and one of the most expressive in the *English* language. The French are always amused with it, they having no similar term.

SHICKERY: shabby, bad.

SOLD UP or **OUT:** broken down, bankrupt.

TIN-POT: "he plays a **TIN-POT** game," *i.e.*, a low or shabby one. —*Billiards*.

SHOWY

BIG: "to look BIG," to assume an inflated dress or manner, "to talk BIG," *i.e.*, boastingly or with an "extensive" air.

BOTTY: conceited, swaggering.

EXTENSIVE: frequently applied in a slang sense to a person's appearance or talk; "rather EXTENSIVE that!" intimating that the person alluded to is showing off or "cutting it fat."

FAST: gay, spreeish, unsteady, thoughtless—an Americanism that has of late ascended from the streets to the drawing-room. The word has certainly now a distinct meaning, which it had not thirty years ago. QUICK is the synonym for FAST, but a QUICK MAN would not convey the meaning of a FAST MAN—a person who by late hours, gaiety, and continual rounds of pleasure, lives too fast and wears himself out. In polite society a FAST young lady is one who affects mannish habits or makes herself conspicuous by some unfeminine accomplishment, —talks slang, drives about in London, smokes cigarettes, is knowing in dogs, horses, &c. An amusing anecdote is told of a FAST young lady, the daughter of a right reverend prelate, who was an adept in *horseflesh*. Being desirous of ascertaining the opinion of a candidate for ordination who had the look of a bird of the same feather, as to the merits of some cattle just brought to her father's palace for her to select from, she was assured by him they were utterly unfit for a lady's use. With a knowing look at the horses' points, she gave her decision in these choice words, "Well, I agree with you; they *are* a rum lot, as the Devil said of the ten commandments."

FLASH: showy, smart, knowing; a word with various meanings. A person is said to be dressed FLASH when his garb is showy, and after a fashion, but without taste. A person is said to be FLASH when he apes the appearance or manners of his betters or when he is trying to be superior to his friends and relations. FLASH also means "fast," roguish, and sometimes infers counterfeit or deceptive—and this, perhaps, is its general signification. "FLASH, my young friend, or slang, as others call it, is the classical language of the Holy Land; in other words, St. Giles' Greek."—*Tom and Jerry, by Moncreiff.* Vulgar language was first termed FLASH in the year 1718, by Hitchin, author of "*The Regulator of Thieves, &c., with accounts of FLASH words.*"

HIGHFALUTEN: showy, affected, tinselled, affecting certain pompous or fashionable airs, stuck up; "come, none of yer **HIGHFALUTEN** games," *i.e.*, you must not show off or imitate the swell here. *American* slang from the *Dutch*, **VERLOOTEN**.

LEARY: flash or knowing.

LEARY BLOAK: a person who dresses showily.

LOUD: flashy, showy, as applied to dress or manner.—*See* **BAGS** *page 96.*

SLANGY: flashy, vulgar; loud in dress, manner, and conversation.

SNOB: a low, vulgar, or affected person. Supposed to be from the nickname usually applied to a Crispin, or a maker of shoes; but believed by a writer in *Notes and Queries* to be a contraction of the *Latin*, Sine obolo. A more probable derivation, however, has just been forwarded by an ingenious correspondent. He supposes the **NOBS**, *i.e.*, *Nobiles*, was appended in lists to the names of persons of gentle birth, whilst those who had not that distinction were marked down as **S. NOB.**, *i.e.*, *sine nobilitate*, without marks of gentility—thus reversing its meaning. Another "word-twister" remarks that, as at college sons of nobleman wrote after their names in the admissions lists, *fil nob.*, son of a lord, and hence all young noblemen were called **NOBS** and what they did **NOBBY**, so those who imitated them would be called *quasi-nobs*, "like a nob," which by a process of contraction would be shortened to *si-nobs*, and then **SNOB**, one who pretends to be what he is not, and apes his betters. The short and expressive terms which many think fitly represent the three great estates of the realm, **NOB**, **SNOB** and **MOB**, were all originally slang words. The last has safely passed through the vulgar ordeal of the streets, and found respectable quarters in the standard dictionaries.

STARCHY: stuck-up, high-notioned, showily dressed, disdainful, cross.

TOFT: a showy individual, a **SWELL**, a person who, according to a Yorkshireman's vocabulary, is **UP-ISH**.

 ## SMART and CUNNING

DODGER: a tricky person or one who, to use the popular phrase, "knows too much." — *See* **DEVIL-DODGERS** *page 125.*

DOWNY: knowing or cunning; "a **DOWNY COVE**," a knowing or experienced sharper.

FLASH: showy, smart, knowing; a word with various meanings. A person is said to be dressed **FLASH** when his garb is showy, and after a fashion, but without taste. A person is said to be **FLASH** when he apes the appearance or manners of his betters, or when he is trying to be superior to his friends and relations. **FLASH** also means "fast," roguish, and sometimes infers counterfeit or deceptive—and this, perhaps, is its general signification. "**FLASH**, my young friend, or slang, as others call it, is the classical language of the Holy Land; in other words, St. Giles' Greek."—*Tom and Jerry, by Moncreiff.* Vulgar language was first termed **FLASH** in the year 1718, by Hitchin, author of "*The Regulator of Thieves, &c., with accounts of* **FLASH** *words.*"

FLYMY: knowing, cunning, roguish.

GNOSTICS: knowing ones or sharpers.—*Nearly obsolete in this vulgar sense.*

KNOWING: a slang term for sharpness; "**KNOWING** codger," or "a **KNOWING** blade," one who can take you in or cheat you, in any transaction you may have with him. It implies also deep cunning and foresight, and generally signifies dishonesty.

> "Who, on a spree with black-eyed Sal, his blowen,
> So swell, so prime, so nutty and so **KNOWING**."
> —*Don Juan*

LEARY: flash or knowing.

SHARP or **SHARPER:** a cunning cheat, a rogue—the opposite of **FLAT**.

SNUFF: "up to **SNUFF**," knowing and sharp; "to take **SNUFF**," to be offended. *Shakespere* uses **SNUFF** in the sense of anger or passion. **SNUFFY**, tipsy.

 ## STUCK-UP

BOTTY: conceited, swaggering.

BULLY: a braggart; but in the language of the streets, a man of the most degraded morals, who protects prostitutes, and lives off their miserable earnings.—*Shakespere*, Midsummer Night's Dream, iii. 1; iv. 2.

CHEEK: impudence, assurance; **CHEEKY**, saucy or forward. *Lincolnshire*, **CHEEK**, to accuse.

COCKY: pert, saucy.

GRANNY: importance, knowledge, pride; "take the **GRANNY** off them as has white hands," viz., remove their self-conceit.—*Mayhew*, vol. i., p. 364.

HIGH JINKS: "**ON THE HIGH JINKS**," taking up an arrogant position, assuming undue superiority.

RIDE: "to **RIDE THE HIGH HORSE**," or **RIDE ROUGH-SHOD** over one, to be overbearing or oppressive; to **RIDE THE BLACK DONKEY**, to be in an ill humour.

RUMBUSTIOUS or **RUMBUSTICAL:** pompous, haughty, boisterous, careless of the comfort of others.

SMALL BEER: "he doesn't think **SMALL BEER** of himself," *i.e.*, he has a great opinion of his own importance. **SMALL COALS** is also used in the same sense.

SNOB: a low, vulgar, or affected person. Supposed to be from the nickname usually applied to a Crispin, or a maker of shoes; but believed by a writer in *Notes and Queries* to be a contraction of the *Latin*, Sine obolo. A more probable derivation, however, has just been forwarded by an ingenious correspondent. He supposes the **NOBS**, *i.e.*, *Nobiles*, was appended in lists to the names of persons of gentle birth, whilst those who had not that distinction were marked down as **S. NOB.**, *i.e.*, *sine nobilitate*, without marks of gentility—thus reversing its meaning. Another "word-twister" remarks that, as at college sons of nobleman wrote after their names in the admissions lists, *fil nob.*, son of a lord, and hence all young noblemen were called **NOBS** and what they did **NOBBY**, so those who imitated them would be called *quasi-nobs*, "like a nob," which by a process of contraction would be shortened to *si-nobs*, and then **SNOB**, one who pretends to be what he is not, and apes his betters. The short and expressive terms which many think fitly represent the three great estates of the realm, **NOB**, **SNOB** and **MOB**, were all originally slang words. The last has safely passed through the vulgar ordeal of the streets, and found respectable quarters in the standard dictionaries.

SNOBBISH: stuck up, proud, make-believe.

STARCHY: stuck-up, high-notioned, showily dressed, disdainful, cross.

STUCK-UP: "purse-proud," —a form of snobbishness very common in those who have risen in the world. Mr. Albert Smith has written some amusing papers on the *Natural History of* STUCK-UP *People.*

SWELL: a man of importance; a person with a showy, jaunty exterior; "a rank SWELL," a very "flashily" dressed person, a man who by excessive dress apes a higher position than he actually occupies. Anything is said to be SWELL or SWELLISH that looks showy, or is many-coloured, or is of a desirable quality. Dickens and Thackeray are termed great SWELLS in literature; so indeed are the first persons in the learned professions.

TIGHT: close, stingy; hard up, short of cash; TIGHT, spruce, strong, active; "a TIGHT lad," a smart, active young fellow; TIGHT, drunk or nearly so; "TIGHT-laced," puritanical, over-precise. Money is said to be TIGHT when the public, from want of confidence in the aspect of affairs, are not inclined to speculate.

UPPISH: proud, arrogant.

 TEMPERAMENTS

CATCHY: (similar formation to *touchy*), inclined to take an undue advantage.

CHATTER-BOX: an incessant talker or chatterer.

CHEEK: impudence, assurance; CHEEKY, saucy or forward. *Lincolnshire,* CHEEK, to accuse.

CHICKEN-HEARTED: cowardly, fearful.

COLT'S TOOTH: elderly persons of juvenile tastes are said to have a colt's tooth.

COWAN: a sneak, an inquisitive or prying person.—*Masonic term. Greek,* κυων, a dog.

CRAB or **GRAB:** a disagreeable old person. *Name of a wild and sour fruit.* "To catch a CRAB," to fall backwards by missing a stroke in rowing.

CRIB BITER: an inveterate grumbler; properly said of a horse which has the habit, a sign of its bad digestion.

CROAKER: one who takes a desponding view of everything; an alarmist. *From the croaking of a raven.* —*Ben Johnson.*

CURE: an odd person; contemptuous term, abridged from CURIOSITY —which was formerly the favourite expression.

DUMPISH: sullen or glumpy.

FAST: gay, spreeish, unsteady, thoughtless—an Americanism that has of late ascended from the streets to the drawing-room. The word has certainly now a distinct meaning, which it had not thirty years ago. QUICK is the synonym for FAST, but a QUICK MAN would not convey the meaning of a FAST MAN—a person who by late hours, gaiety, and continual rounds of pleasure, lives too fast and wears himself out. In polite society a FAST young lady is one who affects mannish habits, or makes herself conspicuous by some unfeminine accomplishment, —talks slang, drives about in London, smokes cigarettes, is knowing in dogs, horses, &c. An amusing anecdote is told of a FAST young lady, the daughter of a right reverend prelate, who was an adept in *horseflesh*. Being desirous of ascertaining the opinion of a candidate for ordination who had the look of a bird of the same feather, as to the merits of some cattle just brought to her father's palace for her to select from, she was assured by him they were utterly unfit for a lady's use. With a knowing look at the horses' points, she gave her decision in these choice words, "Well, I agree with you; they *are* a rum lot, as the Devil said of the ten commandments."

FIDDLER: a sharper, a cheat; also one who dawdles over little matters and neglects great ones.

GAMMY: bad, unfavourable, poor-tempered. Those householders who are known enemies to the street folk and tramps are pronounced by them to be GAMMY. GAMMY sometimes means forged, as "GAMMY MONEKER," a forged signature; GAMMY STUFF, spurious medicine; GAMMY LOWR, counterfeit coin. *Hants,* GAMY, dirty. The hieroglyphic used by beggars and cadgers to intimate to those of the tribe coming after that things are not very favourable, is known as □, or GAMMY.

GLUMPISH: of a stubborn, sulky temper.

HORSE MARINE: an awkward person. In ancient times the "JOLLIES" or Royal Marines, were the butts of the sailors, from their ignorance of seamanship. "Tell that to the MARINES, the blue jackets won't believe it!" was a common rejoinder to a "stiff yarn." Now-a-days they are deservedly appreciated as the finest regiment in the service. A HORSE MARINE (an impossibility) was used to denote one more awkward still.

HUFF: to vex or offend; a poor temper.

HUMP UP: "to have one's HUMP UP," to be cross or ill-tempered—like a cat with its back set up.—*See* MONKEY *page 96.*

KNARK: a hard-hearted or savage person.

LEARY: to look or be watchful; shy.—*Old Cant.*

MAGGOTTY: fanciful, fidgetty. Whims and fancies were formerly termed MAGGOTS, from the popular belief that a maggot in the brain was the cause of any odd notion or caprice a person might exhibit.

OFFISH: distant, not familiar.

PEERY: suspicious or inquisitive.

PIG-HEADED: obstinate.

PUCKER or **PUCKER UP:** to get in a poor temper.

QUIZ: a prying person, an odd fellow. *Oxford slang*; lately admitted into dictionaries. Not noticed by *Johnson.*

RANTIPOLE: a wild, noisy fellow.

RIDE: "to RIDE THE HIGH HORSE," or RIDE ROUGH-SHOD over one, to be overbearing or oppressive; to RIDE THE BLACK DONKEY, to be in an ill humour.

RUMBUMPTIOUS: haughty, pugilistic.

RUMBUSTIOUS or **RUMBUSTICAL:** pompous, haughty, boisterous, careless of the comfort of others.

RUSTY: cross, ill-tempered, morose, one who cannot go through life like a person of easy and *polished* manners.

RUSTY GUTS: a blunt, rough, old fellow. Corruption of RUSTICUS.

SCAB: a worthless person.—*Old. Shakespere* uses SCALD in a similar sense.

SCREW: a mean or stingy person.

SKIN: to abate or lower the value of anything; "thin-SKINNED," sensitive, touchy.

SKIN-FLINT: an old popular simile for a "close-fisted," stingy person.

SKY: a disagreeable person, an enemy.—*Westminster School.*

SLAMMOCK: a slattern or awkward person.—*West*; and *Norfolk.*

SPOFFY: a bustling busy-body is said to be SPOFFY.

THINSKINNED: over nice, petulant, apt to get a "raw."

WHITE FEATHER: "to show the WHITE FEATHER," to evince cowardice. In the times when great attention was paid to the breeding of game-cocks, a white feather in the tail was considered a proof of cross-breeding.

YAY-NAY: "a poor YAY-NAY" fellow, one who has no conversational power, and can only answer *yea* or *nay* to a question.

YELLOW-GLOAK: a jealous man.

TRAITORS

CAT-IN-THE-PAN: a traitor, a turn-coat—derived by some from the *Greek*, Καραπαν, altogether; or from *cake in pan*, a pan cake, which is frequently turned from side to side.

MOUNTER: a false swearer. Derived from the borrowed clothes men used to MOUNT, or dress in, when going to swear for a consideration.

NARK: a person in the pay of the police; a common informer; one who gets his living by laying traps for publicans, &c.

NOSE: a thief who turns informer or Queen's evidence; a spy or watch; "on the NOSE," on the look out.

RAT: a sneak, an informer, a turn-coat, one who changes his party for interest. The late Sir Robert Peel was called the RAT, or the TAMWORTH RATCATCHER, for altering his views on the Roman Catholic question. From rats deserting vessels about to sink.

SNITCHERS: persons who turn queen's evidence or who tell tales. In *Scotland*, SNITCHERS signify handcuffs.

 # UNRELIABLE and CRAZY

BALMY: insane.

BEE: "to have a BEE in one's bonnet," *i.e.*, to be not exactly sane.

DUFFING: false, counterfeit, worthless.

FAST: gay, spreeish, unsteady, thoughtless—an Americanism that has of late ascended from the streets to the drawing-room. The word has certainly now a distinct meaning, which it had not thirty years ago. QUICK is the synonym for FAST, but a QUICK MAN would not convey the meaning of a FAST MAN—a person who by late hours, gaiety, and continual rounds of pleasure, lives too fast and wears himself out. In polite society a FAST young lady is one who affects mannish habits, or makes herself conspicuous by some unfeminine accomplishment— talks slang, drives about in London, smokes cigarettes, is knowing in dogs, horses, &c. An amusing anecdote is told of a FAST young lady, the daughter of a right reverend prelate, who was an adept in *horseflesh*. Being desirous of ascertaining the opinion of a candidate for ordination who had the look of a bird of the same feather, as to the merits of some cattle just brought to her father's palace for her to select from, she was assured by him they were utterly unfit for a lady's use. With a knowing look at the horses' points, she gave her decision in these choice words, "Well, I agree with you; they *are* a rum lot, as the Devil said of the ten commandments."

FISHY: doubtful, unsound, rotten, a term used to denote a suspicion of a "screw being loose," or "something rotten in the state of Denmark," in alluding to an unsafe speculation.

KICKSY: troublesome, disagreeable.

MAGGOTTY: fanciful, fidgetty. Whims and fancies were formerly termed MAGGOTS, from the popular belief that a maggot in the brain was the cause of any odd notion or caprice a person might exhibit.

MEALY-MOUTHED: plausible, deceitful.

OFF AND ON: vacillating; "an OFF AND ON kind of a chap," one who is always undecided.

QUEER: an *Old Cant* word, once in continual use as a prefix, signifying base, roguish, or worthless. The opposite of RUM, which signified good and genuine. QUEER, in all probability, is immediately derived from the *Cant* language. It has been mooted that it came into use from a quœre (?) being set before a man's name; but it is more than probable that it was brought into this country by the Gipseys from Germany, where QUER signifies "*cross*," or "*crooked*." At all events, it is believed to have been first used in England as a *Cant* word.

ROOKY: rascally, rakish, scampish.

SHY: to fight SHY of a person," to avoid his society either from dislike, fear, or any other reason. SHY has also the sense of flighty, unsteady, untrustworthy.

SKY WANNOCKING: unsteady, frolicking. — *Norfolk.*

SLATE: "he has a SLATE loose," *i.e.,* he is slightly crazy.

TILE: a hat; a covering for the head.

> "I'm a gent, I'm a gent,
> In the Regent-street style, —
> Examine my vest,
> And look at my TILE," — *Popular Song.*

Sometimes used in another sense, "Having a TILE loose," *i.e.,* being slightly crazy. — *See* PANTILE *page 127.*

 ## WOMEN

BLOWEN: a showy or flaunting prostitute, a thief's paramour. In *Wilts,* a BLOWEN is a blossom. *Germ.* BLUHEN, to bloom.

> "O du *bulhende* Madchen viel schone Willkomm!"
> — *German Song.*

Possibly however, the street term, BLOWEN may mean one whose reputation has been BLOWN UPON or damaged.

BLOWER: a girl; a contemptuous name in opposition to JOMER.

BURERK: a lady. *Grose* gives BURICK, a prostitute.

CRONY: a termagant or malicious old woman; an intimate friend. *Johnson* calls it *Cant*.

DRAB: a vulgar or low woman. — *Shakespere.*

FAGOT: a term of opprobrium used by low people to children; "you little **FAGOT**, you!" **FAGOT** was originally a term of contempt for a dry, shriveled old woman, whose bones were like a bundle of sticks, only fit to burn. Compare the *French* expression for a heretic, *sentir le fagot.*

FRUMP: a slatternly woman, a gossip. — *Ancient.*

GAD: a trapesing, slatternly woman. — *Gipsey. Anglo Saxon,* **GADELYING.**

GAY: loose, dissipated; "**GAY** woman," a kept mistress or prostitute.

GILL: a homely woman; "Jack and Gill," &c. — *Ben Johnson.*

GRASS-WIDOW: an unmarried mother; a deserted mistress. In the United States, during the gold fever in California, it was common for an adventurer to put both his **GRASS-WIDOW** and his children to *school* during his absence.

HAY BAG: a woman.

JACK: a low prostitute.

KIDDLEYWINK: a small shop where they retail the commodities of a village store. Also, a loose woman.

MOLLISHER: a low girl or woman; generally a female cohabitating with a man, and jointly getting their living by thieving.

MOTT: a girl of indifferent character. Formerly *Mort. Dutch,* **MOTT-KAST,** a harlotry.

MOTT-KAST: a harlotry.

MUTTON: a lewd woman. — *Shakespere.*

PIECE: a contemptuous term for a woman; a strumpet. — *Shakespere.*

QUEAN: (not Queen) a strumpet.

SHAKE: a prostitute, a disreputable man or woman. — *North.*

SHOWFULL PULLET: a "gay" woman.

WORK-RELATED

JACK-AT-A-PINCH: one whose assistance is only sought on an emergency. **JACK IN THE WATER,** an attendant at the watermen's stairs on the river and sea-port towns, who does not mind wetting his feet for a customer's convenience, in consideration of a douceur.

JOHN THOMAS: a generic for "flunkies,"—footmen popularly represented with large calves and bushy whiskers.

NABOB: an Eastern prince, a retired Indian official; hence a slang term for a capitalist.

SHODDY: old cloth worked up into new; also, a term of derision applied to workmen in woolen factories.—*Yorkshire.*

SNOB-STICK: a workman who refuses to join in strikes or trade unions. Query, properly **KNOB-STICK.**

SWEATER: a common term for a "cutting" or "grinding" employer.

TOOL: "a poor **TOOL,**" a bad hand at anything.

OTHER INSULTS

BOUNCE: impudence.

BUCK: a gay or smart man, cuckold.

COMB-CUT: mortified, disgraced, "down on one's luck."—*See* **CUT** *page 479.*

CRAMMER: a lie; or a person who commits a falsehood.

DUFFING: false, counterfeit, worthless.

FUNK: trepidation, nervousness, cowardice. To **FUNK,** to be afraid or nervous.

JAIL-BIRD: a prisoner, one who has been in jail.

LED CAPTAIN: a fashionable spunger, a swell who, by artifice ingratiates himself into the good graces of the master of the house, and lives at his table.

LIP: bounce, impudence; "come, none o' yer **LIP!**"

LOAFER: a lazy vagabond. Generally considered an *Americanism*. LOPER or LOAFER, however, was in general use as a *Cant* term in the early part of the last century. LANDLOPER was a vagabond who begged in the attire of a sailor; and the sea phrase, LAND LUBBER, was doubtless synonymous.—*See the Times*, 3rd November, 1859, for a reference to LOAFER.

NOSE-BAGS: visitors at watering places, and houses of refreshment, who carry their own victuals.—*Term applied by waiters.*

POGRAM: a dissenter, a fanatic, formalist, or humbug.

RATHER OF THE RATHEREST: a phrase applied to anything slightly in excess or defect.

RICH: spicy; also used in the sense of "too much of a good thing;" "a RICH idea," one too absurd or unreasonable to be adopted.

RUGGY: fusty, frowsy.

SALT: "it's rather too SALT," said of an extravagant hotel bill.

SCRATCH: "no great SCRATCH," of little worth.

SEWED-UP: done up, used-up, intoxicated. *Dutch*, SEEUWT, sick.

SHILLY SHALLY: to trifle or fritter away time; irresolute. Corruption of *Shall I, shall I?*

SKY: a disagreeable person, an enemy.—*Westminster School.*

SMUTTY: obscene—vulgar as applied to conversation.

SUCK: a parasite, flatterer of the "nobs."—*University.*

TIGHT: close, stingy; hard up, short of cash; TIGHT, spruce, strong, active; "a TIGHT lad," a smart, active young fellow; TIGHT, drunk or nearly so; "TIGHT-laced," puritanical, over-precise. Money is said to be TIGHT when the public, from want of confidence in the aspect of affairs, are not inclined to speculate.

TUFT-HUNTER: a hanger-on to persons of quality or wealth. Originally *University slang*, but now general.

WALL FLOWER: a person who goes to a ball, and looks on without dancing, either from choice or not being able to obtain a partner.

WHIP JACK: a sham shipwrecked sailor, called also a TURNPIKE SAILOR.

WILD: vexed, cross, passionate. In the United States the word *mad* is supplemented with a vulgar meaning similar to our Cockneyism,

WILD; and to make a man MAD on the other side of the Atlantic is to vex him or "rile" his temper—not to render him a raving maniac or a fit subject for Bedlam.

 # MODIFIERS

ABOUT RIGHT: "to do the thing ABOUT RIGHT," *i.e.*, to do it properly, soundly, correctly; "he guv it 'im ABOUT RIGHT," *i.e.*, he beat him severely.

ALL TO PIECES: utterly excessively; "he beat him ALL TO PIECES," *i.e.*, excelled or surpassed him exceedingly.

ANY HOW: in any way, or at any rate, bad; "he went on ANY HOW," *i.e.*, badly or indifferently.

BENE: good.—*Ancient Cant;* BENAR was the comparative.—*See* BONE *page 20. Latin.*

BLAZES: "like BLAZES," furious or desperate, a low comparison.

BOBBISH: very well, clever, spruce; "how are you doing?" "Oh! Pretty BOBBISH."

BROWN: "to do BROWN," to do well or completely (in allusion to roasting); "doing it BROWN," prolonging the frolic or exceeding sober bounds; "DONE BROWN," taken in, deceived, or surprised.

CHEAP: "doing it on the CHEAP," living economically or keeping up a showy appearance with very little means.

CLEAN: quite or entirely; "CLEAN gone," entirely out of sight or away. —*Old, see Cotgrave.—Shakespere.*

COME: a slang verb used in many phrases; "A'nt he COMING IT," *i.e.*, is he not proceeding at a great rate? "Don't COME TRICKS here," "don't COME THE OLD SOLDIER over me," *i.e.*, we are aware of your practices, and "twig" your manoeuver. COMING IT STRONG, exaggerating, going a-head, the opposite of *"drawing it mild."* COMING IT also means informing or disclosing.

DOG-CHEAP or **DOG-FOOLISH:** very or singularly cheap, or foolish. Latham, in his *English Language*, says: "This has nothing to do with dogs. The first syllable is god = *good* transposed, and the second, the ch—p, is chapman, *merchant*: compare EASTCHEAP." *Old term.*

GINGERLY: to do anything with great care.—*Cotgrave.*

HIGGLEDY-PIGGLEDY: all together, as hogs and pigs lie.

HOG: "to go the whole HOG," to do anything with a person's entire strength, not "by halves," realized by the phrase "in for a penny in for a pound." *Bartlett* claims this to be a pure *American* phrase; whilst *Ker,* of course, give it a *Dutch* origin.—*Old.*

KIDDILY: fashionably or showily; "KIDDILY togg'd," showily dressed.

NATION: very or exceedingly. Corruption of DAMNATION.

NINEPENCE: "right as NINEPENCE," all right, right to a nicety.

NOBBILY: showily.—*See* SNOB *page 51 for derivation.*

PROPER: very, exceedingly, sometimes ironically; "you are a PROPER nice fellow," meaning a great scamp.

QUIET: "on the QUIET," clandestinely, so as to avoid observation, "under the rose."

RIGHT AS A NINEPENCE: quite right, exactly right.

SERENE: all right; "it's all SERENE," a street phrase of very modern adoption, the burden of a song.

SIXTY: "to go along like SIXTY," *i.e.*, at a good rate, briskly.

SLAP: exactly, precisely; "SLAP in the wind's eye," *i.e.*, exactly to windward.

SLAP-BANG: suddenly, violently.

SLAPDASH: immediately or quickly.

SLICK: an *Americanism*, very prevalent in England since the publication of Judge Haliburton's facetious stories. As an *adjective*, SLICK means rapidly, effectually, utterly; as a *verb*, it has the force of "to despatch rapidly," turn off, get done with a thing.

SMACK SMOOTH: even, level with the surface, quickly.

SPANK: to move along quickly; hence a fast horse or vessel is said to be "a SPANKER to go."

STRONG: "to come it STRONG,"—*See* COME *page 63.*

TEETOTALLY: amplification of TOTALLY.

TIDY: tolerably or pretty well; "how did you get on to-day?" — "Oh, TIDY," — *Saxon.*

TOL-LOL or **TOL-LOLISH:** tolerable or tolerably.

WHISTLE: "as clean as a WHISTLE," neatly or "SLICKLY done," as an American would say; "to WET ONE'S WHISTLE," to take a drink. This is a very old term. *Chaucer* says of the Miller of Trumpington's wife (*Canterbury Tales*, 4153) —

> "So was hir joly WHISTAL well Y-WET;"

"to WHISTLE FOR ANYTHING," to stand small chance of getting it, from the nautical custom of *whistling* for a wind in a calm, which of course comes none the sooner for it.

WINKIN: "he went off like WINKIN," *i.e.*, very quickly.

OH, THE HUMANITY

You cannot slander human nature; it is worse than words can paint it.

Charles Haddon Spurgeon

Within this chapter, Body Parts is far and away my favorite section. The "lower orders" as John Camden Hotten called them, may not have had much money or education, but they had a brilliant knack for descriptive and playful language. How could anyone *not* be charmed by such terms as **dumpling depot** for a stomach or **painted peeper** for a black eye?

They even faced death with a colorful sense of humor. Someone on their last legs was a **croaker** and once gone they became a **stiff 'un.**

It is amazing what their words can tell us about how they thought. How interesting that costermongers used the term **mollygrubs** for sorrow as well as for a stomach ache because they believed the stomach to be the seat of emotions. And they used **maggotty** for whims and fanciful notions because they thought such ideas were caused by an actual maggot in the brain. How fortunate they were wrong about that one!

Editor's Faves:

COUNCIL OF TEN: the toes of a man who turns his feet inward.

OLD GOOSEBERRY (*see* **GOOSEBERRY** *page 450*), **OLD HARRY** (query, *Old Hairy?*), **OLD SCRATCH:** all synonyms for the devil.

SHOOT THE CAT: to vomit.

IN THIS CHAPTER

PEOPLE

CHILDREN (GENERIC TERMS)

BANTLING: a child; stated in *Bacchus and Venus*, 1737, and by *Grose*, to be a *Cant* term.

BYE-BLOW: a bastard child.

CHATTER BASKET: common term for a prattling child amongst nurses.

CHICKEN: a young girl.

CHIP OF THE OLD BLOCK: a child who resembles its father. **BROTHER CHIP**, one of the same trade or profession.

CULL: a man or boy.—*Old Cant.*

DEVIL: a printer's youngest apprentice, an errand boy.

DONNA AND FEELES: a woman and children. *Italian* or *Lingua Franca*, **DONNE E FIGLIE.**

DOXY: female companion of a thief or beggar. In the West of England, the women frequently call their little girls **DOXIES**, in a familiar or endearing sense. A learned divine once described *orthodoxy* as being a man's own **DOXY**, and *heterodoxy* another man's **DOXY**.—*Ancient Cant.*

FAGOT: a term of opprobrium used by low people to children; "you little **FAGOT**, you!" **FAGOT** was originally a term of contempt for a dry, shriveled old woman, whose bones were like a bundle of sticks, only fit to burn. Compare the *French* expression for a heretic, *sentir le fagot.*

FEELE: a daughter or child.—*Corrupted French.*

GRIFFIN: in India, a newly arrived cadet; general for an inexperienced youngster. "Fast" young men in London frequently term an umbrella a **GRIFFIN.**

JACK SPRAT: a diminutive boy or man.

KID: an infant or child.

KIDDY: a man or boy. Formerly a low thief.

KINCHIN: a child.—*Old Cant.* From the *German* diminutive **KINDCHEN**, a baby.

LUNAN: a girl. — *Gipsey.*

MOLL: a girl; nickname for Mary. — *Old Cant.*

NIPPER: a small boy. *Old Cant* for a boy cut-purse.

SAUCEBOX: a mouth, also a pert young person.

SHALER: a girl.

SHAVER: a sharp fellow; "a young" or "old **SHAVER,**" a boy or man. — *Sea.*

TIGER: a boy employed to wait on a gentlemen; one who waits on ladies is a page.

TITTER: a girl.

WENCH: provincial and old-fashioned term for a girl, derived from **WINK.** In *America,* negro girls only are termed **WENCHES.**

YOUNKER: in street language, a lad or a boy. Term in general use amongst costermongers, cabmen, and old-fashioned people. *Barnefield's Affectionate Shepherd,* 1594, has the phrase, "a seemelie **YOUNKER.**" *Danish* and *Friesic,* **JONKER.** In the *Navy,* a naval cadet is usually termed a **YOUNKER.**

 # ENTITIES and PERSONAGES

DARBLE: the devil. *French,* **DIABLE.**

DAVY: "on my **DAVY,**" on my affidavit, of which it is a vulgar corruption. Latterly **DAVY** has become synonymous in street language with the name of the Deity; "so help me **DAVY,**" slang rendering of the conclusion of the oath usually exacted of witnesses.

DEUCE: the devil. — *Old.* Stated by *Junius* and others to be from **DEUS.**

DICKENS: synonymous with devil; "what the **DICKENS** are you after?" what the d—l are you doing? Used by *Shakespere* in the *Merry Wives of Windsor.*

GAR: euphuistic corruption of the title of the Deity; "be **GAR,** you don't say so!" — *Franco-English.*

HARRY or OLD HARRY: *(i.e. Old Hairy?)* the Devil; "to play **OLD HARRY** with one," *i.e.,* ruin or annoy him.

NICK or **OLD NICK:** the evil spirit. — *Scandinavian.*

OD DRAT IT, OD RABBIT (*Coleman's broad grins*), **OD'S BLOOD:** and all other exclamations commencing with **OD**, are nothing but softened or suppressed oaths. **OD** is a corruption of **GOD**, and **DRAT** of **ROT**. — *Shakespere.*

OLD GOOSEBERRY (*see* **GOOSEBERRY** *page 450*), **OLD HARRY** (query, *Old Hairy*?), **OLD SCRATCH:** all synonyms for the devil.

SNOOKS: an imaginary personage often brought forward as the answer to an idle question or as the perpetrator of a senseless joke.

VIC.: the Victoria Theatre, London — patronised principally by costermongers and low people; also the street abbreviation of the Christian name of her Majesty the Queen.

GROUPS OF PEOPLE

BARNEY: a mob, a crowd.

GODS: the people in the upper gallery of a theatre; "up amongst the GODS," a seat amongst the low persons in the gallery — so named from the high position of the gallery, and the blue sky generally painted on the ceiling of the theatre; termed by the *French*, **PARADIS**.

HEAP: "a HEAP of people," a crowd; "struck all of a HEAP," suddenly astonished.

MOB: Swift informs us, in his *Art of Polite Conversation*, that MOB was, in his time, the slang abbreviation of *Mobility*, just as NOB is of *Nobility* at the present day. — *See* SCHOOL *below.*

MOBILITY: the populace; or according to *Burke*, the "great unwashed." *Johnson* calls it a *Cant* term, although *Swift* notices it as a proper expression.

PUSH: a crowd. — *Old Cant.*

RISE (or **RAISE**) **A BARNEY:** to collect a mob.

RUCK: the undistinguished crowd; "to come in with the RUCK," to arrive at the winning post among the non-winning horses. — *Racing term.*

SCHOOL or **MOB:** two or more "patterers" working together in the streets.

TAG-RAG-AND-BOB-TAIL: a mixed crowd of low people, mobility.

MEN and WOMEN (GENERIC TERMS)

BLADE: a man—in ancient times the term for a soldier; "knowing BLADE," a wide-awake, sharp, or cunning man.

BLOAK or **BLOKE:** a man; "the BLOAK with a jasey," the man with a wig, *i.e.,* the Judge. *Gipsey* and *Hindoo,* LOKE. *North,* BLOACHER, any large animal.

BURERK: a lady. *Grose* gives BURICK, a prostitute.

CASE: a few years ago the term CASE was applied to persons and things; "what a CASE he is," *i.e.,* what a curious person; "a rum CASE that," or "you are a CASE," both synonymous with the phrase "odd fish," common half a century ago. Among young ladies at boarding schools a CASE means a love affair.

CHUM: an acquaintance. A recognised term, but in such frequent use with the lower orders that it demanded a place in this glossary.

CODGER: an old man; "a rum old CODGER," a curious old fellow. CODGER is sometimes used synonymous with CADGER, and then signifies a person who gets his living in a questionable manner. CAGER or GAGER, was the *Old Cant* term for a man.

COVE or **COVEY:** a boy or man of any age or station. A term generally preceded by an expressive adjective, thus a "flash COVE," a "ruin COVE," a "downy COVE," &c. The feminine, COVESS, was once popular, but it has fallen into disuse. *Ancient Cant,* originally (temp. Henry VIII.) COFE or CUFFIN, altered in *Decker's* time to COVE. Probably connected with CUIF, which, in the North of England, signifies a lout or awkward fellow. Amongst *Negroes,* CUFFEE.

CRONY: a termagant or malicious old woman; an intimate friend. *Johnson* calls it *Cant.*

CULL: a man or boy.—*Old Cant.*

CUSTOMER: synonymous with CHAP, a fellow; "a rum CUSTOMER," *i.e.,* an odd fish or curious person.—*Shakespere.*

DONNA AND FEELES: a woman and children. *Italian* or *Lingua Franca,* DONNE E FIGLIE.

FISH: a person; "a queer **FISH**," "a loose **FISH**," &c.

FLAME: a sweetheart.

FLICK or **OLD FLICK:** an old chap or fellow.

FROW: a girl or wife. *German,* **FRAU**; *Dutch,* **VROUW**.

GLOAK: a man.—*Scotch.*

GOVERNOR: a father, a master or superior person, an elder; "which way, **GUV'NER**, to Cheapside?"

GRASS-WIDOW: an unmarried mother; a deserted mistress. In the United States, during the gold fever in California, it was common for an adventurer to put both his **GRASS-WIDOW** and his children to *school* during his absence.

HAND: a workman or helper, a person. "A cool **HAND**," explained by Sir Thomas Overbury to be "one who accounts bashfulness the wickedest thing in the world, and therefore studies impudence."

JACK SPRAT: a diminutive boy or man.

JAGGER: a gentleman.—*German,* **JAGER**, a sportsman.

JOMER: a sweetheart or favourite girl.—*See* **BLOWER** *page 35.*

KIDDY: a man or boy. Formerly a low thief.

LADDLE: a lady. Term with chimney-sweeps on the 1st of May. A correspondent suggests that the term may come from the brass *ladles* for collecting money, always carried by the sweeps' ladies.

MATE: the term a coster or low person applies to a friend, partner, or companion; "me and my **MATE** did so and so," is a common phrase with a low Londoner.—Originally a *Sea term.*

MOBS: companions; **MOBSMEN**, dressy swindlers.

MURERK: the mistress of the house.—*See* **BURERK** *page 31.*

MUSLIN: a woman or girl; "he picked up a bit of **MUSLIN**."

NAMUS or **NAMOUS:** some one, *i.e.,* "be off, somebody is coming,"—*Back slang,* but general.—*See* **VAMOS** *page 172.*

NUB: a husband.

OMEE: a master or landlord; "the **OMEE** of the cassey's a nark on the pitch," the master of the house will not let us perform. *Italian,* **UOMO**, a man; "**UOMO DELLA CASA**," the master of the house.

PAL: a partner, acquaintance, friend, an accomplice. *Gipsey*, a brother.

PETTICOAT: a woman.

RACLAN: a married woman.—*Gipsey*.

RELIEVING OFFICER: a significant term for a father.—*University*.

RIB: a wife.—*North*.

RUMY: a good woman or girl.—*Gipsey slang*. In the regular *Gipsey* language, ROMI, a woman, a wife, is the feminine of RO, a man; and in the *Robber's Language* of Spain (partly *Gipsey*,) RUMI signifies a harlot.

SHAVER: a sharp fellow; "a young" or "old SHAVER," a boy or man. —*Sea*.

SKIPPER: the master of a vessel. *Dutch*, SCHIFFER, from *schiff* a ship; sometimes used synonymous with "Governor."

TEETOTALLER: a total abstainer from alcoholic drinks.

YOURNIBS: yourself.

NATIONALITIES

BOG-TROTTER: satirical name for an Irishman.—*Miege. Camden*, however, speaking of the "debateable land" on the borders of England and Scotland, says, "both these dales breed notable BOG-TROTTERS."

COCKNEY: a native of London. Originally, a spoilt or effeminate boy, derived from COCKERING, or foolishly petting a person, rendering them of soft or luxurious manners. Halliwelll states, in his admirable essay upon the word, that "some writers trace the word with much probability to the imaginary land of COCKAYGNE, the lubber land of the olden times." *Grose* gives Minsheu's absurd but comical derivation:—A citizen of London being in the country, and hearing a horse neigh, exclaimed, *"Lord! How that horse laughs."* A bystander informed him that that noise was called neighing. The next morning when the cock crowed, the citizen, to show that he had not forgotten what was told him, cried out, *"Do you hear how the COCK NEIGHS?"*

GREEKS: the low Irish. **ST. GILES' GREEK,** slang or *Cant* language. *Cotgrave* gives **MERIE GREEK** as a definition for a roystering fellow, a drunkard. — *Shakespere.* — *See* **MEDICAL GREEK** *page 141.*

PADDY, PAT, or **PADDY WHACK:** An Irishman.

> "I'm **PADDY WHACK,** from Bally hack,
>> Not long ago turned soldier;
> In storm and sack, in front attack,
>> None other can be boulder."
>>>> — *Irish Song.*

QUI-HI: an English resident at Calcutta. — *Anglo Indian.*

ROMANY: a Gipsey or the *Gipsey* language; the speech of the Roma or Zincali. — *Spanish Gipsey.*

SAWNEY, or **SANDY:** a Scotchman. Corruption of Alexander.

SCOT: temper or passion — from the irascible temperament of that nation; "oh what a **SCOT** he was in," *i.e.,* what temper he showed, —especially if you allude to **SCOTCH FIDDLE.** — *See page 87.*

TAFFY: (corruption of *David*), a Welshman. Compare **SAWNEY** (from *Alexander*), a Scotchman.

TEAGUELAND: Ireland.

YELLOW BELLY: a native of the Fens of Lincolnshire or the Isle of Ely, —in allusion to the frogs and a yellow-bellied eel caught there; they are also said to be *web-footed.*

BODILY FUNCTIONS

BLUBBER: to cry in a childish manner. — *Ancient.*

CASCADING: vomiting.

CASTING UP ONE'S ACCOUNTS: vomiting. — *Old.*

CAT: to vomit like a cat. — *See* **SHOOT THE CAT** *below.*

CRAP: to ease oneself, to evacuate. *Old word* for refuse, also *Old Cant,* **CROP.**

DANNA: excrement; **DANNA DRAG,** a nightman's or dustman's cart.

DITHERS: nervous or cold shiverings. "It gave me the **DITHERS**."

DOSS: to sleep, formerly spelt **DORSE**. Perhaps from the phrase to lie on one's *dorsum*, back.

GANDER MONTH: the period when the monthly nurse is in the ascendant, and the husband has to shift for himself.

IN THE ARMS OF MURPHY: fast asleep.

LAG: to void urine.—*Ancient Cant.*

MURPHY: "in the arms of **MURPHY**," *i.e.*, fast asleep. Corruption of **MORPHEUS**.

NAP ONE'S BIB: to cry, shed tears, or carry one's point.

PIPE: to shed tears or bewail; "**PIPE** one's eye."—*Sea term.*

> "He first began to eye his pipe,
> and then to **PIPE HIS EYE**."
>
> —*Old Song.*

Metaphor from the boatswain's pipe, which calls to duty.

PUMP SHIP: to evacuate urine.—*Sea.*

SHOOT THE CAT: to vomit.

SNOOZE or **SNOODGE** (vulgar pronunciation): to sleep or doze.

STALE: to evacuate urine.—*Stable term.*

 # BODY PARTS

 ## ARMS and HANDS

BENDER: the arm; "over the **BENDER**, "synonymous with "over the left,"—*See* **OVER** *page 400*. Also an ironical exclamation similar to **WALKER**.

BUNCH OF FIVES: the hand or fist.

CLICK: knock or blow. **CLICK-HANDED**, left-handed.—*Cornish.*

DADDLES: hands; "tip us your **DADDLES**," *i.e.*, shake hands.

FAMBLES or **FAMMS:** the hands.—*Ancient Cant. German,* **FAUGEN**.

FIN: a hand; "come, tip us your **FIN**," viz., let us shake hands. — *Sea.*

FLIPPER: the hand; "give us your **FLIPPER**," give me your hand. — *Sea.* Metaphor taken from the flipper or paddle of a turtle.

FORKS or **GRAPPLING IRONS:** fingers.

FUNNY-BONE: the extremity of the elbow — or rather, the muscle which passes round it between the two bones, a blow on which causes painful tingling in the fingers. Facetiously derived, from its being the extremity of the *humerus* (humorous).

GRABBERS: the hands.

GRAPPLING IRONS: fingers. — *Sea.*

KIMBO or **A KIMBO:** holding the arms in a bent position from the body, and resting the hands upon the hips, in a bullying attitude. Said to be from **A SCHEMBO**, *Italian*; but more probably from **KIMBAW**, the *Old Cant* for beating or bullying. — *See Grose.*

MAULEY: a fist, that with which one strikes as with a **MALL**. — *Pugilistic.*

MITTENS: fists. — *Pugilistic.*

PAWS: hands.

PICKERS: the hands. — *Shakespere.*

 # BODY

BELLOWS: the lungs.

BREAD BASKET, DUMPLING DEPOT, VICTUALLING OFFICE: &c., are terms given by the "*Fancy*" to the digestive organ.

BUB: a teat, woman's breast.

BUFF: the bare skin; "stripped to the **BUFF**."

BUM: the part on which we sit. — *Shakespere.* **BUMBAGS**, trousers.

COLD MEAT: a corpse.

COLLYWOBBLES: a stomach ache, a person's bowels — supposed by many of the lower orders to be the seat of feeling and nutrition; an idea either borrowed from, or transmitted by, the ancients. — *Devonshire.*

CORPORATION: the protuberant front of an obese person.

MOLLYGRUBS or **MULLIGRUBS:** stomach ache or sorrow—which to the costermongers is much the same, as he believes, like the ancients, that the viscera is the seat of all feeling.

MOOE: the mouth; the female generative organ.—*Gipsey* and *Hindoo*. *Shakespere* has **MOE**, to make mouths.

MY LORD: a nickname given to a hunchback.

OTTOMY: a thin man, a skeleton, a dwarf. Vulgar pronunciation of *Anatomy*, *Shakespere* has '**ATOMY**.

PIPKIN: the stomach—properly, an earthen round-bottomed pot. —*Norwich*.

POSTERIORS: a correspondent insists that the vulgar sense of this word is undoubtedly slang (Swift, I believe, first applied it as such), and remarks that it is curious the word *anterior* has not been so abused.

RIBROAST: to beat till the ribs are sore—*Old*, but still in use:

> "And he departs, not meanly boasting
> Of his magnificent **RIBROASTING**." –*Hudibras*.

STIFF 'UN: a corpse.—*Term used by undertakers*.

WIFFLE-WOFFLES: in the dumps, sorrow, stomach ache.

 # BLOOD

BODMINTON: blood.—*Pugilistic*.

CLARET: blood.—*Pugilistic*.

 # EYES and EARS

BLINKER: a blackened eye.—*Norwich slang*.

BOSS-EYED: a person with one eye, or rather with one eye injured.

BUCKHORSE: a smart blow or box on the ear; derived from the name of a celebrated "bruiser" of that name.

COCK: "to **COCK** your eye," to shut or wink one eye.

COCK-EYE: one that squints.

DAYLIGHTS: eyes; "to darken his **DAYLIGHTS**," to give a person black eyes.

LIGHTS: the eyes.

LUG: the ear.—*Scotch.*

OGLES: eyes. *Old Cant. French* **OEIL**.

PEEPERS: eyes; "painted **PEEPERS**," eyes bruised or blackened from a blow.

SQUINNY-EYED: squinting.—*Shakespere.*

WATTLES: ears.

WINDOWS: the eyes or "peepers."

 ## FACE

CRIBBAGE-FACED: marked with the smallpox, full of holes like a cribbage board.

CUT OF ONE'S GIB: the expression or cast of his countenance (*see* **GIB**).

FIGURE: "to cut a good or bad **FIGURE**," to make a good or indifferent appearance; "what's the **FIGURE**?" how much is to pay? **FIGURE-HEAD**, a person's face.—*Sea term.*

FRONTISPIECE: the face.

GIB-FACE: properly the lower lip of a horse; "**TO HANG ONE'S GIB**," to pout the lower lip, be angry or sullen.

GILLS: the lower part of the face.—*Bacon.* "To grease one's **GILLS**," "to have a good feed," or make a hearty meal.

GRAVEL-RASH: a scratched face—telling its tale of a drunken fall.

JIB: the face or a person's expression; "the cut of his **JIB**," *i.e.*, his peculiar appearance. The sail of a ship, which in position and shape corresponds to the nose on a person's face.—*See* **GIB-FACE**.—*Sea.*

PHYSOG or **PHIZ:** the face. *Swift* uses the latter. Corruption of *physiognomy.*

HAIR

AGGERAWATORS: (corruption of *Aggravators*), the greasy locks of hair in vogue among costermongers and other street folk, worn twisted from the temple back toward the ear. They are also, from a supposed resemblance in form, termed **NEWGATE KNOCKERS.**—*See* **NEWGATE KNOCKERS** *below.*—*Sala's Gaslight*, &c.

BOW- CATCHERS or **KISS CURLS:** small curls twisted on the cheeks or temples of young—and often old—girls, adhering to the face as if gummed or pasted. Evidently a corruption of **BEAU-CATCHERS.** In old times these were called *lovelocks*, when they were the marks at which all the puritan and ranting preachers levelled their pulpit pop-guns, loaded with sharp and virulent abuse. Hall and Pryune looked upon all women as strumpets who dared to let the hair depart from a straight line upon their cheeks. The French prettily term them *accroche-cœurs*, whilst in the United States they are plainly and unpleasantly called **SPIT-CURLS.** Bartlett says: "**SPIT CURL,** a detached lock of hair curled upon the temple; probably from having been first filastered into shape by the saliva. It is now understood that the mucilage of quince seed is used by the ladies for this purpose."

> "You may prate of your lips, and your teeth of pearl,
>   And your eyes so brightly flashing;
> My song shall be of that **SALIVA CURL**
>   Which threatens my heart to smash in."
>   —*Boston Transcript*, October 30, 1858.

When men twist the hair on each side of their faces into ropes they are sometime called **BELL-ROPES**, as being wherewith to *draw the belles*. Whether **BELL-ROPES** or **BOW-CATCHER**, it is singular they should form part of the prisoner's paraphernalia, and that a jaunty little kiss-me quick curl should, of all things in the world, ornament a gaol dock; yet such was formerly the case. Hunt, the murderer of Weare, on his trial, we are informed by the *Athenæum*, appeared at the bar with a highly pomatumed love-lock sticking tight to his forehead. Young ladies, think of this!

CARROTS: the coarse and satirical term for red hair.

COUNTY-CROP: (*i.e.,* COUNTY-PRISON CROP), hair cut close and round, as if guided by a basin — an indication of having been in prison.

COW-LICK: The term given to the lock of hair which costermongers and thieves usually twist forward from the ear; a large greasy curl upon the cheek, seemingly licked into shape. The opposite of NEWGATE-KNOCKER. — *See* NEWGATE KNOCKERS *below.*

CROPPIE: a person who has had his hair cut, or CROPPED, in prison.

GINGER HACKLED: having flaxen light yellow hair. — *See* HACKLE *page* 27.

NEWGATE FRINGE or **FRILL:** the collar of beard worn under the chin; so called from its occupying the position of the rope when Jack Ketch operates. Another name for it is a TYBURN COLLAR.

NEWGATE KNOCKER: the term given to the lock of hair which costermongers and thieves usually twist back towards the ear. The shape is supposed to resemble the knocker on the prisoners' door at Newgate — a resemblance that would appear to carry a rather unpleasant suggestion to the wearer. Sometime termed a COBBLER'S KNOT or COW-LICK. — *See* COW-LICK *above.*

STROMMEL: straw. — *Ancient Cant.* Halliwell says that in Norfolk STRUMMEL is a name for hair.

TYBURN COLLAR: the fringe of beard worn under the chin. — *See* NEWGATE FRINGE *above.*

HEAD

ATTIC: the head; "queer in the ATTIC," intoxicated. — *Pugilistic.*

BLOCK: the head.

CANISTER: the head. — *Pugilistic.*

GARRET: the head.

KNOWLEDGE BOX: the head. — *Pugilistic.*

LOBB: the head. — *Pugilistic.*

LOLLY: the head. — *See* LOBB *above.* — *Pugilistic.*

NOB: the head. — *Pugilistic;* "BOB A NOB," a shilling a head. *Ancient Cant,* NEB. NOB is an early *English* word, and is used in the Romance of

Kynge Alisaunder (thirteenth century) for a head; originally, no doubt, the same as *Knob.*

NUDDIKIN: the head.

SCONCE: the head, judgment, sense. — *Dutch.*

TWOPENNY: the head; "tuck in your TWOPENNY," bend down your head.

UPPER STOREY or **UPPER LOFT:** a person's head; "his UPPER STOREY is unfurnished," *i.e.*, he does not know very much.

LEGS and FEET

BEETLE-CRUSHERS or **SQUASHERS:** large flat feet.

CHUBBY HOCKS: round or clumsy feet.

COUNCIL OF TEN: the toes of a man who turns his feet inward.

GADDING THE HOOF: going without shoes. GADDING, roaming about, although used in an old translation of the Bible, is now only heard amongst the lower orders.

HOCKS: the feet.

PINS: legs.

SCOTCHES: the legs; also synonymous with NOTCHES.

SHANKS: legs.

STEMS: the legs.

STUMPS: feet or legs.

TROTTERS: feet. Sheep's TROTTERS, boiled sheep's feet, a favourite street delicacy.

MOUTH

CHESHIRE CAT: "to grin like a CHESHIRE CAT," to display the teeth and gums when laughing. Formerly the phrase was "to grin like a CHESHIRE CAT *eating* CHEESE." A *hardly satisfactory* explanation has been give of this phrase — that Cheshire is a county palatine, and the cats, when they think of it, are so tickled with the notion that they can't help grinning.

CHOPS: properly CHAPS, the mouth or cheeks; "down in the CHOPS," or down in the mouth," *i.e.*, sad or melancholy.

CLAPPER: the tongue.

DOMINOS: the teeth.

DUBBER: the mouth; "mum your DUBBER," hold your tongue.

GOB: the mouth; mucus or saliva.—*North.* Sometimes used for GAB, talk:

> "There was a man called *Job*,
> Dwelt in the land of Uz;
> He had a good gift of the GOB;
> The same case happen us."
> —*Zach. Boyd.*

GRINDERS: teeth.

IVORIES: teeth; "a box" or "cage of IVORIES," a set of teeth, the mouth; "wash your IVORIES," *i.e.*, "drink." The word is also used to denote DICE.

JIBB: the tongue.—*Gipsey and Hindoo.*

LATCHPAN: the lower lip—properly a dripping pan; "to hang one's LATCHPAN," to pout, be sulky.—*Norfolk.*

MAW: the mouth; "hold your MAW," cease talking.

MOOE: the mouth; the female generative organ.—*Gipsey* and *Hindoo. Shakespere* has MOE, to make mouths.

MUG: the mouth or face.—*Old.*

MUNS: the mouth. *German,* MUND.—*Old Cant.*

MUZZLE: the mouth.

POTATO TRAP: the mouth. A humorous *Hibernicism.*

RED RAG: the tongue.

SAUCEBOX: a mouth, also a pert young person.

SNAGGLE TEETH: uneven and unpleasant looking dental operators. —*West.* SNAGS (*Americanism*) ends of sunken drift-wood sticking out of the water, on which river steamers are often wrecked.

VELVET: the tongue.

 ## NECK and THROAT

GUTTER LANE: the throat.

NECK: to swallow. **NECK-OIL,** drink of any kind.

RED LANE: the throat.

SCRAG: the neck.—*Old Cant. Scotch,* **CRAIG.** Still used by butchers. Hence, **SCRAG,** to hang by the neck, and **SCRAGGING,** an execution. —Also *Old Cant.*

SCRUFF: the back part of the neck seized by the adversary in an encounter.

 ## NOSE

CONK: a nose; **CONKY,** having a projecting or remarkable nose. The Duke of Wellington was frequently termed "Old **CONKY**" in satirical papers and caricatures.

CORK: "to draw a **CORK,**" to give a bloody nose.—*Pugilistic.*

HANDLE: a nose; the title appended to a person's name; also a term in boxing, "**HANDLING** one's fists."

NOSER: a bloody or contused nose.—*Pugilistic.*

PASTE-HORN: the nose. Shoemakers nickname any shopmate with a large nose "old **PASTE-HORN,**" from the horn in which they keep their paste.

POST-HORN: the nose.—*See* **PASTE-HORN** *above.*

SMELLER: a blow on the nose, or a **NOSER.**

SNOT: a term of reproach applied to persons by the vulgar when vexed or annoyed. In a Westminster school vocabulary for boys, published in the last century, the term is curiously applied. Its proper meaning is the glandular mucus discharged through the nose.

 ILLNESS, DEATH, & REMEDIES

ABRAM-SHAM or **SHAM-ABRAHAM:** to feign sickness or distress. From **ABRAM MAN**, the *Ancient Cant* term for a begging impostor or one who pretended to have been mad. — *Burton's Anatomy of Melancholy*, part i., sec. 2, vol. i., p.360. When Abraham Newland was Cashier of the Bank of England, and signed their notes, it was sung:

> "I have heard people say
> That **SHAM ABRAHAM** you may,
> But you mustn't **SHAM ABRAHAM** Newland."

ALL-OVERISH: neither sick nor well, the premonitory symptoms of illness.

BELLY-VENGEANCE: small sour beer, apt to cause gastralgia.

CHATTS: lice or body vermin.

COCK ONE'S TOES: to die.

COLLYWOBBLES: a stomach ache, a person's bowels — supposed by many of the lower orders to be the seat of feeling and nutrition; an idea either borrowed from, or transmitted by, the ancients. — *Devonshire.*

CROAK: to die — from the gurgling sound a person makes when the breath of life is departing. — *Oxfordshire.*

CROAKER: a corpse or dying person beyond hope.

CRUMBS: "to pick up one's **CRUMBS**," to begin to have an appetite after an illness; to improve in health, circumstances, &c., after a loss thereof.

CUSTOMHOUSE OFFICER: an aperient pill. [laxative.]

DAVY'S LOCKER or **DAVY JONES' LOCKER:** the sea, the common receptacle for all things thrown overboard — a nautical phrase for death, the other world.

GARGLE: medical student Slang for physic.

GRASS: "gone to **GRASS**," dead — a coarse allusion to *burial*; absconded or disappeared suddenly; "oh, go to **GRASS**," a common answer to a troublesome or inquisitive person—possibly a corruption of "go to GRACE," meaning, of course, a directly opposite fate.

GRAYS or SCOTCH GRAYS: lice.—*Scotch.*

HOOKS: "dropped off the HOOKS," said of a deceased person. Derived from the ancient practice of suspending on hooks the quarters of a traitor or felon sentenced by the old law to be hung, drawn, and quartered, and which dropped off the hooks as they decayed.

HOOK-UM SNIVEY: (formerly "hook *and* snivey") a low expression meaning to cheat by feigning sickness or other means. Also a piece of thick iron wire crooked at one end, and fastened into a wooden handle, for the purpose of undoing from the outside the wooden bolt of a door.

HOPPING GILES: a cripple. St. Ægidius or Giles, himself similarly afflicted, was their patron saint. The ancient lazar houses were dedicated to him.

KERTEVER-CARTZO: the venereal disease. From the *Lingua Franca*, CATTIVO, bad, and CAZZO, the male generative organ.

KICK THE BUCKET: to die.—*Norfolk.* According to Forby, a metaphor taken from the descent of a well or mine, which is of course absurd. The Rev. E. S. Taylor supplies me with a following note from his MS. additions to the work of the East–Anglian lexicographer:

> "The allusion is to the way in which a slaughtered pig is hung up, viz., by passing the ends of a bent piece of wood behind the tendons of the hind legs, and so suspending it to a hook in a beam above. This piece of wood is locally termed a *bucket,* and so by a coarse metaphor the phrase came to signify to die. Compare the Norfolk phrase "as wrong as a bucket."

The natives of the West Indies have converted the expression into KICKERABOO.

LORD: a humpbacked man.—*See* MY LORD *below.*

LOUSE-TRAP: a small-toothed comb.—*Old Cant.*—*See* CATCH 'EM ALIVE.

MOLLYGRUBS or MULLIGRUBS: stomach ache or sorrow—which to the costermongers is much the same, as he believes, like the ancients, that the viscera is the seat of all feeling.

MY LORD: a nickname given to a hunchback.

NAIL: to steal or capture; "paid on the NAIL," *i.e.*, ready money; NAILED, taken up or caught—probably in allusion to the practice of NAILING bad money to the counter. We say "as dead as a DOORNAIL;"—why? *Shakespere* has the expression in Henry IV:

> "*Falstaff.* What! Is the old king dead?
> *Pistol.* As nail in door."

A correspondent thinks the expression is only alliterative humour, and compares as "*Flat as a flounder*," "straight as a soldier," &c.

PICK: "to PICK oneself up," to recover after a beating or illness; "to PICK a man up," "to do," or cheat him.

POT: "to GO TO POT," to die; from the classic custom of putting the ashes of the dead in an urn; also, to be ruined or broken up—often applied to tradesmen who fail in business. GO TO POT! *i.e.*, go and hang yourself, shut up and be quiet. *L 'Estrange,* to PUT THE POT ON, to overcharge or exaggerate.

PURL: a mixture of hot ale and sugar, with wormwood infused in it, a favourite morning drink to produce an appetite, sometimes with gin and spice added:

> "Two penn'orth o' PURL—
> Good 'early PURL,'
> 'Gin all the world
> To put your hair into a curl,
> When you feel yourself queer of a mornin'."

SCOTCH FIDDLE: the itch; "to play the SCOTCH FIDDLE," to work the index finger of the right hand like a fiddlestick between the index and middle finger of the left. This provokes a Scotchmen in the highest degree, it implying that he is afflicted with the itch.

SCOTCH GRAYS: lice. Our northern neighbours are calumniously reported, from their living on oatmeal, to be peculiarly liable to cutaneous eruptions and parasites.

SHAKY: said of a person of questionable health, integrity, or solvency; at the *University*, of one not likely to pass his examination.

SHAM ABRAHAM: to feign sickness.—*See* ABRAHAM *page 85.*

SHOES: "to die in one's SHOES," to be hung.

SICK AS A HORSE: popular simile—curious, because a horse never vomits.

SICKNER or **SICKENER:** a dose too much of anything.

TWIG: "to hop the TWIG," to decamp, "cut one's stick," to die.

WIFFLE-WOFFLES: in the dumps, sorrow, stomach ache.

WIND: "to raise the WIND," to procure money; "to slip one's WIND," coarse expression meaning to die.

YELLOW-JACK: the yellow fever prevalent in the West Indies.

 # EMOTIONAL STATES

 ## COCKY

BIG: "to look BIG," to assume an inflated dress or manner, "to talk BIG," *i.e.*, boastingly or with an "extensive" air.

BOTTY: conceited, swaggering.

BOUNCE: impudence.

CATCHY: (similar formation to *touchy*), inclined to take an undue advantage.

CHEEK: impudence, assurance; CHEEKY, saucy or forward. *Lincolnshire*, CHEEK, to accuse.

COCKSURE: certain.

COCKY: pert, saucy.

FAST: gay, spreeish, unsteady, thoughtless—an Americanism that has of late ascended from the streets to the drawing-room. The word has certainly now a distinct meaning, which it had not thirty years ago. QUICK is the synonym for FAST, but a QUICK MAN would not convey the meaning of a FAST MAN—a person who by late hours, gaiety, and continual rounds of pleasure, lives too fast and wears himself out. In polite society a FAST young lady is one who affects mannish habits, or makes herself conspicuous by some unfeminine accomplishment, —talks slang, drives about in London, smokes cigarettes, is knowing in dogs, horses, &c. An amusing anecdote is told of a FAST young lady, the daughter of a right reverend prelate, who was an adept in *horseflesh*. Being desirous of ascertaining the opinion of a candidate for ordination who had the look of a bird of the same feather, as to the merits of some cattle just brought to her father's palace for her to select from, she was assured by him they were utterly unfit for a lady's use. With a knowing look at the horses' points, she gave her decision in these choice words, "Well, I agree with you; they *are* a rum lot, as the Devil said of the ten commandments."

GRANNY: importance, knowledge, pride; "take the GRANNY off them as has white hands," viz., remove their self-conceit.—*Mayhew*, vol. i., p. 364.

HAND: a workman or helper, a person. "A cool HAND," explained by Sir Thomas Overbury to be "one who accounts bashfulness the wickedest thing in the world, and therefore studies impudence."

HIGH JINKS: "ON THE HIGH JINKS," taking up an arrogant position, assuming an undue superiority.

RIDE: "TO RIDE THE HIGH HORSE," or RIDE ROUGH-SHOD over one, to be overbearing or oppressive; to RIDE THE BLACK DONKEY, to be in an ill humour.

ROOKY: rascally, rakish, scampish.

RUMBUMPTIOUS: haughty, pugilistic.

RUMBUSTIOUS or **RUMBUSTICAL:** pompous, haughty, boisterous, careless of the comfort of others.

SMALL BEER: "he doesn't think SMALL BEER of himself," *i.e.*, he has a great opinion of his own importance. SMALL COALS is also used in the same sense.

SNOBBISH: stuck up, proud, make-believe.

STARCHY: stuck-up, high-notioned, showily dressed, disdainful, cross.

STUCK-UP: "purse-proud,"—a form of snobbishness very common in those who have risen in the world. Mr. Albert Smith has written some amusing papers on the *Natural History of* STUCK-UP *People*.

UPPISH: proud, arrogant.

CROSS and BAD-TEMPERED

BAD: "to go to the BAD," to deteriorate in character, be ruined. *Virgil* has an exactly similar phrase, *in pejus ruere.*

GAMMY: bad, unfavourable, poor-tempered. Those householders who are known enemies to the street folk and tramps are pronounced by them to be GAMMY. GAMMY sometimes means forged, as "GAMMY MONEKER," a forged signature; GAMMY STUFF, spurious medicine; GAMMY LOWR, counterfeit coin. *Hants*, GAMY, dirty. The hieroglyphic used by beggars and cadgers to intimate to those of the tribe coming after that things are not very favourable, is known as □, or GAMMY.

HUFF: to vex or offend; a poor temper.

NASTY: ill-tempered, cross-grained.

PUCKER or **PUCKER UP:** to get in a poor temper.

RUSTY: cross, ill-tempered, morose, one who cannot go through life like a person of easy and polished manners.

SHIRTY: ill-tempered or cross. When one person makes another in an ill humour he is said to have "got his SHIRT out."

SNAGGY: cross, crotchetty, malicious.

STREAKY: irritated, ill-tempered.

TOUCHY: peevish, irritable. *Johnson* terms it a low word.

WAXY: cross, ill-tempered.

FEARFUL

CHICKEN-HEARTED: cowardly, fearful.

DUTCH COURAGE: false courage, generally excited by drink —*pot-valour.*

FUNK: trepidation, nervousness, cowardice. To FUNK, to be afraid or nervous.

TWITTER: "all in a TWITTER,"in a fright or a fidgetty state.

WHITE FEATHER: "to show the WHITE FEATHER," to evince cowardice. In the times when great attention was paid to the breeding of game-cocks, a white feather in the tail was considered a proof of cross-breeding.

WHITE LIVER'D or **LIVER-FACED:** cowardly, much afraid, very mean.

GRUMPY

CRIB BITER: an inveterate grumbler; properly said of a horse which has the habit, a sign of its bad digestion.

CROAKER: one who takes a desponding view of everything; an alarmist. *From the croaking of a raven.—Ben Johnson.*

CRUSTY: ill-tempered, petulant, morose.—*Old.*

DUMPISH: sullen or glumpy.

GIB-FACE: properly the lower lip of a horse; "To HANG ONE'S GIB," to pout the lower lip, be angry or sullen.

GLUMP: to sulk.

GLUMPISH: of a stubborn, sulky temper.

GREEN: ignorant, not wide-awake, inexperienced.—*Shakespere.* "Do you see any GREEN in my eye?" ironical question in a dispute.

HUMP UP: "to have one's HUMP UP," to be cross or ill-tempered—like a cat with its back set up.—*See* MONKEY *page 96.*

KICKSY: troublesome, disagreeable.

PUCKER: poor temper, difficulty, *deshabille.*

RIDE: "to RIDE THE HIGH HORSE," or RIDE ROUGH-SHOD over one, to be overbearing or oppressive; to RIDE THE BLACK DONKEY, to be in an ill humour.

RUST: "to nab the RUST," to take offense. RUSTY, cross, ill-tempered, morose, one who cannot go through life like a person of easy and *polished* manners.

RUSTY GUTS: a blunt, rough, old fellow. Corruption of RUSTICUS.

SHIRTY: ill-tempered or cross. When one person makes another in an ill humour he is said to have "got his SHIRT out."

SNAGGY: cross, crotchetty, malicious.

SOFT: foolish, inexperienced. An old term for bank notes.

STREAKY: irritated, ill-tempered.

TOUCHY: peevish, irritable. *Johnson* terms it a low word.

WAXY: cross, ill-tempered.

HAPPY and JOLLY

BOBBISH: very well, clever, spruce; "how are you doing?" "Oh! Pretty BOBBISH." — *Old.*

CLOVER: happiness or luck.

COCKLES: "to rejoice the COCKLES of one's heart," a vulgar phrase implying great pleasure. — *See* PLUCK *page 93.*

COXY-LOXY: good-tempered, drunk. — *Norfolk.*

FIZZING: first-rate, very good, excellent; synonymous with STUNNING.

GOLOPSHUS: splendid, delicious, luscious. — *Norwhich.*

KIDDYISH: frolicsome, jovial.

> "Think on the KIDDYISH spree we had on such a day."
> — *Randall's Diary*, 1820.

LUMMY: jolly, first-rate.

PINK: the *acmé* of perfection. — *Shakespere.*

PLUMMY: round, sleek, jolly, or fat; excellent, very good, first-rate.

QUIZZICAL: jocose, humorous.

PASSIONATE and BRAVE

DANDER: passion or temper; "to get one's DANDER up," to rouse his passion. — *Old.*

GAME: a term variously applied; "are you GAME?" have you courage enough? "what's your little GAME?" what are you going to do? "come, none of your GAMES," be quiet, don't annoy me; "on the GAME," out thieving.

GASSY: liable to "flare up" at any offence.

MONKEY: spirit or ill temper; "to get one's MONKEY up," to rouse his passion. A man is said to have his MONKEY up, or the MONKEY on his back, when he is "*riled*" or out of temper; also to have his BACK or HUMP up.

NUTTY: amorous.

PLUCK: the heart, liver, and lungs of an animal—all that is PLUCKED away in connection with the windpipe, from the chest of a sheep or hog; among low persons, courage, valour, and a stout heart.—*See* MOLLYGRUBS *page 78.*

RACKETY: wild or noisy.

RANTIPOLE: a wild, noisy fellow.

SCOT: temper or passion—from the irascible temperament of that nation; "oh what a SCOT he was in," *i.e.*, what temper he showed, —especially if you allude to SCOTCH FIDDLE.—*See page 87.*

SPUNK: spirit, *fire*, courage, mettle.

> "In that snug room, where any man of SPUNK
> would find it a hard matter to get drunk."
>
> —*Peter Pindar, i., 245*

Common in *America*. For derivation *see* SPUNKS *on page 308.*

TAKE: to "TAKE UP for anyone," to protect or defend a person; "to TAKE heart," to have courage; "to TAKE THE FIELD," when said of a *General*, to commence operations against the enemy; when a *racing man* TAKES THE FIELD he stakes his money against the favourite.—*See* TAKE *in the Index for more meanings on page 504.*

WILD: vexed, cross, passionate. In the United States the word *mad* is supplemented with a vulgar meaning similar to our Cockneyism, WILD; and to make a man MAD on the other side of the Atlantic is to vex him or "rile" his temper—not to render him a raving maniac or a fit subject for Bedlam.

WOOL: courage, pluck; "you are not half-**WOOLLED**," term of reproach from one thief to another.

 ## TOUCHY and INQUISITIVE

LEARY: to look or be watchful; shy. — *Old Cant.*

PEERY: suspicious or inquisitive.

QUIZ: a prying person, an odd fellow. *Oxford slang;* lately admitted into dictionaries. Not noticed by *Johnson.*

RAW: a tender point, a foible; "to touch a man up on the **RAW**," is to irritate one by alluding to, or joking him on, anything on which he is peculiarly susceptible or "thin-skinned."

SKIN: to abate or lower the value of anything; "thin-**SKINNED**," sensitive, touchy.

SPOFFY: a bustling busy-body is said to be **SPOFFY**.

THINSKINNED: over nice, petulant, apt to get a "raw."

TIGHT: close, stingy; hard up, short of cash; **TIGHT**, spruce, strong, active; "a **TIGHT** lad," a smart, active young fellow; **TIGHT**, drunk or nearly so; "**TIGHT**-laced," puritanical, over-precise. Money is said to be **TIGHT** when the public, from want of confidence in the aspect of affairs, are not inclined to speculate.

OTHER EMOTIONAL STATES

COCUM: advantage, luck, cunning, or sly, "to fight **COCUM**," to be wily and cautious.

COLT'S TOOTH: elderly persons of juvenile tastes are said to have a colt's tooth.

CRIB BITER: an inveterate grumbler; properly said of a horse which has the habit, a sign of its bad digestion.

CROCODILE TEARS: the tears of a hypocrite. An ancient phrase, introduced into this country by Mandville, or other early English traveler. — *Othello*, iv., 1.

CUT: CUT UP, mortified, to criticize severely or expose. —*See* CUT *in the Index for more meanings on page 479.*

DEAD ALIVE: stupid, dull.

DUTCH CONSOLATION: "thank God it is no worse."

FAST: embarrassed, wanting money. Synonymous with HARD UP. —*Yorkshire.*

FIDDLER: a sharper, a cheat; also one who dawdles over little matters and neglects great ones.

HALF-BAKED: soft, doughy, half-witted, silly.

HALF-ROCKED: silly, half-witted. —Compare HALF-BAKED above.

HORSE MARINE: an awkward person. In ancient times the "JOLLIES" or Royal Marines, were the butts of the sailors, from their ignorance of seamanship. "Tell that to the MARINES, the blue jackets won't believe it!" was a common rejoinder to a "stiff yarn." Now-a-days they are deservedly appreciated as the finest regiment in the service. A HORSE MARINE (an impossibility) was used to denote one more awkward still.

JANNOCK: sociable, fair dealing. —*Norfolk.*

KNARK: a hard-hearted or savage person.

MAGGOTTY: fanciful, fidgetty. Whims and fancies were formerly termed MAGGOTS, from the popular belief that a maggot in the brain was the cause of any odd notion or caprice a person might exhibit.

OFFISH: distant, not familiar.

PIG-HEADED: obstinate.

RUM: like its opposite, QUEER, was formerly a much used prefix signifying fine, good, gallant, or valuable, perhaps in some way connected with ROME. Now-a-days it means indifferent, bad, or questionable, and we often hear even persons in polite society use such a phrase as "what a RUM fellow he is, to be sure," in speaking of a man of singular habits or appearance. The term, from its frequent use, long since claimed a place in our dictionaries; but, with the exception of *Johnson*, who says "RUM, a *Cant* word for a clergyman(?)," no lexicographer has deigned to notice it.

> "Thus **RUMLY** floor'ed, the kind Acestes ran.
> And pitying, rais'd from earth the game old man."
> —*Virgil's Æneid*, book v., Translation by Thomas Moore.

SWEET: loving or fond; "how **SWEET** he was upon the moll," *i.e.*, what marked attention he paid the girl.

TAKE: "to **TAKE ON**," to grieve; *Shakespere* uses the word **TAKING** in this sense.—*See* **TAKE** *in the Index for more meanings on page 504.*

THICK: intimate, familiar. *Scotch,* **CHIEF**; "the two are very **CHIEF** now," *i.e.*, friendly.

 # FINANCIAL STATES

ALL TO SMASH or GONE TO PIECES: bankrupt or smashed to pieces. —*Somersetshire.*

BAGS: trousers. Trousers of an extensive pattern or exaggerated fashionable cut, have lately been termed **HOWLING BAGS**, but only when the style has been very "*loud.*" The word is probably an abbreviation for b-mbags. "To have the **BAGS** off," to be of age and one's own master, to have plenty of money.

BESTED: taken in or defrauded.

BREECHED or TO HAVE THE BAGS OFF: to have plenty of money; "to be well **BREECHED**," to be in good circumstances.

BROSIER: a bankrupt.—*Cheshire.* **BROSIER-MY-DAME**, school term, implying a clearing of the housekeeper's larder of provisions, in revenge for stinginess.—*Eton.*

CLEAN OUT: to thrash or beat; to ruin or bankrupt anyone; to take all they have got, by purchase or force. *De Quincey*, in his article on "Richard Bentley," speaking of the lawsuit between that great scholar and Dr. Colbatch, remarks that the latter "must have been pretty well **CLEANED OUT**."

CRACKED-UP: penniless or ruined.

FAST: embarrassed, wanting money. Synonymous with **HARD UP**. —*Yorkshire.*

FAT: rich, abundant, &c.; "a FAT lot;" "to cut it FAT," to exaggerate, to show off in an extensive or grand manner, to assume undue importance; CUT UP FAT." — *See under* CUT *page 479.* As a *Theatrical* term, a part with plenty of FAT in it, is one which affords the actor an opportunity of effective display.

FEATHERS: money, wealth; "in full FEATHER," rich.

FLAG OF DISTRESS: poverty—when the end of a person's shirt protrudes through his trousers.

GRIEF: "to come to GRIEF," to meet with an accident, be ruined.

HARD UP: in distress, poverty-stricken. — *Sea.*

LUCK: "down on one's LUCK" wanting money or in difficulty.

LUG: "my togs are in LUG," *i.e.,* in pawn.

MAHOGANY: "to have one's feet under another man's MAHOGANY," to sit at his table, be supported on other than one's own resources; "amputate your MAHOGANY," *i.e.,* go away or "cut your stick."

MONKEY WITH A LONG TAIL: a mortgage. — *Legal.*

MUCK OUT: to clean out. Often applied to one utterly ruining an adversary in gambling. From the *Provincial* MUCK, dirt.

MUCK-SNIPE: one who had been "MUCKED OUT" or beggared, at gambling.

PLUM: £100,000, usually applied to the dowry of a rich heiress or a legacy.

POT: "to GO TO POT," to die; from the classic custom of putting the ashes of the dead in an urn; also, to be ruined or broken up—often applied to tradesmen who fail in business. GO TO POT! *i.e.,* go and hang yourself, shut up and be quiet. *L 'Estrange*, to PUT THE POT ON, to overcharge or exaggerate.

QUEER STREET: "in QUEER STREET," in difficulty or in want.

QUISBY: bankrupt, poverty-stricken. — *Household Words*, No.183.

RAG SPLAWGER: a rich man.

RHINOCERAL: rich, wealthy, abounding in RHINO.

SCREW: a mean or stingy person.

SHAKY: said of a person of questionable health, integrity, or solvency; at the *University*, of one not likely to pass his examination.

SHINEY RAG: "to win the SHINEY RAG," to be ruined—said in gambling, when anyone continues betting after "luck has set in against him."

SMASH: to become bankrupt or worthless; "to go all to SMASH;" to break or "go to the dogs."

SOLD UP or **OUT:** broken down, bankrupt.

STUCK-UP: "purse-proud,"—a form of snobbishness very common in those who have risen in the world. Mr. Albert Smith has written some amusing papers on the *Natural History of* STUCK-UP *People.*

STUMPED: bowled out, done for, bankrupt, poverty-stricken. —*Cricketing term.*

TIGHT: close, stingy; hard up, short of cash; TIGHT, spruce, strong, active; "a TIGHT lad," a smart, active young fellow; TIGHT, drunk or nearly so; "TIGHT-laced," puritanical, over-precise. Money is said to be TIGHT when the public, from want of confidence in the aspect of affairs, are not inclined to speculate.

USED-UP: broken-hearted, bankrupt, fatigued.

WARM: rich or well-off.

 # MARITAL STATES

BREAK-DOWN: a jovial, social gathering, a FLARE UP; in Ireland, a wedding.

BREECHES: "to wear the BREECHES," said of a wife who usurps the husband's prerogative.

BUCK: a gay or smart man, cuckold.

FROW: a girl or wife. *German,* FRAU; *Dutch,* VROUW.

GRASS-WIDOW: an unmarried mother; a deserted mistress. In the United States, during the gold fever in California, it was common for an adventurer to put both his GRASS-WIDOW and his children to *school* during his absence.

HEN-PECKED: said of one whose wife "wears the breeches."

INTERESTING: "to be in an INTERESTING situation," applied to females when *enceinte.* [pregnant]

KNOCKED-UP: tired, jaded, used-up, done for. In the United States, amongst females, the phrase is equivalent to being *enceinte*, so that Englishmen often unconsciously commit themselves when amongst our Yankee cousins.

MARRIAGE LINES: a marriage certificate. — *Provincial.*

MOLL'D: followed or accompanied by a woman.

MOLLISHER: a low girl or woman; generally a female cohabitating with a man, and jointly getting their living by thieving.

MURERK: the mistress of the house. — *See* BURERK *page 31.*

NINCOMPOOP: a fool, a hen-pecked husband, a "Jerry Sneak." Corruption of *non compos mentis.*

NUB: a husband.

ON THE SHELF: to be transported. With old maids it has another and very different meaning.

POLL: a prostitute. POLLED UP, living with a woman without being married to her.

RACLAN: a married woman. — *Gipsey.*

RIB: a wife. — *North.*

RUMY: a good woman or girl. — *Gipsey slang.* In the regular *Gipsey* language, ROMI, a woman, a wife, is the feminine of RO, a man; and in the *Robber's Language* of Spain (partly *Gipsey,*) RUMI signifies a harlot.

SCREW LOOSE: when friends become cold and distant towards each other, it is said there is a SCREW LOOSE betwixt them; said also when anything goes wrong with a person's credit or reputation.

SHELF: "on the SHELF," not yet disposed of; young ladies are said to be so situated when they cannot meet with a husband; "on the SHELF," pawned.

SPLICE: to marry, "and the two shall become one flesh." — *Sea.*

SPOONS: "when I was SPOONS with you," i.e., when young, and in our courting days before marriage. — *Charles Mathews*, in the farce of *Everybody's Friend.*

STANGEY: a tailor; a person under petticoat government — derived from the custom of "*riding the* STANG," mentioned in Hudibras:

> "It is a custom used of course
> Where the grey mare is the better horse."

STRAW: married ladies are said to be "in **THE STRAW**" at their *accouchements*. The phrase is a coarse allusion to farm-yard animals in a similar condition.

SWEAT: to extract money from a person, to "bleed," to squander riches. — *Bulwer.*

SWISHED: married.

TIED UP: given over, finished; also married, in allusion to the Hymenial knot, unless a jocose allusion be intended to the *halter* (altar).

TOOTH: "he has cut his eye **TOOTH**," *i.e.*, he is sharp enough or old enough, to be so; "up in the **TOOTH**," far advanced in age — said often of old maids. *Stable term* for aged horses which have lost the distinguishing mark in their teeth.

YORKSHIRE ESTATES: "I will do it when I come into my **YORKSHIRE ESTATES**," — meaning if I ever have the money or the means. The phrase is said to have originated with *Dr. Johnson.*

MENTAL STATES

KIDNEY: "of that **KIDNEY**," of such a stamp; "strange **KIDNEY**," odd humour; "two of a **KIDNEY**," two persons of a sort, or as like as two peas, *i.e.*, resembling each other like two kidneys in a bunch. — *Old.* "Attempting to put their hair out of **KIDNEY**." *Terræ Filius*, 1763.

AWARE

AWAKE or **FLY:** knowing, thoroughly understanding, not ignorant of. The phrase **WIDE-AWAKE** carries the same meaning in ordinary conversation.

CLOCK: "to know what's **O'CLOCK**," a definition of knowingness in general. — *See* **TIME O'DAY** *page 221.*

CUTE: sharp cunning. Abbreviation of **ACUTE**.

DOWN: to be aware of or awake to, any move—in this meaning, synonymous with UP; "DOWN upon one's luck," unfortunate; "DOWN in the mouth," disconsolate; "to be DOWN on one," to treat him harshly or suspiciously, to pounce upon him or detect his tricks.

DOWNY: knowing or cunning; "a DOWNY COVE," a knowing or experienced sharper.

ELEPHANT: "to have SEEN THE ELEPHANT," to be "*up* to the latest move," or "*down* to the last new trick;" to be knowing, and not "green," &c. Possibly a metaphor taken from the travelling menageries, where the ELEPHANT is the *finale* of the exhibition. —Originally an *Americanism. Bartlett* gives conflicting examples. *General* now, however.

FLASH: showy, smart, knowing; a word with various meanings. A person is said to be dressed FLASH when his garb is showy, and after a fashion, but without taste. A person is said to be FLASH when he apes the appearance or manners of his betters or when he is trying to be superior to his friends and relations. FLASH also means "fast," roguish, and sometimes infers counterfeit or deceptive—and this, perhaps, is its general signification. "FLASH, my young friend, or slang, as others call it, is the classical language of the Holy Land; in other words, St. Giles' Greek." —*Tom and Jerry, by Moncreiff.* Vulgar language was first termed FLASH in the year 1718, by Hitchin, author of "*The Regulator of Thieves, &c., with accounts of* FLASH *words.*"

FLY: knowing, wide-awake, fully understanding another's meaning.

FLYMY: knowing, cunning, roguish.

GUMPTION: or **RUMGUMPTION:** comprehension, capacity. From GUAM, to comprehend; "I canna GAUGE, and I canna GUAM it," as a Yorkshire exciseman said of a hedgehog.

KNOWING: a slang term for sharpness, "KNOWING codger," or "a KNOWING blade," one who can take you in or cheat you, in any transaction you may have with him. It implies also deep cunning and foresight, and generally signifies dishonesty.

> Who, on a spree with black-eyed Sal, his blowen,
> So swell, so prime, so nutty and so KNOWING."
> —*Don Juan*

LEARY: flash or knowing.

O'CLOCK or **A'CLOCK:** "like ONE O'CLOCK," a favourite comparison with the lower orders, implying briskness; "to know what O'CLOCK it is," to be wide-awake, sharp or experienced.

P'S AND Q'S: particular points, precise behaviour; "mind your P'S AND Q'S," be very careful. Originating, according to some, from the similarity of p's and q's in the hornbook alphabet, and therefore the warning of an old dame to her pupils; or, according to others, of a French dancing master to his pupils, to mind their *pieds* (feet) and *queues* (wigs) when making a bow.

RUMGUMPTION or **GUMPTION:** knowledge, capacity, capability, —hence, RUMGUMPTIOUS, knowing, wide-awake, forward, positive, pert, blunt.

SNUFF: "up to SNUFF," knowing and sharp; "to take SNUFF," to be offended. *Shakespere* uses SNUFF in the sense of anger or passion. SNUFFY, tipsy.

TRAP: "up to TRAP," knowing, wide-awake—synonymous with "up to SNUFF."

UP: "to be UP to a thing or two," to be knowing or understanding; "to put a man UP to a move," to teach him a trick; "it's all UP with him," *i.e.*, it is all over with him, often pronounced U.P., naming the two letters separately; "UP a tree." —*See* TREE *page 110*. "UP to TRAP," "UP to SNUFF," wide-awake, acquainted with the last new move; "UP to one's GOSSIP," to be a match for one who is trying to take you in; —"UP to SLUM," proficient in roguery, capable of committing a theft successfully.

WIDO: wide-awake, no fool.

CRAZY and CONFUSED

BALMY: insane.

BEE: "to have a BEE in one's bonnet," *i.e.*, to be not exactly sane.

BLUE: confounded or surprised; "to look BLUE," to be astonished or disappointed.

BUTTONS: "not to have all one's BUTTONS," to be deficient in intellect.

FISHY: doubtful, unsound, rotten—a term used to denote a suspicion of a "screw being loose," or "something rotten in the state of Denmark," in alluding to an unsafe speculation.

FLUMMUX: to perplex, hinder; FLUMMUXED, stopped, used-up.

GRAVEL: to confound, to bother; "I'm GRAVELLED," *i.e.,* perplexed or confused.—*Old.*

HEAP: "a HEAP of people," a crowd; "struck all of a HEAP," suddenly astonished.

MAGGOTTY: fanciful, fidgetty. Whims and fancies were formerly termed MAGGOTS, from the popular belief that a maggot in the brain was the cause of any odd notion or caprice a person might exhibit.

NILLY-WILLY: *i.e., Nill ye, will ye,* whether you will or no, a familiar version of the *Latin,* NOLENS VOLENS.

OFF AND ON: vacillating; "an OFF AND ON kind of a chap," one who is always undecided.

QUEER: an *Old Cant* word, once in continual use as a prefix, signifying base, roguish, or worthless. The opposite of RUM, which signified good and genuine. QUEER, in all probability, is immediately derived from the *Cant* language. It has been mooted that it came into use from a quœre (?) being set before a man's name; but it is more than probable that it was brought into this country by the Gipseys from Germany, where QUER signifies *"cross,"* or *"crooked."* At all events, it is believed to have been first used in England as a *Cant* word.

SIXES AND SEVENS: articles in confusion are said to be all SIXES AND SEVENS. The Deity is mentioned in the Towneley Mysteries as He that "sett all on seven," *i.e.,* set or appointed everything in seven days. A similar phrase at this early date implies confusion and disorder, and from these, *Halliwell* thinks, has been derived the phrase "to be at SIXES AND SEVENS." A Scotch correspondent, however, states that the phrase probably came from the workshop, and that amongst needle makers when the points and eyes are "heads and tails" ("heeds and thraws") or in confusion, they are said to be SIXES AND SEVENS, because those numbers are the sizes most generally used, and in the course of manufacture have frequently to be distinguished.

SKY WANNOCKING: unsteady frolicking.—*Norfolk.*

SLATE: "he has a SLATE loose," *i.e.,* he is slightly crazy.

STUNNERS: feelings of great astonishment "it put the stunners on me," it confounded me.

TILE: a hat; a covering for the head.

> "I'm a gent, I'm a gent,
>   In the Regent-street style, —
> Examine my vest,
>   And look at my TILE," — *Popular Song.*

Sometimes used in another sense, "Having a TILE loose," *i.e.*, being slightly crazy. — *See* PANTILE *page 127.*

 # PHYSICAL STATES

BANDED: hungry.

BEAT-OUT or **DEAD-BEAT:** tired or fagged.

BELLOWS-TO-MEND: out of breath.

BOSS-EYED: a person with one eye, or rather with one eye injured.

BUFFED: stripped to the skin.

BUTTER-FINGERED: apt to let things fall.

CHATTY: a filthy person, one whose clothes are not free from vermin; CHATTY DOSS, a lousy bed.

CHUBBY: round-faced, plump.

COCK-EYE: one that squints.

CRIBBAGE-FACED: marked with the smallpox, full of holes like a cribbage board.

CRUMMY: fat, plump. — *North.*

DIMBER DAMBER: very pretty; a clever rogue who excels his fellows; chief of a gang. *Old Cant* in the latter sense. — *English Rogue.*

DISHABBILLY: the ridiculous corruption of the *French*, DESHABILLE, [Stripped] amongst fashionably affected, but ignorant "stuck-up" people.

DUMPY: short and stout.

FIGURE: "to cut a good or bad FIGURE," to make a good or indifferent appearance; "what's the FIGURE?" how much is to pay? FIGURE-HEAD, a person's face.—*Sea term.*

FOXING: to pretend to be asleep like a fox, which is said to take its rest with one eye open.

GROGGY: tipsy; when a prize-fighter becomes "weak on his pins," and nearly beaten, he is said to be GROGGY.—*Pugilistic.* The same term is applied to horses in a similar condition. *Old English,* AGGROGGYD, weighed down, oppressed.—*Prompt. Parvulorum.*

GUMMY: thick, fat, generally applied to a woman's ankles or to a man whose flabby person betokens he's a drunk.

HOPPING GILES: a cripple. St. Ægidius or Giles, himself similarly afflicted, was their patron saint. The ancient lazar houses were dedicated to him.

HUMPTY DUMPTY: short and thick.

INTERESTING: "to be in an INTERESTING situation," applied to females when *enceinte.* [pregnant]

KNOCKED-UP: tired, jaded, used-up, done for. In the United States, amongst females, the phrase is equivalent to being *enceinte,* so that Englishmen often unconsciously commit themselves when amongst our Yankee cousins.

LOP-SIDED: uneven, one side larger than the other.—*Old.*

NUTTY: amorous.

OFF ONE'S FEED: real or pretended want of appetite.—*Stable slang.*

PECKISH: hungry. *Old Cant,* PECKIDGE, meat.

PODGY: drunk; dumpy, short and fat.

RANDY: rampant, violent, warm, amorous. *North,* RANDYBEGGAR, a Gipsey tinker.

SHAKY: said of a person of questionable health, integrity, or solvency; at the *University,* of one not likely to pass his examination.

SHALLOWS: "to go on the SHALLOWS," to go half-naked.

SHUT UP!: be quiet, don't make a noise; to stop short, to make cease in a summary manner, to silence effectually. "Only the other day we heard of a preacher who, speaking of the scene with the doctors in the

Temple, remarked that the Divine disputant completely SHUT THEM UP!"—*Athen.* 30th July, 1859. SHUT UP, utterly exhausted, done for.

SKY-SCRAPER: a tall man; "are you cold up there, old SKY-SCRAPER?" Properly a sea term; the light sails which some adventurous skippers set above the royals in calm latitudes are termed SKY-SCRAPERS and MOON-RAKERS.

SPRY: Active, strong, manly.—*Americanism.*

SQUABBY: flat, short, and thick.

SQUINNY-EYED: squinting.—*Shakespere.*

STRAW: married ladies are said to be "in THE STRAW" at their *accouchements.* The phrase is a coarse allusion to farm-yard animals in a similar condition.

TEETH: "he has cut his *eye* TEETH," *i.e.*, is old and cute enough.

THUMPING: large, fine, or strong.

TIGHT: close, stingy; hard up, short of cash; TIGHT, spruce, strong, active; "a TIGHT lad," a smart, active young fellow; TIGHT, drunk or nearly so; "TIGHT-laced," puritanical, over-precise. Money is said to be TIGHT when the public, from want of confidence in the aspect of affairs, are not inclined to speculate.

TONGUED: talkative; "to TONGUE a person," *i.e.*, talk him down.

TOOTH: "he has cut his eye TOOTH," *i.e.*, he is sharp enough or old enough, to be so; "up in the TOOTH," far advanced in age—said often of old maids. *Stable term* for aged horses which have lost the distinguishing mark in their teeth.

TRUCK-GUTTED: pot-bellied, corpulent.—*Sea.*

TWIST: appetite; "Will's got a capital TWIST."

TWITCHETTY: nervous, fidgetty.

TWO-HANDED: awkward.

USED-UP: broken-hearted, bankrupt, fatigued.

GOOD FORTUNE

BREECHED or **TO HAVE THE BAGS OFF:** to have plenty of money; "to be well **BREECHED**," to be in good circumstances.

CROW: "a regular **CROW**," a success, a stroke of luck—equivalent to a **FLUKE**.

CUT: **CUT AND COME AGAIN**, plenty, if one cut does not suffice, plenty remains to "come again;" **CUT YOUR LUCKY**, to run off;—*Cambridge. Old* **CUTTE**, to say.—*See* **CUT** *in the Index for more meanings p. 479.*

FLUKE: at billiards, playing for one thing and getting another. Hence, generally what one gets accidentally, an unexpected advantage, "more by luck than wit."

PULL: an advantage or hold upon another; "I've the **PULL** over you," *i.e.,* you are in my power—perhaps an oblique allusion to the judicial sense.—*See* **PULL** *page 140.*

SWIM: "a good **SWIM**," a good run of luck, a long time out of the policeman's clutches.—*Thieves' term.*

T: "to suit to a **T**," to fit to a nicety.—*Old.* Perhaps from the **T**-square of carpenters, by which the accuracy of work is tested.

TICKET: "that's the **TICKET**," *i.e.,* what was wanted or what is best. Corruption of "that is not *etiquette*," by adding, in vulgar pronunciation, *th* to the first *e* of etiquette; or, perhaps from **TICKET**, a bill or invoice. This phrase is sometimes extended into "that's the **TICKET FOR SOUP**," in allusion to the card given to beggars for immediate relief at soup kitchens.—*See* **TICK** *page 185.*

WOE

BAD: "to go to the **BAD**," to deteriorate in character, be ruined. *Virgil* has an exactly similar phrase, *in pejus ruere.*

BESTED: taken in or defrauded.

BLUES: a fit of despondency.—*See* **BLUE DEVILS** *page 340.*

BOTHER: (from the *Hibernicism* **POTHER**), trouble or annoyance. *Grose* has the singular derivation, **BOTHER** or **BOTH-EARED**, from two persons talking at the same time or to both ears. **BLOTHER,** an old word, signifying to chatter idly. — *See Halliwell.*

CATEVER: a queer or singular affair; anything poor or very bad. From the *Lingua Franca,* and *Italian,* **CATTIVO,** bad. Variously spelled by the lower orders. — *See* **KERTEVER** *page 86.*

CHOPS: properly **CHAPS,** the mouth or cheeks; "down in the **CHOPS,**" or down in the mouth," *i.e.*, sad or melancholy.

CLEAN OUT: to thrash or beat; to ruin or bankrupt anyone; to take all they have got, by purchase or force. *De Quincey,* in his article on "Richard Bentley," speaking of the lawsuit between that great scholar and Dr. Colbatch, remarks that the latter "must have been pretty well **CLEANED OUT.**"

COLLAR: "out of **COLLAR,**" *i.e.*, out of place, no work.

COMB-CUT: mortified, disgraced, "down on one's luck." — *See* **CUT.**

COON: abbreviation of Racoon. — *American.* A **GONE COON** — *ditto,* one in an awful fix, past praying for. This expression is said to have originated in the American war with a spy, who dressed himself in a racoon skin, and ensconced himself in a tree. An English rifleman taking him for a veritable coon levelled his piece at him, upon which he exclaimed, "Don't shoot, I'll come down of myself, I know I'm a **GONE COON.**" The Yankees say the Britisher was so flummuxed that he flung down his rifle and "made tracks" for home. The phrase is pretty usual in England.

CORNERED: hemmed in a corner, placed in a position from which there is no escape. — *Americanism.*

DICKEY: bad, sorry, or foolish; food or lodging is pronounced **DICKEY** when of a poor description; "it's all **DICKEY** with him," *i.e.*, all over with him.

DOLDRUMS: difficulties, low spirits, dumps. — *Sea.*

DOWN: to be aware of or awake to, any move — in this meaning, synonymous with **UP;** "**DOWN** upon one's luck," unfortunate; "**DOWN** in the mouth," disconsolate; "to be **DOWN** on one," to treat him harshly or suspiciously, to pounce upon him or detect his tricks.

DUTCH CONSOLATION: "thank God it is no worse."

FIX: a predicament, dilemma; "an awful FIX," a terrible position; "to FIX one's flint for him," *i.e.*, to "settle his *hash*," "put a spoke in his wheel."

GRIEF: "to come to GRIEF," to meet with an accident, be ruined.

HARD LINES: hardship, difficulty.—*Soldiers' term* for hard duty on the LINES in front of the enemy.

HARD UP: in distress, poverty-stricken.—*Sea.*

IN FOR IT: in trouble or difficulty of any kind.

KNOCKED-UP: tired, jaded, used-up, done for. In the United States, amongst females, the phrase is equivalent to being *enceinte,* so that Englishmen often unconsciously commit themselves when amongst our Yankee cousins.

LUCK: "down on one's LUCK" wanting money or in difficulty.

MOLLYGRUBS or **MULLIGRUBS:** stomach ache or sorrow—which to the costermongers is much the same, as he believes, like the ancients, that the viscera is the seat of all feeling.

NECK OR NOTHING: desperate.—*Racing phrase.*

PICKLE: a miserable or comical position; "he is in a sad PICKLE," said of anyone who has fallen into the gutter or got besmeared. "A PICKLE herring," a comical fellow, a merry Andrew.—*Old.*

PUCKER: poor temper, difficulty, *deshabille.*

QUEER STREET: "in QUEER STREET," in difficulty or in want.

ROW: a noisy disturbance, tumult, or trouble. Originally *Cambridge,* now universal. Seventy years ago it was written ROUE, which would indicate a *French* origin from *roue,* a profligate or disturber of the peace.—*Vide George Parker's Life's Painter,* 1789, p. 122.

RUB: a quarrel or impediment: "there's the RUB," *i.e.,* that is the difficulty.—*Shakespere and L'Estrange.*

SCRAPE: a difficulty; SCRAPE, low wit for a shave.

SEEDY: worn out, poverty-stricken, used-up, shabby. Metaphorical expression from the appearance of flowers when off bloom and running to *seed*: hence said of one who wears clothes until they crack and become shabby; "how SEEDY he looks," said of any man whose clothes are worn threadbare, with greasy facings, and hat brightened up by perspiration and continual polishing and wetting. When a

man's coat begins to look worn out and shabby he is said to look
SEEDY and ready for *cutting*. This term has been "on the streets" for
nearly two centuries, and latterly has found its way into most
dictionaries. Formerly slang, it is now a recognised word, and one of
the most expressive in the *English* language. The French are always
amused with it, they having no similar term.

SEWED-UP: done up, used-up, intoxicated. *Dutch*, SEEUWT, sick.

SOLD UP or **OUT:** broken down, bankrupt.

STINK: a disagreeable exposure.

TAKE: "to TAKE ON," to grieve; *Shakespere* uses the word TAKING in this
sense. "to TAKE IN," to cheat or defraud, from the lodging-house
keepers' advertisements, "single men TAKEN IN AND DONE FOR;" an
engagement which is as frequently performed in a bad as a good
sense. — *See* TAKE *in the Index for more meanings on page 504.*

TIED UP: given over, finished; also married, in allusion to the Hymenial
knot, unless a jocose allusion be intended to the *halter* (altar).

TO-DO: (pronounced quickly, and as one word) a disturbance, trouble;
"here's a pretty TO-DO," here is an unpleasant difficulty. This exactly
tallies with the *French* word AFFAIRE (*a faire*). — *See Forby's Vocabulary
of East Anglia.*

TREE: "up in a TREE," in temporary difficulties — out of the way.
American expression, derived from RACCOON or BEAR-HUNTING. When
Bruin is TREED or is forced UP A TREE by the dogs, it means that then
the tug of war begins. — *See* 'COON *page 108*. Hence when an opponent
is fairly run to bay, and can by no evasion get off, he is said to be
TREED. These expressions originated with Colonel Crockett. In
Scotland the phrase is "up a CLOSE," *i.e.*, a passage, out of the usual
track, or removed from observation.

USED-UP: broken-hearted, bankrupt, fatigued.

WIFFLE-WOFFLES: in the dumps, sorrow, stomach ache.

ꙅᎯ OTHER PHYSICAL STATES

BAR or **BARRING:** excepting; in common use in the betting ring; "I bet
against the field BAR two." The Irish use of BARRIN' is very similar.

BEND: "That's above my **BEND**," *i.e.*, beyond my power, too expensive, or too difficult for me to perform.

BLEWED: got rid of, disposed of, spent; "I **BLEWED** all my blunt last night," I spent all my money.

BOOKED: caught, fixed, disposed of.—Term in *Book-keeping*.

CRIB: a situation.

DARK: "keep it **DARK**," *i.e.*, secret. **DARK HORSE**, in racing phraseology a horse whose chance of success is unknown, and whose capabilities have not been made the subject of comment.

FADGE: to suit or fit; "it won't **FADGE**," it will not do. Used by *Shakespere*, but now heard only in the streets.

GALORE: abundance. *Irish*, **GO LEOR**, in plenty.

LEEF: "I'd as **LEEF** do it as not," *i.e.*, I have no objection to do it.
—*Corruption* of **LIEF** or **LEAVE**. *Old English*, **LIEF**, inclined to.

POT-LUCK: just as it comes; to take **POT-LUCK**, *i.e.*, one's chance of a dinner—a hearty term used to signify whatever the pot contains you are welcome to.

ROSE: "under the **ROSE**" (frequently used in its *Latin* form, *Sub rosa*), *i.e.*, under obligation of silence and secrecy, of which the rose was anciently an emblem, perhaps, as Sir Thomas Browne remarks, from the closeness with which its petals are enfolded in the bud. The Rose of Venus was given, says the classic legend, to Harpocrates, the God of Silence, by Cupid, as a bribe not to "peach" about the Goddess' amours. It was commonly sculptured on the ceilings of banqueting rooms, as a sign that what was said in free conversation there was not afterwards to be divulged and about 1526 was placed over the Roman confessionals as an emblem of secrecy. The White Rose was also an emblem of the Pretender, whose health, as king, his secret adherents used to drink "under the **ROSE**."

SHUT OF or **SHOT OF:** rid of.

UNDER THE ROSE:—*See* **ROSE** *above*.

WHAT'S MY LINE?

Slang is a language that rolls up its sleeves, spits on its hands and goes to work.

Carl Sandburg

've included begging in this section, though technically it was illegal unless you had permission from the government. That permission was generally given to well-off people who suffered a devastating loss from a fire or other disaster. Begging papers were a social safety net not usually extended to the people who really needed them.

While many of these words are amusing, some are appalling. Honest people were forced to do horrible things to make ends meet. **Pure-finders** collected dog dung, **bone-grubbers** hunted dust-holes and gutters for bones to sell. Consider that the next time you want to complain about your desk job!

Is it any wonder so many of the "lower order" turned to a life of crime? Breaking the law was dangerous. Punishments were harsh, but then, so was the toll on your health if you made an honest living by groveling through the refuse-laden mud of the Thames for trinkets.

Editor's Faves:

SAINT MONDAY: a holiday most religiously observed by journeymen shoemakers and other mechanics. An Irishman observed that this saint's anniversary happened every week. —*North*, where it is termed **COBBLER'S MONDAY**.

SHIVERING JEMMY: the name given by street folk to any cadger who exposes himself, half-naked, on a cold day, to excite pity and procure alms. The "game" is unpleasant, but exceedingly lucrative.

SKIPPER-BIRDS or **KEYHOLE WHISTLERS:** persons who sleep in barns or outhouses in preference to lodging-houses.

IN THIS CHAPTER

WORKING IN GENERAL

ATTACK: to carve or commence operations on; "ATTACK that beef, and oblige!"

BONES: "he made no BONES of it," he did not hesitate, *i.e.*, undertook and finished work without difficulty, "found no BONES in the jelly." —*Ancient, vide Cotgrave.*

BROWN: "to do BROWN," to do well or completely (in allusion to roasting); "doing it BROWN," prolonging the frolic or exceeding sober bounds; "DONE BROWN," taken in, deceived, or surprised.

BUCKLE-TO: to bend to one's work, to begin at once and with great energy.

CHIP OF THE OLD BLOCK: a child who resembles its father. **BROTHER CHIP**, one of the same trade or profession.

COLLAR: "out of COLLAR," *i.e.*, out of place, no work.

CRACK: first-rate, excellent; "a CRACK HAND," an adept; a "CRACK article," a good one. —*Old.*

CUT: to CUT AND RUN, to quit work or occupation and start off at once. —*Cambridge. Old* CUTTE, *to say.* —*See* CUT *in the Index for more meanings on page 479.*

CUT: to compete in business.

DAGS: feat or performance; "I'll do your DAGS," *i.e.*, I will do something that you cannot do.

DEAD HORSE: "to draw the DEAD HORSE," DEAD-HORSE work —working for wages already paid; also any thankless or unassisted service.

DRIVE: a term used by tradesmen in speaking of business; "he's DRIVING a *roaring* trade," *i.e.*, a very good one; hence, to succeed in a bargain, "I DROVE a good bargain," *i.e.*, got the best end of it.

ELBOW GREASE: labour or industry.

FIDDLING: doing any odd jobs in the street, holding horses, carrying parcels, &c. for a living. Among the middle classes, FIDDLING means idling away time or trifling; and amongst sharpers, it means gambling.

GRAFT: to work; "where are you GRAFTING?" *i.e.*, where do you live or work?

HAND: a workman or helper, a person. "A cool HAND," explained by Sir Thomas Overbury to be "one who accounts bashfulness the wickedest thing in the world, and therefore studies impudence."

HOOK IT: "get out of the way," or "be off about your business," "TO HOOK IT," to run away, to decamp; "on one's own HOOK," depending upon one's own exertions.—*See* HOOK OR BY CROOK *page 240.*

JANNOCK: sociable, fair dealing.—*Norfolk.*

JOB: a short piece of work, a prospect of employment. *Johnson* describes JOB as a low word, without etymology. It is, and was, however, a *Cant* word, and a JOB, two centuries ago, was an arranged robbery. Even at the present day it is mainly confined to the street, in the sense of employment for a short time. Amongst undertakers a JOB signifies a funeral; "to do a JOB," conduct anyone's funeral; "by the JOB," *i.e.*, *piece*-work, as opposed to *time*-work. A JOB in political phraseology is a government office or contract, obtained by secret influence or favouritism.

KNIGHT: a common and ironical prefix to a man's calling—thus, "KNIGHT of the whip," a coachman; "KNIGHT of the thimble," a tailor.

KNOCK OFF: to give over or abandon. A saying used by workmen about dinner or other meal times, for upwards of two centuries.

LINE: calling, trade, profession; "what LINE are you in?" "the building LINE."

MOOCHING or **ON THE MOOCH:** on the look-out for any article or circumstances which may be turned to a profitable account; watching in the streets for odd jobs, scraps, horses to hold, &c.

ROARING TRADE: a very successful business.

ROUND: "ROUND dealing," honest trading; "ROUND sum," a large sum. Synonymous also in a *slang* sense with SQUARE.—*See* SQUARE *below.*

SACK: "to get the SACK," to be discharged by an employer.

SAINT MONDAY: a holiday most religiously observed by journeymen shoemakers and other mechanics. An Irishman observed that this saint's anniversary happened every week.—*North*, where it is termed COBBLER'S MONDAY.

SCREW: salary or wages.

SHICE: nothing; "to do anything for **SHICE**," to get no payment. The term was first used by the Jews in the last century. *Grose* gives the phrase **CHICE-AM-A-TRICE**, which has a synonymous meaning. *Spanish*, **CHICO**, little; *Anglo Saxon*, **CHICHE**, niggardly.

SNAPPS: share, portion; any articles or circumstances out of which money may be made; "looking for **SNAPPS**," waiting for windfalls or odd jobs.—*Old. Scotch*, **CHITS**—term also used for "coppers," or halfpence.

SPIRT or SPURT: "to put on a **SPIRT**," to make an increased exertion for a brief space, to attain one's end; a nervous effort.

SQUARE: honest; "on the **SQUARE**," *i.e.*, fair and strictly honest; "to turn **SQUARE**," to reform, and get one's living in an honest manner. The opposite of **CROSS**.

SWELL: a man of importance; a person with a showy, jaunty exterior; "a rank **SWELL**," a very "flashily" dressed person, a man who by excessive dress apes a higher position than he actually occupies. Anything is said to be **SWELL** or **SWELLISH** that looks showy, or is many-coloured, or is of a desirable quality. Dickens and Thackeray are termed great **SWELLS** in literature; so indeed are the first persons in the learned professions.

TOP-SAWYER: the principal of a party or profession. "A **TOP-SAWYER** signifies a man that is a master genius in any profession. It is a piece of *Norfolk* slang, and took its rise from Norfolk being a great timber county, where the *top* sawyers get double the wages of those beneath them."—*Randall's Diary*, 1820.

PROFESSIONS

BEGGARS and TRAMPS

CAD or CADGER (from which it is shortened): a mean or vulgar fellow; a beggar; one who would rather live on other people than work for himself; a man trying to worm something out of another, either money or information. *Johnson* uses the word, and gives *huckster* as the meaning, but I never heard it used in this sense. CAGER or GAGER, the *Old Cant* term for a man. The exclusives in the Universities apply the term CAD to all non-members.

CROAKER: a beggar.

DOXY: female companion of a thief or beggar. In the West of England, the women frequently call their little girls DOXIES, in a familiar or endearing sense. A learned divine once described *orthodoxy* as being a man's own DOXY, and *heterodoxy* another man's DOXY.—*Ancient Cant.*

HIGH FLY: "on the HIGH FLY," on the begging or cadging system.

HIGH-FLYER: a genteel beggar or swindler.

LOAFER: a lazy vagabond. Generally considered an *Americanism*. LOPER or LOAFER, however, was in general use as a *Cant* term in the early part of the last century. LANDLOPER was a vagabond who begged in the attire of a sailor; and the sea phrase, LAND LUBBER, was doubtless synonymous.—*See the Times*, 3rd November, 1859, for a reference to LOAFER.

MUCK-SNIPE: one who had been "MUCKED OUT" or beggared, at gambling.

MUMPER: a beggar.—*Gipsey*. Possibly a corruption of MUMMER.

NEEDY: a nightly lodger or tramp.

NEEDY MIZZLER: a shabby person; a tramp who runs away without paying for his lodging.

SHALLOW-COVE: a begging rascal who goes about the country half-naked—with the most limited amount of rags upon his person, wearing neither shoes, stockings, nor hat.

SHALLOW-MOT: a ragged woman, the frequent companion of the SHALLOW-COVE.

SHIVERING JEMMY: the name given by street folk to any cadger who exposes himself, half-naked, on a cold day, to excite pity and procure alms. The "game" is unpleasant, but exceedingly lucrative.

SKATES LURK: a begging impostor dressed as a sailor.

TRAVELLER: name given by one tramp to another. "A TRAVELLER at her Majesty's expense," *i.e.*, a transported felon, a convict.

TURNPIKE-SAILORS: beggars who go about dressed as sailors.

WHIP JACK: a sham shipwrecked sailor, called also a TURNPIKE SAILOR.

BEGGING TERMS

BLOB: (from **BLAB**), to talk. Beggars are of two kinds—those who **SCREEVE** (introduce themselves with a **FAKEMENT**, or false document), and those who **BLOB**, or state their case in their own truly "unvarnished" language.

BONE: good, excellent. ◊, the vagabond's hieroglyphic for **BONE** or good, chalked by them on houses and street corners, as a hint to succeeding beggars. *French,* **BON**.

CADGE: to beg in an artful or wheedling manner.—*North.*

CADGING: begging of the lowest degree.

DEE: a pocket book, term used by tramps.—*Gipsey.*

DODGE: a cunning trick. "**DODGE**, that homely but expressive phrase."—*Sir Hugh Cairns on the Reform Bill*, 2nd March, 1859. *Anglo Saxon*, **DEOGIAN**, to colour, to conceal. The **TIDY DODGE**, as it is called by street-folk, consists in dressing up a family clean and tidy, and parading the streets to excite compassion and obtain alms. A correspondent suggests that the verb **DODGE** may have been formed (like *wench* from *wink*) from **DOG**, *i.e.,* to double quickly and unexpectedly, as in coursing.

FAKEMENT: a false begging petition, any act of robbery, swindling, or deception.

FLATTY-KEN: a public house, the landlord of which is ignorant of the practices of the thieves and tramps who frequent it.

FLUMMUXED: done up, sure of a month in **QUOD**, or prison. In mendicant freemasonry, the sign chalked by rogues and tramps upon a gate-post or house corner, to express to succeeding vagabonds that it is unsafe for them to call there, is known as Θ, or **FLUMMUXED**, which signifies that the only thing they would be likely to get upon applying for relief would be a "a month in **QUOD**."—*See* **QUOD** *p. 258.*

GAMMY: bad, unfavourable, poor-tempered. Those householders who are known enemies to the street folk and tramps are pronounced by them to be **GAMMY**. **GAMMY** sometimes means forged, as "**GAMMY MONEKER**," a forged signature; **GAMMY STUFF**, spurious medicine; **GAMMY LOWR**, counterfeit coin. *Hants,* **GAMY**, dirty. The hieroglyphic used by beggars and cadgers to intimate to those of the tribe coming after that things are not very favourable, is known as □, or **GAMMY**.

GLIM LURK: a begging paper, giving a certified account of a dreadful fire—which never happened.

MACE: to spunge, swindle or beg, in a polite way; "give it him (a shopkeeper) on the **MACE**," *i.e.*, obtain goods on credit and never pay for them; also termed "striking the **MACE**."

MAUND: to beg; "**MAUNDERING** on the fly," begging of people in the streets.—*Old Cant.* **MAUNG**, to beg, is a term in use amongst the Gipseys, and may also be found in the *Hindoo* vocabulary. **MAUND**, however, is pure *Anglo Saxon*, from **MAND**, a basket. Compare "beg," which is derived from **BAG**, a curious parallel.

MONKEY'S ALLOWANCE: to get blows instead of alms, more kicks than half-pence.

MOON: a month—generally used to express the length of time a person has been sentenced by the magistrate; thus "**ONE MOON**" is one month.—*See* **DRAG** *page 259*. It is a curious fact that the Indians of America and the roaming vagabonds of England should both calculate time by the **MOON**.

MUNGARLY CASA: a baker's shop; evidently a corruption of some *Lingua Franca* phrase for an eating house. The well-known "Nix mangiare" stairs at Malta derive their name from the endless beggars who lie there and shout **NIX MANGIARE**, *i.e.*, "nothing to eat," to excite the compassion of the English who land there—an expression which exhibits remarkably the mongrel composition of the *Lingua Franca*, **MANGIARE** being *Italian*, and *Nix* an evident importation from Trieste or other Austrian seaport.

MUNGING or **MOUNGING:** whining, begging, muttering.—*North.*

PAD: "to stand **PAD**," to beg with a small piece of paper pinned on the breast, inscribed "I'm starving."

PAD: the highway; a tramp.—*Lincolnshire.*

PAD THE HOOF: to walk not ride; "**PADDING THE HOOF** on the high toby," tramping or walking on the high road.

> "Trudge, plod away o' the hoof."
> —*Merry Wives*, i., 3.

PADDING KENS or **CRIBS:** tramps' and boys' lodging houses.

PALAVER: to ask or talk—not deceitfully, as the term usually signifies; "**PALAVER** to the nibs for a shant of bivvy," ask the

master for a quart of beer. In this sense used by *tramps.*—Derived from *French,* **PARLER.**

SCALDRUM DODGE: burning the body with a mixture of acids and gunpowder, so as to suit the hues and complexions of the accident to be deplored.

SCRAN: pieces of meat, broken victuals. Formerly the reckoning at a public-house. **SCRANNING,** begging for broken victuals. Also, an *Irish* malediction of a mild sort, "Bad **SCRAN** to yer!"

SCREEVE: a letter, a begging petition.

SHAKE LURK: a false paper carried by an impostor, giving an account of a "dreadful shipwreck."

SHANKS' NAG: "to ride **SHANKS' NAG**," to go on foot.

SHOOL: to saunter idly, become a vagabond, beg rather than work. —*Smollett's Roderick Random,* vol. i., p.262.

SITTING PAD: sitting on the pavement in a begging position.

SKIPPER IT: to sleep in the open air or in a rough way.

SKIPPER-BIRDS or **KEYHOLE WHISTLERS:** persons who sleep in barns or outhouses in preference to lodging-houses.

STAG: to demand money, to "cadge."

STAND: "to **STAND** treat," to pay for a friend's entertainment; to bear expense; to put up with treatment, good or ill; "this house **STOOD** me in £1,000," *i.e.,* cost that sum; "to **STAND PAD**," to beg on the curb with a small piece of paper pinned on the breast, inscribed *"I'm starving."*

START: "**THE START**," London, the great starting point for beggars and tramps.

TICKET: "that's the **TICKET**," *i.e.,* what was wanted or what is best. Corruption of "that is not *etiquette*," by adding, in vulgar pronunciation, *th* to the first *e* of etiquette; or, perhaps from **TICKET**, a bill or invoice. This phrase is sometimes extended into "that's the **TICKET FOR SOUP**," in allusion to the card given to beggars for immediate relief at soup kitchens.—*See* **TICK** *page 185.*

WILD: a village.—*Tramps' term.*—*See* **VILE** *page 135.*

BOXERS

ATTIC: the head; "queer in the ATTIC," intoxicated.—*Pugilistic.*

BELCHER: a kind of handkerchief.—*See* BILLY *page 285.*

BLUE-BILLY: the handkerchief (blue ground with white spots) worn and used at prize fights. Before a SET TO, it is common to take it from the neck and tie it around the leg as a garter, or round the waist, to "keep in the wind." Also, the refuse ammoniacal lime from gas factories.

BODMINTON: blood.—*Pugilistic.*

BOTTLE-HOLDER: an assistant to a "Second,"—*Pugilistic*; an abettor; also, the bridegroom's man at a wedding.

BRUISER: a fighting man, a pugilist.—*Pugilistic. Shakespere* uses the word BRUISING in a similar sense.

BUCKHORSE: a smart blow or box on the ear; derived from the name of a celebrated "bruiser" of that name.

BUFFER: a dog. Their skins were formerly in great request—hence the term, BUFF meaning in *Old English* to skin. It is still used in the ring, BUFFED meaning stripped to the skin. In Irish Cant, BUFFER is a *boxer.* The BUFFER of a railway carriage doubtless received its very appropriate name from the old pugilistic application of this term.

BUNG: to give, pass, hand over, drink, or indeed to perform any action; BUNG UP, to close up—*Pugilistic*; "BUNG over the rag," hand over the money—*Old*, used by *Beaumont and Fletcher*, and *Shakespere.* Also, to deceive one by a lie, to CRAM.—*See page 176.*

CANISTER: the head.—*Pugilistic.*

CANISTER-CAP: a hat.—*Pugilistic.*

CLARET: blood.—*Pugilistic.*

CORINTHIANISM: a term derived from the classics, much in vogue some years ago, implying pugilism, high life, SPREES, roistering, &c. —*Shakespere.* The immorality of *Corinth* was proverbial in Greece. to Κορινθιάζ εσθαι, *Corinthianise,* indulge in the company of courtesans, was a *Greek* slang expression. Hence the proverb:

Οὐ παντὸς ἀνδρὸς εἰς Κόρινθον ἔσθ' ὁ πλοῦς,

and *Horace*, Epist. Lib. 1, xvii. 36:

Non cuivis homini contingit adire Corinthum,

In allusion to the spoliation practiced by the "hetæræ" on those who visited them.

CORK: "to draw a CORK," to give a bloody nose.—*Pugilistic.*

DO: this useful and industrious verb has for many years done service as a slang term. To DO a person is to cheat him. Sometimes another tense is employed, such as I DONE him," meaning I cheated or "paid him out;" DONE BROWN, cheated thoroughly, befooled; DONE OVER, upset, cheated, knocked down, ruined; DONE UP, used-up, finished, or quieted. DONE also means convicted or sentenced; so does DONE FOR. To DO a person in pugilism is to excel him in fisticuffs. Humphreys, who fought Mendoza, a Jew, wrote this laconic note to his supporter: "Sir, I have DONE the Jew, and am in good health. Rich. Humphries." Tourists use the expression "I have DONE France and Italy," meaning I have completely explored those countries.

FANCY: the favourite sports, pets, or pastime of a person, *the tan of low life.* Pugilists are sometime termed THE FANCY. *Shakespere* uses the word in the sense of a favourite or pet; and the paramour of a prostitute is still called her FANCY-MAN.

FLOOR: to knock down.—*Pugilistic.*

GROGGY: tipsy; when a prize-fighter becomes "weak on his pins," and nearly beaten, he is said to be GROGGY.—*Pugilistic.* The same term is applied to horses in a similar condition. *Old English*, AGGROGGYD, weighed down, oppressed.—*Prompt. Parvulorum.*

HANDER: a second or assistant, in a prize fight.

HANDLE: a nose; the title appended to a person's name; also a term in boxing, "HANDLING one's fists."

KNOWLEDGE BOX: the head.—*Pugilistic.*

LOBB: the head.—*Pugilistic.*

LOLLY: the head.—*See* LOBB *above.*—*Pugilistic.*

MAULEY: a fist, that with which one strikes as with a MALL.—*Pugilistic.*

MITTENS: fists.—*Pugilistic.*

MUGGING: a thrashing. Synonymous with SLOGGING, both terms of the "ring," and frequently used by fighting men.

NOB: the head.—*Pugilistic;* "BOB A NOB," a shilling a head. *Ancient Cant,* NEB. NOB is an early *English* word, and is used in the Romance of Kynge Alisaunder (thirteenth century) for a head; originally, no doubt, the same as *Knob.*

NOSER: a bloody or contused nose.—*Pugilistic.*

PEEL: to strip or disrobe.—*Pugilistic.*

PEPPER: to thrash or strike.—*Pugilistic,* but used by *Shakespere.*—*East.*

POLISH OFF: to finish off anything quickly—a dinner for instance; also to finish off an adversary.—*Pugilistic.*

RING: a generic term given to horse racing and pugilism. The latter is sometimes termed the PRIZE-RING. From the practice of forming the crowd into a RING around the combatants or outside the racecourse.

RUMBUMPTIOUS: haughty, pugilistic.

SCRATCH: a fight, contest, point of dispute; "coming up to the **Scratch**," going or preparing to fight—in reality, approaching the line usually chalked on the ground to divide the ring.—*Pugilistic.*

SET TO: a sparring match, a fight; "a dead set," a determined stand, in argument or in movement.

SLASHER: a powerful roisterer, a pugilist; "the TIPTON SLASHER."

SPONGE: "to throw up the SPONGE," to submit, give over the struggle—from the practice of throwing up the SPONGE used to cleanse the combatants' faces, at a prize fight, as a signal that the "mill" is concluded.

STICK: to cheat; "he got STUCK," he was taken in; STICK, to forget one's part in a performance.—*Theatrical.* STICK ON, to overcharge or defraud; STICK UP FOR, to defend a person, especially when slandered in his absence; STICK UP TO, to preserver in courting or attacking, whether in fisticuffs or argument; "to STICK in one's gizzard," to rankle in one's heart; "to STICK TO a person," to adhere to one, be his friend through adverse circumstances.

WHITECHAPEL: the "upper-cut," or strike.—*Pugilistic.*

 CLERGY and RELIGIOUS PEOPLE

BRISKET BEATER: a Roman Catholic.

CAMISTER: a preacher, clergyman, or master.

CHERUBS or **CHERUBIMS:** the chorister boys who chaunt in the services at the abbeys.

CHOKER: a cravat, a neckerchief. **WHITE-CHOKER**, the white neckerchief worn by mutes at a funeral and waiters at a tavern. Clergymen are frequently termed **WHITE-CHOKERS**.

CODDS: the "poor brethren" of the Charter house. At p. 133 of the *Newcomes*, Mr. Thackeray writes, "The Cistercian lads call these old gentlemen **CODDS**, I know not wherefore." An abbreviation of **CODGER**.

COMMISTER: a chaplain or clergyman.

CUSHION-THUMPER: polite rendering of **TUB-THUMPER**, a clergyman, a preacher.

DEVIL-DODGERS: clergymen; also people who go sometimes to church and sometimes to meeting.

DOMINE: a parson.

EARWIG: clergyman, also one who prompts another maliciously.

GOSPEL GRINDER: a city missionary or tract distributor.

GRAY-COAT-PARSON: a lay impropriator or lessee of great tithes.

ONE IN TEN: a parson.

OWNED: a canting expression used by the ultra-Evangelicals when a popular preacher makes many converts. The converts themselves are called his "**SEALS**."

PADRE: a clergyman. — *Anglo Indian.*

PANTILER: a dissenting preacher. Probably from the practice of the Quakers, and many dissenters, of not removing the hat in a place of worship.

PSALM-SMITER: a "Ranter," one who sings at a conventicle. — *See* **BRISKET BEATER** *above.*

PUSSEY CATS: corruption of *Puseyites*, the name constantly, but improperly, given to the "Tractarian" party in the Church, from the Oxford Regius Professor of Hebrew, who by no means approved of the Romanising tendencies of some of its leaders.

RAT: term amongst printers to denote one who works under price. *Old Cant* for a clergyman.

ROOK: a clergyman, not only from his black attire, but also, perhaps, from the old nursery favourite, the *History of Cock Robin*.

> "I, says the **ROOK**,
> With my little book,
> I'll be the parson."

SEALS: a religious slang term for converts.—*See* **OWNED** *page 125*.

SIM: one of a Methodistical turn in religion; a low- church-man; originally a follower of the late Rev. Charles Simeon.—*Cambridge*.

SPOUT: to preach or make speeches; **SPOUTER**, a preacher or lecturer.

SWADDLER: a Wesleyan Methodist; a name originally given to members of that body by the Irish mob; said to have originated with an ignorant Romanist, to whom the words of the English Bible were a novelty, and who, hearing one of John Wesley's preachers mention the *swaddling clothes* of the Holy Infant, in the sermon on Christmas-day at Dublin, shouted out in derision, "*A swaddler! A swaddler*" as if the whole story were the preacher's invention.—*Southey's Life of Wesley*, vol. ii., p. 109.

W. P. or **WARMING PAN:** a clergyman who holds a living *pro tempore*, under a bond of resignation, is styled a **W. P.** or **WARMING PAN** rector, because he keeps the place warm for his successor.—*Clerical slang*.

WET QUAKER: a drunkard of that sect; a man who pretends to be religious, and is a dram drinker on the sly.

RELIGIOUS TERMS

BROAD AND SHALLOW: an epithet applied to the so-called "Broad church," in contradiction to the "High: and "Low" Church.—*See* **HIGH AND DRY** *below*.

CRACK A KIRK: to break into a church or chapel.

DEAD-LURK: entering a dwelling-house during divine service.

DUST: money; "down with the DUST," put down the money.—*Ancient.* Dean Swift once took for his text, "He who giveth to the poor lendeth to the Lord." His sermon was short. "Now, my brethren," said he, "if you are satisfied with the security, down with the DUST."

GIN AND GOSPEL GAZETTE: the *Morning Advertiser*, so called from its being the organ of the dissenting party, and of the Licensed Victuallers' Association. Sometimes termed the TAP TUB, or the 'TIZER.

HIGH AND DRY: an epithet applied to the *soi disant* "orthodox" clergy of the last century, for whom, while ill-paid curates did the work, the *comforts* of the establishment were its greatest charms.

> "Wherein are various ranks, and due degrees,
> The Bench for honour, and the Stall for ease."

Though often confounded with, they are utterly dissimilar to, the modern High Church or Anglo-Catholic party. Their equally uninteresting opponents deserve the corresponding appellation of LOW AND SLOW; while the so-called "Broad Church" is defined with equal felicity as the BROAD AND SHALLOW.

JAPAN: to ordain.—*University.*

M. B. COAT: *i.e., Mark of the Beast*, a name given to the long surtout worn by the clergy—a modern Puritan form of abuse, said to have been accidentally disclosed to a Tractarian customer by a tailor's orders to his foreman.

PANTILE: a hat. The term PANTILE is properly applied to the mould into which the sugar is poured which is afterwards known as "loaf sugar." Thus, PANTILE, from whence comes the phrase "a sugar loaf hat," originally signified a tall, conical hat, in shape similar to that usually represented as the head gear of a bandit. From PANTILE, the more modern slang term TILE has been derived.—*Halliwell* gives PANTILE SHOP, a meeting-house.

PATTER: a speech or discourse, a pompous street oration, a judge's summing up, a trial. *Ancient* word for muttering. Probably from the *Latin*, PATER NOSTER, or Lord's Prayer. This was said, before the

Reformation, in a *low voice* by the priest, until he came to, "and lead us not into temptation," to which the choir responded, "but deliver us from evil." In our reformed Prayer Book this was altered, and the Lord's Prayer directed to be said "with a *loud voice.*" — *Dr. Pusey* takes this view of the derivation in his *Letter to the Bishop of London*, P 78, 1851. Scott uses the word twice in *Ivanhoe* and the *Bride of Lammermoor.*

PYGOSTOLE: the least irreverent of names for the peculiar "M. B." coats worn by Tractarian curates.

> "It is true that the wicked make sport
> Of our **PYGOSTOLES**, as we go by;
> And one gownsman, in Trinity Court,
> Went so far as to call me a 'Guy,'"

SCHISM-SHOP: a dissenters' meeting-house. — *University.*

SHITTEN-SATURDAY: (corruption of SHUT-IN-SATURDAY), the Saturday between Good Friday and Easter Sunday, when our Lord's body was enclosed in the tomb.

SIT UNDER: a term employed in Dissenters' meeting houses, to denote attendance on the ministry of any particular preacher.

STIR UP SUNDAY: the Sunday next before Advent, the collect for that day commencing with the words "Stir up." Schoolboys, growing excited at the prospect of the vacation, irreverently commemorate it by stirring up—pushing and poking each other. **CRIB CRUST MONDAY** and **TUG BUTTON TUESDAY** are distinguished by similar tricks; while on **PAY-OFF WEDNESDAY** they retaliate small grudges in a playful facetious way. Forby says, good housewives in Norfolk consider themselves reminded by the name to mix the ingredients for their Christmas mince pies.

TUB-THUMPING: preaching or speech-making.

 # CRAFTSMEN

ALL-THERE: in strict fashion, first-rate, "up to the mark." A vulgar person would speak of a spruce, showily-dressed female as being

ALL-THERE. An artisan would use the same phrase to express the capabilities of a skillful fellow workman.

BLUE-PIGEON FLYERS: journeymen plumbers, glaziers, and others, who, under the plea of repairing houses, strip off the lead, and make way with it. Sometimes they get off with it by wrapping it round their bodies.

BOILERS: the slang name given to the New Kensington Museum and School of Art, in allusion to the peculiar form of the buildings, and the fact of their being mainly composed of, and covered with, sheet iron. — *See* **PEPPER-BOXES** *page 271.*

BROTHER-CHIP: fellow carpenter. Also, **BROTHER-WHIP**, a fellow coachman; and **BROTHER-BLADE**, of the same occupation or calling — originally a fellow soldier.

CHIVE: to cut, saw, or file.

DAB or **DABSTER**: an expert person. Johnson says, "in low language, an artist."

SCREEVER: a man who draws with coloured chalks on the pavement figures of our Saviour crowned with thorns, specimens of elaborate writing, thunderstorms, ships on fire, &c. The men who attend these pavement chalkings, and receive halfpence and sixpences from the admirers of street art, are not always the draughtsmen. The artist, or **SCREEVER**, drew perhaps in half-a-dozen places that very morning, and rented the spots out to as many cadaverous looking men.

SHALLOW-SCREEVER: a man who sketches and draws on the pavement. — *See* **SCREEVER** *above.*

T: "to suit to a **T**," to fit to a nicety. — *Old*. Perhaps from the T-square of carpenters, by which the accuracy of work is tested.

TOP-SAWYER: the principal of a party or profession. "A **TOP-SAWYER** signifies a man that is a master genius in any profession. It is a piece of *Norfolk* slang, and took its rise from Norfolk being a great timber county, where the *top* sawyers get double the wages of those beneath them." — *Randall's Diary*, 1820.

WHIPPING THE CAT: when an operative works at a private house by the day. Term used amongst tailors and carpenters.

⌒◯ DRIVERS

BONE-PICKER: a footman.

BROTHER-CHIP: fellow carpenter. Also, BROTHER-WHIP, a fellow coachman; and BROTHER-BLADE, of the same occupation or calling —originally a fellow soldier.

CABBY: the driver of a cab.

CAD: an onminbus conductor.

CHARIOT-BUZZING: picking pockets in an omnibus.

CULLING or **CULING:** stealing from the carriages on racecourses.

DAISY-KICKERS: the name hostlers at large inns used to give each other, now *nearly obsolete*. DAISY-KICKER or GROGHAM was likewise the *Cant* term for a horse. The DAISY-KICKERS were sad rogues in the old posting days; frequently the landlords rented the stables to them, as the only plan to make them return a profit.

DRAG: a cart of any kind, a coach; gentlemen drive to the races in DRAGS.

DRAGGING: robbing carts, &c.

DRAGSMEN: fellows who cut trunks from the backs of carriages. They sometimes have a light cart, and "drop behind" the plundered vehicle, and then drive off in an opposite direction with the booty.

FIDDLE: a whip.

FLOGGER: a whip.—*Obsolete.*

HORSE'S NIGHTCAP: a halter; "to die in the HORSE'S NIGHTCAP," to be hung.

HUNTING THE SQUIRREL: when hackney and stage coachmen try to upset each other's vehicles on the public roads.—*Nearly obsolete.*

JARVEY: the driver of a hackney coach; JARVEY'S UPPER BENJAMIN, a coachman's over-coat.

JEHU: old slang term for a coachman or one fond of driving.

KNIGHT: a common and ironical prefix to a man's calling—thus, "KNIGHT of the whip," a coachman; "KNIGHT of the thimble," a tailor.

NURSE: a curious term lately applied to competition in omnibuses. Two omnibuses are placed on the road to **NURSE** or oppose, each opposition "buss," one before, the other behind. Of course, the central or **NURSED** buss has very little chance, unless it happens to be a favourite with the public. **NURSE**, to cheat or swindle; trustees are said to **NURSE** property, *i.e.*, gradually eat it up themselves.

PEG: "to **PEG** away," to strike, run, or drive away; "**PEG** a hack," to drive a cab; "take down a **PEG** or two," to check an arrogant or conceited person.

PETERER or PETERMAN: one who follows hackney and stage coaches, and cuts off the portmanteaus and trunks from behind.—*Nearly obsolete. Ancient* term for a fisherman, still used at Gravesend.

RIBBONS: the reins.—*Middlesex.*

SPILT: thrown from a horse or chaise.—*See* **PURL** *page 133.*

TOOL: to drive a mail coach.

TOUCHER: "as near as a **TOUCHER**," as near as possible without actually touching.—Co*aching term.* The old jarveys, to show their skill, used to drive against things so close as absolutely to *touch*, yet without injury. This they called a **TOUCHER** or, **TOUCH AND GO**, which was hence applied to anything which was within an ace of ruin.

TURN OUT: personal show or appearance; a man with a showy carriage and horses is said to have a good **TURN OUT**.

UNICORN: a style of driving with two wheelers abreast, and one leader, termed in the *United States*, a **SPIKE TEAM**. **TANDEM** is one wheeler and one leader. **RANDOM**, three horses in line.

HORSES and DONKEYS

BUFFER: a familiar expression for a jolly acquaintance, probably from the *French*, **BOUFFARD**, a fool or clown; a "jolly old **BUFFER**," said of a good-humoured or liberal old man. In 1737, a **BUFFER** was a "rogue that killed good sound horses for the sake of their skins, by running a long wire into them."—*Bacchus and Venus.* The term was once applied to those who took false oaths for a consideration.

COPER: properly **HORSE-COUPER**, a Scotch horse dealer—used to denote a dishonest one.

CRIB BITER: an inveterate grumbler; properly said of a horse which has the habit, a sign of its bad digestion.

DAISY-CUTTER: a horse which trots or gallops without lifting its feet much from the ground.

DAISY-KICKERS: the name hostlers at large inns used to give each other, now *nearly obsolete*. **DAISY-KICKER** or **GROGHAM** was likewise the *Cant* term for a horse. The **DAISY-KICKERS** were sad rogues in the old posting days; frequently the landlords rented the stables to them, as the only plan to make them return a profit.

DARK: "keep it **DARK**," *i.e.*, secret. **DARK HORSE**, in racing phraseology a horse whose chance of success is unknown, and whose capabilities have not been made the subject of comment.

DEVOTIONAL HABITS: horses weak in the knees and apt to stumble and fall are said to have these. — *Stable.*

DICKEY: a donkey.

DIGGERS: spurs; also the spades on cards.

FIDDLE: a whip.

FIG: "to **FIG** a horse," to play improper tricks with one in order to make him lively.

FLOGGER: a whip. — *Obsolete.*

FOALED: "thrown from a horse." — *Hunting term.* — *See* **PURL** *page 133, and* **SPILT** *page 131.*

FREE: to steal; generally applied to horses.

GIB-FACE: properly the lower lip of a horse; "**TO HANG ONE'S GIB**," to pout the lower lip, be angry or sullen.

GINGER: a showy, fast horse—as if he had been **FIGGED** with **GINGER** under his tail.

GROGGY: tipsy; when a prize-fighter becomes "weak on his pins," and nearly beaten, he is said to be **GROGGY**. — *Pugilistic.* The same term is applied to horses in a similar condition. *Old English*, **AGGROGGYD**, weighed down, oppressed. — *Prompt. Parvulorum.*

HORSE CHAUNTER: a dealer who takes worthless horses to country fairs and disposes of them by artifice. He is flexible in his ethics, and will put in a glass-eye or perform other tricks. — *See* **COPER** *page 131.*

HORSE'S NIGHTCAP: a halter; "to die in the **HORSE'S NIGHTCAP**," to be hung.

JERUSALEM PONY: a donkey.

JIB or **JIBBER:** a horse that starts or shrinks. *Shakespere* uses it in the sense of a worn-out horse.

KNACKER: an old horse; a horse slaughterer.—*Gloucestershire.*

LEG IT: to run; **LEG BAIL**, to run off, "to give a **LEG**," to assist, as when one mounts a horse; "making a **LEG**," a countryman's bow, —projecting the leg from behind as a balance to the head bent forward.—*Shakespere.*

MOKE: a donkey.—*Gipsey.*

NEDDY: a donkey.

OFF ONE'S FEED: real or pretended want of appetite.—*Stable slang.*

OUT-SIDER: a person who does not habitually bet or is not admitted to the "Ring." Also, a horse whose name does not appear among the "favourites."

PEACOCK HORSE: amongst undertakers, is one with a showy tail and mane, and holds its head up well.—*che va favor-reggiando, &c., Italian.*

PERSUADERS: spurs.

PLUNDER: a common word in the horse trade to express profit. Also an *American* term for baggage, luggage.

PRAD: a horse.

PRAD NAPPING: horse stealing.

PRANCER: a horse.—*Ancient Cant.*

PURL: hunting term for a fall, synonymous with **FOALED** or **SPILT**; "he'll get **PURLED** at the rails."

RACKS: the bones of a dead horse. Term used by horse slaughterers.

RANDOM: three horses driven in line, a very appropriate term.—*See* **UNICORN** *below.*

RIBBONS: the reins.—*Middlesex.*

ROARER: a broken-winded horse.

RUCK: the undistinguished crowd; "to come in with the **RUCK**," to arrive at the winning post among the non-winning horses.—*Racing term.*

SCRATCH: to strike a horse's name out of the list of runners in a particular race. "Tomboy was SCRATCHED for the Derby, at 10, a.m., on Wednesday," from which period all bets made in reference to him (with one exception) are void.—*See* P.P.—*Turf*.

SCREW: an unsound or broken-down horse, that requires both whip and spur to get him along.

SICK AS A HORSE: popular simile—curious, because a horse never vomits.

SNAFFLED: arrested, "pulled up;" so termed from a kind of horse's bit, called a SNAFFLE. In *East Anglia*, to SNAFFLE is to talk foolishly.

SPANK: to move along quickly; hence a fast horse or vessel is said to be "a SPANKER to go."

SPILT: thrown from a horse or chaise.—*See* PURL *page 133*.

STALE: to evacuate urine.—*Stable term.*

TIT: favourite name for a horse.

TOOTH: "he has cut his eye TOOTH," *i.e.*, he is sharp enough or old enough, to be so; "up in the TOOTH," far advanced in age—said often of old maids. *Stable term* for aged horses which have lost the distinguishing mark in their teeth.

UNICORN: a style of driving with two wheelers abreast, and one leader, termed in the *United States*, a SPIKE TEAM. TANDEM is one wheeler and one leader. RANDOM, three horses in line.

WALK OVER: a re-election without opposition.—*Parliamentary*, but derived from the *Turf*, where a horse—which has no rivals entered—WALKS OVER the course, and wins without exertion.

ROADS and TOWNS

DRAG: a street or road; BACK-DRAG, back-street.

GAMMY-VIAL: (Ville) a town where the police will not let persons hawk.

HUEY: a town or village.

KNAPPING-JIGGER: a turnpike-gate; "to dub at the KNAPPING-JIGGER," to pay money at the turnpike.

MAIN-TOBY: the highway or the main road.

MONKERY: the country or rural districts. *Old* word for a quiet or monastic life.—*Hall*.

PAD: the highway; a tramp.—*Lincolnshire*.

PIKE: a turnpike: "to bilk a PIKE," to cheat the keeper of the toll-gate.

RATTLERS: a railway; "on the RATTLERS to the stretchers," *i.e.*, going to the races by railway.

RECENT INCISION: the busy thoroughfare on the Surrey side of the Thames, known by sober people as the NEW CUT.

TOBY: a road; "high TOBY," the turnpike road. "High TOBY spice," robbery on horse-back.—*Don Juan*, canto xi., 19.

TOBY CONSARN: a highway expedition.

VILLE or VILE: a town or village.—pronounced *phial* or *vial*.—*French*.

WILD: a village.—*Tramps' term.—See* VILE *page 135*.

VEHICLES

BIRD-CAGE: a four-wheeled cab.

BOUNDER: a four-wheeled cab. *Lucus a non lucendo?*

BUGGY: a gig or light chaise. Common term in America and in Ireland.

BUSS: an abbreviation of "omnibus," a public carriage. Also, a kiss.

CAB: in statutory language, "a hackney carriage drawn by one horse." Abbreviated from CABRIOLET, *French*; originally meaning "a light low chaise." The wags of Paris playing upon the word (quasi *cabri* au lait) used to call a superior turn-out of the kind a *cabri au creme*. Our abbreviation, which certainly smacks of slang, has been stamped with the authority of "George, *Ranger*." See the notices affixed to the carriage entrances of St. James' Park.

CASK: fashionable slang for a brougham or other private carriage. —*Household Words*, No. 183.

DRAG: a cart of any kind, a coach; gentlemen drive to the races in DRAGS.

HUM-DRUM: tedious, tiresome, boring; "a society of gentleman who used to meet near the Charter house or at the King's Head, St. John's Street. They were characterised by less mystery and more pleasantry than the Freemasons." — *Bacchus and Venus*, 1737. In the *West,* a low cart.

KNIFE-BOARD: the seat running along the roof of an omnibus.

MAB: a cab or hackney coach.

RATTLER: a cab, coach, or cart. — *Old Cant.*

SHOWFULL or **SCHOFELL:** a Hansom cab — said to have been from the name of the inventor. — *Led de hor qu.*

SULKY: a one-horse chaise, having only room for one person.

TRAP: a "fast" term for a carriage of any kind. **TRAPS,** goods and chattels of any kind, but especially luggage and personal effects; in Australia, **SWAG.**

TROLLY or **TROLLY-CARTS:** term given by costermongers to a species of narrow cart, which can either be drawn by a donkey or driven by hand.

TURN OUT: personal show or appearance; a man with a showy carriage and horses is said to have a good **TURN OUT.**

WHITECHAPEL or **WESTMINSTER BROUGHAM:** a costermonger's donkey-barrow.

 LAW ENFORCEMENT

POLICEMEN

BEAK: a magistrate, judge, or policeman; "baffling the **BEAK,**" to get remanded. *Ancient Cant,* **BECK.** *Saxon,* **BEAG,** a necklace or gold collar — emblem of authority. Sir John Fielding was called the **BLIND-BEAK** in the last century. Query, if connected with the *Italian* **BECCO,** which means a (bird's) *beak,* and also a *blockhead.*

BLUE: a policeman; "disguised in **BLUE** and liquor." — *Boots at the Swan.*

BLUE-BOTTLE: a policeman. It is singular that this well-known slang term for a London constable should have been used by Shakespere. In part ii. of King Henry IV., act v., scene 4, Doll Tearsheet calls the beadle, who is dragging her in, a "thin man in a censer, a **BLUE-BOTTLE** rogue."

BOBBY: a policeman. Both **BOBBY** and **PEELER** were nicknames given to the new police, in allusion to the christian and surnames of the late *Sir Robert Peel*, who was the prime mover in effecting their introduction and improvement. The term **BOBBY** is, however, older than the *Saturday Reviewer*, in his childish and petulant remarks, imagines. The official square-keeper, who is always armed with a cane to drive away idle and disorderly urchins, has, time out of mind, been called by the said urchins, **BOBBY** *the Beadle*. **BOBBY** is also, I may remark, an *Old English* word for striking or hitting, a quality not unknown to policemen.—*See Halliwell's Dictionary.*

COPPER: a policeman, *i.e.*, one who **COPS**.—*See* **COP** *page 253.*

COSSACK: a policeman.

CRUSHER: a policeman.

DUBSMAN or **SCREW:** a turnkey.

FROG: a policeman.

LEATHER: to beat or thrash. From the leather belt worn by soldiers and policemen, often used as a weapon in street rows.

LOBSTER: a soldier. A *policeman* from the colour of his coat is styled an *unboiled* or *raw* **LOBSTER**.

NAM: a policeman. Evidently *back slang.*

PEELER: a policeman; so called from Sir Robert Peel (*see* **BOBBY** *above*); properly applied to the Irish constabulary rather than the City police, the former force having been established by Sir Robert Peel.

POLE-AXE: vulgar corruption of policeman.

SCUFTER: a policeman.—*North country.*

SHARPING-OMEE: a policeman.

SLOP: a policeman. Probably at first *back slang*, but now general.

STOP: a detective policeman.

OTHER LAW MEN

BEAK: a magistrate, judge, or policeman; "baffling the BEAK," to get remanded. *Ancient Cant*, BECK. *Saxon*, BEAG, a necklace or gold collar—emblem of authority. Sir John Fielding was called the BLIND-BEAK in the last century. Query, if connected with the *Italian* BECCO, which means a (bird's) *beak*, and also a *blockhead*.

BODY-SNATCHERS: bailiffs and runners: SNATCH, the trick by which the bailiff captures the delinquent.

BUM-BAILIFF: a sheriff's officer; a term, some say, derived from the proximity which this gentleman generally maintains to his victims. *Blackstone* says it is a corruption of "bound bailiff."

CHARLEY: a watchman, a beadle.

CHARLIE: a watchman, a beadle.

JIGGER-DUBBERS: term applied to jailors or turnkeys.

KETCH or **JACK KETCH:** the popular name for a public hangman —derived from a person of that name who officiated in the reign of Charles II.—*See Macaulay's History of England*, p. 626.

LAND-SHARK: sailor's definition of a lawyer.

LIMB OF THE LAW: a lawyer or clerk articled to that profession.

MOUTHPIECE: a lawyer or counsel.

NARK: a person in the pay of the police; a common informer; one who gets his living by laying traps for publicans, &c.

QUEER CUFFEN: a justice of the peace or magistrate—a very ancient term, mentioned in the earliest slang dictionary.

RAT: a sneak, an informer, a turn-coat, one who changes his party for interest. The late Sir Robert Peel was called the RAT, or the TAMWORTH RATCATCHER, for altering his views on the Roman Catholic question. From rats deserting vessels about to sink.

SNATCHER: bailiffs and runners.

SNIPE: a long bill; also a term for attorneys, a race remarkable for their propensity to long bills.

SNITCHERS: persons who turn queen's evidence or who tell tales. In *Scotland*, **SNITCHERS** signify handcuffs.

STIPE: a stipendiary magistrate.—*Provincial.*

TRAP: a sheriff's officer.

LAW MEN'S TERMS

BEAT: the allotted range traversed by a policeman on duty.

BONE: to steal or pilfer. **BONED**, seized, apprehended.—*Old.*

BRACELETS: handcuffs.

DARBIES: handcuffs.—*Old Cant.*

DOG-LATIN: barbarous *Latin*, such as was formerly used by lawyers in their pleadings.

DRIVE-AT: to aim at; "what is he **DRIVING AT?**" what does he intend to imply? A phrase often used when a circuitous line of argument is adopted by a barrister, or a strange set of questions asked, the purpose of which in not very evident.

FRISK: to search; **FRISKED**, searched by a constable or other officer.

FULLY: "to be **FULLIED**," to be committed for trial. From the slang of the penny-a-liner, "the prisoner was *fully* committed for trial."

GRABBED: caught, apprehended.

HUSH-MONEY: a sum given to quash a prosecution or evidence.

IN FOR PATTER: waiting for trial.

KIDMENT: a pocket-handkerchief fastened to the pocket and partially hung out to entrap thieves.

NOSE: a thief who turns informer or Queen's evidence; a spy or watch; "on the **NOSE**," on the look out.

PATTER: a speech or discourse, a pompous street oration, a judge's summing up, a trial. *Ancient* word for muttering. Probably from the *Latin*, **PATER NOSTER**, or Lord's Prayer. This was said, before the Reformation, in a *low voice* by the priest, until he came to, "and lead us not into temptation," to which the choir responded, "but deliver us from evil." In our reformed Prayer Book this was altered, and the Lord's Prayer directed to be said "with a *loud voice.*"—*Dr. Pusey* takes this view of the derivation in his *Letter to the Bishop of London*, P 78, 1851. Scott uses the word twice in *Ivanhoe* and the *Bride of Lammermoor*.

PULL: to have one apprehended; "to be PULLED up," to be taken before a magistrate.

QUEER BAIL: worthless persons who for a consideration would stand bail for anyone in court. Insolvent Jews generally performed this office, which gave rise to the term JEW-BAIL. — *See* MOUNTERS *page 57*: both *nearly obsolete*.

SCROBY: "to get SCROBY," to be whipped in prison before the justices.

SNAFFLED: arrested, "pulled up;" so termed from a kind of horse's bit, called a SNAFFLE. In *East Anglia*, to SNAFFLE is to talk foolishly.

SNITCHERS: persons who turn queen's evidence or who tell tales. In *Scotland*, SNITCHERS signify handcuffs.

SPOTTED: to be known or marked by the police.

SQUARING HIS NIBS: giving a policeman money.

STRETCHER: a contrivance with handles, used by the police to carry off persons who are violent or drunk.

THEATRE: a police court.

TURNED OVER: to be stopped and searched by the police.

TURNED UP: acquitted by the magistrate or judge for want of evidence.

WIFE: a fetter fixed to one leg. — *Prison*.

MEDICAL MEN

CROCUS or **CROAKUS:** a quack or traveling doctor; CROCUS-CHOVEY, a chemist shop.

DUMMIES: empty bottle and drawers in an apothecary's shop, labelled so as to give an idea of an extensive stock.

GARGLE: medical student Slang for physic.

GRIND: to work up for an examination, to cram with a GRINDER, or private tutor. — *Medical*.

HALF AND HALF: a mixture of ale and porter, much affected by medical students; occasionally *Latinized* into DIMIDIUM DIMIDIUMQUE. — *See* **COOPER** *page 332.*

LOBLOLLY BOY: a derisive term for a surgeon's mate in the navy.

MARROWSKYING: — *See* **MEDICAL GREEK** *page 141.*

MEDICAL GREEK: the slang used by medical students at the hospitals. At the London University they have a way of disguising *English*, described by Albert Smith as the *Gowerstreet Dialect*, which consists in transposing the initials of words, *e.g.*, *"poke a smipe"* —smoke a pipe, *"flutter-by"* —butterfly, &c. This disagreeable nonsense is often termed MORROWSKYING. — *See* **GREEK**, St. Giles' Greek, or the *"Ægidiac"* dialect, Language of **ZIPH** below, &c.

OINTMENT: medical student slang for butter.

PILL: a doctor. — *Military.* **PILL-DRIVER**, a peddling apothecary.

SAWBONES: a surgeon.

SQUIRT: a doctor or chemist.

ZIPH: "LANGUAGE OF," a way of disguising *English* in use among the students at *Winchester College.* Compare **MEDICAL GREEK** above.

MERCANTILE

BAZAAR: a shop or counter. *Gipsey* and *Hindoo*, a market.

BOUNCER: a person who steals whilst bargaining with a tradesmen; a lie.

BOX-HARRY: a term with bagmen or commercial travellers, implying dinner and tea at one meal; also dining with Humphrey, *i.e.*, going without. — *Lincolnshire.*

BUSK (or **BUSKING**): to sell obscene songs and books at the bars and in the tap-rooms of public houses. Sometimes implies selling any articles.

CHOVEY: a shop.

DAMPER: a shop till; to **DRAW A DAMPER**, *i.e.*, rob a till.

LOB: a till or money drawer.

PLEBS: a term used to stigmatise a tradesman's son at Westminster School. *Latin*, PLEBS, the vulgar.

SHOPPING: purchasing at shops. Termed by *Todd* a slang word, but used by *Cowper* and *Byron*.

STAR THE GLAZE: to break the window or show glass of a jeweller or other tradesman, and take any valuable articles, and run away. Sometimes the glass is cut with a diamond, and a strip of leather fastened to the piece of glass cut to keep it from falling in and making a noise. Another plan is to cut the sash.

STRIKE ME LUCKY!: an expression used by the lower orders when making a bargain, derived from the old custom of striking hands together, leaving in that of the seller a LUCK PENNY as an earnest that the bargain is concluded. In Ireland, at cattle markets, &c., a penny or other small coin, is always given by the buyer to the seller to ratify the bargain.—*Hudibras.* Anciently this was called a GOD'S PENNY.

"With that he cast him a God's Peny."—*Heir of Linne.*

The origin of the phrase being lost sight of, like that of many others, it is often corrupted now-a-days into STRIKE ME SILLY.

BUTCHERS and FOOD SELLERS

BAKER'S DOZEN: this consists of thirteen or fourteen; the surplus number, called the *inbread*, being thrown in for fear of incurring the penalty for short weight. To "give a man a BAKER'S DOZEN," in a slang sense, means to give him an extra good beating or pummelling.

BLOCK ORNAMENTS: the small dark coloured pieces of meat exposed on the cheap butchers' blocks or counters—debatable points to all the sharp-visaged, argumentative old women in low neighbourhoods.

CAKEY-PANNUM-FENCER: a man who sells street pastry.

COSTER: the short and slang term for a costermonger or costard-monger, who was originally an apple seller. COSTERING, *i.e.*, costermongering.

COSTERMONGERS: street sellers of fish, fruit, vegetables, poultry, &c. The London costermongers number more than 30,000. They form a distinct class, occupying whole neighbourhoods, and are cut off from the rest of metropolitan society by their low habits, general improvidence, pugnacity, love of gambling, total want of education, disregard for lawful marriage ceremonies, *and their use of Cant* (or so-called *back slang*) *language.*

CRACK-FENCER: a man who sells nuts.

CUT-THROAT: a butcher, a cattle slaughterer; a ruffian.

KIDDIER: a pork-butcher.

KNACKER: an old horse; a horse slaughterer.—*Gloucestershire.*

SCRAG: the neck.—*Old Cant. Scotch,* **CRAIG.** Still used by butchers. Hence, **SCRAG,** to hang by the neck, and **SCRAGGING,** an execution. —Also *Old Cant.*

SPUDDY: a seller of bad potatoes. In *Scotland,* a **SPUD** is a raw potato; and roasted **SPUDS** are those cooked in the cinders with their jackets on.

STICKINGS: bruised or damaged meat sold to sausage makers and penny pie shops.—*North.*

TURKEY-MERCHANTS: dealers in plundered or contraband silk. Poulterers are sometimes termed **TURKEY MERCHANTS,** in memory of Home Tooke's answer to the boys at Eton, who wished in an aristocratic way to know who his father was—a **TURKEY MERCHANT,** replied Tooke. His father was a poulterer. **TURKEY MERCHANT,** also, was formerly slang for a driver of turkeys or geese to market.

PAWNBROKERS

BLUE or **BLEW:** to pawn or pledge.

BRACE UP: to pawn stolen goods.

BRIEF: a pawnbroker's duplicate.

DOLLY SHOP: an illegal pawnshop where goods or stolen property, not good enough for the pawnbroker, are received and charged at so much per day. If not redeemed the third day, the goods are forfeited. *Anglo Saxon,* **DAEL,** a part—to dole?—*See* **NIX** *page 371.* A correspondent thinks it may have been derived from the *black doll*, the usual sign of a rag shop.

FENCE: to sell or pawn stolen property to a FENCER.

LAVENDER: "to be laid up in LAVENDER," in pawn; or, when a person is out of the way for an especial purpose.—*Old*.

LEAVING SHOP: an unlicensed house where goods are taken in to pawn at exorbitant rates of interest.—*Daily Telegraph*, 1st August, 1859.

LUG: "my togs are in LUG," *i.e.*, in pawn.

LUG CHOVEY: a pawnbroker's shop.

LUMBER: to pawn or pledge.—*Household Words*, No. 183.

MY UNCLE: the pawnbroker; generally used when any person questions the whereabouts of a domestic article, "Oh! Only at MY UNCLE'S" is the reply. UP THE SPOUT has the same meaning.

POP: to pawn or pledge; "to POP up the spout," to pledge at the pawnbroker's—an allusion to the spout up which the broker sends the ticketed article until such time as they shall be redeemed. The spout runs from the ground floor to the wareroom at the top of the house.

RAFE or **RALPH:** a pawnbroker's duplicate.—*Norwich*.

RAISE THE WIND: to obtain credit or money; generally by pawning or selling off property.

SHELF: "on the SHELF," not yet disposed of; young ladies are said to be so situated when they cannot meet with a husband; "on the SHELF," pawned.

SPOUT: "up the SPOUT," at the pawnbroker's; SPOUTING, pawning. —*See* POP *above* for origin.

UNCLE: the pawnbroker.—*See* MY UNCLE *above*.

PRINTERS and NEWSPAPERS

BALAAM: printers' slang for matter kept in type about monsterous productions of nature, &c., to fill up spaces in newspapers that would otherwise be vacant. The term **BALAAM-BOX** has long been used in *Blackwood* as the name of the depository for rejected articles.

COCK ROBIN SHOP: a small printer's office where low wages are paid to journeymen who have never served a regular apprenticeship.

DEVIL: a printer's youngest apprentice, an errand boy.

FAT: a printer's term signifying the void spaces on a page, for which he is paid at the same rate as full or unbroken pages. This work afforded much **FAT** for the printers.

FLIMSY: the thin, prepared copying paper used by newspaper reporters and "penny-a-liners" for making several copies at once, thus enabling them to supply different papers with the same article without loss of time.—*Printers' term.*

FLYING STATIONERS: paper workers, hawkers of penny ballad; "Printed for the Flying Stationers" is the *imprimatur* on hundreds of penny histories and sheet songs of the last and present centuries.

GIN AND GOSPEL GAZETTE: the *Morning Advertiser*, so called from its being the organ of the dissenting party, and of the Licensed Victuallers' Association. Sometimes termed the **TAP TUB**, or the '**TIZER.**

GODS: the quadrats used by printers in throwing on the imposing stone, similar to the movement of cast dice.—*Printers' term.*

HELL: a fashionable gambling house. In printing offices, the term is generally applied to the old tin box in which is thrown the broken or spoilt type, purchased by the founders for re-casting. *Nearly obsolete.*

JEAMES: (a generic for "flunkies,") the *Morning Post* newspaper—the organ of Belgravia and the "Haristocracy."

MRS. HARRIS and **MRS. GAMP:** nicknames of the *Morning Herald* and *Standard* newspapers, while united under the proprietorship of Mr. Baldwin. **MRS. GAMP**, a monthly nurse, was a character in Mr. Charles Dickens' popular novel of *Martin Chuzzlewit*, who continually quoted an imaginary *Mrs. Harris* in attestation of the superiority of her qualifications, and the infallibility of her opinions; and thus afforded a parallel to the two newspapers, who appealed to each other as independent authorities, being all the while the production of the same editorial staff.

PAPER WORKERS: the wandering vendors of street literature; street folk who sell ballads, dying speeches and confessions, sometimes termed RUNNING STATIONERS.

PENNY-A-LINER: a contributor of local news, accidents, fires, scandal, political and fashionable gossip, club jokes, and anecdotes to a newspaper; not regularly "on the paper," one who is popularly believed to be paid for each contribution at the rate of a *penny a line*, and whose interest is, therefore, that his article should be horribly stuffed with epithets.

RAT: term amongst printers to denote one who works under price. *Old Cant* for a clergyman.

SHEEP'S FOOT: an iron hammer used in a printing office, the end of the handle being made like a sheep's foot.

TAP TUB: the *Morning Advertiser.*

THUNDERER: the *Times* newspaper.

'TIZER: the *Morning Advertiser.*

TAILORS and SHOEMAKERS

BANDY or **CRIPPLE:** a sixpence, so called from this coin being generally bent or crooked; old term for flimsy or bad cloth, temp. Q. Elizabeth.

BRADS: money. Properly, a small kind of nails used by cobblers. —Compare HORSE NAILS page 194.

CABBAGE: pieces of cloth said to be purloined by tailors.

COUNTER JUMPER: a shopman, a draper's assistant.

DRAWERS: formerly the *Ancient Cant* name for very long stockings, now a hosier's term.

DRIZ: lace. In a low lodging house, this singular autograph inscription appears over the mantelpiece, "Scotch Mary, with DRIZ (lace), bound to Dover and back, please God."

GOOSE: a tailor's pressing iron.—Originally a slang term, but now in most dictionaries.

KNIGHT: a common and ironical prefix to a man's calling—thus, "KNIGHT of the whip," a coachman; "KNIGHT of the thimble," a tailor.

PASTE-HORN: the nose. Shoemakers nickname any shopmate with a large nose "old PASTE-HORN," from the horn in which they keep their paste.

PEAKING: remnants of cloth.

POST-HORN: the nose. — *See* PASTE-HORN *above.*

ROLL OF SNOW: a piece of Irish linen.

SANK WORK: making soldiers' clothes. *Mayhew* says from the *Norman,* Sanc, blood — in allusion either to the soldier's calling or the colour of his coat.

SHODDY: old cloth worked up into new; also, a term of derision applied to workmen in woolen factories. — *Yorkshire.*

SIXES AND SEVENS: articles in confusion are said to be all SIXES AND SEVENS. The Deity is mentioned in the Towneley Mysteries as He that "sett all on seven," *i.e.,* set or appointed everything in seven days. A similar phrase at this early date implies confusion and disorder, and from these, *Halliwell* thinks, has been derived the phrase "to be at SIXES AND SEVENS." A Scotch correspondent, however, states that the phrase probably came from the workshop, and that amongst needle makers when the points and eyes are "heads and tails" ("heeds and thraws") or in confusion, they are said to be SIXES AND SEVENS, because those numbers are the sizes most generally used, and in the course of manufacture have frequently to be distinguished.

SNIP: a tailor.

SNYDER: a tailor. *German,* SCHNEIDER.

SPIFFS: the percentage allowed by drapers to their young men when they effect a sale of old-fashioned or undesirable stock.

SPRINGER-UP: a tailor who sells low-priced, ready-made clothing, and gives starvation wages to the poor men and women who "make up" for him. The clothes are said to be SPRUNG-UP or "blown together."

SQUEEZE: silk.

STANGEY: a tailor; a person under petticoat government — derived from the custom of *"riding the STANG,"* mentioned in Hudibras:

"It is a custom used of course
Where the grey mare is the better horse."

STEEL BAR DRIVERS or **FLINGERS:** journeymen tailors.

SUFFERER: a tailor.

TINGE: the percentage allowed by drapers and clothiers to their assistants, upon the sale of old-fashioned articles. — *See* SPIFFS *p. 147.*

TROTTER: a tailor's man who goes 'round for orders. — *University.*

WHIPPING THE CAT: when an operative works at a private house by the day. Term used amongst tailors and carpenters.

OTHER MERCHANTS

BAGMAN: A commercial traveller.

BLINK FENCER: a person who sells spectacles.

BUMMAREE: this term is given to a class of speculating salesmen at Billingsgate market, not recognized as such by the trade, but who get a living by buying large quantities of fish of the salesmen and re-selling it to smaller buyers. The word has been used in the statutes and bye-laws of the market for upwards of 100 years. It has been variously derived, but is most probably from the *French*, BONNE MAREE, good fresh fish! "Marée signifie toute sorts de poisson de mer qûi n'est pas salé; bonne marée — *maree fraiche*, vendeur de marée." — *Dict. De l'Acad. Franc.* The BUMMAREES are accused of many trade tricks. One of them is to blow up cod-fish with a pipe until they look double their actual size. Of course, when the fish come to the table they are flabby, shrunken, and half-dwindled away. In Norwich, TO BUMMAREE ONE is to run up a score at a public house just open, and is equivalent to "running into debt with one."

BUNG: the landlord of a public-house.

COPER: properly HORSE-COUPER, a Scotch horse dealer — used to denote a dishonest one.

DAMPER: a shop till; to DRAW A DAMPER, *i.e.*, rob a till.

DRIZ-FENCER: a person who sells lace.

DUFFER: a hawker of "Brummagem" or sham jewelry; a sham of any kind; a fool or worthless person. **DUFFER** was formerly synonymous with **DUDDER**, and was a general term given to pedlars. It is mentioned in the *Frauds of London* (1760), as a word in frequent use in the last century to express cheats of all kinds. From the *German,* **DURFEN,** to want?

DUMP FENCER: a man who sells buttons.

FIG: "to **FIG** a horse," to play improper tricks with one in order to make him lively.

HORSE CHAUNTER: a dealer who takes worthless horses to country fairs and disposes of them by artifice. He is flexible in his ethics, and will put in a glass-eye or perform other tricks.—*See* **COPER** *page 131.*

KIDDLEYWINK: a small shop where they retail the commodities of a village store. Also, a loose woman.

OMEE: a master or landlord; "the **OMEE** of the cassey's a nark on the pitch," the master of the house will not let us perform. *Italian,* **UOMO,** a man; "**UOMO DELLA CASA,**" the master of the house.

PINNERS-UP: sellers of old songs pinned against a wall or framed canvas.

PLUNDER: a common word in the horse trade to express profit. Also an *American* term for baggage, luggage.

SKULL-THATCHERS: straw bonnet makers—sometimes called "bonnet-**BUILDERS.**"

SPUNK-FENCER: a lucifer match seller.

STRETCHER FENCER: one who sells braces.

SWAG-SHOP: a warehouse where "Brummagem" and general wares are sold—fancy trinkets, plated goods, &c. Jews are the general proprietors, and the goods are excessively low priced, trashy, and showy. **SWAG-SHOPS** were formerly plunder depots.—*Old Cant.*

TIMBER MERCHANT or **SPUNK-FENCER:** a lucifer match seller.

TURKEY-MERCHANTS: dealers in plundered or contraband silk. Poulterers are sometimes termed **TURKEY MERCHANTS**, in memory of Home Tooke's answer to the boys at Eton, who wished in an aristocratic way to know who his father was—a **TURKEY MERCHANT**, replied Tooke. His father was a poulterer. **TURKEY MERCHANT**, also, was formerly slang for a driver of turkeys or geese to market.

TYE or **TIE:** a neckerchief. Proper hosier's term now, but slang thirty years ago, and as early as 1718. Called also, **SQUEEZE**.

PERFORMERS

BARKER: a man employed to cry at the doors of "gaffs," shows, and puffing shops, to entice people inside.

BARN-STORMERS: theatrical performers who travel the country and act in barns, selecting short and frantic pieces to suit the rustic taste. — *Theatrical.*

BELL: a song.

BEN: a benefit. — *Theatrical.*

BILLY–BARLOW: a street clown; sometimes termed a **JIM CROW** or **SALTIMBANCO** — so called from the hero of a slang song. — *Bulwer's Paul Clifford.*

BOSH: a fiddle.

BOSH-FAKER: a violin player.

BUSKER: a man who sings or performs in a public house. — *Scotch.*

CATCH-PENNY: any temporary contrivance to obtain money from the public, penny shows, or cheap exhibitions.

CATGUT-SCRAPER: a fiddler.

CHAUNTER-CULLS: a singular body of men who used to haunt certain well-known public-houses, and write satirical or libellous ballads on any person or body of persons, for a consideration. 7s. 6d. was the usual fee, and in three hours the ballad might be heard in St. Paul's Churchyard or other public spot. There are two men in London at the present day who gain their living in this way.

CHERUBS or **CHERUBIMS:** the chorister boys who chaunt in the services at the abbeys.

CLAP-TRAP: high-sounding nonsense. An *Ancient Theatrical* term for a "**TRAP** to catch a **CLAP** by way of applause from the spectators at a play." — *Bailey's Dictionary.*

CORPSE: to confuse or put out the actors by making a mistake. — *Theatrical.*

CUT: in theatrical language, means to strike out portions of a dramatic piece, so as to render it shorter for representation. A late treasurer of one of the so-called *Patent Theatres*, when asked his opinion of a new play, always gave utterance to the brief, but safe piece of criticism "*wants* CUTTING."

DUTCH CONCERT: where each performer plays a different tune.

FAT: rich, abundant, &c.; "a FAT lot;" "to cut it FAT," to exaggerate, to show off in an extensive or grand manner, to assume undue importance; "CUT UP FAT." — *See under* CUT *page 479.* As a *Theatrical* term, a part with plenty of FAT in it, is one which affords the actor an opportunity of effective display.

FIDDLERS' MONEY: a sixpence. — *Household Words*, No. 183.

FIDDLERS' MONEY: a lot of sixpences; 6d. was the remuneration to fiddlers from each of the company in old times.

GAFF: a fair or penny-playhouse. — *See* PENNY GAFF *page 152.*

GHOST: "the GHOST doesn't walk," *i.e.*, the manager is too poor to pay salaries as yet. — *Theatrical; Household Words, No.*183.

GODS: the people in the upper gallery of a theatre; "up amongst the GODS," a seat amongst the low persons in the gallery — so named from the high position of the gallery, and the blue sky generally painted on the ceiling of the theatre; termed by the *French*, **PARADIS.**

GOOSE: to ruin or spoil. Also, to hiss a play. — *Theatrical.*

HA'PURTH OF LIVELINESS: the music at a low concert or theatre.

HOP-MERCHANT: a dancing master.

HURDY-GURDY: a droning musical instrument shaped like a large fiddle and turned by a crank, used by Savoyards and itinerant foreign musicians in England, now nearly superseded by the hand-organ. A correspondent suggests that the name is derived from being *girded* on the HARDIES, loins or buttocks. — *Scotch; Tam o'Shanter.* In *Italy* the instrument is called **VIOLA.**

LENGTH: forty-two lines of a dramatic composition. — *Theatrical.*

MAKE UP: personal appearance. — *Theatrical.*

MENAGERY: the orchestra of a theatre. — *Theatrical.*

MUG-UP: to paint one's face.—*Theatrical*. To "cram" for an examination. —*Army*.

MUMMER: a performer at a travelling theatre.—*Ancient*. Rustic performers at Christmas in the West of England.

MUTTONWALK: the saloon at Drury Lane Theatre.

OUT OF COLLAR: out of place—in allusion to servants. When in place, the term is COLLARED UP.—*Theatrical* and *general*.

PARADIS: *French* slang for the gallery of a theatre, "up amongst the GODS,"—*See* GODS *above*.

PENNY GAFFS: shops turned into temporary theatres (admission one penny), where dancing and singing take place every night. Rude pictures of the performers are arranged outside to give the front a gaudy and attractive look, and at nighttime coloured lamps and transparencies are displayed to draw an audience.

PRO: a professional.—*Theatrical*.

PROSS: breaking in or instructing a stage-infatuated youth.—*Theatrical*.

RUN: (good or bad), the success of a performance.—*Theatrical*.

SADDLE: an additional charge made by the manager to a performer upon his benefit night.—*Theatrical*.

SAL: a salary.—*Theatrical*.

SALAMANDERS: street acrobats and jugglers who eat fire.

SCHWASSLE BOX: the street performance of Punch and Judy. —*Household Words*, No. 183.

SCREAMING: first-rate, splendid. Believed to have been first used in the *Adelphi* play-bills; "a SCREAMING farce," one calculated to make the audience scream with laughter. Now a general expression.

SLANG: a travelling show.

SLAP: paint for the face, rouge.

SPELLKEN or **SPEELKEN:** a playhouse. *German*, SPIELEN.—*See* KEN *page 269*.—*Don Juan*.

STALL: to lodge or put up at a public house. Also, to act a part. —*Theatrical*.

STAR IT: to perform as the centre of attraction, with inferior subordinates to set off one's abilities. — *Theatrical.*

STICK: to cheat; "he got STUCK," he was taken in; STICK, to forget one's part in a performance. — *Theatrical.* STICK ON, to overcharge or defraud; STICK UP FOR, to defend a person, especially when slandered in his absence; STICK UP TO, to preserver in courting or attacking, whether in fisticuffs or argument; "to STICK in one's gizzard," to rankle in one's heart; "to STICK TO a person," to adhere to one, be his friend through adverse circumstances.

SUP: abbreviation of *supernumerary.* — *Theatrical.*

SURF: an actor who frequently pursues another calling. — *Theatrical.*

TAKE: to succeed or be patronised; "do you think the new opera will TAKE?" "No, because the same company TOOK so badly under the old management;" "to TAKE OFF," to mimic. — *See* TAKE *in the Index for more meanings on page 504.*

TOM-TOM: a street instrument, a small kind of drum beaten with the fingers, somewhat like the ancient tabor; a performer on this instrument. It was imported, doubtless, with the *Negro* melodies, —TOM-TOMS being a favourite instrument with the darkies.

VIC.: the Victoria Theatre, London—patronised principally by costermongers and low people; also the street abbreviation of the Christian name of her Majesty the Queen.

POLITICIANS and STOCKBROKERS

BEAR: one who contracts to deliver or sell a certain quantity of stock in the public fund on a forthcoming day at a stated place, but who does not possess it, trusting to a decline in public securities to enable him to fulfill the agreement and realise a profit. — *See* BULL *below.* Both words are slang terms on the Stock Exchange, and are frequently used in the business columns of newspapers.

> "He who sells that of which he is not possessed is proverbially said to sell the skin before he has caught, the BEAR. It was the practice of stock-jobbers, in the year 1720 to enter into a contract for transferring South Sea Stock at a future time for a

certain price; but he who contracted to sell had frequently no stock to transfer, nor did he who bought intend to receive any in consequence of his bargain; the seller was, therefore, called a BEAR in allusion to the proverb, and the buyer a BULL, perhaps only as a similar distinction. The contract was merely a wager, to be determined by the rise or fall of stock; if it rose, the seller paid the difference to the buyer, proportioned to the sum determined by the same computation to the seller." — *Dr. Warton on Pope.*

BULL: one who agrees to purchase stock at a future day, at a stated price, but who does not possess money to pay for it, trusting to a rise in public securities to render the transaction a profitable one. Should stocks fall, the bull is then called upon to pay the difference. — *See* BEAR, who is the opposite of a BULL, the former selling, the latter purchasing — the one operating for a *fall* or a *pull down*, whilst the other operates for a *rise* or *toss up*.

CAUCUS: a private meeting held for the purpose of concerting measures, agreeing upon candidates for office before an election, &c. — *See Pickering's Vocabulary.*

JOB: a short piece of work, a prospect of employment. *Johnson* describes JOB as a low word, without etymology. It is, and was, however, a *Cant* word, and a JOB, two centuries ago, was an arranged robbery. Even at the present day it is mainly confined to the street, in the sense of employment for a short time. Amongst undertakers a JOB signifies a funeral; "to do a JOB," conduct anyone's funeral; "by the JOB," *i.e.*, *piece*-work, as opposed to *time*-work. A JOB in political phraseology is a government office or contract, obtained by secret influence or favouritism.

LAME DUCK: a stock jobber who speculates beyond his capital and cannot pay his losses. Upon retiring from the Exchange he is said to "waddle out of the Alley."

MASSACRE OF THE INNOCENTS: when the leader of the House of Commons goes through the doleful operation of devoting to extinction a number of useful measures at the end of the session, for want of time to pass them. — *Vide Times,* 20th July, 1859: Mr. C. Foster, on altering the time of the legislative sessions. — *Parliamentary slang.*

NABOB: an Eastern prince, a retired Indian official; hence a slang term for a capitalist.

PLUMPER: a single vote at an election, not a "split ticket."

POT-WALLOPERS: electors in certain boroughs before the passing of the Reform Bill, whose qualification consisted in being housekeepers—to establish which, it was only necessary to boil a pot within the limits of the borough, by the aid of any temporary erection. This implied that they were able to provide for themselves, and not necessitated to apply for parochial relief. WALLOP, a word of *Anglo Saxon* derivation, from the same root as *wall*.

QUOCKERWODGER: a wooden toy figure, which, when pulled by a string, jerks its limbs about. The term is used in a slang sense to signify a pseudo-politician, one whose strings of action are pulled by somebody else.—*West*.

RAG-SHOP: a bank.

STAG: a term applied during the railway mania to a speculator without capital, who took "scrip" in "*Diddlesex Junction*" and other lines, *ejus et sui generis*, got the shares up to a premium, and then sold out. *Punch* represented the house of Hudson, "the Railway King," at Albert Gate, with a STAG on it, in allusion to this term.

WALK OVER: a re-election without opposition.—*Parliamentary*, but derived from the *Turf*, where a horse—which has no rivals entered —WALKS OVER the course, and wins without exertion.

SAILORS and SAILING

A 1: first-rate, the very best; "she's a prime girl she is; she is **A 1**."—*Sam Slick*. The highest classification of ships at Lloyd's; common term in the United States, also at Liverpool and other English seaports. Another even more intensive form, is "first-class, letter A, No. 1."

AVAST: a sailor's phrase for stop, shut up, go away—apparently connected with the *Old Cant*, BYNGE A WASTE.

BANYAN-DAY: a day on which no meat is served out for rations; probably derived from the BANIANS, a Hindoo caste, who abstain from animal food.—*Sea*.

BOOM: "to tip one's **BOOM** off," to be off or start in a certain direction. —*Sea.*

BULL-THE-CASK: to pour hot water into an empty rum puncheon, and let it stand until it extracts the spirit from the wood. The result is drunk by sailors in default of something stronger. —*Sea.*

BUM-BOATS: shore boats which supply ships with provisions, and serve as means of communication between the sailors and the shore.

CHALKS: to walk one's **CHALKS**," to move off or run away. An ordeal for drunkenness used on board ship, to see whether the suspected person can walk on a chalked line without overstepping it on either side.

CRAB or **GRAB:** a disagreeable old person. *Name of a wild and sour fruit.* "To catch a **CRAB**," to fall backwards by missing a stroke in rowing.

DAVY'S LOCKER or **DAVY JONES' LOCKER:** the sea, the common receptacle for all things thrown overboard—a nautical phrase for death, the other world.

DOLDRUMS: difficulties, low spirits, dumps. —*Sea.*

DOUSE: to put out; "**DOUSE** that glim," put out that candle. —*Sea.*

DUDDERS or **DUDSMEN:** persons who formerly travelled the country as pedlars, selling gown-pieces, silk waistcoats, &c., to countrymen. In selling a waistcoat-piece for thirty shillings or two pounds, which cost them perhaps five shillings, they would show great fear of the revenue officer, and beg of the purchasing clodhopper *to kneel down in a puddle of water, crook his arm, and swear that it might never become straight if he told an exciseman, or even his own wife.* The term and practice are *nearly obsolete.* In Liverpool, however, and at the east end of London, men dressed up as sailors with pretended silk handkerchiefs and cigars "only just smuggled from the Indies," are still to be plentifully found.

DUFF: pudding; vulgar pronunciation of **DOUGH**. —*Sea.*

DUNNAGE: baggage, clothes. Also, a *Sea* term for wood or loose faggots laid at the bottom of ships, upon which is placed the cargo.

FIGURE: "to cut a good or bad **FIGURE**," to make a good or indifferent appearance; "what's the **FIGURE**?" how much is to pay? **FIGURE-HEAD**, a person's face. —*Sea term.*

FIN: a hand; "come, tip us your **FIN**," viz., let us shake hands. —*Sea.*

FLIPPER: the hand; "give us your **FLIPPER**," give me your hand. — *Sea.* Metaphor taken from the flipper or paddle of a turtle.

GLIM: a light, a lamp; "dowse the **GLIM**," put the candle out. — *Sea, and Old Cant.*

GRAPPLING IRONS: fingers. — *Sea.*

HALF SEAS OVER: reeling drunk. — *Sea.* Used by *Swift.*

HARD UP: in distress, poverty-stricken. — *Sea.*

HAWSE HOLES: the apertures in a ship's bows through which the cables pass; "he has crept in through the **HAWSE HOLES**," said of an officer who has risen from the grade of an ordinary seaman. — *Navy.*

HORSE MARINE: an awkward person. In ancient times the "**JOLLIES**" or Royal Marines, were the butts of the sailors, from their ignorance of seamanship. "Tell that to the **MARINES**, the blue jackets won't believe it!" was a common rejoinder to a "stiff yarn." Now-a-days they are deservedly appreciated as the finest regiment in the service. A **HORSE MARINE** (an impossibility) was used to denote one more awkward still.

JACK TAR: a sailor.

JIB: the face or a person's expression; "the cut of his **JIB**," *i.e.*, his peculiar appearance. The sail of a ship, which in position and shape corresponds to the nose on a person's face. — *See* **GIB-FACE**. — *Sea.*

JUNK: salt beef. — *See* **OLD HORSE** *page 158.*

KEEL-HAULING: a good thrashing or mauling, rough treatment — from the old nautical custom of punishing offenders by throwing them overboard with a rope attached and hauling them up from under the ship's keel.

LAGGER: a sailor.

LAND LUBBER: sea term for a landsman. — *See* **LOAFER** *below.*

LAND-SHARK: sailor's definition of a lawyer.

LARK: fun, a joke; "let's have a jolly good **LARK**," let us have a piece of fun. *Mayhew* calls it "a convenient word covering much mischief." — *Anglo Saxon,* **LAC**, sport; but more probably from the nautical term **SKYLARKING**, *i.e.*, mounting to the highest yards and sliding down the ropes for amusement, which is allowed on certain occasions.

LOAFER: a lazy vagabond. Generally considered an *Americanism*. LOPER or LOAFER, however, was in general use as a *Cant* term in the early part of the last century. LANDLOPER was a vagabond who begged in the attire of a sailor; and the sea phrase, LAND LUBBER, was doubtless synonymous.—*See the Times*, 3rd November, 1859, for a reference to LOAFER.

LOBLOLLY: gruel.—*Old*: used by *Markham* as a sea term for grit gruel or hasty pudding.

LOBLOLLY BOY: a derisive term for a surgeon's mate in the navy.

LUBBER'S HOLE: an aperture in the maintop of a ship, by which a timid climber may avoid the difficulties of the "futtock shrouds" —hence, a sea term for a cowardly way of evading duty.

LUMPER: a contractor. On the river, more especially a person who contracts to deliver a ship laden with timber.

LUMPERS: low thieves who haunt wharves and docks, and rob vessels; persons who sell old goods for new.

MATE: the term a coster or low person applies to a friend, partner, or companion; "me and my MATE did so and so," is a common phrase with a low Londoner.—Originally a *Sea term*.

MIDDY: abbreviation of MIDSHIPMAN.—*Naval*.

MUFTI: the civilian dress of a naval or military officer when off duty. —*Anglo Indian*.

NEDDY: a life preserver.—Contraction of KENNEDY, the name of the first man, it is said in St. Giles', who had his head broken by a poker. —*Vide Mornings at Bow Street*.

OLD HORSE: salt junk or beef.—*Sea*.

PAY: to beat a person or "serve them out." Originally a nautical term, meaning to stop the seams of a vessel with pitch (*French*, POIX); "here's the devil to PAY and no pitch hot," said when any catastrophe occurs which there is no means of averting; "to PAY over face and eyes, as the cat did the monkey;" "to PAY through the nose," to give a ridiculous price—whence the origin? *Shakespere* uses PAY in the sense of to beat or thrash.

PIPE: to shed tears or bewail; "PIPE one's eye."—*Sea term*.

"He first began to eye his pipe,
and then to PIPE HIS EYE."

—Old Song.

Metaphor from the boatswain's pipe, which calls to duty.

PUMP SHIP: to evacuate urine. *—Sea.*

RIGGED: "well-RIGGED," well-dressed. *Old slang,* in use in 1736. *—See Bailey's Dictionary. —Sea.*

SALT JUNK: navy salt beef. *—See* OLD HORSE *page 158.*

SHAVER: a sharp fellow; "a young" or "old SHAVER," a boy or man. *—Sea.*

SHIP-SHAPE: proper, in good order; sometimes the phrase is varied to "SHIP-SHAPE and *Bristol* fashion." *—Sea.*

SING OUT: to call aloud. *—Sea.*

SKATES LURK: a begging impostor dressed as a sailor.

SKILIGOLEE: prison gruel, also sailors' soup of many ingredients.

SKIPPER: the master of a vessel. *Dutch,* SCHIFFER, from *schiff* a ship; sometimes used synonymous with "Governor."

SKY-LARK: *—See* LARK *page 157.*

SKY-SCRAPER: a tall man; "are you cold up there, old SKY-SCRAPER?" Properly a sea term; the light sails which some adventurous skippers set above the royals in calm latitudes are termed SKY-SCRAPERS and MOON-RAKERS.

SLEWED: drunk or intoxicated. *—Sea term.* When a vessel changes the tack she, as it were, staggers, the sails flap, she gradually heels over and, the wind catching the waiting canvas, she glides off at another angle. The course pursued by an intoxicated, or SLEWED man, is supposed to be analogous to that of the ship.

SLIP: "to give the SLIP," to run away or elude pursuit. *Shakespere* has "you *gave me the counterfeit,*" in Romeo and Juliet. GIVING THE SLIP, however, is a *Sea phrase,* and refers to fastening an anchor and chain cable to a floating buoy or water cask, until such a time arrives that is convenient to return and take them on board. In fastening the cable, the home end is *slipped* through the hawse pipe. Weighing anchor is a noisy task, so that giving it the SLIP infers to leave it in quietness.

SLOP: cheap or ready made, as applied to clothing, is generally supposed to be a modern appropriation; but it was used in this sense in 1691 by *Maydman* in his *Naval Speculations*; and by *Chaucer* two centuries before that. **SLOPS** properly signify sailors' working clothes.

SLUSHY: a ship's cook.

SNAGGLE TEETH: uneven and unpleasant looking dental operators. —*West.* **SNAGS** (*Americanism*) ends of sunken drift-wood sticking out of the water, on which river steamers are often wrecked.

SOFT TACK: Bread.—*Sea.*

SPANK: to move along quickly; hence a fast horse or vessel is said to be "a **SPANKER** to go."

SPLICE: to marry, "and the two shall become one flesh." —*Sea.*

SPLICE THE MAIN BRACE: to take a drink.—*Sea.*

SQUARE-RIGGED: well-dressed.—*Sea.*

SWIPES: sour or small beer. **SWIPE**, to drink.—Sea.

TACKLE: clothes.—*Sea.*

THREE SHEETS IN THE WIND: unsteady from drink.—*Sea.*

TIP: a douceur; also to give, lend, or hand over anything to another person; "come, **TIP** up the tin," *i.e.*, hand up the money; "**TIP** the wink," to inform by winking; "**TIP** us your fin," *i.e.*, give me your hand; "**TIP** one's boom off," to make off, depart.—*Sea.* "To miss one's **TIP**," to fail in a scheme.—*Old Cant.*

TOSHERS: men who steal copper from ships' bottoms in the Thames.

TRUCK-GUTTED: pot-bellied, corpulent.—*Sea.*

TURNPIKE-SAILORS: beggars who go about dressed as sailors.

WHIP: To "**WHIP** anything *up*," to take it up quickly; from the method of hoisting heavy goods or horses on board ship by a **WHIP** or running tackle, from the yard-arm. Generally used to express anything dishonestly taken.—*L' Estrange* and *Johnson.*

WHIP JACK: a sham shipwrecked sailor, called also a **TURNPIKE SAILOR**.

WHISTLE: "as clean as a **WHISTLE**," neatly or "slickly done," as an American would say; "to **WET ONE'S WHISTLE**," to take a drink. This is a very old term. *Chaucer* says of the Miller of Trumpington's wife (*Canterbury Tales*, 4153)—

"So was hir joly **WHISTAL** well **Y-WET**;"

"to **WHISTLE FOR ANYTHING**," to stand small chance of getting it, from the nautical custom of *whistling* for a wind in a calm, which of course comes none the sooner for it.

YARN: a long story or tale; "a tough **YARN**," a tale hard to be believed; "spin a **YARN**," tell a tale.—*Sea.*

YOUNKER: in street language, a lad or a boy. Term in general use amongst costermongers, cabmen, and old-fashioned people. *Barnefield's Affectionate Shepherd*, 1594, has the phrase, "a seemelie **YOUNKER**." *Danish* and *Friesic*, **JONKER**. In the *Navy*, a naval cadet is usually termed a **YOUNKER**.

SERVANTS and SERVICE PROVIDERS

BONE-PICKER: a footman.

BUM-BOATS: shore boats which supply ships with provisions, and serve as means of communication between the sailors and the shore.

BUTTONS: a page—from the rows of gilt buttons which adorn his jacket.

CHOKER: a cravat, a neckerchief. **WHITE-CHOKER**, the white neckerchief worn by mutes at a funeral and waiters at a tavern. Clergymen are frequently termed **WHITE-CHOKERS**.

CHUMMY: a chimney sweep; also a low-crowned felt hat.

COLD COOK: an undertaker.

COOLIE: a soldier; in allusion to the *Hindoo* **COOLIES**, or day labourers.

DANNA: excrement; **DANNA DRAG**, a nightman's or dustman's cart.

DEVIL: a printer's youngest apprentice, an errand boy.

DOLLYMOP: a tawdrily dressed maidservant, a street-walker.

FAG: a schoolboy who performs a servant's offices to a superior schoolmate. *Grose* thinks **FAGGED OUT** is derived from this.

FANTAIL: a dustman's hat.

FLINT: an operative who works for a "society" master, *i.e.*, for full wages.

FLUE FAKERS: chimney sweeps; also low sporting characters, who are so termed from their chiefly betting on the *Great Sweeps.*

FLUNKEY: a footman, servant.—*Scotch.*

FOGEY or **OLD FOGEY:** a dullard, an old-fashioned or singular person. *Grose* says it is a nickname for an invalid soldier, from the *French,* FOURGEAUX, fierce or fiery, but it has lost this signification now. FOGGER, *old word* for a huckster or servant.

GYP: an undergraduate's valet at *Cambridge.* Corruption of GYPSEY JOE (*Saturday Review*); popularly derived by Cantabs from the *Greek,* GYPS, (γυψ) a vulture, from their dishonest rapacity. At *Oxford* they are called SCOUTS.

HUMBLE PIE: to "eat HUMBLE PIE," to knock under, be submissive. The UMBLES, or entails of a deer, were anciently made into a dish for servants, while their masters feasted off the haunch.

JACK-AT-A-PINCH: one whose assistance is only sought on an emergency; JACK-IN-THE-WATER: an attendant at the watermen's stairs on the river and sea-port towns, who does not mind wetting his feet for a customer's convenience, in consideration of a douceur.

JEAMES: (a generic for "flunkies,") the *Morning Post* newspaper—the organ of Belgravia and the "Haristocracy."

JOB: a short piece of work, a prospect of employment. *Johnson* describes JOB as a low word, without etymology. It is, and was, however, a *Cant* word, and a JOB, two centuries ago, was an arranged robbery. Even at the present day it is mainly confined to the street, in the sense of employment for a short time. Amongst undertakers a JOB signifies a funeral; "to do a JOB," conduct anyone's funeral; "by the JOB," *i.e., piece*-work, as opposed to *time*-work. A JOB in political phraseology is a government office or contract, obtained by secret influence or favouritism.

JOHN THOMAS: generic for "flunkies,"—footmen popularly represented with large calves and bushy whiskers.

KNULLER: old term for a chimney-sweep, who solicited jobs by ringing a bell. From the *Saxon,* CNYLLAN, to knell, or sound a bell.—*See* QUERIER *below.*

LADDLE: a lady. Term with chimney-sweeps on the 1st of May. A correspondent suggests that the term may come from the brass *ladles* for collecting money, always carried by the sweeps' ladies.

LOOF FAKER: a chimney-sweep.— *See* **FLUE FAKER** *page 162.*

MARINE or **MARINE RECRUIT:** an empty bottle. This expression having once been used in the presence of an officer of marines, he was at first inclined to take it as an insult, until someone adroitly appeased his wrath by remarking that no offence could be meant, as all that it could possibly imply was, "one who had done his duty, and was ready to do it again." — *See* **HORSE MARINE** *page 55.* — *Naval.*

MOP: a hiring place (or fair) for servants. Steps are being taken to put down these assemblies, which have been proved to be greatly detrimental to the morality of the poor.

MUSH (or MUSHROOM) FAKER: an itinerant mender of umbrellas.

OUT OF COLLAR: out of place—in allusion to servants. When in place, the term is **COLLARED UP.** — *Theatrical* and *general.*

PEACOCK HORSE: amongst undertakers, is one with a showy tail and mane, and holds its head up well. — *che va favor-reggiando, &c., Italian.*

QUERIER: a chimney-sweep who calls from house to house—formerly termed **KNULLER.** — *See* **KNULLER** *above.*

QUILL-DRIVER: a scrivener, a clerk—satirical phrase similar to **STEEL BAR-DRIVER**, a tailor.

SALOOP, SALEP, or **SALOP:** a greasy-looking beverage, formerly sold on stalls at early morning, prepared from a powder made of the root of the *Orchis mascula*, or Red-handed Orchis. Within a few years coffee stands have superseded **SALOOP** stalls, but Charles Lamb, in one of his papers, has left some account of this drinkable, which he says was of all preparations the most grateful to the stomachs of young chimney sweeps.

SCOUT: a college valet or waiter. — *Oxford.* — *See* **GYP** *page 173.*

SLAVEY: a maid servant.

STIFF 'UN: a corpse. — *Term used by undertakers.*

SWAG: a lot or plenty of anything, a portion or division of property. In Australia the term is used for the luggage carried by diggers: in India the word **LOOT** is used. *Scotch,* **SWEG** or **SWACK**; *German,* **SWEIG**, a flock. *Old Cant* for a shop.

TAPE: gin—term with female servants.

TIGER: a boy employed to wait on a gentlemen; one who waits on ladies is a page.

WHITE TAPE: gin—term used principally by female servants.

⟨ SOLDIERS

BLADE: a man—in ancient times the term for a soldier; "knowing BLADE," a wide-awake, sharp, or cunning man.

BROTHER-CHIP: fellow carpenter. Also, BROTHER-WHIP, a fellow coachman; and BROTHER-BLADE, of the same occupation or calling —originally a fellow soldier.

BROWN BESS: the old Government regulation musket.

COOLIE: a soldier; in allusion to the *Hindoo* COOLIES, or day labourers.

CORKS: money; "how are you off for CORKS?" a soldier's term of a very expressive kind, denoting the means of "keeping afloat."

CRIMPS: men who trepan others into the clutches of the recruiting sergeant. They generally pretend to give employment in the colonies, and in that manner cheat those mechanics who are half famished. —*Nearly obsolete.*

FLYING-MESS: "to be in FLYING MESS" is a soldier's phrase for being hungry and having to mess where he can.—*Military.*

FOGEY or **OLD FOGEY:** a dullard, an old-fashioned or singular person. *Grose* says it is a nickname for an invalid soldier, from the *French*, FOURGEAUX, fierce or fiery, but it has lost this signification now. FOGGER, *old word* for a huckster or servant.

GRIFFIN: in India, a newly arrived cadet; general for an inexperienced youngster. "Fast" young men in London frequently term an umbrella a GRIFFIN.

HARD LINES: hardship, difficulty.—*Soldiers' term* for hard duty on the LINES in front of the enemy.

HORSE MARINE: an awkward person. In ancient times the "JOLLIES" or Royal Marines, were the butts of the sailors, from their ignorance of seamanship. "Tell that to the MARINES, the blue jackets won't believe it!" was a common rejoinder to a "stiff yarn." Now-a-days they are deservedly appreciated as the finest regiment in the service. A **HORSE MARINE** (an impossibility) was used to denote one more awkward still.

JOLLY: a Royal Marine.—*See* **HORSE MARINE** *page 55.*

LEATHER: to beat or thrash. From the leather belt worn by soldiers and policemen, often used as a weapon in street rows.

LOBSTER: a soldier. A *policeman* from the colour of his coat is styled an *unboiled* or *raw* **LOBSTER.**

LOBSTER BOX: a barrack or military station.

MONKEY: the instrument which drives a rocket.—*Army.*

MUFTI: the civilian dress of a naval or military officer when off duty. —*Anglo Indian.*

MUG-UP: to paint one's face.—*Theatrical.* To "cram" for an examination. —*Army.*

PILL: a doctor.—*Military.* **PILL-DRIVER,** a peddling apothecary.

POT: to finish; "don't **POT** me," term used at billiards. This word was much used by our soldiers in the Crimea, for firing at the enemy from a hole or ambush. These were called **POT-SHOTS.**

RED HERRING: a soldier.

ROOKERY: a low neighbourhood inhabited by dirty Irish and thieves; as **ST. GILES' ROOKERY.**—*Old.* In *Military slang* that part of the barracks occupied by subalterns, often by no mean a pattern of good order.

SANK WORK: making soldiers' clothes. *Mayhew* says from the *Norman,* **SANC,** blood—in allusion either to the soldier's calling or the colour of his coat.

SON OF A GUN: a contemptuous title for a man. In the army it is sometimes applied to an artilleryman.

SPIN: to reject from an examination.—*Army.*

SWADDY or **COOLIE:** a soldier. The former was originally applied to a discharged soldier, and perhaps came from **SHODDY,** of which soldiers' coats are made.

SWOT: mathematics; also a mathematician; as a verb, to work hard for an examination, to be diligent in one's studies.—*Army.* This word originated at the great slang manufactory for the army, the Royal

Military College, Sandhurst, in the broad Scotch pronunciation of Dr. Wallace, one of the Professors, of the word *sweat.—See Notes and queries*, vol. i., p. 369.

TAKE: "to **TAKE THE FIELD**," when said of a General, to commence operations against the enemy; when a racing man **TAKES THE FIELD** he stakes his money against the favourite.—*See* **TAKE** *in the Index for more meanings on page 504.*

STREET SELLERS and COSTERMONGERS

BIBLE CARRIER: a person who sells songs without singing them.

BLACKBERRY-SWAGGER: a person who hawks tapes, boot laces, &c.

BONE-GRUBBERS: persons who hunt dust-holes, gutters, and all likely spots for refuse bones, which they sell at the rag shops or to the bone-grinders.

CAKEY-PANNUM-FENCER: a man who sells street pastry.

CHAUNTERS: those street sellers of ballads, last copies of verses, and other broadsheets, who sing or bawl the contents of their papers. They often term themselves **PAPER WORKERS**.—*Anglo-Norman.*—*See* **HORSE CHAUNTERS** *page 132.*

CHEAP JACKS or **JOHNS:** oratorical hucksters and patterers of hardware, &c., at fairs and races. They put an article up at a high price, and then cheapen it by degrees, indulging in volleys of coarse wit, until it becomes to all appearances a bargain, and as such it is bought by one of the crowd. The popular idea is that the inverse method of auctioneering saves them paying for the auction license.

CHIVE-FENCER: a street hawker of cutlery.

COSTER: the short and slang term for a costermonger or costard-monger, who was originally an apple seller. **COSTERING,** *i.e.,* costermongering.

COSTERMONGERS: street sellers of fish, fruit, vegetables, poultry, &c. The London costermongers number more than 30,000. They form a distinct class, occupying whole neighbourhoods, and are cut off from the rest of metropolitan society by their low habits, general improvidence, pugnacity, love of gambling, total want of education, disregard for lawful marriage ceremonies, *and their use of Cant* (or so-called *back slang*) *language.*

DEATH-HUNTERS: running patterers, who vend last dying speeches and confessions.

DUDDERS or **DUDSMEN:** persons who formerly travelled the country as pedlars, selling gown-pieces, silk waistcoats, &c., to countrymen. In selling a waistcoat-piece for thirty shillings or two pounds, which cost them perhaps five shillings, they would show great fear of the revenue officer, and beg of the purchasing clodhopper *to kneel down in a puddle of water, crook his arm, and swear that it might never become straight if he told an exciseman, or even his own wife.* The term and practice are *nearly obsolete.* In Liverpool, however, and at the east end of London, men dressed up as sailors with pretended silk handkerchiefs and cigars "only just smuggled from the Indies," are still to be plentifully found.

DUFFER: a hawker of "Brummagem" or sham jewelry; a sham of any kind; a fool or worthless person. DUFFER was formerly synonymous with DUDDER, and was a general term given to pedlars. It is mentioned in the *Frauds of London* (1760), as a word in frequent use in the last century to express cheats of all kinds. From the *German,* DURFEN, to want?

FLYING STATIONERS: paper workers, hawkers of penny ballad; "Printed for the Flying Stationers" is the *imprimatur* on hundreds of penny histories and sheet songs of the last and present centuries.

GRIDDLER: a person who sings in the streets without a printed copy of the words.

HAND-SAW or **CHIVE-FENCER:** a man who sells razors and knives in the streets.

HANDSELLER or **CHEAP JACK:** a street or open-air seller, a man who carries goods to his customers instead of waiting for his customers to visit him.

HARD-UPS: cigar-end finders, who collect the refuse pieces of smoked cigars from the gutter and, having dried them, sell them as tobacco to the very poor.

JEW-FENCER: a Jew street salesman.

MATE: the term a coster or low person applies to a friend, partner, or companion; "me and my MATE did so and so," is a common phrase with a low Londoner.—Originally a *Sea term.*

PAPER WORKERS: the wandering vendors of street literature; street folk who sell ballads, dying speeches and confessions, sometimes termed RUNNING STATIONERS.

PATTERERS: men who cry last dying speeches, &c., in the streets, and those who help off their wares by *long harangues* in the public thoroughfares. These men, to use their own term "are the haristocracy of the street sellers," and despise the costermongers for their ignorance, boasting that they live by their intellect. The public, they say, do not expect to receive from them an equivalent for their money—they pay to hear them talk.—*Mayhew.* PATTERERS were formerly termed "mountebanks."

RUNNING PATTERER: a street seller who runs or moves briskly along, calling aloud his wares.

RUNNING STATIONERS: hawkers of books, ballads, dying speeches, and newspapers. They, formerly used to run with newspapers, blowing a horn, when they were also termed FLYING STATIONERS.

SCHOOL or MOB: two or more "patterers" working together in the streets.

SPUDDY: a seller of bad potatoes. In *Scotland*, a SPUD is a raw potato; and roasted SPUDS are those cooked in the cinders with their jackets on.

STANDING PATERERS: men who take a stand on the curb of a public thoroughfare, and deliver prepared speeches to effect a sale of any article they have to vend. — *See* PATTERERS *above.*

STIFF FENCER: a street seller of writing paper.

STREET PITCHERS: negro minstrels, ballad singers, long song men, men "working a board" on which have been painted various exciting scenes in some terrible drama, the details of which the STREET PITCHER is bawling out, and selling in a little book or broadsheet (price one penny); or any persons who make a stand in the streets, and sell articles for their living.

SWELL FENCER: a street salesman of needles.

STREET SELLERS' TERMS

AGGERAWATORS: (corruption of *Aggravators*), the greasy locks of hair in vogue among costermongers and other street folk, worn twisted from the temple back toward the ear. They are also, from a supposed resemblance in form, termed NEWGATE KNOCKERS. — *See* NEWGATE KNOCKERS *below.* — *Sala's Gaslight*, &c.

BOWLAS: round tarts made of sugar, apple, and bread, sold in the streets.

BUNTS: costermongers' perquisites; the money obtained by giving light weight, &c.; costermonger's goods sold by boys on commission. Probably a corruption of *bonus*, BONE being the slang for good. BUNCE, *Grose* gives as the *Cant* word for money.

CALL-A-GO: in street "patter," is to remove to another spot or address the public in different vein.

CHAUNT: to sing the contents of any paper in the streets. CANT, as applied to vulgar language, was derived from CHAUNT.

CHONKEYS: a kind of mince meat baked in a crust and sold in the streets.

CHUCKING A JOLLY: when a costermonger praises the inferior article his mate or partner is trying to sell.

CHUFF IT: be off or take it away, in answer to a street seller who is importuning you to purchase. *Halliwell* mentions CHUFF as a "term of reproach," surly, &c.

COCKS: fictitious narratives, in verse or prose, of murders, fires, and terrible accidents, sold in the streets as true accounts. The man who hawks them, a patterer, often changes the scene of the awful event to suit the taste of the neighbourhood he is trying to delude. Possibly a corruption of *cook*, a cooked statement or, as a correspondent suggests, the COCK LANE Ghost may have given rise to the term. This had a great run, and was a rich harvest to the running stationers.

COW-LICK: The term given to the lock of hair which costermongers and thieves usually twist forward from the ear; a large greasy curl upon the cheek, seemingly licked into shape. The opposite of NEWGATE-KNOCKER. — *See below.*

CROAKS: last dying speeches and murderers' confessions.

DIES: last dying speeches and criminal trials.

DOUBLE-SHUFFLE: a low, shuffling, noisy dance, common amongst costermongers.—*See* **FLIP-FLAPS** *page 329.*

GAMMY-VIAL: (Ville) a town where the police will not let persons hawk.

GAWFS: cheap red-skinned apples, a favourite fruit with costermongers, who rub them well with a piece of cloth, and find ready purchasers.

HANDSEL or **HANDSALE:** the *lucky money,* or first money taken in the morning by a pedlar.—*Cocker's Dictionary*, 1724. "Legs of mutton (street term for sheep's trotters or feet) two for a penny; who'll give me a **HANSEL**? Who'll give me a **HANSEL**," —*Cry at Cloth Fair at the present day.* Hence, earnest money, first fruits, &c. In Norfolk, **HANSELLING** a thing is using it for the first time, as wearing a new coat, taking seizin of it, as it were.—*Anglo Saxon. N. Bailey.*

HOLY LAND: Seven Dials—where the St. Giles' Greek is spoken.

KINGSMAN: the favourite coloured neckerchief of the costermongers. The women wear them thrown over their shoulders. With both sexes they are more valued than any other article of clothing. A coster's *caste*, or position, is at stake, he imagines, if his **KINGSMAN** is not of the most approved pattern. When he fights, his **KINGSMAN** is tied either around his waist as a belt or as a garter around his leg. This very singular partiality for a peculiar coloured neckcloth was doubtless derived from the Gipseys, and probably refers to an Oriental taste or custom long forgotten by these vagabonds. A singular similarity of taste for certain colours exists amongst the Hindoos, Gipseys, and London costermongers. Red and yellow (or orange) are the great favourites, and in these hues the Hindoo selects his turban and his robe; the Gipsey his breeches, and his wife her shawl or gown; and the costermonger his plush waistcoat and favourite **KINGSMAN**. Amongst either class, when a fight takes place, the greatest regard is paid to the favourite coloured article of dress. The Hindoo lays aside his turban, the Gipsey folds up his scarlet breeches or coat, whilst the pugilistic costermonger of Covent Garden or Billingsgate, as we have just seen, removes his favourite neckerchief to a part of his body, by the rules of the "ring" comparatively out of danger. Amongst the various patterns of kerchiefs worn by the wandering tribes of London, red and yellow are the oldest and most in fashion. Blue, intermixed with spots, is a late importation, probably from the Navy, through sporting characters.

MIKE: to loiter; or, as a costermonger defined it, to "lazy about." The term probably originated at St. Giles', which used to be thronged with Irish labourers (Mike being so common a term with them as to become a generic appellation for Irishmen with the vulgar) who used to loiter about the Pound, and lean against the public-houses in the "Dials" waiting for hire.

NEWGATE KNOCKER: the term given to the lock of hair which costermongers and thieves usually twist back towards the ear. The shape is supposed to resemble the knocker on the prisoners' door at Newgate—a resemblance that would appear to carry a rather unpleasant suggestion to the wearer. Sometime termed a **COBBLER'S KNOT**, or **COW-LICK**.—*See above.*

PITCH: a fixed locality where a patterer can hold forth to a gaping multitude for at least some few minutes continuously; "to do a **PITCH** in the drag," to perform in the street.

PLANT: a dodge, a preconcerted swindle; a position in the street to sell from. **PLANT**, a swindle, may be thus described: a coster will join a party of gaming costers that he never saw before, and commence tossing. When sufficient time has elapsed to remove all suspicions of companionship, his mate will come up and commence betting on each of his **PAL'S** throws with those standing around. By a curious quickness of hand, a coster can make the toss tell favourably for his wagering friend, who meets him in the evening after the play is over and shares the spoils.

ROUNDS: (in the language of the streets): the **BEATS** or usual walks of the costermonger to sell his stock. A term used by street folks generally.

> "Watchmen, sometimes they made their sallies,
> And walk'd their **ROUNDS** through streets and allies."
> —*Ned Ward's Vulgus Britannicus*, 1710.

SELL: to deceive, swindle, or play a practical joke upon a person. A sham is a **SELL** in street parlance. "**SOLD** again, and got the money," a costermonger cries after having successfully deceived somebody. *Shakespere* uses SELLING in a similar sense, viz., blinding or deceiving.

SHAKESTER or **SHICKSTER:** a prostitute. Amongst costermongers this term is invariably applied to *ladies* or the wives of tradesmen, and females generally of the classes immediately above them.

SHALLOW: a flat basket used by costers.

SLANG: counterfeit or short weights and measures. A SLANG quart is a pint and a half. SLANG measures are lent out at 2d. per day. The term is used principally by costermongers.

STANDING: the position at a street corner or on the curb of a market street, regularly occupied by a costermonger or street seller.

STRAWING: *selling* straws in the streets (generally for a penny) and *giving* the purchaser a paper (indecent or political) or a gold (!) ring —neither of which the patterer states he is allowed to sell.

THREE-UP: a gambling game played by costers. Three halfpennies are thrown up, and when they fall all "heads," or all "tails," it is a mark; and the man who gets the greatest number of marks out of a given amount—three, five, or more—wins. The costers are very quick and skillful at this game, and play fairly at it amongst themselves; but should a stranger join in they invariably unite to cheat him.

TOPS: dying speeches and gallows broadsides.

TROLLY or **TROLLY-CARTS:** term given by costermongers to a species of narrow cart, which can either be drawn by a donkey or driven by hand.

TROTTERS: feet. Sheep's TROTTERS, boiled sheep's feet, a favourite street delicacy.

VAMOS or **VAMOUS:** to go or be off. *Spanish,* VAMOS, "let us go!" Probably NAMUS or NAMOUS the costermonger's word, was from this, although it is generally considered back slang.

VIC.: the Victoria Theatre, London—patronised principally by costermongers and low people; also the street abbreviation of the Christian name of her Majesty the Queen.

WHITECHAPEL or **WESTMINSTER BROUGHAM:** a costermonger's donkey-barrow.

WORK: to plan or lay down and execute any course of action, to perform anything; "to WORK the BULLS," *i.e.*, to get rid of false crown pieces;

"to **WORK** the **ORACLE**," to succeed by maneuvering, to concert a wily plan, to victimise—a possible reference to the stratagems and bribes used to corrupt the *Delphic oracle*, and cause it to deliver a favourable response. "To **WORK** a street or neighborhood," trying at each house to sell all one can, or so bawling that every housewife may know what you have to sell. The general plan is to drive a donkey barrow a short distance, and then stop and cry. The term implies thoroughness; To "**WORK** a street well" is a common saying with a coster.

YOUNKER: in street language, a lad or a boy. Term in general use amongst costermongers, cabmen, and old-fashioned people. *Barnefield's Affectionate Shepherd*, 1594, has the phrase, "a seemelie **YOUNKER**." *Danish* and *Friesic*, **JONKER**. In the *Navy*, a naval cadet is usually termed a **YOUNKER**.

STUDENTS and TEACHERS

BUM-BRUSHER: a schoolmaster

CHERUBS or **CHERUBIMS:** the chorister boys who chaunt in the services at the abbeys.

COACH: a *Cambridge* term for a private tutor.

FAG: a schoolboy who performs a servant's offices to a superior schoolmate. *Grose* thinks **FAGGED OUT** is derived from this.

FAG: to beat, also one boy working for another at school.

GRIND: to work up for an examination, to cram with a **GRINDER**, or private tutor.—*Medical.*

GYP: an undergraduate's valet at *Cambridge*. Corruption of **GYPSEY JOE** (*Saturday Review*); popularly derived by Cantabs from the *Greek*, **GYPS**, (γυψ) a vulture, from their dishonest rapacity. At *Oxford* they are called **SCOUTS**.

HARRY-SOPH: (εϱϭοψος, very wise indeed), an undergraduate in his last year of residence.—*Cambridge.*

HIVITE: a student of St. Begh's College, Cumberland; pronounced **ST. BEE'S.**—*University.*

PLEBS: a term used to stigmatise a tradesman's son at Westminster School. *Latin,* PLEBS, the vulgar.

POKERS: the *Cambridge* slang term for the Esquire Bedels, who carry the silver maces (also called POKERS) before the Vice-Chancellor.

POLL: the "ordinary degree" candidates for the B.A. Examination, who do not aspire to the "Honours" list. From the *Greek,* "the many." Some years ago, at *Cambridge,* Mr. Hopkins being the most celebrated "honour coach," or private tutor for the wranglers, and Mr. Potts the principle "crammer" of the non-honour men, the latter was facetiously termed the "POLLY HOPKINS" by the undergraduates.

RELIEVING OFFICER: a significant term for a father.—*University.*

SCOUT: a college valet or waiter.—*Oxford.*—*See* GYP *page 173.*

SCULL or **SKULL:** the head or master of a college.—*University,* but *nearly obsolete*; the gallery, however, in St. Mary's (the University church), where the "Heads of Houses" sit in solemn state, is still nicknamed the GOLGOTHA by the undergraduates.

SIM: one of a Methodistical turn in religion; a low- church-man; originally a follower of the late Rev. Charles Simeon.—*Cambridge.*

SIZERS or **SIZARS:** are certain poor scholars at *Cambridge,* annually elected, who get their dinners (including *sizings*) from what is left at the upper, or Fellows' table, free or nearly so. They pay rent of rooms, and some other fees, on a lower scale than the "Pensiouers" or ordinary students, and answer to the "battlers" and "servitors" at Oxford.

SKY: a disagreeable person, an enemy.—*Westminster School.*

SOPH: (abbreviation of SOPHISTER) a title peculiar to the University of *Cambridge.* Undergraduates are *junior* SOPHS before passing their "Little Go," or first University examination, *senior* SOPHS after that.

SUCK: a parasite, flatterer of the "nobs."—*University.*

TUFT-HUNTER: a hanger-on to persons of quality or wealth. Originally *University slang,* but now general.

TUFTS: fellow commoners, *i.e.,* wealthy students at the University, who pay higher fees, dine with the Dons, and are distinguished by golden TUFTS, or tassels, in their caps.

WOODEN SPOON: the last junior optime who takes a University degree; denoting one who is only fit to stay at home, and stir porridge.—*Cambridge*.

WOODEN WEDGE: the last name in the classical honours list at *Cambridge*. The last in mathematical honours had long been known as the **WOODEN SPOON**; but when the classical Tripos was instituted in 1824, it was debated among the undergraduates what *sobriquet* should be given to the last on the examination list. Curiously enough, the name that year which happened to be last was **WEDGEWOOD** (a distinguished Wrangler). Hence the title.

EDUCATION TERMS

BATTLES: the students' term at Oxford for rations. At *Cambridge*, **COMMONS**.

BITCH: tea, "a **BITCH** party," a tea-drinking.—*University*.

BOG or **BOG-HOUSE:** a water-closet.—*School term*. In the Inns of Court, I am informed, this term is very common.

BOILERS: the slang name given to the New Kensington Museum and School of Art, in allusion to the peculiar form of the buildings, and the fact of their being mainly composed of, and covered with, sheet iron.—*See* **PEPPER-BOXES** *page 271*.

BROSIER: a bankrupt.—*Cheshire*. **BROSIER-MY-DAME**, school term, implying a clearing of the housekeeper's larder of provisions, in revenge for stinginess.—*Eton*.

BUZ-NAPPER'S ACADEMY: school in which young thieves are trained. Figures are dressed up, and experienced tutors stand in various difficult attitudes for the boys to practice upon. When clever enough they are sent on the streets. It is reported that a house of this nature is situated in a court near Hatton Garden. The system is well explained in *Dickens' Oliver Twist*.

BY GOLLY: an ejaculation or oath; a compromise for "by God." In the United States, small boys are permitted by their guardians to say **GOL DARN** anything, but they are on no account allowed to commit the profanity of G—d d—ing anything. An effective ejaculation and moral waste pipe for interior passion or wrath is seen in the exclamation: BY THE EVER-LIVING-JUMPING-MOSES—a harmless phrase, that from its length expends a considerable quantity of fiery anger.

CAD or **CADGER** (from which it is shortened): a mean or vulgar fellow; a beggar; one who would rather live on other people than work for himself; a man trying to worm something out of another, either money or information. *Johnson* uses the word, and gives *huckster* as the meaning, but I never heard it used in this sense. CAGER or GAGER, the *Old Cant* term for a man. The exclusives in the Universities apply the term CAD to all non-members.

CASE: a few years ago the term CASE was applied to persons and things; "what a CASE he is," *i.e.*, what a curious person; "a rum CASE that," or "you are a CASE," both synonymous with the phrase "odd fish," common half a century ago. Among young ladies at boarding schools a CASE means a love affair.

CHUCK: a schoolboy's treat.—*Westminster school.* Food, provisions for an entertainment.—*Norwich.*

COMMONS: rations, because eaten *in common.*—*University.* SHORT COMMONS (derived from the University slang term), a scanty meal, a scarcity.

COPUS: a *Cambridge* drink consisting of ale combined with spices and varied by spirits, wines, &c. Corruption of HIPPOCRAS.

CRAM: to lie or deceive, implying to fill up or CRAM a person with false stories; to acquire learning quickly, to "*grind*" or prepare for an examination.

CRIB: a literal translation of a classic author.—*University.*

DICKEY: formerly the *Cant* for a worn-out shirt, but means now-a-days a front or half-shirt. DICKEY was originally TOMMY (from the Greek, τομη, a section), a name which I understand was formerly used in Trinity College, Dublin. The students are said to have invented the term, and the GYPS change it to DICKEY, in which dress it is supposed to have been imported into England.

DOG-ON-IT: a form of mild swearing used by boys. It is just worthy of mention that DOGONE, in *Anglo-Norman*, is equivalent to a term of contempt. *Friesic,* DOGENIET.

FORAKERS: a water-closet or house of office. — Term used by the boys at *Winchester school.*

FOURTH or **FOURTH COURT:** the court appropriated to the water-closets at *Cambridge*; from its really being No. 4 at Trinity College. A man leaving his room to go to this **FOURTH COURT** writes on his door *"gone to the* **FOURTH***,"* or, in algebraic notation, **"GONE 4"** — the *Cambridge* slang phrase.

FOX: to cheat or rob. — *Eton College.*

GARGLE: medical student Slang for physic.

GRIND: "to take a **GRIND**," *i.e.,* a walk or constitutional. — *University.*

GRIND: to work up for an examination, to cram with a **GRINDER,** or private tutor. — *Medical.*

GULFED: a university term, denoting that a man is unable to enter for the classical examination, from having failed in the mathematical. Candidates for classical honours were compelled to go in for both examinations. From the alteration of the arrangements the term is now obsolete. — *Cambridge.*

HALF AND HALF: a mixture of ale and porter, much affected by medical students; occasionally *Latinized* into **DIMIDIUM DIMIDIUMQUE.** — *See* **COOPER** *page 332.*

HOAX: to deceive or ridicule — *Grose* says was originally a *University Cant* word. Corruption of **HOCUS,** to cheat.

HOT TIGER: an Oxford mixture of hot-spiced ale and sherry.

JAPAN: to ordain. — *University.*

LITTLE GO: the "Previous Examination," at *Cambridge* the first University examination for undergraduates in their second year of matriculation. At Oxford, the corresponding term is **THE SMALLS.**

MARROWSKYING: — *See* **MEDICAL GREEK** *page 141.*

MEDICAL GREEK: the slang used by medical students at the hospitals. At the London University they have a way of disguising *English,* described by Albert Smith as the *Gowerstreet Dialect,* which consists in transposing the initials of words, *e.g.,* *"poke a smipe"* — smoke a pipe, *"flutter-by"* — butterfly, &c. This disagreeable nonsense is often termed **MORROWSKYING.** — *See* **GREEK,** St. Giles' Greek, or the "Ægidiac" dialect, Language of **ZIPH** *page 141,* &c.

MORTAR-BOARD: the term given by the vulgar to the square college caps.

MUDFOG: "the British Association for the Promotion of Science." —*University.*

NIX!: the signal word of school boys to each other that the master or other person in authority, is approaching.

OAK: the outer door of college rooms; to "sport one's **OAK**," to be "not at home" to visitors.—*See* **SPORT** *page 179.*—*University.*

OINTMENT: medical student slang for butter.

PINDARIC HEIGHTS: studying the odes of Pindar.—*Oxford.*

PLOUGHED: drunk.—*Household Words*, No. 183. Also a *University* term equivalent to **PLUCKED**.

PLUCKED: turned back at an examination.—*University.*

POST-MORTEM: at *Cambridge*, the second examination which men who have been "plucked" have to undergo.—*University.*

PROS: a water-closet. Abbreviated form of $\pi\rho\sigma\varsigma\ \tau\iota\nu\alpha\ \tau\sigma\pi\sigma\nu$.—*Oxford University.*

RIDER: in a University examination, a problem or question appended to another, as directly arising from or dependent on it;—beginning to be generally used for any corollary or position which naturally arises from any previous statement or evidence.

SCHISM-SHOP: a dissenters' meeting-house.—*University.*

SCRAPE: cheap butter; "bread and **SCRAPE**," the bread and butter issued to school-boys—so called from the butter being laid on, and then *scraped* off again, for economy's sake.

SCRATCH-RACE: (on the *Turf*), a race where any horse, aged, winner, or loser, can run with any weights; in fact, a race without restrictions. At *Cambridge* a boat-race, where the crews are drawn by lot.

SHAKY: said of a person of questionable health, integrity, or solvency; at the *University*, of one not likely to pass his examination.

SHAVE: a narrow escape. At *Cambridge*, "just **SHAVING** through," or "making a **SHAVE**," is just escaping a "pluck" by coming out at the bottom of the list.

"My terms are anything but dear,

> Then read with me, and never fear;
> The examiners we're sure to queer,
> And get through, if you make a SHAVE on't."
> —*The Private Tutor.*

SHORT COMMONS: short allowance of food.—*See* COMMONS *p. 176.*

SIZE: to order extras over and above the usual commons at the dinner in college halls. Soup, pastry, &c. are SIZINGS, and are paid for at a certain specified rate *per* SIZE, or portion, to the college cook.—*Peculiar to Cambridge. Minsheu says,* "SIZE, a farthing which schollers in *Cambridge* have at the buttery, noted with the letter *s.*"

SKY: a disagreeable person, an enemy.—*Westminster School.*

SLOGGERS: *i.e.,* SLOW-GOERS, the second division of race-boats at *Cambridge.* At *Oxford* they are called TORPIDS.—*University.*

SNOT: a term of reproach applied to persons by the vulgar when vexed or annoyed. In a Westminster school vocabulary for boys, published in the last century, the term is curiously applied. Its proper meaning is the glandular mucus discharged through the nose.

SPIN: to reject from an examination.—*Army.*

SPORT: to exhibit, to wear, &c.; a word which is made to do duty in a variety of senses, especially at the University.—*See the Gradus ad Cantabrigiam.* "To SPORT a new title," "to SPORT an Ægrotat" (*i.e.,* a permission from the "Dons" to abstain from lectures, &c., on account of illness); "to SPORT ONE'S OAK," to shut the outer door and exclude the public—especially *duns* and boring acquaintants. Common also in the Inns of Court.—*See Notes and Queries,* 2nd series, vol. viii. P. 492, and *Gentleman's Magazine,* December, 1794.

SPORTING DOOR: the outer door of chambers, also called the OAK.—*See* under SPORT *page 179.*—*University.*

STINKOMALEE: a name given to the then New London University by Theodore Hook. Some question about *Trincomalee* was agitated at the same time. It is still applied by the students of the old Universities, who regard it with disfavour from its admitting all denominations.

SUCK: a parasite, flatterer of the "nobs."—*University.*

SWOT: mathematics; also a mathematician; as a verb, to work hard for an examination, to be diligent in one's studies.—*Army.* This word originated at the great slang manufactory for the army, the Royal

Military College, Sandhurst, in the broad Scotch pronunciation of Dr. Wallace, one of the Professors, of the word *sweat.—See Notes and queries*, vol. i., p. 369.

TORPIDS: the second-class race-boats at Oxford, answering to the *Cambridge* SLOGGERS.

TROTTER: a tailor's man who goes 'round for orders.—*University.*

TUCK: a schoolboy's term for fruit, pastry, &c. TUCK IN or TUCK OUT, a good meal.

TUFT-HUNTER: a hanger-on to persons of quality or wealth. Originally *University slang*, but now general.

TURKEY-MERCHANTS: dealers in plundered or contraband silk. Poulterers are sometimes termed TURKEY MERCHANTS, in remembrance of Horne Tooke's answer to the boys at Eton, who wished in an aristocratic way to know who *his* father was—a TURKEY MERCHANT, replied Tooke. His father was a poulterer. TURKEY MERCHANT, also, was formerly slang for a driver of turkeys or geese to market.

WATERMAN: a light blue silk handkerchief. The Oxford and *Cambridge* boats' crews always wear these—light blue for *Cambridge*, and a darker shade for Oxford.

ZIPH: "LANGUAGE OF," a way of disguising *English* in use among the students at *Winchester College.* Compare MEDICAL GREEK above.

WOMEN

DOLLYMOP: a tawdrily dressed maidservant, a street-walker.

MURERK: the mistress of the house.—*See* BURERK *page 31.*

RIB: a wife.—*North.*

SHAKESTER or **SHICKSTER:** a prostitute. Amongst costermongers this term is invariably applied to *ladies* or the wives of tradesmen, and females generally of the classes immediately above them.

SLAVEY: a maid servant.

# OTHER JOBS and WORK TERMS

BIG-HOUSE: the work-house.

BILLY-HUNTING: buying old metal.

BLACK-SHEEP: a "bad lot," "*mauvais sujet;*" also a workman who refuses to join in a strike.

BLUE-BILLY: the handkerchief (blue ground with white spots) worn and used at prize fights. Before a **SET TO**, it is common to take it from the neck and tie it around the leg as a garter, or round the waist, to "keep in the wind." Also, the refuse ammoniacal lime from gas factories.

BOOKED: caught, fixed, disposed of.—Term in *Book-keeping.*

BOS-KEN: farm-house. *Ancient.—See* **KEN** *page 269.*

BOSMAN: a farmer; "faking a **BOSMAN** on the main toby," robbing a farmer on the highway. **BOSS**, a master.—*American.* Both terms from the *Dutch*, **BOSCH-MAN**, one who lives in the woods; otherwise *Boshjeman* or *Bushman.*

DAISY-KICKERS: the name hostlers at large inns used to give each other, now *nearly obsolete.* **DAISY-KICKER** or **GROGHAM** was likewise the *Cant* term for a horse. The **DAISY-KICKERS** were sad rogues in the old posting days; frequently the landlords rented the stables to them, as the only plan to make them return a profit.

DUNG: an operative who works for an employer who does not give full or "society" wages.

EVERLASTING STAIRCASE: the treadmill. Sometimes called "Colonel Chesterton's everlasting staircase," from the gallant inventor or improver.

FIDDLE: a whip.

FLOGGER: a whip.—*Obsolete.*

FOXING: watching in the streets for any occurrence which may be turned to a profitable account.—*See* **MOOCHING** *below.*

GRUBBING-KEN or SPINIKIN: a workhouse; a cook-shop.

LED CAPTAIN: a fashionable spunger, a swell who, by artifice ingratiates himself into the good graces of the master of the house, and lives at his table.

LUMP WORK: work contracted for or taken by the *lump*.

LUMPER: a contractor. On the river, more especially a person who contracts to deliver a ship laden with timber.

MIKE: to loiter; or, as a costermonger defined it, to "lazy about." The term probably originated at St. Giles', which used to be thronged with Irish labourers (Mike being so common a term with them as to become a generic appellation for Irishmen with the vulgar) who used to loiter about the Pound, and lean against the public-houses in the "Dials" waiting for hire.

MOOCHING or **ON THE MOOCH:** on the look-out for any article or circumstances which may be turned to a profitable account; watching in the streets for odd jobs, scraps, horses to hold, &c.

MUD-LARKS: men and women who, with their clothes tucked above knee, grovel through the mud on the banks of the Thames, when the tide is low, for silver spoons, old bottle, pieces of iron, coal, or any article of the least value, deposited by the retiring tide, either from passing ships or the sewers. Occasionally those men who cleanse the sewers, with great boots and sou'wester hats.

NIBS: the master or chief person; a man with no means but high pretensions—a "shabby genteel."

OMEE: a master or landlord; "the OMEE of the cassey's a nark on the pitch," the master of the house will not let us perform. *Italian*, UOMO, a man; "UOMO DELLA CASA," the master of the house.

OUT ON THE PICKAROON: PICARONE is *Spanish* for a thief, but this phrase does not necessarily mean anything dishonest, but ready for anything in the way of excitement to turn up; also to be in search of anything profitable.

PAPER MAKERS: rag gatherers and gutter rakers—similar to the chiffonniers of Paris. Also, those men who tramp through the country, and collect rags on the pretense that they are agents to a paper mill.

PETERER or **PETERMAN:** one who follows hackney and stage coaches, and cuts off the portmanteaus and trunks from behind. — *Nearly obsolete.* Ancient term for a fisherman, still used at Gravesend.

PIG: a mass of metal; so called from its being poured in a fluid state from a **SOW.** — *See* **SOW** *below.* — *Workmen's term.*

POT-HUNTER: a sportsman who shoots anything he comes across, having more regard to filling his bag than to the rules which regulate the sport.

PUDDING SNAMMER: one who robs a cook shop.

PURE FINDERS: street collectors of dogs' dung.

RACKS: the bones of a dead horse. Term used by horse slaughterers.

RED LINER: an officer of the Mendicity Society.

SETTER: a person employed by the vendor at an auction to run the bidding up; to bid against *bonâ fide* bidders.

SHODDY: old cloth worked up into new; also, a term of derision applied to workmen in woolen factories. — *Yorkshire.*

SHOE: to free, or initiate a person a practice common in most trades to a newcomer. The **SHOEING** consists in paying for beer or other drink, which is drunk by the older hands. The cans emptied, and the bill paid, the stranger is considered properly **SHOD.**

SKIPPER: a barn. — *Ancient Cant.*

SLAP-BANG SHOPS: Low eating houses, where you have to pay down the ready money with a **SLAP-BANG.** — *Grose.*

SNAGGLING: angling for geese with a hook and line, the bait being a worm or snail. The goose swallows the bait, and is quietly landed and bagged.

SNAPPS: share, portion; any articles or circumstances out of which money may be made; "looking for **SNAPPS,**" waiting for windfalls or odd jobs. — *Old. Scotch,* **CHITS** — term also used for "coppers," or halfpence.

SNOB-STICK: a workman who refuses to join in strikes or trade unions. Query, properly **KNOB-STICK.**

SOW: the receptacle into which the liquid iron is poured in a gun-foundry. The melted metal poured from it is termed **PIG.** — *Workmen's terms.*

SPIN-EM ROUNDS: a street game consisting of a piece of brass, wood, or iron, balanced on a pin, and turned quickly around on a board, when the point, arrow-shaped, stops at a number and decides the bet one way or the other. The contrivance very much resembles a sea compass, and was formerly the gambling accompaniment of London piemen. The apparatus then was erected on the tin lids of their pie cans, and the bets were ostensibly for pies, but more frequently for "coppers," when no policeman frowned upon the scene, and when two or three apprentices or porters happened to meet.

SPINIKEN: a workhouse.

SWEATER: a common term for a "cutting" or "grinding" employer.

TATTING: gathering old rags.

TOMMY SHOP: where wages are generally paid to mechanics or others, who are expected to "take out" a portion of the money in goods.

TOMMY-MASTER: one who pays his workmen in goods or gives them tickets upon tradesmen, with whom he shares the profit.

TOOL: "a poor **Tool**," a bad hand at anything.

TOUTER: a looker out, one who watches for customers, a hotel runner.

TRANSLATOR: a man who deals in old shoes or clothes, and refits them for cheap wear.

TURNOVER: an apprentice who finishes with a second master the indentures he commenced with the first.

WOOL-HOLE: the workhouse.

WORMING: removing the beard of an oyster or muscle.

EXCHANGING MONEY or GOODS

BORROWING and OBTAINING CREDIT

BREAKING SHINS: borrowing money.

CHALK UP: to credit, make entry in account books of indebtedness; "I can't pay you now, but you can **CHALK IT UP**, *i.e.,* charge me with the article of your day-book. From the old practice of chalking one's score for drink behind the bar-doors of public houses.

FLY THE KITE or **RAISE THE WIND:** to obtain money on bills, whether good or bad, alluding to tossing paper about like children do a kite.

LIGHT: "to be able to get a LIGHT at a house," is to get credit.

RAISE THE WIND: to obtain credit or money; generally by pawning or selling off property.

SCORE: "to run up a SCORE at a public house," to obtain credit there until pay day, or a fixed time when the debt must be WIPED OFF.

SCRAN: pieces of meat, broken victuals. Formerly the reckoning at a public-house. SCRANNING, begging for broken victuals. Also, an *Irish* malediction of a mild sort, "Bad SCRAN to yer!"

SCREW: "to put on the SCREW," to limit one's credit, to be more exact and precise.

SCREW LOOSE: when friends become cold and distant towards each other, it is said there is a SCREW LOOSE betwixt them; said also when anything goes wrong with a person's credit or reputation.

TICK: credit, trust. *Johnson* says it is a corruption of *ticket*—tradesmen's bills being formerly written on tickets or cards. ON TICK, therefore, is equivalent to *on ticket*, or on trust. In use 1668. Cuthbert Bede, in *Notes and Queries*, supplies me with an earlier date, from the *Gradus ad Canabrigiam*.

> "No matter upon landing whether you have money or no —you may swim in twentie of their boats over the river UPON TICKET."
>
> —*Decker's Gul's Hornbook*, 1609.

WIND: "to raise the WIND," to procure money; "to slip one's WIND," coarse expression meaning to die.

GETTING PAID

BLEED: to victimise or extract money from a person, to spunge on, to make suffer vindictively.

DONKEY: "three more and up goes the DONKEY," a vulgar street phrase for extracting as much money as possible before performing any task. The phrase had its origin with a travelling showman, the *finale* of whose performance was the hoisting of a DONKEY on a pole or ladder; but this consummation was never arrived at unless the required number of "browns" was first paid up, and "three more" was generally the unfortunate deficit.

DUN: to solicit payment.—*Old Cant*, from the *French* DONNEZ, give; or from JOE DUN, the famous bailiff of Lincoln; or simply a corruption of DIN, from the *Anglo Saxon* DUNAN, to clamour?

NOBBING: collecting money; "what NOBBINGS?" *i.e.*, how much have you got?

SAL: a salary.—*Theatrical.*

STAG: to see, discover, or watch—like a STAG at gaze; "STAG the push," look at the crowd. Also, to dun, or demand payment.

SWEAT: to extract money from a person, to "bleed," to squander riches. —*Bulwer.*

TIP: a douceur; also to give, lend, or hand over anything to another person; "come, TIP up the tin," *i.e.*, hand up the money; "TIP the wink," to inform by winking; "TIP us your fin," *i.e.*, give me your hand; "TIP one's boom off," to make off, depart.—*Sea.* "To miss one's TIP," to fail in a scheme.—*Old Cant.*

 GOING INTO DEBT

BLUE or **BLEW:** to pawn or pledge.

BROSIER: a bankrupt.—*Cheshire.* BROSIER-MY-DAME, school term, implying a clearing of the housekeeper's larder of provisions, in revenge for stinginess.—*Eton.*

BUMMAREE: this term is given to a class of speculating salesmen at Billingsgate market, not recognized as such by the trade, but who get a living by buying large quantities of fish of the salesmen and re-selling it to smaller buyers. The word has been used in the statutes and bye-laws of the market for upwards of 100 years. It has been variously derived, but is most probably from the *French*, BONNE MAREE, good fresh fish! "Marée signifie toute sorts de poisson de mer

qûi n'est pas salé; bonne marée—*maree fraiche*, vendeur de marée."
—*Dict. De l'Acad. Franc.* The **BUMMAREES** are accused of many trade tricks. One of them is to blow up cod-fish with a pipe until they look double their actual size. Of course, when the fish come to the table they are flabby, shrunken, and half-dwindled away. In Norwich, **TO BUMMAREE ONE** is to run up a score at a public house just open, and is equivalent to "running into debt with one."

CONSTABLE: "to overrun the **CONSTABLE**," to exceed one's income, get deep in debt.

DIPPED: mortgaged.—*Household Words*, No. 183.

LEVANTER: a card sharper or defaulting gambler. A correspondent states that it was formerly the custom to give out to the creditors, when a person was in pecuniary difficulties, and it was convenient for him to keep away, that he was gone to the *East*, or the **LEVANT**; hence, when one loses a bet and decamps without settling, he is said to **LEVANT**.

LUG: "my togs are in **LUG**," *i.e.*, in pawn.

LUMBER: to pawn or pledge.—*Household Words*, No. 183.

MUCK-SNIPE: one who had been "**MUCKED OUT**" or beggared, at gambling.

POP: to pawn or pledge; "to **POP** up the spout," to pledge at the pawnbroker's—an allusion to the spout up which the broker sends the ticketed article until such time as they shall be redeemed. The spout runs from the ground floor to the wareroom at the top of the house.

POT: "to **GO TO POT**," to die; from the classic custom of putting the ashes of the dead in an urn; also, to be ruined or broken up—often applied to tradesmen who fail in business. **GO TO POT!** *i.e.*, go and hang yourself, shut up and be quiet. *L 'Estrange*, to **PUT THE POT ON**, to overcharge or exaggerate.

RAISE THE WIND: to obtain credit or money; generally by pawning or selling off property.

RING: "to go through the **RING**," to take advantage of the Insolvency Act, or be *whitewashed*.

SHELF: "on the SHELF," not yet disposed of; young ladies are said to be so situated when they cannot meet with a husband; "on the SHELF," pawned.

SHINEY RAG: "to win the SHINEY RAG," to be ruined—said in gambling, when anyone continues betting after "luck has set in against him."

SOLD UP or OUT: broken down, bankrupt.

SPOUT: "up the SPOUT," at the pawnbroker's; SPOUTING, pawning. —*See* POP *above* for origin.

STUMPED: bowled out, done for, bankrupt, poverty-stricken.— *Cricketing term.*

TIP THE DOUBLE: to "bolt," or run away from a creditor or officer. Sometimes TIP THE DOUBLE TO SHERRY, *i.e.,* to the sheriff.

WHITEWASH: when a person has taken the benefit of the Insolvency Act he is said to have been WHITEWASHED.

ILLEGAL PRACTICES

COOK: a term well known in the Bankruptcy Courts, referring to accounts that have been meddled with, or COOKED, by the bankrupt; also the forming a balance sheet from general trade inferences; stated by a correspondent to have been first used in reference to the celebrated alteration of the accounts of the Eastern Counties Railway, by George Hudson, the Railway King.

DOCTOR: to adulterate or drug liquor; also to falsify accounts.—*See* COOK *above.*

GREASING: GREASING a man is bribing; SOAPING is flattering him.

HUSH-MONEY: a sum given to quash a prosecution or evidence.

RIG: a trick, SPREE, or performance; "run a RIG," to play a trick—*Gipsey*; "RIG the market." In reality to play tricks with it—a mercantile slang phrase often used in the newspapers.

RUN: (good or bad), the success of a performance.—*Theatrical.*

SHOWFULL PITCHING: passing bad money.

SLUMMING: passing bad money.

SMASH: to pass counterfeit money.

SQUARING HIS NIBS: giving a policeman money.

STICK: to cheat; "he got STUCK," he was taken in; STICK, to forget one's part in a performance.—*Theatrical.* STICK ON, to overcharge or defraud; STICK UP FOR, to defend a person, especially when slandered in his absence; STICK UP TO, to preserver in courting or attacking, whether in fisticuffs or argument; "to STICK in one's gizzard," to rankle in one's heart; "to STICK TO a person," to adhere to one, be his friend through adverse circumstances.

SPENDING and PAYING

BLEWED: got rid of, disposed of, spent; "I BLEWED all my blunt last night," I spent all my money.

COME DOWN: to pay down.

DUB: to pay or give; "DUB UP," pay up.

DUCKS AND DRAKES: "to make DUCKS AND DRAKES of one's money," to throw it away childishly—derived from children "shying" flat stones on the surface of a pool, which they call DUCKS AND DRAKES, according to the number of skips they make.

FIGURE: "to cut a good or bad FIGURE," to make a good or indifferent appearance; "what's the FIGURE?" how much is to pay? FIGURE-HEAD, a person's face.—*Sea term.*

FORK OUT: bring out one's money, to pay the bill, to STAND FOR or treat a friend; to hand over what does not belong to you.—*Old Cant* term for picking pockets, and very curious it is to trace its origin. In the early part of the last century, a little book on purloining was published, and of course it had to give the latest modes. FORKING was the newest method, and it consisted in thrusting the fingers stiff and open into the pocket, and then quickly closing them and extracting any article.

MAULEY: a signature, from MAULEY, a fist; "put your FIST to it," is sometimes said by a low tradesman when desiring a fellow trader to put his signature to a bill or note.

NOSE: "to pay through the NOSE," to pay an extravagant price.

PAY: to beat a person or "serve them out." Originally a nautical term, meaning to stop the seams of a vessel with pitch (*French*, **POIX**); "here's the devil to **PAY** and no pitch hot," said when any catastrophe occurs which there is no means of averting; "to **PAY** over face and eyes, as the cat did the monkey;" "to **PAY** through the nose," to give a ridiculous price—whence the origin? *Shakespere* uses **PAY** in the sense of to beat or thrash.

PRIG: a thief. Used by *Addison* in the sense of a coxcomb. *Ancient Cant*, probably from the *Saxon*, **PRICC-AN**, to filch, &c.—*Shakespere*. **PRIG**, to steal or rob. **PRIGGING**, thieving. In *Scotland* the term **PRIG** is used in a different sense from what it is in England. In Glasgow, or at Aberdeen, "to **PRIG** a salmon," would be to cheapen it, or seek for an abatement in the price. A story is told of two Scotchmen, visitors to London, who got into sad trouble a few years ago by announcing their intention of "**PRIGGING** a hat" which they had espied in a fashionable manufacture's window, and which one of them thought he would like to possess.

RABBIT: when a person gets the worst of a bargain he is said "to have bought the **RABBIT**."

SAM: to "stand **SAM**," to pay for refreshment or drink, to stand paymaster for anything. An *Americanism*, originating in the letter U.S. on the knapsacks of the United States soldiers, which letters were jocularly said to be the initials of *Uncle Sam* (the Government), who pays for all. In use in this country as early as 1827.

SHELL OUT: to pay or count out money.

SNIPE: a long bill; also a term for attorneys, a race remarkable for their propensity to long bills.

STAND: "to **STAND** treat," to pay for a friend's entertainment; to bear expense; to put up with treatment, good or ill; "this house **STOOD** me in £1,000," *i.e.*, cost that sum; "to **STAND PAD**," to beg on the curb with a small piece of paper pinned on the breast, inscribed "*I'm starving*."

STUMP UP: to pay one's share, to pay the reckoning, to bring forth the money reluctantly.

WIPE: to strike; "he fetcht me a **WIPE** over the knuckles," he struck me on the knuckles; "to **WIPE** a person down," to flatter or pacify a person; to **WIPE** off a score, to pay one's debts, in allusion to the slate or chalk methods of account keeping; "to **WIPE** a person's eye," to shoot game which he has missed—*Sporting term*; hence to gain an advantage by superior activity.

OTHER EXCHANGES

DRIVE: a term used by tradesmen in speaking of business; "he's DRIVING a *roaring* trade," *i.e.*, a very good one; hence, to succeed in a bargain, "I DROVE a good bargain," *i.e.*, got the best end of it.

FLASH IT: "show it;" said when any bargain is offered.

MOOCH: to sponge; to obtrude yourself upon friends just when they are about to sit down to dinner or other lucky time—of course quite accidentally.—Compare HULK. To slink away, and allow your friends to pay for the entertainment. *In Wiltshire*, on the MOUTCH is to shuffle.

POKE: a bag or sack; "to buy a pig in a POKE," to purchase anything without seeing it.—*Saxon.*

RAG: to divide or share; "let's RAG IT," or GO RAGS, *i.e.*, share it equally between us.—*Norwich.*

RINGING THE CHANGES: changing bad money for good.

ROUND: "ROUND dealing," honest trading; "ROUND sum," a large sum. Synonymous also in a *slang* sense with SQUARE.—*See* SQUARE *p. 117.*

SHAKE or SHAKES: a bad bargain is said to be "no great SHAKES;" "pretty fair SHAKES" is anything good or favourable.—*Byron.* In America, a fair SHAKE is a fair trade or a good bargain.

SHICE: nothing; "to do anything for SHICE," to get no payment. The term was first used by the Jews in the last century. *Grose* gives the phrase CHICE-AM-A-TRICE, which has a synonymous meaning. *Spanish*, chico, little; *Anglo Saxon*, CHICHE, niggardly.

SHORT: when spirit is drunk without any admixture of water, it is said to be taken "short;" "summat SHORT," a dram. A similar phrase is used at the counters of banks: upon presenting a cheque, the clerk asks, "how will you take it?" *i.e.*, in gold or in notes? Should it be desired to receive it in as small a compass as possible, the answer is, "SHORT."

SHOT: from the once *English*, but now provincial word, to SHOOT, to subscribe, contribute in fair proportion; a share, the same as SCOT, both being from the *Anglo Saxon* word, SCEAT; "to pay one's SHOT," *i.e.*, share of the reckoning, &c.

SKIN: to abate or lower the value of anything; "thin-SKINNED," sensitive, touchy.

STAG: to demand money, to "cadge."

STRIKE ME LUCKY!: an expression used by the lower orders when making a bargain, derived from the old custom of striking hands together, leaving in that of the seller a LUCK PENNY as an earnest that the bargain is concluded. In Ireland, at cattle markets, &c., a penny or other small coin, is always given by the buyer to the seller to ratify the bargain.—*Hudibras*. Anciently this was called a GOD'S PENNY.

"With that he cast him a God's Peny." —*Heir of Linne*.

The origin of the phrase being lost sight of, like that of many others, it is often corrupted now-a-days into STRIKE ME SILLY.

SWAP: to exchange. *Grose* says it is *Irish Cant*, but the term is now included in most dictionaries as an allowed vulgarism.

TAKE: to succeed or be patronized; "do you think the new opera will TAKE?" "No, because the same company TOOK so badly under the old management;" "to TAKE IN," to cheat or defraud, from the lodging-house keepers' advertisements, "single men TAKEN IN AND DONE FOR;" an engagement which is as frequently performed in a bad as a good sense.—*See* TAKE *in the Index for more meanings on page 504.*

TIP: a douceur; also to give, lend, or hand over anything to another person; "come, TIP up the tin," *i.e.*, hand up the money; "TIP the wink," to inform by winking; "TIP us your fin," *i.e.*, give me your hand; "TIP one's boom off," to make off, depart.—*Sea.* "To miss one's TIP," to fail in a scheme.—*Old Cant*.

TIT FOR TAT: an equivalent.

TOMMY: a truck, barter, the exchange of labour for goods, not money. Both term and practice general among English operatives for half a century.

TOMMY-MASTER: one who pays his workmen in goods or gives them tickets upon tradesmen, with whom he shares the profit.

TRUCK: to exchange or barter.

MONEY

ALMIGHTY DOLLAR: an *American* expression for the "power of money," first introduced by Washington Irving in 1837.

BEANS: money; "a haddock of **BEANS**," a purse of money; formerly **BEAN** meant a guinea; *French*, **BIENS**, property; also used as a synonym for **BRICK**.—*See* **BRICK** *page 23.*

BIT: a purse or any sum of money.

BIT: fourpence; in America 12 ½ cents is called a **BIT**, and a defaced 20 cent piece is termed a **LONG BIT**. A **BIT** is the smallest coin in Jamaica, equal to 6d.

BLUNT: money. It has been said that this term is from the *French* **BLOND**, sandy or golden color, and that a parallel may be found in **BROWN** or **BROWNS**, the slang for half-pence. The etymology seems far-fetched however.

BRADS: money. Properly, a small kind of nails used by cobblers. —Compare **HORSE NAILS** below.

BRASS: money.

BUNTS: costermongers' perquisites; the money obtained by giving light weight, &c.; costermonger's goods sold by boys on commission. Probably a corruption of *bonus*, **BONE** being the slang for good. **BUNCE,** *Grose* gives as the *Cant* word for money.

BUSTLE: money; "to draw the **BUSTLE**."

CHINK or **CHINKERS:** money.—*Ancient.*—*See Florio.*

CHIPS: money.

CORKS: money; "how are you off for **CORKS**?" a soldier's term of a very expressive kind, denoting the means of "keeping afloat."

DIBBS: money; so called from the buckle bones of sheep, which have been used from the earliest times for gambling purposes, being thrown up five at a time and caught on the back of the hand like halfpence.

DIMMOCK: money; "how are you off for **DIMMOCK**," diminutive of **DIME**, a small foreign silver coin.

DINARLY: money; "NANTEE DINARLY," I have no money, corrupted from the *Lingua franca*, "NIENTE DINARO," not a penny. *Turkish*, DENARI; *Spanish*, DINERO; *Latin*, DENARIUS.

DUST: money; "down with the DUST," put down the money.—*Ancient*. Dean Swift once took for his text, "He who giveth to the poor lendeth to the Lord." His sermon was short. "Now, my brethren," said he, "if you are satisfied with the security, down with the DUST."

FEATHERS: money, wealth; "in full FEATHER," rich.

FLUSH: the opposite of HARD UP, in possession of money, not poverty-stricken.—*Shakespere*.

GILT: money. *German*, GELD; *Dutch*, GELT.

HANDSEL or **HANDSALE:** the *lucky money*, or first money taken in the morning by a pedlar.—*Cocker's Dictionary*, 1724. "Legs of mutton (street term for sheep's trotters or feet) two for a penny; who'll give me a HANSEL? Who'll give me a HANSEL,"—*Cry at Cloth Fair at the present day*. Hence, earnest money, first fruits, &c. In Norfolk, HANSELLING a thing is using it for the first time, as wearing a new coat, taking seizin of it, as it were.—*Anglo Saxon. N. Bailey*.

HORSE NAILS: money.—Compare BRADS above.

INNINGS: earnings, money coming in; "he's had long INNINGS," *i.e.*, a good run of luck, plenty of cash flowing in.

KING'S PICTURES: (now, of course, QUEEN'S PICTURES), money.

LOAVER: money.—*See* LOUR *below*.

LOUR or **LOWR:** money; "gammy LOWR," bad money.—*Ancient Cant*, and *Gipsey*.

MOPUSSES: money; "MOPUSSES ran taper," money ran short.

NAIL: to steal or capture; "paid on the NAIL," *i.e.*, ready money; NAILED, taken up or caught—probably in allusion to the practice of NAILING bad money to the counter. We say "as dead as a DOORNAIL;"—why? *Shakespere* has the expression in Henry IV:

> "*Falstaff*. What! Is the old king dead?
> *Pistol*. As nail in door."

A correspondent thinks the expression is only alliterative humour, and compares as "*Flat as a flounder*," "straight as a soldier," &c.

NEEDFUL: money, cash.

OCHRE: money, generally applied to *gold* for a very obvious reason.

OIL OF PALMS or **PALM OIL:** money.

PALM SOAP: money.

PEWTER: money, like TIN, used generally to signify silver; also, a pewter-pot.

POSH: a halfpenny or trifling coin. Also a generic term for money.

QUID or **THICK UN:** a sovereign; "half a QUID," half a sovereign; QUIDS, money generally; "QUID for a QUOD," one good turn for another. The word is used by *Old French* writers:

> "Des testamens qu'on dit le maistre
> De mon fait n'aura QUID ne QUOD. "
> —*Grand Testament de Villon.*

RAG-SHOP: a bank.

RAP: a halfpenny; frequently used generically for money, thus; "I hav'nt a RAP," *i.e.*, I have no money whatever; "I don't care a RAP," &c. Originally a species of counterfeit coin used for small change in *Ireland*, against the use of which a proclamation was issued, 5th May, 1737. Small copper or base metal coins are still called RAPPEN in the Swiss cantons, Irish robbers are called RAPPAREES.

READY or **READY GILT:** (properly GELT), money. Used by *Arbuthnot*, "Lord Strut was not very *flush* in READY."

RHINO: ready money.

RHINOCERAL: rich, wealthy, abounding in RHINO.

ROWDY: money. In *America*, a ruffian, a brawler, "rough."

SHINERS: sovereigns or money.

STUFF: money.

STUMPY: money.

TIN: money—generally applied to silver.

YELLOW-BOY: a sovereign or any gold coin.

BANK NOTES

FINUF: a five-pound note. **DOUBLE FINUF**, a ten-pound note.—*German, Funf*, five.

FLIMSIES: bank notes.

LONG-TAILED-ONES: bank notes or **FLIMSIES**, for a large amount.

RAGS: bank notes.

SOFT: foolish, inexperienced. An old term for bank notes.

COUNTERFEIT MONEY

BIT-FAKER or **TURNER OUT:** a coiner of bad money.

BRUMS: counterfeit coins.—*Nearly obsolete*. Corruption of *Brummagem* (Bromwicham), the ancient name of *Birmingham*, the great emporium of plated goods and imitation jewellery.

CASE: a bad crown piece. **HALF-A-CASE**, a counterfeit half crown. There are two sources, either of which may have this slang term. **CASER** is the Hebrew word for a crown; and silver coin is frequently counterfeited by coating or **CASING** pewter or iron imitations with silver.

COVER-DOWN: a tossing coin with a false cover, enabling either head or tail to be shown, according as the cover is left on or taken off.

GRAYS: halfpennies, with either two "heads" or two "tails," both sides alike. *Low gamblers* use **GRAYS**, and they cost from 2d. to 6d. each.

LOUR or **LOWR:** money; "gammy **LOWR**," bad money.—*Ancient Cant*, and *Gipsey*.

QUEER BIT-MAKERS: coiners.

QUEER SCREENS: forged bank notes.

QUEER SOFT: bad money.

RAP: a halfpenny; frequently used generically for money, thus; "I hav'nt a **RAP**," *i.e.*, I have no money whatever; "I don't care a **RAP**," &c. Originally a species of counterfeit coin used for small change in *Ireland*, against the use of which a proclamation was issued, 5th May,

1737. Small copper or base metal coins are still called **RAPPEN** in the Swiss cantons, Irish robbers are called **RAPPAREES**.

SCHOFEL: bad money.—*See* **SHOW-FULL** *below.*

SHEEN: bad money.—*Scotch.*

SHOW-FULL or **SCHOFUL:** bad money. *Mayhew* thinks this word is from the *Danish,* **SKUFFE**, to shove, to deceive, cheat; *Saxon,* **SCUFAN** —whence the *English,* **SHOVE**. The term, however, is possibly one of the many street words from the *Hebrew* (through the low Jews), **SHEPHEL**, in that language, signifying a *low* or debased estate. *Chaldee,* **SHAPHAL**.—*See* Psalm cxxxvi. 23, "in our *low estate.*" A correspondent suggests another very probable derivation, from the *German,* **SCHOFEL**, trash, rubbish—the *German* adjective, **SCHOFELIG**, being the nearest possible translation of our *shabby.*

SHOWFULL PITCHING: passing bad money.

SHOWFULL-PITCHER: a passer of counterfeit money.

SINKERS: bad money.

SLUMMING: passing bad money.

SMASH: to pass counterfeit money.

SMASHER: one who passes bad coin.

SMASHFEEDER: a Britannia metal spoon—the best imitation shillings are made from this metal.

TURNER OUT: a coiner of bad money.

 # CROWN

ALDERMAN: half-crown—possibly from its rotundity.

BULL: a crown piece; formerly, **BULL'S EYE**.

CASE: a bad crown piece. **HALF-A-CASE**, a counterfeit half crown. There are two sources, either of which may have contributed this slang term. **CASER** is the Hebrew word for a crown; and silver coin is frequently counterfeited by coating or **CASING** pewter or iron imitations with silver.

COACH WHEEL: crown piece or five shillings.

HALF A TUSHEROON: half a crown.

THICK-UN: a sovereign; a crown piece or five shillings.

TUSHEROON: a crown piece, five shillings.

FARTHING

FADGE: a farthing.

FIDDLER: a farthing.

GIG: a farthing. Formerly, GRIG.

QUARTEREEN: a farthing.—*Gibraltar term, Italian,* QUATTRINO.

PENNY, HALFPENNY, and PENCE

BANDY or **CRIPPLE:** a sixpence, so called from this coin being generally bent or crooked; old term for flimsy or bad cloth, temp. Q. Elizabeth.

BENDER: a sixpence—from its liability to bend.

BIT: fourpence; in America 12 ½ cents is called a BIT, and a defaced 20 cent piece is termed a LONG BIT. A BIT is the smallest coin in Jamaica, equal to 6d.

BROWN: a half penny.—*See* BLUNT *page 193.*

COPPER: a penny. COPPERS, mixed pence.

CRIPPLE: a bent sixpence.

DACHA SALTEE: tenpence. Probably from the *Lingua Franca.* Modern *Greek,* STICA; *Italian,* DIECI SOLDI, tenpence; *Gipsey,* DIK, ten. So also DACHA-ONE, *i.e.,* dieciuno, elevenpence.—*See* SALTEE *page 199.*

DEUCE: twopence; DEUCE at cards or dice, one with two pips or holes.

DOWNER: a sixpence; apparently the *Gipsey* word, TAWNO, "little one," in course of metamorphosis into the more usual "*tanner.*"

FIDDLER: a sixpence.—*Household Words,* No. 183.

FIDDLERS' MONEY: a lot of sixpences; 6d. was the remuneration to fiddlers from each of the company in old times.

FYE-BUCK: a sixpence.—*Nearly obsolete.*

HALF A HOG: sixpence; sometimes termed **HALF A GRUNTER.**

HANGMAN'S WAGES: thirteenpence halfpenny.

JOEY: a fourpenny piece. The term is derived (like **BOBBY** from Sir Robert Peel) from Joseph Hume, the late respected M.P. The explanation is thus given in *Hawkins' History of the Silver Coinage of England*:

> "These pieces are said to have owed their existence to the pressing insistance of Mr. Hume, from whence they, for some time, bore the nickname of **JOEYS.** As they were very convenient to pay short cab fares, the Hon. M.P. was extremely unpopular with the drivers, who frequently received only *a groat* where otherwise they would have received a sixpence without any demand for change." The term originated with the London cabmen, who have invented many others.

KICK: a sixpence; "two and a **KICK,**" two shillings and sixpence.

LORD OF THE MANOR: a sixpence.

MAG: a halfpenny. — *Ancient Cant*, **MAKE. MEGGS** were formerly guineas. — *B.M. Carew.*

NOBBA SALTEE: ninepence. *Lingua Franca*, **NOVE SOLDI.**

OTTER: eightpence. — *Italian*, **OTTO,** eight.

PIG or **SOW'S BABY:** a sixpence.

POSH: a half penny or trifling coin. Also a generic term for money.

POT: a sixpence, *i.e.*, the price of a pot or quart of half-and-half. A half-crown, in medical student slang, is a **FIVE-POT PIECE.**

RAP: a halfpenny; frequently used generically for money, thus; "I hav'nt a **RAP,**" *i.e.*, I have no money whatever; "I don't care a **RAP,**" &c. Originally a species of counterfeit coin used for small change in *Ireland*, against the use of which a proclamation was issued, 5th May, 1737. Small copper or base metal coins are still called **RAPPEN** in the Swiss cantons, Irish robbers are called **RAPPAREES.**

SALTEE: a penny. Pence, &c., are thus reckoned:

ONEY SALTEE: a penny, from the *Italian*, **UNO SOLDO.**

DOOE SALTEE: twopence, from the *Italian*, **DUE SOLDI.**

THAY SALTEE: threepence, from the *Italian*, **TRE SOLDI.**

QUARTERER SALTEE: fourpence, from the *Italian*, QUATTRO SOLDI.

CHINKER SALTEE: fivepence, from the *Italian*, CINQUE SOLDI.

SAY SALTEE: sixpence, from the *Italian*, SEI SOLDI.

SAY ONEY SALTEE or **SETTER SALTEE:** sevenpence, from the *Italian*, SETTE SOLDI.

SAY DOOE SALTEE or **OTTER SALTEE:** eightpence, from the *Italian*, OTTO SOLDI.

SAY TRAY SALTEE or **NOBBA SALTEE:** ninepence, from the *Italian*, NOVE SOLDI.

SAY QUARTERER SALTEE or **DACHA SALTEE:** tenpence, from the *Italian*, DIECI SOLDI.

SAY CHINKER SALTEE or **DACHA ONE SALTEE:** elevenpence, from the *Italian*, DIECI UNO SOLDI, &c.

ONEY BEONG: one shilling.

A BEONG SAY SALTEE: one shilling and sixpence.

DOOE BEONG SAY SALTEE or **MADZA CAROON:** half-a-crown or two shillings and sixpence.

> *This curious list of numerals in use among the London street folk is, strange as it may seem, derived from the *Lingua Franca*, or bastard *Italian*, of the Mediterranean seaports, of which other examples may be found in the pages of this Dictionary. SALTEE, the *Cant* term used by the costermongers and others for a penny, is no other than the *Italian*, SOLDO (plural SOLDI), and the numerals —as may be seen by the *Italian* equivalents—are a tolerably close imitation of the originals. After the number six, a curious variation occurs, which is peculiar to the London *Cant*, seven, being reckoned as SAY ONEY, *six-one*, SAY DOOE, *six-two = 8*, and so on. DACHA, I may remark, is perhaps from the *Greek*, DEKA, ten, which, in the Constantinopolitan *Lingua Franca*, is likely enough to have been substituted for the *Italian*. MADZA, is clearly the *Italian* MEZZA. The origin of BEONG I have not been so fortunate as to discover, unless it be the *French*, BIEN, the application of which to a shilling is not so evident; but amongst costermongers and other street folk, it is quite immaterial what foreign tongue contributes to their secret language. Providing the terms are unknown to the police and the public generally, they

care not a rushlight whether the polite French, the gay Spaniards, or the cloudy Germans helped to swell their vocabulary. The numbers of low foreigners, however, dragging out a miserable existence in our crowded neighbourhoods, organ grinders and image sellers, foreign seamen from the vessels in the river, and our own connections with Malta and the Ionian Isles may explain, to a certain extent, the phenomenon of these Southern phrases in the mouths of costers and tramps.

SETTER: seven pence. *Italian*, **SETTE.** —*See* **SALTEE** *page 199*.

SIMON: a sixpenny piece.

SNID: a sixpence. —*Scotch.*

SOW'S BABY: a pig; sixpence.

SPRAT: sixpence.

TANNER: a sixpence. *Gipsey*, **TAWNO**, little, or *Latin*, **TENER**, slender?

TESTER: sixpence. From **TESTONE**, a shilling in the reign of Henry VIII., but a sixpence in the time of Q. Elizabeth. —*Shakespere. French*, **TESTE** or **TETE**, the head of the monarch on the coin.

THRUMMER: a threepenny bit.

THRUMS: threepence.

THRUPS: threepence.

TIZZY: a sixpence. Corruption of **TESTER.**
WINN: a penny. —*Ancient Cant.*

 # SHILLING

BEONG: a shilling. —*See* **SALTEE** *page 199*.

BOB: a shilling. Formerly **BOBSTICK**, which may have been the original.

BREAKY-LEG: a shilling.

CAROON: five shillings. *French*, **COUBONNE**; *Gipsey*, **COURNA**, *Spanish* **COURNA**, half-a-crown.

CART WHEEL: a five shilling piece.

DEANER: a shilling. *Provincial Gipsey*, **DEANEE**, a pound.

GEN: a shilling. Also, **GENT**, silver. Abbreviation of the *French*, **ARGENT**.

HOG: a shilling.—*Old Cant.*

JAMES: a sovereign or twenty shillings.

PEG: a shilling.—*Scotch.*

SMASHFEEDER: a Britannia metal spoon—the best imitation shillings are made from this metal.

STAG: a shilling.

TEVISS: a shilling.

THICK-UN: a sovereign; a crown piece or five shillings.

TUSHEROON: a crown piece, five shillings.

TWELVER: a shilling.

SOVEREIGN

CANARY: a sovereign. This is stated by a correspondent to be a Norwich term, that city being famous for its breed of those birds.

COUTER: a sovereign. **HALF-A-COUTER**, half-a-sovereign.

FOONT: a sovereign or 20s.

GOLDFINCH: a sovereign.

HALF A BEAN: half a sovereign.

HALF A COUTER: half a sovereign.

JACKS and **HALF-JACKS:** card counters, resembling in size and appearance sovereigns and half-sovereigns, for which they are occasionally passed to simple persons. In large gambling establishments the "heaps of gold" are frequently composed mainly of **JACKS**.

JAMES: a sovereign or twenty shillings.

POONA: a sovereign.—Corruption of *pound*; or from the *Lingua Franca?*

QUID or **THICK UN:** a sovereign; "half a **QUID**," half a sovereign; **QUIDS**, money generally; "**QUID** for a **QUOD**," one good turn for another. The word is used by *Old French* writers:

"Des testamens qu'on dit le maistre
De mon fait n'aura **QUID** ne **QUOD**"
                              —*Grand Testament de Villon.*

ROULEAU: a packet of sovereigns.—*Gaming.*

SHINERS: sovereigns or money.

SKID: a sovereign. Fashionable slang.

THICK-UN: a sovereign; a crown piece or five shillings.

YELLOW-BOY: a sovereign or any gold coin.

OTHER MONEY

BUNTS: costermongers' perquisites; the money obtained by giving light weight, &c.; costermonger's goods sold by boys on commission. Probably a corruption of *bonus*, **BONE** being the slang for good. **BUNCE**, *Grose* gives as the *Cant* word for money.

COPPER: a penny. **COPPERS**, mixed pence.

FLAG: a groat or 4d.—*Ancient Cant.*

HALF A BULL: two shillings and sixpence.

JACKS, HALF-JACKS: card counters, resembling in size and appearance sovereigns and half-sovereigns, for which they are occasionally passed to simple persons. In large gambling establishments the "heaps of gold" are frequently composed mainly of **JACKS**.

MARYGOLD: one million sterling.—*See* **PLUM** *below.*

MONKEY: £500.

NEDS: guineas. **HALF-NEDS**, half-guineas.

PLUM: £100,000, usually applied to the dowry of a rich heiress or a legacy.

PLUNDER: a common word in the horse trade to express profit. Also an *American* term for baggage, luggage.

PONY: twenty-five pounds.—*Sporting.*

ROUND: "ROUND dealing," honest trading; "ROUND sum," a large sum. Synonymous also in a *slang* sense with SQUARE. — *See* SQUARE *p. 117.*

SCRATCH: "no great SCRATCH," of little worth.

SCREW: salary or wages.

STIFF: paper, a bill of acceptance, &c.; "how did you get it, STIFF or *hard?*" *i.e.*, did he pay you cash or give a bill.

TIP: a douceur; also to give, lend, or hand over anything to another person; "come, TIP up the tin," *i.e.*, hand up the money; "TIP the wink," to inform by winking; "TIP us your fin," *i.e.*, give me your hand; "TIP one's boom off," to make off, depart. — *Sea.* "To miss one's TIP," to fail in a scheme. — *Old Cant.*

GUILTY AS CHARGED

Honesty pays, but it doesn't seem to pay enough to suit some people.

Kin Hubbard

*T*his chapter is my favorite. The slang terms for crime are colorful and fun. As I imagine were the characters perpetrating some of them.

The section on thieves is by far the longest, and I love how specialized some of the thieves are, like the **body-snatchers** who stole cats, or the **stook buzzer** who stole pocket-handkerchiefs. It's hard to believe you could make a living at either, and I really don't want to know what they did with the cats.

The section on cons and scams is also eye-opening. I imagine many of these cons are still practiced by modern-day grifters. My favorite is the story of a pair of thieves that robbed a shoemaker and even got the shoemaker to cheer one of them on.

But it wasn't all fun and games. The law was harsh and executions and transportation to penal colonies were common occurrences. Yet even here a sense of humor prevailed. An execution was a **stretching match** and to be transported was to be **marinated.**

Editor's Faves:

LITTLE SNAKES-MAN: a little thief, who is generally passed through a small aperture to open any door to let in the rest of the gang.

SUCK THE MONKEY: to rob a cask of liquor by inserting a straw through a gimlet hole, and sucking a portion of the contents.

THIMBLE TWISTERS: thieves who rob persons of their watches.

IN THIS CHAPTER

BOOTY and SHARES

CHEEK: share or portion; "where's my **CHEEK**?" where is my allowance?

CHOUSE: to cheat out of one's share or portion. Hackluyt, **CHAUS**; Massinger, **CHIAUS**. From the Turkish, in which language it signifies an interpreter. Gifford gives a curious story as to its origin:

> In the year 1609 there was attached to the Turkish embassy in England an interpreter, or **CHIAOUS**, who by cunning, aided by his official position, managed to cheat the Turkish and Persian merchants then in London out of the large sum of £4,000, then deemed an enormous amount. From the notoriety which attended the fraud, and the magnitude of the swindle, anyone who cheated or defrauded was said to *chiaous*, or *chause*, or **CHOUSE;** to do, that is, as this *Chiaous* had done.—*See Trench, English. Past and Present,* p. 87.

DOLLOP: to **DOLE UP**, give up a share.—*Ib.*

LOOT: swag or plunder.—*Hindoo.*

NAP THE REGULARS: to divide the booty.

POLL or **POLLING:** one thief robbing another of part of their booty. —*Hall's Union,* 1548.

RAG: to divide or share; "let's **RAG IT**," or **GO RAGS**, *i.e.*, share it equally between us.—*Norwich.*

REGULARS: a thief's share of plunder. "They were quarrelling about the **REGULARS**." —*Times,* 8th January, 1856.

SCOT: a quantity of anything, a lot, a share.—*Anglo Saxon,* **SCEAT**, pronounced **SHOT**.

SHOT: from the once *English,* but now provincial word, to **SHOOT**, to subscribe, contribute in fair proportion; a share, the same as **SCOT**, both being from the *Anglo Saxon* word, **SCEAT**; "to pay one's **SHOT**," *i.e.*, share of the reckoning, &c.

SNACK: booty or share. Also, a light repast.—*Old Cant* and *Gipsey* term.

SNAPPS: share, portion; any articles or circumstances out of which money may be made; "looking for **SNAPPS**," waiting for windfalls or odd jobs.—*Old. Scotch*, CHITS—term also used for "coppers," or halfpence.

SWAG: a lot or plenty of anything, a portion or division of property. In Australia the term is used for the luggage carried by diggers: in India the word LOOT is used. *Scotch,* SWEG or SWACK; *German*, SWEIG, a flock. *Old Cant* for a shop.

SWAG: booty, or plundered property; "collar the SWAG," seize the booty.

WHACK: a share or lot; "give me my WHACK," give me my share. *Scotch,* SWEG or SWACK.

 # CRIMINALS and CRIMES

 ## BOYS' CRIMES

AREA-SNEAK: a boy thief who commits depredations upon kitchens and cellars.—*See* CROW *page 235.*

BROSIER: a bankrupt.—*Cheshire.* BROSIER-MY-DAME, school term, implying a clearing of the housekeeper's larder of provisions, in revenge for stinginess.—*Eton.*

BUZ-BLOAK: a pickpocket, who principally confines his attention to purses and loose cash. *Grose* gives BUZ-GLOAK (or CLOAK?), an ancient *Cant* word. BUZ-NAPPER, a young pickpocket.

BUZ-NAPPER'S ACADEMY: school in which young thieves are trained. Figures are dressed up, and experienced tutors stand in various difficult attitudes for the boys to practice upon. When clever enough they are sent on the streets. It is reported that a house of this nature is situated in a court near Hatton Garden. The system is well explained in *Dickens' Oliver Twist.*

KIDDEN: a low lodging house for boys.

KIDSMAN: one who trains boys to thieve and pick pockets successfully.

LITTLE SNAKES-MAN: a little thief, who is generally passed through a small aperture to open any door to let in the rest of the gang.

PADDING KENS or **CRIBS:** tramps' and boys' lodging houses.

SIGHT: "to take a SIGHT at a person," a vulgar action employed by street boys to denote incredulity or contempt for authority, by placing the thumb against the nose and closing all the fingers except the little one, which is agitated in token of derision. — *See* WALKER *p. 400.*

SMUGGINGS: snatching or purloining — shouted out by boys, when snatching the tops or small play property, of other lads, and then running off at full speed.

> "Tops are in; spin 'em agin.
> Tops are out; SMUGGING about."

 ## CHEATS

BABES: the lowest order of KNOCK-OUTS (see below), who are prevailed upon not to give opposing biddings at auctions, in consideration of their receiving a small sum (from one shilling to half-a-crown), and a certain quantity of beer. BABES exist in Baltimore, U.S., where they are known as blackguards and "rowdies."

BESTER: a low betting cheat.

BILK: a cheat or a swindler. Formerly in frequent use, now confined to the streets, where it is very general. *Gothic*, BILAICAN.

BITE: a cheat; "a Yorkshire BITE," a cheating fellow from that county. — *North*; also *old slang*, used by *Pope*. Swift says it originated with a nobleman in his day.

BLACK-LEG: a rascal, swindler, or card cheat.

BONNET: a gambling cheat. "A man who sits at a gaming table, and appears to be playing against the table; when a stranger enters, the BONNET generally wins." — *Times*, Nov. 17, 1856. Also, a pretense or make-believe, a sham bidder at auctions.

BOUNCE: a showy swindler.

BOUNETTER: a fortune-telling cheat. — *Gipsey.*

BROADS: cards. BROADSMAN, a card sharper.

BUMMAREE: this term is given to a class of speculating salesmen at Billingsgate market, not recognized as such by the trade, but who get a living by buying large quantities of fish of the salesmen and re-selling it to smaller buyers. The word has been used in the statutes and bye-laws of the market for upwards of 100 years. It has been variously derived, but is most probably from the *French*, **BONNE MAREE**, good fresh fish! "Marée signifie toute sorts de poisson de mer qûi n'est pas salé; bonne marée—*maree fraiche*, vendeur de marée." —*Dict. De l'Acad. Franc.* The **BUMMAREES** are accused of many trade tricks. One of them is to blow up cod-fish with a pipe until they look double their actual size. Of course, when the fish come to the table they are flabby, shrunken, and half-dwindled away. In Norwich, to **BUMMAREE ONE** is to run up a score at a public house just open, and is equivalent to "running into debt with one."

BUTTON: a decoy, sham purchaser, &c. At any mock or sham auction seedy specimens may be seen. Probably from the connection of *buttons* with *Brummagem*, which is often used as a synonym for a sham.

CARRIER PIGEONS: swindlers, who formerly used to cheat Lottery Office Keepers.—*Nearly obsolete.*

CHARLEY-PITCHERS: low, cheating gamblers.

DIDDLER or **JEREMY DIDDLER:** an artful swindler.

DOWNY: knowing or cunning; "a **DOWNY COVE**," a knowing or experienced sharper.

DUDDERS or **DUDSMEN:** persons who formerly travelled the country as pedlars, selling gown-pieces, silk waistcoats, &c., to countrymen. In selling a waistcoat-piece for thirty shillings or two pounds, which cost them perhaps five shillings, they would show great fear of the revenue officer, and beg of the purchasing clodhopper *to kneel down in a puddle of water, crook his arm, and swear that it might never become straight if he told an exciseman, or even his own wife.* The term and practice are *nearly obsolete.* In Liverpool, however, and at the east end of London, men dressed up as sailors with pretended silk handkerchiefs and cigars "only just smuggled from the Indies," are still to be plentifully found.

DUFFER: a hawker of "Brummagem" or sham jewelry; a sham of any kind; a fool or worthless person. **DUFFER** was formerly synonymous with **DUDDER**, and was a general term given to pedlars. It is mentioned in the *Frauds of London* (1760), as a word in frequent use in the last century to express cheats of all kinds. From the *German*, DURFEN, to want?

FAKER: one who makes or FAKES anything.

FIDDLER: a sharper, a cheat; also one who dawdles over little matters and neglects great ones.

HIGH-FLYER: a genteel beggar or swindler.

HORSE CHAUNTER: a dealer who takes worthless horses to country fairs and disposes of them by artifice. He is flexible in his ethics, and will put in a glass-eye or perform other tricks. — *See* COPER *page 131.*

KNOCK-OUTS or KNOCK-INS: disreputable persons who visit auction rooms and unite to buy the articles at their own prices. One of their number is instructed to buy for the rest, and after a few small bids as blinds to the auctioneer and bystanders, the lot is knocked down to the KNOCK-OUT bidders, at a nominal price—the competition to result from an auction being thus frustrated and set aside. At the conclusion of the sale the goods are paid for, and carried to some neighbouring public house, where they are re-sold or KNOCKED-OUT, and the difference between the first purchase and the second—or taproom KNOCK-OUT—is divided amongst the gang. As generally happens with ill-gotten gains, the money soon finds its way to the landlord's pocket, and the KNOCK-OUT is rewarded with a red nose or a bloated face. Cunning tradesmen join the KNOCK-OUTS when an opportunity for money making presents itself. The lowest description of KNOCK-OUTS, fellows with more tongue than capital, are termed BABES. — *See above.*

LED CAPTAIN: a fashionable spunger, a swell who, by artifice ingratiates himself into the good graces of the master of the house, and lives at his table.

LURKER: an impostor who travels the country with false certificates of fires, shipwrecks, &c.

MACE: a dressy swindler who victimizes tradesmen.

MAGSMAN: a street swindler, who watches for countrymen and "gullible" persons.

MOBS: companions; MOBSMEN, dressy swindlers.

MOUNTER: a false swearer. Derived from the borrowed clothes men used to MOUNT, or dress in, when going to swear for a consideration.

NEEDY MIZZLER: a shabby person; a tramp who runs away without paying for his lodging.

NOBBLERS: confederates of thimble-rigs, who play earnestly as if strangers to the "Rig," and thus draw unsuspecting persons into a game.

ROOK: a cheat or tricky gambler; the opposite of PIGEON. — *Old.*

SHARK: a sharper, a swindler. *Bow-street* term in 1785, now in most dictionaries. — *Friesic* and *Danish,* SCHURK. — *See* LAND-SHARK *p. 138.*

SHARP or **SHARPER:** a cunning cheat, a rogue — the opposite of FLAT.

SPUDDY: a seller of bad potatoes. In *Scotland,* a SPUD is a raw potato; and roasted SPUDS are those cooked in the cinders with their jackets on.

SWINDLER: although a recognized word in respectable dictionaries, commenced service as a slang term. It was used as such by the poor Londoners against the German Jews who set up in London about the year 1762, also by our soldiers in the German War about that time. SCHWINDEL, in *German,* signifies to cheat.

◆ CHEATING

BALLYRAG: to scold vehemently, to swindle one out of his money by intimidation and sheer abuse, as alleged in a late cab case (*Evans* v. *Robinson*).

BAMBOOZLE: to deceive, make fun of, or cheat a person; abbreviated to BAM, which is used also as a substantive, a deception, a sham, a "sell." *Swift* says BAMBOOZLE was invented by a nobleman in the reign of Charles II. But this I conceive to be an error. The probability is that a nobleman first *used* it in polite society. The term is derived from the Gipseys.

BESTING: excelling, cheating. BESTED, taken in or defrauded.

BILK: to defraud, or obtain goods, &c. without paying for them; "to BILK the schoolmaster," to get information or experience without paying for it.

BITE: to cheat; "to be BITTEN," to be taken in or imposed upon. Originally a *Gipsey* term. — *See Bacchus and Venus.*

BOUNCE: to boast, cheat, or bully.—*Old Cant.*

BROWN: "to do BROWN," to do well or completely (in allusion to roasting); "doing it BROWN," prolonging the frolic or exceeding sober bounds; "DONE BROWN," taken in, deceived, or surprised.

CHISEL: to cheat.

CHOUSE: to cheat out of one's share or portion. Hackluyt, CHAUS; Massinger, CHIAUS. From the Turkish, in which language it signifies an interpreter. Gifford gives a curious story as to its origin:

> In the year 1609 there was attached to the Turkish embassy in England an interpreter, or CHIAOUS, who by cunning, aided by his official position, managed to cheat the Turkish and Persian merchants then in London out of the large sum of 4,000, then deemed an enormous amount. From the notoriety which attended the fraud, and the magnitude of the swindle, anyone who cheated or defrauded was said to *chiaous, or chause*, or CHOUSE; to do, that is, as this *Chiaous* had done.—*See Trench, English. Past and Present*, p. 87.

COG: to cheat at dice.—*Shakespere.* Also, to agree with, as one cog-wheel does with another.

COOPER: to forge or imitate in writing; "COOPER a moniker," to forge a signature.

DESPATCHES: false "dice with two sides, double four, double five, and double six."—*Times*, 27th November, 1856.

DIDDLE: to cheat or defraud.—*Old.*

DO: this useful and industrious verb has for many years done service as a slang term. To DO a person is to cheat him. Sometimes another tense is employed, such as I DONE him," meaning I cheated or "paid him out;" DONE BROWN, cheated thoroughly, befooled; DONE OVER, upset, cheated, knocked down, ruined; DONE UP, used-up, finished, or quieted. DONE also means convicted or sentenced; so does DONE FOR. To DO a person in pugilism is to excel him in fisticuffs. Humphreys, who fought Mendoza, a Jew, wrote this laconic note to his supporter: "Sir, I have DONE the Jew, and am in good health. Rich. Humphries." Tourists use the expression "I have DONE France and Italy," meaning I have completely explored those countries.

FAKE: to cheat or swindle; to do anything; to go on or continue; to make or construct; to steal or rob—a verb variously used. **FAKED**, done or done for; "**FAKE AWAY**, there's no down," go on, there is nobody looking. *Mayhew* says it is from the *Latin*, **FACIMENTUM**.

FLIMP: to hustle or rob.

FOX: to cheat or rob.—*Eton College.*

FOXING: watching in the streets for any occurrence which may be turned to a profitable account.—*See* **MOOCHING** *page 116.*

FULLAMS: false dice, which always turn up high.—*Shakespere.*

HOAX: to deceive or ridicule—*Grose* says was originally a *University Cant* word. Corruption of **HOCUS**, to cheat.

HOOK-UM SNIVEY: (formerly "hook *and* snivey") a low expression meaning to cheat by feigning sickness or other means. Also a piece of thick iron wire crooked at one end, and fastened into a wooden handle, for the purpose of undoing from the outside the wooden bolt of a door.

LET IN: to cheat or victimize.

MACE: to spunge, swindle, or beg, in a polite way; "give it him (a shopkeeper) on the **MACE**," *i.e.*, obtain goods on credit and never pay for them; also termed "striking the **MACE**."

NOBBLE: to cheat, to overreach; to discover.

NURSE: a curious term lately applied to competition in omnibuses. Two omnibuses are placed on the road to **NURSE**, or oppose, each opposition "buss," one before, the other behind. Of course, the central or **NURSED** buss has very little chance, unless it happens to be a favourite with the public. **NURSE**, to cheat or swindle; trustees are said to **NURSE** property, *i.e.*, gradually eat it up themselves.

OFFICE: "to give the **OFFICE**," to give a hint dishonestly to a confederate, thereby enabling him to win a game or bet, the profits being shared.

PICK: "to **PICK** oneself up," to recover after a beating or illness; "to **PICK** a man up," "to do," or cheat him.

PIKE: a turnpike: "to bilk a **PIKE**," to cheat the keeper of the toll-gate.

PINCH: to steal or cheat; also, to catch or apprehend.

PUT UPON: cheated, deluded, oppressed.

RISE: "to take a RISE out of a person," to mortify, outwit, or cheat him, by superior cunning.

SELL: to deceive, swindle, or play a practical joke upon a person. A sham is a SELL in street parlance. "SOLD again, and got the money," a costermonger cries after having successfully deceived somebody. *Shakespere* uses SELLING in a similar sense, viz., blinding or deceiving.

SHOOT THE MOON: to remove furniture from a house in the night, without paying the landlord.

SLANG: to cheat, to abuse in foul language.

SLUM THE GORGER: to cheat on the sly, to be an eye servant. SLUM in this sense is *Old Cant*.

SOLD: "SOLD again! and the money taken," gulled, deceived.—*Vide* SELL.

STICK: to cheat; "he got STUCK," he was taken in; STICK, to forget one's part in a performance.—*Theatrical*. STICK ON, to overcharge or defraud; STICK UP FOR, to defend a person, especially when slandered in his absence; STICK UP TO, to preserver in courting or attacking, whether in fisticuffs or argument; "to STICK in one's gizzard," to rankle in one's heart; "to STICK TO a person," to adhere to one, be his friend through adverse circumstances.

STRAWING: *selling* straws in the streets (generally for a penny) and *giving* the purchaser a paper (indecent or political) or a gold (!) ring —neither of which the patterer states he is allowed to sell.

TAKE: "to TAKE IN," to cheat or defraud, from the lodging-house keepers' advertisements, "single men TAKEN IN AND DONE FOR;" an engagement which is as frequently performed in a bad as a good sense.—*See* TAKE *in the Index for more meanings on page 504.*

TAKE IN: a cheating or swindling transaction—sometimes termed "a DEAD TAKE IN." *Shakespere* has TAKE IN in the sense of conquering. TO BE HAD or TO BE SPOKE TO, were formerly synonymous phrases with TO BE TAKEN IN.

YORKSHIRE: "to YORKSHIRE," or "come YORKSHIRE over any person," is to cheat or BITE them.—*North*.

CONS and SCAMS

BABES: the lowest order of **KNOCK-OUTS** (see below), who are prevailed upon not to give opposing biddings at auctions, in consideration of their receiving a small sum (from one shilling to half-a-crown), and a certain quantity of beer. **BABES** exist in Baltimore, U.S., where they are known as blackguards and "rowdies."

BAMBOOZLE: deceive, make fun of or cheat a person; abbreviated to **BAM**, which is used also as a substantive, a deception, a sham, a "sell." *Swift* says **BAMBOOZLE** was invented by a nobleman in the reign of Charles II. But this I conceive to be an error. The probability is that a nobleman first *used* it in polite society. The term is derived from the Gipseys.

CHURCH A YACK: (or watch), to take the works of a watch from its original case and put them into another one, to avoid detection.—*See* **CHRISTENING** *page 239.*

COCKS: fictitious narratives, in verse or prose, of murders, fires, and terrible accidents, sold in the streets as true accounts. The man who hawks them, a patterer, often changes the scene of the awful event to suit the taste of the neighbourhood he is trying to delude. Possibly a corruption of *cook*, a cooked statement, or, as a correspondent suggests, the **COCK LANE** Ghost may have given rise to the term. This had a great run, and was a rich harvest to the running stationers.

COVER-DOWN: a tossing coin with a false cover, enabling either head or tail to be shown, according as the cover is left on or taken off.

DODGE: a cunning trick. "**DODGE**, that homely but expressive phrase."—*Sir Hugh Cairns on the Reform Bill,* 2nd March, 1859. *Anglo Saxon*, **DEOGIAN**, to colour, to conceal. The **TIDY DODGE**, as it is called by street-folk, consists in dressing up a family clean and tidy, and parading the streets to excite compassion and obtain alms. A correspondent suggests that the verb **DODGE** may have been formed (like *wench* from *wink*) from **DOG**, *i.e.*, to double quickly and unexpectedly, as in coursing.

DONKEY: "three more and up goes the **DONKEY**," a vulgar street phrase for extracting as much money as possible before performing any task.

The phrase had its origin with a travelling showman, the *finale* of whose performance was the hoisting of a DONKEY on a pole or ladder; but this consummation was never arrived at unless the required number of "browns" was first paid up, and "three more" was generally the unfortunate deficit.

DOOKIN: fortune telling. *Gipsey,* DUKKERIN.

DURRYNACKING: offering lace or any other article as an introduction to fortune-telling; generally pursued by women.

FAKEMENT: a false begging petition, any act of robbery, swindling, or deception.

FAWNEY or **FAWNEY RIG:** ring dropping. A few years ago, this practice or RIG, was very common. A fellow purposely dropped a ring or a pocket book with some little articles of jewellery, &c., in it, and when he saw any person pick it up, ran to claim half. The ring found, the questions of how the booty was to be divided had then to be decided. The *Fawney* says, "if you will give me eight or nine shilling for my share the things are yours." This the FLAT thinks very fair. The ring of course is valueless, and the swallower of the bait discovers the trick too late.

FAWNEY BOUNCING: selling rings for a wager. This practice is founded upon the old tale of a gentleman laying a wager that if he was to offer "real gold sovereigns" at a penny a piece at the foot of London Bridge, the English public would be too incredulous to buy. The story states that the gentleman stationed himself with sovereigns in a tea tray, and sold only two within the hour—winning the bet. This tale the FAWNEY BOUNCERS tell the public, only offering brass, double gilt rings, instead of sovereigns.

FIG: "to FIG a horse," to play improper tricks with one in order to make him lively.

GLIM LURK: a begging paper, giving a certified account of a dreadful fire—which never happened.

HUFF: a dodge or trick; "don't try that HUFF on me," or "that HUFF won't do." — *Norwich.*

KID-RIG: cheating children in the streets sent on errands or entrusted with packages. — *Nearly obsolete.*

KNOCK-OUTS or **KNOCK-INS:** disreputable persons who visit auction rooms and unite to buy the articles at their own prices. One of their number is instructed to buy for the rest, and after a few small bids as blinds to the auctioneer and bystanders, the lot is knocked down to the KNOCK-OUT bidders, at a nominal price—the competition to result from an auction being thus frustrated and set aside. At the conclusion of the sale the goods are paid for, and carried to some neighbouring public house, where they are re-sold or KNOCKED-OUT, and the difference between the first purchase and the second—or taproom KNOCK-OUT—is divided amongst the gang. As generally happens with ill-gotten gains, the money soon finds its way to the landlord's pocket, and the KNOCK-OUT is rewarded with a red nose or a bloated face. Cunning tradesmen join the KNOCK-OUTS when an opportunity for money making presents itself. The lowest description of KNOCK-OUTS, fellows with more tongue than capital, are termed **BABES.**—*See above.*

LURK: a sham, swindle, or representation of feigned distress.

MAKE: a successful theft or swindle.

MOVE: a "dodge," or cunning trick; "up to a **MOVE** or two," acquainted with tricks.

NOBBLERS: confederates of thimble-rigs, who play earnestly as if strangers to the "Rig," and thus draw unsuspecting persons into a game.

PALMING: robbing shops by pairs—one thief bargaining with apparent intent to purchase, whilst the other watches his opportunity to steal. An amusing example of **PALMING** came off some time since. A man entered a "ready made" boot and shoe shop and desired to be shown a pair of boots—his companion staying outside and amusing himself by looking in at the window. The one who required to be fresh shod was apparently of a humble and deferential turn, for he placed his hat on the floor directly he stepped in the shop. Boot after boot was tried on until at last a fit was obtained—when lo, forth came a man, snatched up the customer's hat left near the door, and down the street he ran as fast as his legs could carry him. Away went the customer after his hat, and Crispin, standing at the door, clapped his hands and shouted, "go it, you'll catch him,"—little thinking that it was a concerted trick, and that neither his boots nor the customer would ever return. **PALMING** sometimes refers to secreting money or rings in the hand.

PLANT: a dodge, a preconcerted swindle; a position in the street to sell from. **PLANT**, a swindle, may be thus described: a coster will join a party of gaming costers that he never saw before, and commence tossing. When sufficient time has elapsed to remove all suspicions of companionship, his mate will come up and commence betting on each of his **PAL'S** throws with those standing around. By a curious quickness of hand, a coster can make the toss tell favourably for his wagering friend, who meets him in the evening after the play is over and shares the spoils.

PRICK THE GARTER or **PITCH THE NOB:** a gambling and cheating game common at fairs, and generally practiced by thimble riggers. It consists of a "garter" or a piece of list doubled, and then folded up tight. The bet is made upon your asserting that you can, with a pin, "prick" the point at which the garter is doubled. The garter is then unfolded, and nine times out of ten you will find that you have been deceived, and that you pricked one of the false folds. The owner of the garter, I should state, holds the ends tightly with one hand. This was, doubtless, originally a Gipsey game, and we are informed by *Brand* that it was much practiced by the Gipseys in the time of *Shakespere*. In those days, it was termed **PRICKING AT THE BELT** or **FAST AND LOOSE**.

RACKET: a dodge, maneuver, exhibition; a disturbance.

RING DROPPING:—*See* **FAWNEY** *page 218.*

SCALDRUM DODGE: burning the body with a mixture of acids and gunpowder, so as to suit the hues and complexions of the accident to be deplored.

SELL: a deception, disappointment; also a lying joke.

SHAKE LURK: a false paper carried by an impostor, giving an account of a "dreadful shipwreck."

SHAVE: a false alarm, a hoax, a sell. This was much used in the Crimea during the Russian campaign.

STALL or **STALL OFF:** a dodge, a blind, or an excuse. **STALL** is *Ancient Cant.*

THIMBLE-RIG: a noted cheating game played at fairs and places of great public thronging, consisting of two or three thimbles rapidly and dexterously placed over a pea, when the **THIMBLE-RIGGER,** suddenly ceasing, asks you under which thimble the pea is found. If you are not a practiced hand you will lose nine times out of ten any bet you may happen to make with him. The pea is sometimes concealed under his nail.

TIME O' DAY: a dodge, the latest aspect of affairs; "that's your **TIME O' DAY,**" i.e., *Euge*, well done; to **PUT A PERSON UP TO THE TIME O' DAY,** let him know what is o' clock—to instruct him in the knowledge needful for him.

GAMBLERS

BESTER: a low betting cheat.

BLACK-LEG: a rascal, swindler, or card cheat.

BONNET: a gambling cheat. "A man who sits at a gaming table, and appears to be playing against the table; when a stranger enters, the **BONNET** generally wins." — *Times*, Nov. 17, 1856. Also, a pretense or make-believe, a sham bidder at auctions.

BONNETTER: one who induces another to gamble.

BROAD-FENCER: card seller at races.

BROADS: cards. **BROADSMAN,** a card sharper.

BROWN PAPERMEN: low gamblers.

BUTTONER: a man who entices another to play.—*See* **BONNETTER** *above.*

CHARLEY-PITCHERS: low, cheating gamblers.

FLUE FAKERS: chimney sweeps; also low sporting characters, who are so termed from their chiefly betting on the *Great Sweeps*.

LEGS or **BLACKLEGS:** disreputable sporting characters and racecourse *habitues*.

LEVANTER: a card sharper or defaulting gambler. A correspondent states that it was formerly the custom to give out to the creditors, when a person was in pecuniary difficulties, and it was convenient for him to keep away, that he was gone to the *East*, or the **LEVANT;**

hence, when one loses a bet and decamps without settling, he is said to LEVANT.

MUCK-SNIPE: one who had been "MUCKED OUT" or beggared, at gambling.

OUT-SIDER: a person who does not habitually bet or is not admitted to the "Ring." Also, a horse whose name does not appear among the "favourites."

ROOK: a cheat or tricky gambler; the opposite of PIGEON.—*Old.*

◆ GAMBLING

BAR or **BARRING:** excepting; in common use in the betting ring; "I bet against the field **BAR** two." The Irish use of **BARRIN'** is very similar.

BOOK: an arrangement of bets for and against, chronicled in a pocket-book made for that purpose; "making a **BOOK** upon it," common phrase to denote the general arrangement of a person's bets on a race. "That does not suit my **BOOK**," *i.e.*, does not accord with my other arrangements. *Shakespere* uses **BOOK** in the sense of "a paper of conditions."

DIBBS: money; so called from the buckle bones of sheep, which have been used from the earliest times for gambling purposes, being thrown up five at a time and caught on the back of the hand like halfpence.

DRUM: a house, a lodging, a street; **HAZARD-DRUM**, a gambling house; **FLASH-DRUM**, a house of ill-fame.

FIDDLING: doing any odd jobs in the street, holding horses, carrying parcels, &c. for a living. Among the middle classes, **FIDDLING** means idling away time or trifling; and amongst sharpers, it means gambling.

HEDGE: to secure a doubtful bet by making others.—*Turf.*

HELL: a fashionable gambling house. In printing offices, the term is generally applied to the old tin box in which is thrown the broken or spoilt type, purchased by the founders for re-casting. *Nearly obsolete.*

MUCK OUT: to clean out. Often applied to one utterly ruining an adversary in gambling. From the *Provincial* **MUCK**, dirt.

OFFICE: "to give the OFFICE," to give a hint dishonestly to a confederate, thereby enabling him to win a game or bet, the profits being shared.

OUT-SIDER: a person who does not habitually bet or is not admitted to the "Ring." Also, a horse whose name does not appear among the "favourites."

PLANT: a dodge, a preconcerted swindle; a position in the street to sell from. **PLANT**, a swindle, may be thus described: a coster will join a party of gaming costers that he never saw before and commence tossing. When sufficient time has elapsed to remove all suspicions of companionship, his mate will come up and commence betting on each of his PAL'S throws with those standing around. By a curious quickness of hand, a coster can make the toss tell favourably for his wagering friend, who meets him in the evening after the play is over and shares the spoil.

PONY: twenty-five pounds. — *Sporting.*

PUT THE POT ON: to bet too much upon one horse. — *Sporting.*

ROULEAU: a packet of sovereigns. — *Gaming.*

SCHOOLING: a low gambling party.

SHINEY RAG: "to win the SHINEY RAG," to be ruined — said in gambling, when anyone continues betting after "luck has set in against him."

TAKE: "to TAKE THE FIELD," when said of a General, to commence operations against the enemy; when a racing man TAKES THE FIELD he stakes his money against the favourite. — *See* TAKE *in the Index for more meanings on page 504.*

GAMES WITH CARDS

BLACK-LEG: a rascal, swindler, or card cheat.

BLIND-HOOKEY: a gambling game at cards.

BONNET: a gambling cheat. "A man who sits at a gaming table and appears to be playing against the table; when a stranger enters, the BONNET generally wins." — *Times*, Nov. 17, 1856. Also, a pretense or make-believe, a sham bidder at auctions.

BRAD-FAKING: playing at cards.

BROADS: cards. **BROADSMAN**, a card sharper.

CURSE OF SCOTLAND: the Nine of Diamonds. Various hypotheses have been set up as to the appellation—that it was the card on which the "Butcher Duke" wrote a cruel order with respect to the rebels after the battle of Culloden; that the diamonds are the nine lozenges in the arms of Dalrymple, Earl of Stair, detested for his share in the Massacre of Glencoe; that it is a corruption of *Cross of Scotland*, the nine diamonds being arranged somewhat after the fashion of the St. Andrew's Cross; but the most probable explanation is, that in the game of Pope Joan the nine of diamonds is the Pope, of whom the Scotch have an especial horror.

DECK: a pack of cards.—*Old*. Used by Bulwer as a *Cant* term. General in the *United States*.

DEUCE: twopence; **DEUCE** at cards or dice, one with two pips or holes.

DIGGERS: spurs; also the spades on cards.

DUMMY: in three-handed whist the person who holds two hands plays **DUMMY**.

EARL OF CORK: the ace of diamonds.—*Hibernicism*.

> "What do you mean by the Earl of Cork?" asked Mr. Squander. "The ace of diamonds, your honour. It's the worst ace, and the poorest card in the pack, and is called the Earl of Cork, because he's the poorest nobleman in Ireland."—*Carleton's Traits and Stories of the Irish Peasantry*.

ELBOW: "to shake one's **ELBOW**," to play at cards.

GRACE-CARD: the ace of hearts.

JACKS, HALF-JACKS: card counters, resembling in size and appearance sovereigns and half-sovereigns, for which they are occasionally passed to simple persons. In large gambling establishments the "heaps of gold" are frequently composed mainly of **JACKS**.

JOGUL: to play up, at cards or other game. *Spanish*, **JUGAR**.

KNOCK-IN: the game of *loo*.

LEVANTER: a card sharper or defaulting gambler. A correspondent states that it was formerly the custom to give out to the creditors, when a person was in pecuniary difficulties and it was convenient for him to keep away, that he was gone to the *East,* or the LEVANT; hence, when one loses a bet and decamps without settling, he is said to LEVANT.

NED STOKES: the four of spades.—*North Hampshire.—See Gentleman's Magazine* for 1791, p.141.

PAM: the knave of clubs; or, in street phraseology, Lord Palmerston.

PUT: a game at cards.

QUEEN BESS: the Queen of Clubs—perhaps because that queen, history says, was of a swarthy complexion.—*North Hampshire.—See Gentleman's Magazine* for 1791, p. 141.

RUBBER: a term at whist, &c., two games out of three.—*Old,* 1677.

HORSE RACING and OTHER RACING

BOOK: an arrangement of bets for and against, chronicled in a pocketbook made for that purpose; "making a BOOK upon it," common phrase to denote the general arrangement of a person's bets on a race. "That does not suit my BOOK," *i.e.,* does not accord with my other arrangements. *Shakespere* uses BOOK in the sense of "a paper of conditions."

BROAD-FENCER: card seller at races.

CART: a racecourse.

CULLING or **CULING:** stealing from the carriages on racecourses.

DARK: "keep it DARK," *i.e.,* secret. **DARK HORSE,** in racing phraseology a horse whose chance of success is unknown and whose capabilities have not been made the subject of comment.

DRAG: a cart of any kind, a coach; gentlemen drive to the races in DRAGS.

HEDGE: to secure a doubtful bet by making others.—*Turf.*

LEGS or **BLACKLEGS:** disreputable sporting characters and racecourse *habitues.*

NECK OR NOTHING: desperate.—*Racing phrase.*

OUT-SIDER: a person who does not habitually bet or is not admitted to the "Ring." Also, a horse whose name does not appear among the "favourites."

PUT THE POT ON: to bet too much upon one horse. — *Sporting.*

RING: a generic term given to horse racing and pugilism. The latter is sometimes termed the PRIZE-RING. From the practice of forming the crowd into a RING around the combatants or outside the racecourse.

RUCK: the undistinguished crowd; "to come in with the RUCK," to arrive at the winning post among the non-winning horses. — *Racing term.*

SCRATCH: to strike a horse's name out of the list of runners in a particular race. "Tomboy was SCRATCHED for the Derby, at 10, a.m., on Wednesday," from which period all bets made in reference to him (with one exception) are void. — *See P.P. — Turf.*

SCRATCH-RACE: (on the *Turf*), a race where any horse, aged, winner, or loser, can run with any weights; in fact, a race without restrictions. At *Cambridge* a boat-race, where the crews are drawn by lot.

SLOGGERS: *i.e.,* SLOW-GOERS, the second division of race-boats at *Cambridge.* At *Oxford* they are called TORPIDS. — *University.*

TAKE: "to TAKE THE FIELD," when said of a General, to commence operations against the enemy; when a racing man TAKES THE FIELD he stakes his money against the favourite. — *See* TAKE *in the Index for more meanings on page 504.*

TORPIDS: the second-class race-boats at Oxford, answering to the *Cambridge* SLOGGERS.

TURF: horse racing and betting thereon; "on the TURF," one who occupies himself with racecourse business; said also of a street-walker, nymph of the pavé.

WALK OVER: a re-election without opposition. — *Parliamentary*, but derived from the *Turf*, where a horse — which has no rivals entered — WALKS OVER the course and wins without exertion.

TOSSING DICE and COINS

BONES: dice; also called ST. HUGH'S BONES.

BRAD-FAKING: playing at cards.

CHATTS: dice—formerly the gallows; a bunch of seals.

COG: to cheat at dice.—*Shakespere*. Also, to agree with, as one cog-wheel does with another.

COVER-DOWN: a tossing coin with a false cover, enabling either head or tail to be shown, according as the cover is left on or taken off.

DESPATCHES: false "dice with two sides, double four, double five, and double six."—*Times*, 27th November, 1856.

DEUCE: twopence; DEUCE at cards or dice, one with two pips or holes.

DEVIL'S TEETH: dice.

DIBBS: money; so called from the buckle bones of sheep, which have been used from the earliest times for gambling purposes, being thrown up five at a time and caught on the back of the hand like halfpence.

FULLAMS: false dice, which always turn up high.—*Shakespere*.

GAFFING: tossing halfpence or counters.—*North*, where it means tossing up three pennies.

GRAYS: halfpennies, with either two "heads" or two "tails," both sides alike. *Low gamblers* use GRAYS, and they cost from 2d. to 6d. each.

IVORIES: teeth; "a box" or "cage of IVORIES," a set of teeth, the mouth; "wash your IVORIES," *i.e.*, "drink." The word is also used to denote DICE.

NEWMARKET: in tossing halfpence, when it is agreed that the first toss shall be decisive, the play is said to be NEWMARKET.

ODD MAN: a street or public-house game at tossing. The number of players is three. Each tosses up a coin, and if two come down head and one tail or *vice versa*, the last is ODD MAN, and loses or wins as may have been agreed upon. Frequently used to victimise a "flat." If all three be alike, then the toss goes for nothing and the coppers are again "*skied.*"

PLANT: a dodge, a preconcerted swindle; a position in the street to sell from. PLANT, a swindle, may be thus described: a coster will join a party of gaming costers that he never saw before and commence tossing. When sufficient time has elapsed to remove all suspicions of companionship, his mate will come up and commence betting on each of his PAL'S throws with those standing around. By a curious quickness of hand, a coster can make the toss tell favourably for his wagering friend, who meets him in the evening after the play is over and shares the spoil.

SHOVE-HALFPENNY: a gambling street game.

SICES or **SIZES:** a throw of sixes at dice.

SINKS: a throw of fives at dice. *French,* CINQS.

SKIE: to throw upwards, to toss "coppers." — *See* **ODD MAN** *above.*

TAT BOX: a dice box.

TATS: dice.

THREE-UP: a gambling game played by costers. Three halfpennies are thrown up and when they fall all "heads," or all "tails," it is a mark; and the man who gets the greatest number of marks out of a given amount—three, five, or more—wins. The costers are very quick and skillful at this game and play fairly at it amongst themselves; but should a stranger join in they invariably unite to cheat him.

OTHER GAMES

AUNT SALLY: A favourite game on racecourses and at fairs, consisting of a wooden head mounted on a stick, firmly fixed in the ground; in the nose of which, or rather in that part of the facial arrangement of AUNT SALLY which is generally considered incomplete without a nasal projection, a tobacco pipe is inserted. The fun consists on standing at a distance and demolishing AUNT SALLY'S pipe-clay projection with short bludgeons, very similar to the half of a broom handle. The Duke of Beaufort is a "crack hand" at smashing pipe noses, and his performances two years ago on Brighton racecourse are yet fresh in remembrance. The noble Duke, in the summer months, frequently drives the old London and Brighton four-horse mail coach, "Age"—a whim singular enough now, but common forty years ago.

BOWL-OUT: to put out of the game, to remove out of one's way, to detect. — *Cricketing term.*

COCKSHY: a game at fairs and races, where trinkets are set upon sticks, and for one penny three throws at them are accorded, the thrower keeping whatever he knocks off. From the ancient game of throwing or "shying" at live cocks.

DOWN THE DOLLY: a favourite gambling contrivance, often seen in the tap rooms of public houses, at racecourses, and fairs, consisting of a round board and the figure of an old man or "doll," down which is a spiral hole. A marble is dropped "down the doll," and stops in one of the small holes or pits (numbered) on the board. The bet is decided according as the marble stops on a high or low figure.

FID FAD: a game similar to chequers or drafts, played in the West of England.

FLUKE: at billiards, playing for one thing and getting another. Hence, generally what one gets accidentally, an unexpected advantage, "more by luck than wit."

HUNTER PITCHING: cockshies or three throws a penny. — *See* **COCKSHY** *above.*

JIGGER: a door; "dub the **JIGGER**," shut the door. *Ancient Cant,* **GYGER**. In billiards the *bridge* on the table is often termed the **JIGGER**."

KNOCK-IN: the game of *loo.*

LOVE: at billiards, "five to none" would be "five **LOVE**," —a **LOVE** being the same as when one player does not score at all.

POT: to finish; "don't **POT** me," term used at billiards. This word was much used by our soldiers in the Crimea, for firing at the enemy from a hole or ambush. These were called **POT-SHOTS**.

PRICK THE GARTER or **PITCH THE NOB:** a gambling and cheating game common at fairs and generally practiced by thimble riggers. It consists of a "garter" or a piece of list doubled and then folded up tight. The bet is made upon your asserting that you can, with a pin, "prick" the point at which the garter is doubled. The garter is then unfolded and nine times out of ten you will find that you have been deceived, and that you pricked one of the false folds. The owner of the garter, I should state, holds the ends tightly with one hand. This was, doubtless, originally a Gipsey game, and we are informed by *Brand* that it was much practiced by the Gipseys in the time of *Shakespere.* In those days, it was termed **PRICKING AT THE BELT** or **FAST AND LOOSE**.

RING: a generic term given to horse racing and pugilism. The latter is sometimes termed the PRIZE-RING. From the practice of forming the crowd into a RING around the combatants or outside the racecourse.

SHOVE-HALFPENNY: a gambling street game.

SHY: to fling; COCK-SHY, a game at fairs, consisting of throwing short sticks at trinkets set upon other sticks—both name and practice derives from the old game of throwing or SHYING at live cocks.

SKITTLES: a game similar to Ten Pins, which, when interdicted by the Government was altered to Nine Pins, or SKITTLES. They are set up in an alley and are *thrown at* (not bowled) with a round piece of hard wood, shaped like a small flat cheese. The costers consider themselves the best players in London.

SMUGGINGS: snatching or purloining—shouted out by boys, when snatching the tops or small play property, of other lads, and then running off at full speed.

> "Tops are in; spin 'em agin.
> Tops are out; SMUGGING about."

SPIN-EM ROUNDS: a street game consisting of a piece of brass, wood, or iron, balanced on a pin, and turned quickly around on a board, when the point, arrow-shaped, stops at a number and decides the bet one way or the other. The contrivance very much resembles a sea compass and was formerly the gambling accompaniment of London piemen. The apparatus then was erected on the tin lids of their pie cans, and the bets were ostensibly for pies, but more frequently for "coppers," when no policeman frowned upon the scene, and when two or three apprentices or porters happened to meet.

STUMPED: bowled out, done for, bankrupt, poverty-stricken. —*Cricketing term.*

TAW: a large or principal marble; "I'll be one on your TAW," I will pay you out or be even with you—a simile taken from boys aiming always at winning the TAW when playing at marbles.

THIMBLE-RIG: a noted cheating game played at fairs and places of great public thronging, consisting of two or three thimbles rapidly and dexterously placed over a pea, when the THIMBLE-RIGGER, suddenly ceasing, asks you under which thimble the pea is found. If you are not a practiced hand you will lose nine times out of ten any bet you may happen to make with him. The pea is sometimes concealed under his nail.

TIBBING OUT: going out of bounds.—*Charterhouse*.

TIN-POT: "he plays a TIN-POT game," *i.e.*, a low or shabby one. —*Billiards*.

PICKPOCKETS

BUZ: to pick pockets; BUZ-FAKING, robbing.

BUZ-BLOAK: a pickpocket, who principally confines his attention to purses and loose cash. *Grose* gives BUZ-GLOAK (or CLOAK?), an *Ancient Cant* word. BUZ-NAPPER, a young pickpocket.

BUZ-NAPPER'S ACADEMY: school in which young thieves are trained. Figures are dressed up, and experienced tutors stand in various difficult attitudes for the boys to practice upon. When clever enough they are sent on the streets. It is reported that a house of this nature is situated in a court near Hatton Garden. The system is well explained in *Dickens' Oliver Twist*.

BUZZERS: pickpockets. *Grose* gives BUZ COVE and BUZ GLOAK, the latter is very *Ancient Cant*.

CHARIOT-BUZZING: picking pockets in an omnibus.

CHUCKING A STALL: where one rogue walks in front of a person while another picks his pockets.

CLY-FAKER: a pickpocket.

CONVEYANCER: a pickpocket. *Shakespere* uses the *Cant* expression, **Conveyer,** a thief. The same term is also *French slang*.

DIVE: to pick pockets.

DIVERS: pickpockets.

FAKING A CLY: picking a pocket.

FORK OUT: bring out one's money, to pay the bill, to STAND FOR or treat a friend; to hand over what does not belong to you.—*Old Cant* term for picking pockets, and very curious it is to trace its origin. In the early part of the last century, a little book on purloining was published, and of course it had to give the latest modes. FORKING was the newest method, and it consisted in thrusting the fingers stiff and open into the pocket, and then quickly closing them and extracting any article.

FRISK A CLY: to empty a pocket.

GONNOF or **GUN:** a fool, a bungler, an amateur pickpocket. A correspondent thinks this may be a corruption of *gone off*, on the analogy of **GO-ALONG**; but the term is really as old as *Chaucer's* time. During Kett's rebellion in Norfolk, in the reign of Edward VI., a song was sung by the insurgents in which the term occurs—

> The country GNOFFES, Hob, Dick, and Hick,
>   With clubbes and clouted shoou,
> Shall fill up Dussyn dale
>   With slaughtered bodies soone.

KIDSMAN: one who trains boys to thieve and pick pockets successfully.

KNUCKLE: to pick pockets after the most approved method.

KNUCKLER: a pickpocket.

LIFT: to steal, pick pockets; "there's a clock been **LIFTED**," said when a watch has been stolen. The word is as old as the Border forays, and is used by *Shakespere.* **SHOPLIFTER** is a recognized term.

MOLL-TOOLER: a female pickpocket.

NIPPER: a small boy. *Old Cant* for a boy cut-purse.

PATENT COAT: a coat with pockets inside the skirts—termed **PATENT** from the difficulty of picking them.

PENISULAR or **MOLL-TOOLER:** a female pickpocket.

SNOTTER or **WIPE-HAULER:** a pickpocket who commits great depredations upon gentlemen's pocket handkerchiefs.—*North.*

STOOK HAULER or **BUZZER:** a thief who takes pocket-handkerchiefs.

TAIL BUZZER: a thief who picks coat pockets.

TOOL: to pick pockets.

TOOLER: a pickpocket. **MOLL-TOOLER**, a female pickpocket.

WATCHMAKER: a pickpocket or stealer of watches.

WIRE: a thief with long fingers, expert at picking ladies' pockets.

PROSTITUTES

BLOWEN: a showy or flaunting prostitute, a thief's paramour. In *Wilts*, a BLOWEN is a blossom. *Germ.* **BLUHEN**, to bloom.

> "O du *bulhende* Madchen viel schone Willkomm!"
> —*German Song.*

Possibly however, the street term, BLOWEN may mean one whose reputation has been BLOWN UPON, or damaged.

CUTTY PIPE: a short clay pipe. *Scotch*, CUTTY, short. *Cutty-sark*, a scantily draped lady is so called by *Burns*.

DEMIREP (or RIP): a courtesan. Contraction of DEMI-REPUTATION —*Grose.*

DOLLYMOP: a tawdrily dressed maidservant, a street-walker.

GAD: a trapesing, slatternly woman.—*Gipsey. Anglo Saxon,* GADELYING.

GAY: loose, dissipated; "GAY woman," a kept mistress or prostitute.

JACK: a low prostitute.

KIDDLEYWINK: a small shop where they retail the commodities of a village store. Also, a loose woman.

NYMPH OF THE PAVE: (*French*, PAVE) a street-walker, a girl of the town.

POLL: a prostitute. POLLED UP, living with a woman without being married to her.

SHAKE: a prostitute, a disreputable man or woman.—*North.*

SHAKESTER or **SHICKSTER:** a prostitute. Amongst costermongers this term is invariably applied to *ladies* or the wives of tradesmen, and females generally of the classes immediately above them.

PROSTITUTION

BAWDYKEN: a brothel.—*See* KEN *page 269.*

BULLY: a braggart; but in the language of the streets, a man of the most degraded morals, who protects prostitutes, and lives off their miserable earnings. — *Shakespere*, Midsummer Night's Dream, iii. 1; iv. 2.

DRUM: a house, a lodging, a street; HAZARD-DRUM, a gambling house; FLASH-DRUM, a house of ill-fame.

FANCY: the favourite sports, pets, or pastime of a person, *the tan of low life*. Pugilists are sometime termed THE FANCY. *Shakespere* uses the word in the sense of a favourite or pet; and the paramour of a prostitute is still called her FANCY-MAN.

To **JOE BLAKE THE BARTLEMY:** to visit a low woman.

KNOCKING-SHOP: a brothel or disreputable house frequented by prostitutes.

LOOSE: — *See* ON THE LOOSE *below.*

MOTT: a girl of indifferent character. Formerly *Mort. Dutch,* MOTT-KAST, a harlotry.

NANNY-SHOP: a disreputable house.

ON THE LOOSE: obtaining a living by prostitution, in reality, on the streets. The term is applied to females only, excepting in the case of SPREES, when men carousing are sometimes said to be ON THE LOOSE.

PENSIONER: a man of the lowest morals who lives off the miserable earnings of a prostitute.

TRAPESING: gadding or gossiping about in a slatternly way. — *North.*

TURF: horse racing and betting thereon; "on the TURF," one who occupies himself with racecourse business; said also of a street-walker, nymph of the pavé.

THIEVES

BEAKER-HUNTER: a stealer of poultry.

BLOWEN: a showy or flaunting prostitute, a thief's paramour. In *Wilts*, a BLOWEN is a blossom. *Germ.* BLUHEN, to bloom.

"O du *bulhende* Madchen viel schone Willkomm!"
—*German Song.*

Possibly however, the street term, **BLOWEN** may mean one whose reputation has been **BLOWN UPON**, or damaged.

BLUDGERS: low thieves, who use violence.

BLUE-PIGEON FLYERS: journeymen plumbers, glaziers, and others, who, under the plea of repairing houses, strip off the lead, and make way with it. Sometimes they get off with it by wrapping it round their bodies.

BODY-SNATCHERS: cat stealers.

BUG-HUNTERS: low wretches who plunder drunken men.

CONVEYANCER: a pickpocket. *Shakespere* uses the *Cant* expression, **CONVEYER,** a thief. The same term is also *French slang.*

CRACKSMAN: a burglar.

CROSS-COVE and **MOLLISHER:** a man and woman who live by thieving.

CROW: one who watches whilst another commits a theft, a confederate in a robbery. The **CROW** looks to see that the way is clear, whilst the **SNEAK**, his partner, commits the depredation.

CUTTER: a ruffian, a cut purse. Of *Robin Hood* it was said:

> "So being outlawed (as 'tis told),
>   He with a crew went forth
> Of lusty **CUTTERS**, bold and strong,
>   And robbed in the north."

This *Ancient Cant* word now survives in the phrase, "to swear like a **CUTTER.**"

DOXY: female companion of a thief or beggar. In the West of England, the women frequently call their little girls **DOXIES**, in a familiar or endearing sense. A learned divine once described *orthodoxy* as being a man's own **DOXY**, and *heterodoxy* another man's **DOXY**.—*Ancient Cant.*

DRAGSMEN: fellows who cut trunks from the backs of carriages. They sometimes have a light cart, and "drop behind" the plundered vehicle, and then drive off in an opposite direction with the booty.

DRUMMER: a robber who first makes his victims insensible by drugs or violence, and then plunders them.

DUNAKER: a stealer of cows or calves.—*Nearly obsolete.*

FAMILY MEN or **PEOPLE:** thieves or burglars.

FATHER or **FENCE** a buyer of stolen property.

FENCE or **FENCER:** a purchaser or receiver of stolen goods; FENCE, the shop or warehouse of a FENCER.—*Old Cant.*

FIDLUM BEN: thieves who take anything they can lay their hands upon.

FINDER: one who FINDS bacon and meat at the market before they are lost, *i.e.*, steals them.

GO-ALONG: a thief.—*Household Words*, No. 183.

KEN-CRACKERS: housebreakers.

KIDDY: a man or boy. Formerly a low thief.

KIDNAPPER: one who steals children or adults. From KID, a child, and NAB (corrupted to NAP), to steal or seize.

KIDSMAN: one who trains boys to thieve and pick pockets successfully.

KINCHIN COVE: a man who robs children; a little man.—*Ancient Cant.*

LITTLE SNAKES-MAN: a little thief, who is generally passed through a small aperture to open any door to let in the rest of the gang.

LULLY PRIGGERS: rogues who steal wet clothes hung on lines to dry.

LUMPERS: low thieves who haunt wharves and docks, and rob vessels; persons who sell old goods for new.

MOLLISHER: a low girl or woman; generally a female cohabitating with a man, and jointly getting their living by thieving.

NIBBLE: to take or steal. NIBBLER, a petty thief.

NOSE: a thief who turns informer or Queen's evidence; a spy or watch; "on the NOSE," on the look out.

PANNY: a house—public or otherwise; "flash PANNY," a public-house used by thieves; PANNY MEN, housebreakers.

PETERER or **PETERMAN:** one who follows hackney and stage coaches, and cuts off the portmanteaus and trunks from behind.—*Nearly obsolete. Ancient* term for a fisherman, still used at Gravesend.

PRIG: a thief. Used by *Addison* in the sense of a coxcomb. *Ancient Cant*, probably from the *Saxon*, PRICC-AN, to filch, &c.—*Shakespere*. PRIG, to steal or rob. PRIGGING, thieving. In *Scotland* the term PRIG is used in a different sense from what it is in England. In Glasgow, or at Aberdeen, "to PRIG a salmon," would be to cheapen it, or seek for an abatement in the price. A story is told of two Scotchmen, visitors to London, who got into sad trouble a few years ago by announcing their intention of "PRIGGING a hat" which they had espied in a fashionable manufacture's window, and which one of them thought he would like to possess.

PROP-NAILER: a man who steals, or rather snatches, pins from gentlemen's scarfs.

PUDDING SNAMMER: one who robs a cook shop.

PULLEY: a confederate thief—generally a woman.

RAMPSMAN: a highway robber who uses violence when necessary.

RAP: a halfpenny; frequently used generically for money, thus; "I hav'nt a RAP," *i.e.*, I have no money whatever; "I don't care a RAP," &c. Originally a species of counterfeit coin used for small change in *Ireland*, against the use of which a proclamation was issued, 5th May, 1737. Small copper or base metal coins are still called RAPPEN in the Swiss cantons, Irish robbers are called RAPPAREES.

SAWNEY: bacon. SAWNEY HUNTER, one who steals bacon.

SCAMP: a graceless fellow, a rascal; formerly the *Cant* term for plundering and thieving. A ROYAL-SCAMP was a highwayman, whilst a FOOT-SCAMP was an ordinary thief with nothing but his legs to trust to in case of an attempt at capture. Some have derived SCAMP from *qui ex campo exit*, viz., one who leaves the field, a deserter.

SHOP BOUNCER or **SHOP LIFTER:** a person generally respectably attired, who, while being served with a small article at a shop, steals one of more value. *Shakespere* has the word LIFTER, a thief.

SNEAKSMAN: a shoplifter, a petty, cowardly thief.

SNEEZE LURKER: a thief who throws snuff in a person's face and then robs him.

SNOW GATHERERS or **SNOW-DROPPERS:** rogues who steal linen from hedges and drying grounds.

STAGGER: one who looks out or watches.

STALLSMAN: an accomplice.

STOOK HAULER or **BUZZER:** a thief who takes pocket-handkerchiefs.

SWAGSMAN: one who carries the booty after a burglary.

THIMBLE TWISTERS: thieves who rob persons of their watches.

TOSHERS: men who steal copper from ships' bottoms in the Thames.

TOUT: to look-out or watch.—*Old Cant.*

WATCHMAKER: a pickpocket or stealer of watches.

THIEVING

ARGOT: a term used amongst London thieves for their secret or *Cant* language. *French* term for slang.

BLEED: to victimise or extract money from a person, to spunge on, to make suffer vindictively.

BLOW UP: to make a noise or scold; formerly a *Cant* expression used amongst thieves, now a recognized and respectable phrase. **BLOWING UP**, a jobation, a scolding.

BONE: to steal or pilfer. **BONED**, seized, apprehended.—*Old.*

BOSMAN: a farmer; "faking a **BOSMAN** on the main toby," robbing a farmer on the highway. **BOSS**, a master.—*American*. Both terms from the *Dutch*, **BOSCH-MAN**, one who lives in the woods; otherwise *Boshjeman* or *Bushman*.

BOTTLE-HOLDER: an assistant to a "Second," —*Pugilistic*; an abettor; also, the bridegroom's man at a wedding.

BRACE UP: to pawn stolen goods.

BUZ: to pick pockets; **BUZ-FAKING**, robbing.

CABBAGE: pieces of cloth said to be purloined by tailors.

CABBAGE: to pilfer or purloin. Termed by Johnson a *Cant* word, but adopted by later lexicographers as a respectable term. Said to have been first used in this sense by *Arbuthnot*.

CAT AND KITTEN SNEAKING: stealing pint and quart pots from public-houses.

CAT: a lady's muff; "to free a **CAT**," *i.e.*, steal a muff.

CHRISTENING: erasing the name of the maker from a stolen watch, and inserting a fictitious one in its place.

CHURCH A YACK: (or watch), to take the works of a watch from its original case and put them into another one, to avoid detection. — *See* **CHRISTENING** *above.*

CLIFT: to steal.

CLINK-RIG: stealing tankards from public-houses, taverns, &c.

CLY: a pocket. — *Old Cant* for to steal. A correspondent derives this word from the *Old English,* **CLEYES,** claw; *Anglo Saxon,* **CLEA.** This pronunciation is still retained in Norfolk; thus, to **CLY** would mean to pounce upon, snatch. — *See* **FRISK** *page 139.*

CONVEY: to steal; "**CONVEY**, the wise it call."

COW-LICK: The term given to the lock of hair which costermongers and thieves usually twist forward from the ear; a large greasy curl upon the cheek, seemingly licked into shape. The opposite of **NEWGATE-KNOCKER.** — *See page 242.*

CRACK A KIRK: to break into a church or chapel.

CRIB: to steal or purloin.

CROSS: a general term amongst thieves expressive of their plundering profession, the opposite of **SQUARE.** "To get anything on the **CROSS**" is to obtain it surreptitiously. "**CROSS-FANNING** in a crowd," robbing persons of their scarf pins.

CROSS-CRIB: a house frequented by thieves.

CULLING or **CULING:** stealing from the carriages on racecourses.

DAMPER: a shop till; to **DRAW A DAMPER**, *i.e.*, rob a till.

DEAD-LURK: entering a dwelling-house during divine service.

DONE FOR A RAMP: convicted for thieving.

DOSE: three months' imprisonment as a known thief. — *See* **BRAGGADOCIO** *page 259.*

DRAGGING: robbing carts, &c.

DRAWING TEETH: wrenching off knockers.

EASE: rob; "**EASING** a bloak," robbing a man.

FAKE: to cheat or swindle; to do anything; to go on or continue; to make or construct; to steal or rob—a verb variously used. **FAKED,** done or done for; "**FAKE AWAY,** there's no down," go on, there is nobody looking. *Mayhew* says it is from the *Latin*, **FACIMENTUM.**

FAKEMENT: a false begging petition, any act of robbery, swindling, or deception.

FAKEMENT CHARLEY: the owner's private mark.

FENCE or FENCER: a purchasher or reciever of stolen goods; **FENCE,** the shop or warehouse of a **FENCER.**—*Old Cant.*

FENCE: to sell or pawn stolen property to a **FENCER.**

FILCH: to steal or purloin. Originally a *Cant* word, derived from the **FILCHES,** or hooks, thieves used to carry, to hook clothes or any portable articles from open windows.—*Vide Decker.* It was considered a *Cant* or *Gipsey* term up to the beginning of the last century. *Harman* has "**FYLCHE,** to robbe."

FLATTY-KEN: a public house, the landlord of which is ignorant of the practices of the thieves and tramps who frequent it.

FLIMP: to hustle or rob.

FOX: to cheat or rob.—*Eton College.*

FOXING: watching in the streets for any occurrence which may be turned to a profitable account.—*See* **MOOCHING** *page 116.*

FREE: to steal; generally applied to horses.

GAME: a term variously applied; "are you **GAME?**" have you courage enough? "what's your little **GAME?**" what are you going to do? "come, none of your **GAMES,**" be quiet, don't annoy me; "on the **GAME,**" out thieving.

GIFT: any article which has been stolen and afterwards sold at a low price.

GIVE: to strike or scold; "I'll **GIVE** it to you," I will thrash you. Formerly, *to rob.*

HOCUS: to drug a person, and then rob him. The **HOCUS** generally consists of snuff and beer.

HOISTING: shoplifting.

HOOK OR BY CROOK: by fair means or foul—in allusion to the hook which footpads used to carry to steal from open windows, &c., and from which **HOOK**, to take or steal, has been derived. Mentioned in *Hudibras* as a *Cant* term.

HOOK: to steal or rob.—*See the following.*

HOOK-UM SNIVEY: (formerly "hook *and* snivey") a low expression meaning to cheat by feigning sickness or other means. Also a piece of thick iron wire crooked at one end, and fastened into a wooden handle, for the purpose of undoing from the outside the wooden bolt of a door.

IT'S GOOD ON THE STAR: it's easy to open.

JEMMY: a crowbar.

JILT: a crowbar or housebreaking implement.

JOB: a short piece of work, a prospect of employment. *Johnson* describes **JOB** as a low word, without etymology. It is, and was, however, a *Cant* word, and a **JOB**, two centuries ago, was an arranged robbery. Even at the present day it is mainly confined to the street, in the sense of employment for a short time. Amongst undertakers a **JOB** signifies a funeral; "to do a **JOB**," conduct anyone's funeral; "by the **JOB**," *i.e.*, *piece*-work, as opposed to *time*-work. A **JOB** in political phraseology is a government office or contract, obtained by secret influence or favouritism.

JUMP: to seize or rob; "to **JUMP** a man," to pounce upon him, and either rob or maltreat him; "to **JUMP** a house," to rob it.—*See* **GO** *page 334.*

KIDMENT: a pocket-handkerchief fastened to the pocket and partially hung out to entrap thieves.

KNAP: to receive, to take, to steal.

LAY: to watch; "on the **LAY**," on the look out.—*Shakespere.*

LIFT: to steal, pick pockets; "there's a clock been **LIFTED**," said when a watch has been stolen. The word is as old as the Border forays, and is used by *Shakespere.* **SHOPLIFTER** is a recognized term.

MAKE: a successful theft or swindle.

MAKE: to steal.

NAP or NAB: to take, steal, or receive; "You'll **NAP** it," *i.e.*, you will catch a beating!—*North*; also *Old Cant.*—*Bulwer's Paul Clifford.*

NEWGATE KNOCKER: the term given to the lock of hair which costermongers and thieves usually twist back towards the ear. The shape is supposed to resemble the knocker on the prisoners' door at Newgate—a resemblance that would appear to carry a rather unpleasant suggestion to the wearer. Sometime termed a COBBLER'S KNOT or COW-LICK.—*See* COW-LICK *above.*

NIBBLE: to take or steal. NIBBLER, a petty thief.

NIMMING: stealing. Immediately from the *German*, NEHMEN. Motherwell, the Scotch poet, thought the old word NIM (to snatch or pick up) was derived from *nam, nam,* the tiny words or cries of an infant, when eating anything which pleases its little palate. A negro proverb has the word:

> "Buckra man *nam* crab,
> Crab *nam* buckra man."

Or, in the buckra man's language—

> "White man eat (or steal) the crab,
> And the crab eats the white man."

NIP: to steal, to take up quickly.

OGLE: to look or reconnoitre.

ON THE FLY: getting one's living by thieving or other illegitimate means; the phrase is applied to men the same as ON THE LOOSE is to women.

ON THE NOSE: on the watch or look out.—*See* NOSE *page 57.*

PALMING: robbing shops by pairs—one thief bargaining with apparent intent to purchase, whilst the other watches his opportunity to steal. An amusing example of PALMING came off some time since. A man entered a "ready made" boot and shoe shop and desired to be shown a pair of boots—his companion staying outside and amusing himself by looking in at the window. The one who required to be fresh shod was apparently of a humble and deferential turn, for he placed his hat on the floor directly he stepped in the shop. Boot after boot was tried on until at last a fit was obtained—when lo, forth came a man, snatched up the customer's hat left near the door, and down the street he ran as fast as his legs could carry him. Away went the customer after his hat, and Crispin, standing at the door, clapped his hands and shouted, "go it, you'll catch him,"—little thinking that it was a concerted trick, and that neither his boots nor the customer would ever return. **PALMING** sometimes refers to secreting money or rings in the hand.

PANNY: a house—public or otherwise; "flash **PANNY**," a public-house used by thieves; **PANNY MEN**, housebreakers.

PANTILE: a hat. The term **PANTILE** is properly applied to the mould into which the sugar is poured which is afterwards known as "loaf sugar." Thus, **PANTILE**, from whence comes the phrase "a sugar loaf hat," originally signified a tall, conical hat, in shape similar to that usually represented as the head gear of a bandit. From **PANTILE**, the more modern slang term **Tile** has been derived.—*Halliwell* gives **PANTILE SHOP**, a meeting-house.

PATTER: to talk. **PATTER FLASH**, to speak the language of thieves, *Cant*.

PIGEON or **BLUEY CRACKING:** breaking into empty houses and stealing lead.

PINCH: to steal or cheat; also, to catch or apprehend.

PLANT: to mark a person out for plunder or robbery, to conceal, or place.—*Old Cant*.

POLL or **POLLING:** one thief robbing another of part of their booty. —*Hall's Union*, 1548.

PRAD NAPPING: horse stealing.

PRIG: a thief. Used by *Addison* in the sense of a coxcomb. *Ancient Cant*, probably from the *Saxon*, **PRICC-AN**, to filch, &c.—*Shakespere*. **PRIG**, to steal or rob. **PRIGGING**, thieving. In *Scotland* the term **PRIG** is used in a different sense from what it is in England. In Glasgow, or at Aberdeen, "to **PRIG** a salmon," would be to cheapen it or seek for an abatement in the price. A story is told of two Scotchmen, visitors to London, who got into sad trouble a few years ago by announcing their intention of "**PRIGGING** a hat" which they had espied in a fashionable manufacture's window, and which one of them thought he would like to possess.

PRIME PLANT: a good subject for plunder.—*See* **PLANT** *above.*

RAMP: to thieve or rob with violence.

ROOKERY: a low neighbourhood inhabited by dirty Irish and thieves —as **ST. GILES' ROOKERY**.—*Old*. In *Military slang* that part of the barracks occupied by subalterns, often by no mean a pattern of good order.

SHAKE: to take away, to steal, or run off with any thing; "what SHAKES, Bill?" "None," *i.e.*, no chance of committing a robbery.—*See* SHAKE OR SHAKES *page 191.*

SHOE LEATHER!: a thief's warning cry, when he hears footsteps. This exclamation is used in the same spirit as Bruce's friend, who, when he suspected treachery towards him at King Edward's court, in 1306, sent him a purse and a pair of spurs, as a sign that he should use them in making his escape.

SLUMS or **BACK SLUMS:** dark retreats, low neighbourhoods; "the Westminster SLUMS," favourite haunts for thieves.

SMUG: to snatch another's property and run.

SMUGGINGS: snatching or purloining—shouted out by boys, when snatching the tops or small play property, of other lads, and then running off at full speed.

> "Tops are in; spin 'em agin.
> Tops are out; SMUGGING about."

SNAM: to snatch or rob from the person.

SPEEL: to run away, make off; "SPEEL the drum," to go off with stolen property.—*North.*

STALL OFF: to blind, excuse, hide, to screen a robbery during the perpetration of it by an accomplice.

STAR THE GLAZE: to break the window or show glass of a jeweller or other tradesman, and take any valuable articles, and run away. Sometimes the glass is cut with a diamond, and a strip of leather fastened to the piece of glass cut to keep it from falling in and making a noise. Another plan is to cut the sash.

STRIKE THE JIGGER: to pick the lock or break open the door.

SUCK THE MONKEY: to rob a cask of liquor by inserting a straw through a gimlet hole, and sucking a portion of the contents.

SUPER: a watch; SUPER-SCREWING, stealing watches.

SWIM: "a good SWIM," a good run of luck, a long time out of the policeman's clutches.—*Thieves' term.*

TEETH-DRAWING: wrenching off knockers.

TIKE or **BUFFER LURKING:** dog stealing.

TOBY: a road; "high **TOBY**," the turnpike road. "High **TOBY** spice," robbery on horse-back.—*Don Juan,* canto xi., 19.

UNBETTY: to unlock.—*See* **BETTY** *page 308.*

WHIP: To "**WHIP** anything *up*," to take it up quickly; from the method of hoisting heavy goods or horses on board ship by a **WHIP**, or running tackle, from the yard-arm. Generally used to express anything dishonestly taken.—*L' Estrange* and *Johnson.*

YACK: a watch, to "*church* a **YACK**," to take it out of its case to avoid detection.

⊂ℵℂ COUNTERFEITERS and FORGERS

BIT-FAKER or **TURNER OUT:** a coiner of bad money.

BLOB: (from **BLAB**), to talk. Beggars are of two kinds—those who **Screeve** (introduce themselves with a **FAKEMENT**, or false document), and those who **BLOB**, or state their case in their own truly "unvarnished" language.

BRUMS: counterfeit coins.—*Nearly obsolete.* Corruption of *Brummagem* (Bromwicham), the ancient name of *Birmingham,* the great emporium of plated goods and imitation jewellery.

CASE: a bad crown piece. **HALF-A-CASE,** a counterfeit half crown. There are two sources, either of which may have contributed this slang term. **CASER** is the Hebrew word for a crown; and silver coin is frequently counterfeited by coating or **CASING** pewter or iron imitations with silver.

COOPER: to forge or imitate in writing; "**COOPER** a moniker," to forge a signature.

COVER-DOWN: a tossing coin with a false cover, enabling either head or tail to be shown, according as the cover is left on or taken off.

DUFFING: false, counterfeit, worthless.

GAMMY: bad, unfavourable, poor-tempered. Those householders who are known enemies to the street folk and tramps are pronounced by them to be **GAMMY**. **GAMMY** sometimes means forged, as "**GAMMY MONEKER**," a forged signature; **GAMMY STUFF**, spurious medicine; **GAMMY LOWR**, counterfeit coin. *Hants,* **GAMY**, dirty. The hieroglyphic used by beggars and cadgers to intimate to those of the tribe coming after that things are not very favourable, is known as □, or **GAMMY**.

GRAYS: halfpennies, with either two "heads" or two "tails," both sides alike. *Low gamblers* use **GRAYS**, and they cost from 2d. to 6d. each.

LOUR or **LOWR:** money; "gammy **LOWR**," bad money.—*Ancient Cant*, and *Gipsey*.

NAIL: to steal or capture; "paid on the **NAIL**," *i.e.*, ready money; **NAILED**, taken up or caught—probably in allusion to the practice of **NAILING** bad money to the counter. We say "as dead as a **DOORNAIL**;"—why? *Shakespere* has the expression in Henry IV:

> "*Falstaff*. What! Is the old king dead?
> *Pistol*. As nail in door."

A correspondent thinks the expression is only alliterative humour, and compares as "*Flat as a flounder*," "straight as a soldier," &c.

QUEER BIT-MAKERS: coiners.

QUEER SCREENS: forged bank notes.

QUEER SOFT: bad money.

RINGING THE CHANGES: changing bad money for good.

SCHOFEL: bad money.—*See* **SHOW-FULL** *below*.

SHEEN: bad money.—*Scotch*.

SHOW-FULL or **SCHOFUL:** bad money. *Mayhew* thinks this word is from the *Danish*, **SKUFFE**, to shove, to deceive, cheat; *Saxon*, **SCUFAN**, —whence the *English*, **SHOVE**. The term, however, is possibly one of the many street words from the *Hebrew* (through the low Jews), **SHEPHEL**, in that language, signifying a *low* or debased estate. *Chaldee*, **SHAPHAL**.—*See* Psalm cxxxvi. 23, "in our *low estate*." A correspondent suggests another very probable derivation, from the *German*, **SCHOFEL**, trash, rubbish—the *German* adjective, **SCHOFELIG**, being the nearest possible translation of our *shabby*.

SHOWFULL PITCHING: passing bad money.

SHOWFULL-PITCHER: a passer of counterfeit money.

SINKERS: bad money.

SLANG: counterfeit or short weights and measures. A SLANG quart is a pint and a half. SLANG measures are lent out at 2d. per day. The term is used principally by costermongers.

SLUMMING: passing bad money.

SMASH: to pass counterfeit money.

SMASHER: one who passes bad coin.

SMASHFEEDER: a Britannia metal spoon—the best imitation shillings are made from this metal.

TURNER OUT: a coiner of bad money.

 OTHER BAD PEOPLE

BLACKGUARD: a low or dirty fellow.

> "A *Cant* word amongst the vulgar, by which is implied a dirty fellow of the meanest kind. Dr. Johnson says, and he cites only the modern authority of Swift. But the introduction of this word into our language belongs not to the vulgar, and is more than a century prior to the time of Swift. Mr. Malone agrees with me in exhibiting the two first of the following examples. The *black-guard* is evidently designed to imply a fit attendant on the devil. Mr. Gilford, however, in his late edition of Ben Johnson's works, assigns an origin of the name different from what the old examples which I have cited seem to countenance. It has been formed, he says, from those 'mean and dirty dependents, in great houses, who were selected to carry coals to the kitchen, halls, &c. To this smutty regiment, who attended the progresses, and rode in the carts with the pots and kettles, which, with every other article of furniture, were then moved from palace to palace, the people, in derision, gave the name of *black guards*; a term since become sufficiently familiar, and never properly explained.'
> —Ben Johnson, ii. 169, vii. 250" —*Todd's Johnson's Dictionary.*

BLACK-SHEEP: a "bad lot," "*mauvais sujet*;" also a workman who refuses to join in a strike.

BOUNCER: a person who steals whilst bargaining with a tradesmen; a lie.

BUFFER: a familiar expression for a jolly acquaintance, probably from the *French*, BOUFFARD, a fool or clown; a "jolly old BUFFER," said of a good-humoured or liberal old man. In 1737, a BUFFER was a "rogue that killed good sound horses for the sake of their skins, by running a long wire into them." — *Bacchus and Venus.* The term was once applied to those who took false oaths for a consideration.

CHOKER or **WIND-STOPPER:** a garrotter.

COPER: properly HORSE-COUPER, a Scotch horse dealer — used to denote a dishonest one.

COWAN: a sneak, an inquisitive or prying person. — *Masonic term. Greek,* κυων, a dog.

CRAMMER: a lie; or a person who commits a falsehood.

CRIMPS: men who trepan others into the clutches of the recruiting sergeant. They generally pretend to give employment in the colonies, and in that manner cheat those mechanics who are half famished. — *Nearly obsolete.*

CUT-THROAT: a butcher, a cattle slaughterer; a ruffian.

DOOKIN: fortune telling. *Gipsey,* DUKKERIN.

GYP: an undergraduate's valet at *Cambridge.* Corruption of GYPSEY JOE (*Saturday Review*); popularly derived by Cantabs from the *Greek,* GYPS, (γυψ) a vulture, from their dishonest rapacity. At *Oxford* they are called SCOUTS.

KIDNAPPER: one who steals children or adults. From KID, a child, and NAB (corrupted to NAP), to steal or seize.

LEGS or **BLACKLEGS:** disreputable sporting characters and racecourse *habitues.*

QUEER BAIL: worthless persons who for a consideration would stand bail for anyone in court. Insolvent Jews generally performed this office, which gave rise to the term JEW-BAIL. — *See* MOUNTERS *page 57:* both *nearly obsolete.*

RAT: a sneak, an informer, a turn-coat, one who changes his party for interest. The late Sir Robert Peel was called the RAT, or the TAMWORTH RATCATCHER, for altering his views on the Roman Catholic question. From rats deserting vessels about to sink.

ROUGHS: coarse or vulgar men.

ROWDY: money. In *America*, a ruffian, a brawler, "rough."

RUM MIZZLERS: persons who are clever at making their escape or getting out of a difficulty.

SETTER: a person employed by the vendor at an auction to run the bidding up; to bid against *bonâ fide* bidders.

OTHER BAD BEHAVIOUR

BAD: "to go to the BAD," to deteriorate in character, be ruined. *Virgil* has an exactly similar phrase, *in pejus ruere*.

BLEED: to victimise or extract money from a person, to spunge on, to make suffer vindictively.

BUNTS: costermongers' perquisites; the money obtained by giving light weight, &c.; costermonger's goods sold by boys on commission. Probably a corruption of *bonus*, BONE being the slang for good. BUNCE, *Grose* gives as the *Cant* word for money.

BURKE: to kill, to murder, by pitch plaster or other foul means. From Burke, the notorious Whitechapel murderer, who with others used to waylay people, kill them, and sell their bodies for dissection at the hospitals.

CLEAN OUT: to thrash or beat; to ruin or bankrupt anyone; to take all they have got, by purchase or force. *De Quincey*, in his article on "Richard Bentley," speaking of the lawsuit between that great scholar and Dr. Colbatch, remarks that the latter "must have been pretty well CLEANED OUT."

COOK ONE'S GOOSE: to kill or ruin any person.—*North.*

DEAD-SET: a pointed attack on a person.

DOCTOR: to adulterate or drug liquor; also to falsify accounts.—*See* COOK *page 188.*

JIGGER: a secret still, illicit spirits.—*Scotch.*

KENNEDY: to strike or kill with a poker. A St. Giles' term, so given from a man of that name being killed by a poker. Frequently shortened to NEDDY.

KID-ON: to entice or incite a person on to the perpetration of an act.

KNIFE: "to KNIFE a person," to stab, an un-English but now-a-days a very common expression.

LAY: to watch; "on the LAY," on the look out.—*Shakespere.*

MOONLIGHT or **MOONSHINE:** smuggled gin.

OLD GOWN: smuggled tea.

PAL: a partner, acquaintance, friend, an accomplice. *Gipsey*, a brother.

PINK: to stab or pierce.

SETTLE: to kill, ruin, or effectually quiet a person.

SWEAT: to extract money from a person, to "bleed," to squander riches. —*Bulwer.*

TOMMY SHOP: where wages are generally paid to mechanics or others, who are expected to "take out" a portion of the money in goods.

TOUT: to look-out or watch.—*Old Cant.*

TRAPESING: gadding or gossiping about in a slatternly way.—*North.*

WHITE-COLLAR CRIME

BEAR: one who contracts to deliver or sell a certain quantity of stock in the public fund on a forthcoming day at a stated place, but who does not possess it, trusting to a decline in public securities to enable him to fulfill the agreement and realise a profit.—*See* BULL *below.* Both words are slang terms on the Stock Exchange, and are frequently used in the business columns of newspapers.

> "He who sells that of which he is not possessed is proverbially said to sell the skin before he has caught, the BEAR. It was the practice of stock-jobbers, in the year 1720 to enter into a contract for transferring South Sea Stock at a future time for a certain price; but he who contracted to sell had frequently no stock to transfer, nor did he who bought intend to receive any in consequence of his bargain; the seller was, therefore, called a BEAR in allusion to the proverb, and the buyer a BULL, perhaps only as a similar distinction. The contract was merely a wager, to be determined by the rise or fall of stock; if it rose, the seller paid the difference to the buyer, proportioned to the sum

determined by the same computation to the seller." — *Dr. Warton on Pope.*

BULL: one who agrees to purchase stock at a future day, at a stated price, but who does not possess money to pay for it, trusting to a rise in public securities to render the transaction a profitable one. Should stocks fall, the bull is then called upon to pay the difference. — *See* BEAR, who is the opposite of a BULL, the former selling, the latter purchasing — the one operating for a *fall* or a *pull down,* whilst the other operates for a *rise* or *toss up.*

COOK: a term well known in the Bankruptcy Courts, referring to accounts that have been meddled with, or COOKED, by the bankrupt; also the forming a balance sheet from general trade inferences; stated by a correspondent to have been first used in reference to the celebrated alteration of the accounts of the Eastern Counties Railway, by George Hudson, the Railway King.

CROCUS or CROAKUS: a quack or traveling doctor; CROCUS-CHOVEY, a chemist shop.

DOCTOR: to adulterate or drug liquor; also to falsify accounts. — *See* COOK *above.*

DOLLY SHOP: an illegal pawnshop where goods or stolen property, not good enough for the pawnbroker, are received and charged at so much per day. If not redeemed the third day, the goods are forfeited. *Anglo Saxon,* DAEL, a part — to dole? — *See* NIX *page 371.* A correspondent thinks it may have been derived from the *black doll,* the usual sign of a rag shop.

GREASING: GREASING a man is bribing; SOAPING is flattering him.

HUSH-MONEY: a sum given to quash a prosecution or evidence.

LAME DUCK: a stock jobber who speculates beyond his capital and cannot pay his losses. Upon retiring from the Exchange he is said to "waddle out of the Alley."

LEAVING SHOP: an unlicensed house where goods are taken in to pawn at exorbitant rates of interest. — *Daily Telegraph,* 1st August, 1859.

POT-WALLOPERS: electors in certain boroughs before the passing of the Reform Bill, whose qualification consisted in being housekeepers — to establish which, it was only necessary to boil a pot within the limits of the borough, by the aid of any temporary erection. This implied that they were able to provide for themselves, and not necessitated to apply for parochial relief. **WALLOP**, a word of *Anglo Saxon* derivation, from the same root as *wall*.

RIG: a trick, **SPREE**, or performance; "run a **RIG**," to play a trick—*Gipsey*; "**RIG** the market." In reality to play tricks with it—a mercantile slang phrase often used in the newspapers.

ROUND ROBIN: a petition or paper of remonstrance, with the signatures written in a circle—to prevent the first signer, or ringleader, from being discovered.

SQUARING HIS NIBS: giving a policeman money.

STAG: a term applied during the railway mania to a speculator without capital, who took "scrip" in *"Diddlesex Junction"* and other lines, *ejus et sui generis*, got the shares up to a premium, and then sold out. *Punch* represented the house of Hudson, "the Railway King," at Albert Gate, with a **STAG** on it, in allusion to this term.

STICK: to cheat; "he got **STUCK**," he was taken in; **STICK**, to forget one's part in a performance.—*Theatrical*. **STICK ON**, to over charge or defraud; **STICK UP FOR**, to defend a person, especially when slandered in his absence; **STICK UP TO**, to preserver in courting or attacking, whether in fisticuffs or argument; "to **STICK** in one's gizzard," to rankle in one's heart; "to **STICK TO** a person," to adhere to one, be his friend through adverse circumstances.

 # PRISON and PUNISHMENT

GETTING CAUGHT

BEAK: a magistrate, judge, or policeman; "baffling the **BEAK**," to get remanded. *Ancient Cant*, **BECK**. *Saxon*, **BEAG**, a necklace or gold collar—emblem of authority. Sir John Fielding was called the **BLIND-BEAK** in the last century. Query, if connected with the *Italian* **BECCO**, which means a (bird's) *beak*, and also a *blockhead*.

BODY-SNATCHERS: bailiffs and runners: SNATCH, the trick by which the bailiff captures the delinquent.

BONE: to steal or pilfer. BONED, seized, apprehended.—*Old*.

BOOKED: caught, fixed, disposed of.—Term in *Book-keeping*.

CHUMMING-UP: an old custom amongst prisoners when a fresh culprit is admitted to their number, consisting of a noisy welcome —rough music made with pokers, tongs, sticks, and saucepans. For this ovation the initiated prisoner has to pay, or FORK OVER, half a crown —or submit to a loss of coat and waistcoat. The practice is ancient.

COLLAR: to seize, to lay hold of.

COP: to seize or lay hold of anything unpleasant; used in the similar sense to *catch* in the phrase "to cop (or catch) a beating," "to get COPT."

DONE FOR A RAMP: convicted for thieving.

FRISK: to search; FRISKED, searched by a constable or other officer.

FULLY: "to be FULLIED," to be committed for trial. From the slang of the penny-a-liner, "the prisoner was *fully* committed for trial."

GRABB: to clutch or seize.

GRABBED: caught, apprehended.

IN FOR PATTER: waiting for trial.

KIDMENT: a pocket-handkerchief fastened to the pocket and partially hung out to entrap thieves.

NAIL: to steal or capture; "paid on the NAIL," *i.e.*, ready money; NAILED, taken up or caught—probably in allusion to the practice of NAILING bad money to the counter. We say "as dead as a DOORNAIL;"—why? *Shakespere* has the expression in Henry IV:

> *"Falstaff.* What! Is the old king dead?
> *Pistol.* As nail in door."

A correspondent thinks the expression is only alliterative humour, and compares as *"Flat as a flounder,"* "straight as a soldier," &c.

PATTER: a speech or discourse, a pompous street oration, a judge's summing up, a trial. *Ancient* word for muttering. Probably from the *Latin*, PATER NOSTER, or Lord's Prayer. This was said, before the

Reformation, in a *low voice* by the priest, until he came to, "and lead us not into temptation," to which the choir responded, "but deliver us from evil." In our reformed Prayer Book this was altered, and the Lord's Prayer directed to be said "with a *loud voice.*" —*Dr. Pusey* takes this view of the derivation in his *Letter to the Bishop of London*, P 78, 1851. Scott uses the word twice in *Ivanhoe* and the *Bride of Lammermoor*.

PINCH: to steal or cheat; also, to catch or apprehend.

PULL: to have one apprehended; "to be PULLED up," to be taken before a magistrate.

QUEER BAIL: worthless persons who for a consideration would stand bail for anyone in court. Insolvent Jews generally performed this office, which gave rise to the term JEW-BAIL.—*See* MOUNTERS *page 57*: both *nearly obsolete*.

SNAFFLED: arrested, "pulled up;" so termed from a kind of horse's bit, called a SNAFFLE. In *East Anglia*, to SNAFFLE is to talk foolishly.

SPOTTED: to be known or marked by the police.

STRETCHER: a contrivance with handles, used by the police to carry off persons who are violent or drunk.

TIP THE DOUBLE: to "bolt," or run away from a creditor or officer. Sometimes TIP THE DOUBLE TO SHERRY, *i.e.*, to the sheriff.

TURNED OVER: to be stopped and searched by the police.

TURNED UP: acquitted by the magistrate or judge for want of evidence.

INFORMING

BLEW or **BLOW:** to inform or peach.

BLOW: to expose or inform; "BLOW the gaff," to inform against a person. In *America*, to BLOW is slang for to taunt.

BUDGE: to move, to inform, to SPLIT, or tell tales.

BUFF: to swear to or accuse; to SPLIT, or peach upon. *Old* word for boasting, 1582.

BUST or **BURST:** to tell tales, to SPLIT, to inform. BUSTING, informing against accomplices when in custody.

CAT-IN-THE-PAN: a traitor, a turn-coat—derived by some from the *Greek*, Καταπαν, altogether; or from *cake in pan*, a pan cake, which is frequently turned from side to side.

CHEEK: impudence, assurance; **CHEEKY**, saucy or forward. *Lincolnshire*, **Cheek**, to accuse.

COME: a slang verb used in many phrases; "A'nt he **COMING IT**," *i.e.*, is he not proceeding at a great rate? "Don't **COME TRICKS** here," "don't **COME THE OLD SOLDIER** over me," *i.e.*, we are aware of your practices, and "twig" your manoeuver. **COMING IT STRONG**, exaggerating, going a-head, the opposite of *"drawing it mild."* **COMING IT** also means informing or disclosing.

CRAB: to offend or insult; to expose or defeat a robbery, to inform against.

CUT: **CUT UP**, mortified, to criticize severely or expose; **CUT OUT OF**, done out of; **CUT ONE'S CART**, to expose their tricks.—*Cambridge*. Old **CUTTE**, to say.—*See* **CUT** *in the Index for more meanings on page 479.*

MOUNTER: a false swearer. Derived from the borrowed clothes men used to **MOUNT**, or dress in, when going to swear for a consideration.

NARK: a person in the pay of the police; a common informer; one who gets his living by laying traps for publicans, &c.

NOSE: a thief who turns informer or Queen's evidence; a spy or watch; "on the **NOSE**," on the look out.

PEACH: to inform against or betray. *Webster* states that *impeach* is now the modification mostly used, and that **PEACH** is confined principally to the conversation of thieves and the lower orders.

RAT: a sneak, an informer, a turn-coat, one who changes his party for interest. The late Sir Robert Peel was called the **RAT**, or the **TAMWORTH RATCATCHER**, for altering his views on the Roman Catholic question. From rats deserting vessels about to sink.

ROUND: to tell tales, to "**SPLIT**,"(*see below*); "to **ROUND** on a man," to swear to him as being the person, &c. Synonymous with "**BUFF**." —*See* **BUFF** *above*. *Shakespere* has **ROUNDING**, whispering.

SNITCHERS: persons who turn queen's evidence or who tell tales. In *Scotland*, **SNITCHERS** signify handcuffs.

SPLIT: to inform against one's companions, to tell tales. "To **SPLIT** with a person," to cease acquaintanceship, to quarrel.

TIP: a douceur; also to give, lend, or hand over anything to another person; "come, TIP up the tin," *i.e.*, hand up the money; "TIP the wink," to inform by winking; "TIP us your fin," *i.e.*, give me your hand; "TIP one's boom off," to make off, depart.—*Sea*. "To miss one's TIP," to fail in a scheme.—*Old Cant*.

WHIDDLE: to enter into parley or hesitate with many words, &c.; to inform or discover.

 # PRISONERS and PRISON TERMS

BALL: prison allowance, viz., six ounces of meat.

BRACELETS: handcuffs.

BULL: term amongst prisoners for meat served to them in jail.

CHIVE: a knife, a sharp tool of any kind.—*Old Cant*. This term is particularly applied to the tin knives used in goals.

COCKCHAFER: the treadmill.

COUNTY-CROP: (*i.e.*, COUNTY-PRISON CROP), hair cut close and round, as if guided by a basin—an indication of having been in prison.

CROPPIE: a person who has had his hair cut, or CROPPED, in prison.

DARBIES: handcuffs.—*Old Cant*.

DO: this useful and industrious verb has for many years done service as a slang term. To DO a person is to cheat him. Sometimes another tense is employed, such as I DONE him," meaning I cheated or "paid him out;" DONE BROWN, cheated thoroughly, befooled; DONE OVER, upset, cheated, knocked down, ruined; DONE UP, used-up, finished, or quieted. DONE also means convicted or sentenced; so does DONE FOR. To DO a person in pugilism is to excel him in fisticuffs. Humphreys, who fought Mendoza, a Jew, wrote this laconic note to his supporter: "Sir, I have DONE the Jew, and am in good health. Rich. Humphries." Tourists use the expression "I have DONE France and Italy," meaning I have completely explored those countries.

EVERLASTING STAIRCASE: the treadmill. Sometimes called "Colonel Chesterton's everlasting staircase," from the gallant inventor or improver.

FIDDLE: a whip.

FLOGGER: a whip.—*Obsolete.*

FLUMMUXED: done up, sure of a month in QUOD, or prison. In mendicant freemasonry, the sign chalked by rogues and tramps upon a gate-post or house corner, to express to succeeding vagabonds that it is unsafe for them to call there, is known as Θ, or FLUMMUXED, which signifies that the only thing they would be likely to get upon applying for relief would be a "a month in QUOD."—*See* QUOD *p. 258.*

JAIL-BIRD: a prisoner, one who has been in jail.

JIGGER-DUBBERS: term applied to jailors or turnkeys.

LEGGED: in irons.

MILL: the tread*mill,* prison.

MILL-TOG: a shirt—most likely the prison garment.

NAP THE TEAZE: to be privately whipped in prison.

PANNAM-BOUND: stopping the prison food or rations to a prisoner. PANNAM-STRUCK, very hungry.

SCREW: a key—skeleton or otherwise.

SCROBY: "to get SCROBY," to be whipped in prison before the justices.

SKILIGOLEE: prison gruel, also sailors' soup of many ingredients.

SKILLY: broth served on board the hulks to convicts.—*Line.*

SLOUR: to lock or fasten.

SLOWED: to be locked up—in prison.

SMIGGINS: soup served to convicts on board the hulks.

SNITCHERS: persons who turn queen's evidence or who tell tales. In *Scotland,* SNITCHERS signify handcuffs.

STUNNED ON SKILLY: to be sent to prison and compelled to eat SKILLY or SKILLIGOLEE.

UNBETTY: to unlock.—*See* BETTY *page 308.*

VERTICAL-CARE-GRINDER: the treadmill.

WIFE: a fetter fixed to one leg.—*Prison.*

PRISONS and PLACES of PUNISHMENT

BURDON'S HOTEL: Whitecross-street prison, of which the Governor is or was a Mr. Burdon.

CAGE: a minor kind of prison.—*Shakespere*, part ii. Of Henry IV., iv. 2.

CHATTS: dice—formerly the gallows; a bunch of seals.

DOWN'S: Tothill Fields' prison.

GOVERNMENT SIGNPOST: the gallows.

HORSE: contraction of Horsemonger-lane Gaol.

JUG: a prison or jail.

QUOD: a prison or lock up; QUODDED, put in prison. A slang expression used by Mr. Hughes, in *Tom Brown's Schooldays* (Macmillan's Magazine, January, 1860), throws some light upon the origin of this now very common street term;—"Flogged or whipped in QUAD," says the delineator of student life, in allusion to chastisement inflicted within the *Quadrangle* of a college. Quadrangle is the term given to the prison enclosure within which culprits are allowed to walk, and where whippings were formerly inflicted. Quadrangle also represents a building of four sides; and to be "within FOUR WALLS," or prison, is the frequent slang lament of unlucky vagabonds.

SALT BOX: the condemned cell in Newgate.

SPUNGING-HOUSE: the sheriff's officer's house, where prisoners, when arrested for debt, are sometimes taken. As extortionate charges are made there for accommodation, the name is far from inappropriate.

STEEL: the house of corrections in London, formerly named the *Bastile*, but since shortened to STEEL.

STIR: a prison, a lock-up; "IN STIR," in jail. *Anglo Saxon*, STYR, correction, punishment.

STONE JUG: a prison.

STURABAN: a prison. *Gipsey*, DISTARABIN.

THEATRE: a police court.

SENTENCES

AUTUMN: a slang term for execution by hanging. When the drop was introduced instead of the old gallows, cart, and ladder, and a man was for the first time "turned-off" in the present fashion, the mob were so pleased with the invention that they spoke of the operation as at **AUTUMN**, or the **FALL OF THE LEAF** (*sc.* The drop), with the man about to be hung.

BELLOWSED or LAGGED: transported.

BRAGGADOCIO: three months' imprisonment as a reputed thief or old offender—sometimes termed a **DOSE** or a **DOLLOP.**—*Household Words*, vol. i., p. 579.

CRAPPED: hanged.

CROPPED: hanged.

DANCE UPON NOTHING: to be hanged.

DOSE: three months' imprisonment as a known thief.—*See* **BRAGGADOCIO** *above.*

DRAG or THREE MOON: three months in prison.

FLICK or FLIG: to whip by striking, and drawing the lash back at the same time, which causes a stinging blow.

FLOG: to whip. Cited both by *Grose* and the author of *Bacchus and Venus* as a *Cant* word. It would be curious to ascertain the earliest use; *Richardson* cites Lord Chesterfield.—*Latin.*

GALLOWS: very or exceedingly, a disgusting exclamation; "**GALLOWS** poor," very poor.

HALF A STRETCH: six months in prison.

HANGMAN'S WAGES: thirteenpence halfpenny.

HERRING POND: the sea; "to be sent across the **HERRING POND**," to be transported.

HOOKS: "dropped off the **HOOKS**," said of a deceased person. Derived from the ancient practice of suspending on hooks the quarters of a traitor or felon sentenced by the old law to be hung, drawn, and quartered, and which dropped off the hooks as they decayed.

HORSE'S NIGHTCAP: a halter; "to die in the HORSE'S NIGHTCAP," to be hung.

KETCH or JACK KETCH: the popular name for a public hangman —derived from a person of that name who officiated in the reign of Charles II.—*See Macaulay's History of England, p. 626.*

LAG: a returned transport, or ticket-of-leave convict.

LAGGED: transported for a crime.

LENGTH: six months' imprisonment.—*See* STRETCH *below.*

LIFER: a convict who is sentenced to transportation *for life.*

LUMP THE LIGHTER: to be transported.

MARINATED: transported;—from the salt-pickling fish undergo in Cornwall.—*Old Cant.*

MOON: a month—generally used to express the length of time a person has been sentenced by the magistrate; thus "ONE MOON" is one month.—*See* DRAG *above.* It is a curious fact that the Indians of America and the roaming vagabonds of England should both calculate time by the MOON.

ON THE SHELF: to be transported. With old maids it has another and very different meaning.

SALT BOX: the condemned cell in Newgate.

SCRAG: the neck.—*Old Cant. Scotch,* CRAIG. Still used by butchers. Hence, SCRAG, to hang by the neck, and SCRAGGING, an execution. —Also *Old Cant.*

SETTLED: transported.

SEVEN PENNORTH: transported for seven years.

SHOES: "to die in one's SHOES," to be hung.

STRETCH: abbreviation of "STRETCH one's neck." to hang, be executed as a malefactor.—*Bulwer's Paul Clifford.*

STRETCH: twelve months—generally used to intimate the time anyone has been sentenced by the judge or magistrate. ONE STRETCH is to be imprisoned for twelve months, TWO STRETCH is two years, THREE STRETCH is three years, and so on.

STRETCHING MATCH: an execution.—*See* STRETCH *above.*

SWING: to be hanged.

TOPPED: hung or executed.

TRAVELLER: name given by one tramp to another. "A TRAVELLER at her Majesty's expense," *i.e.,* a transported felon, a convict.

TRINE: to hang.—*Ancient Cant.*

WINDED-SETTLED: transported for life.

LOCATION, LOCATION, LOCATION

When you write things down, they sometimes take you places you hadn't planned.
Melanie Benjamin

*T*he local pub, or public house, in London was the place to hang out and have fun. There are ten terms for a public house and a few more for beer or liquor shops without licenses. We even get a slang term for a specific tavern. The well-known "Elephant and Castle" was perhaps affectionately called the **Pig and Tinder-box.**

There are also eleven terms for jails of different kinds, and the main prisons all had slang names - **Burdon's Hotel** was Whitecross-street prison, of which the Governor was Mr. Burdon, **Down's** was Tothill Fields' prison, and the house of corrections in London was called **Steel.**

We also get a whopping thirteen terms for a water-closet or bathroom, which is not too surprising since they'd only come into fashion a few years earlier. The Great Exhibition of 1851 saw the first public toilets installed in the "retiring rooms" of the Crystal Palace.

Editor's Faves:

HOUSE OF COMMONS: a water-closet.

KIDDLEYWINK: a small shop where they retail the commodities of a village store. Also, a loose woman.

WOBBLESHOP: where beer is sold without a license.

IN THIS CHAPTER

FOOD or ENTERTAINMENT PLACES

BAWDYKEN: a brothel. — *See* KEN *page 269.*

CART: a racecourse.

DRUM: a house, a lodging, a street; HAZARD-DRUM, a gambling house; FLASH-DRUM, a house of ill-fame.

FLOWERY: lodging or house entertainment; "square the omee for the FLOWERY," pay the master for the lodging.

GAFF: a fair or penny-playhouse. — *See* PENNY GAFFS *below.*

GRUBBING-KEN or **SPINIKIN:** a workhouse; a cook-shop.

HELL: a fashionable gambling house. In printing offices, the term is generally applied to the old tin box in which is thrown the broken or spoilt type, purchased by the founders for re-casting. *Nearly obsolete.*

KNOCKING-SHOP: a brothel or disreputable house frequented by prostitutes.

MUNGARLY CASA: a baker's shop; evidently a corruption of some *Lingua Franca* phrase for an eating house. The well-known "Nix mangiare" stairs at Malta derive their name from the endless beggars who lie there and shout NIX MANGIARE, *i.e.,* "nothing to eat," to excite the compassion of the English who land there — an expression which exhibits remarkably the mongrel composition of the *Lingua Franca*, MANGIARE being *Italian*, and *Nix* an evident importation from Trieste or other Austrian seaport.

NANNY-SHOP: a disreputable house.

PARADIS: *French slang* for the gallery of a theatre, "up amongst the Gods." — *See page 363.*

PENNY GAFFS: shops turned into temporary theatres (admission one penny), where dancing and singing take place every night. Rude pictures of the performers are arranged outside to give the front a gaudy and attractive look, and at nighttime coloured lamps and transparencies are displayed to draw an audience.

RING: a generic term given to horse racing and pugilism. The latter is sometimes termed the PRIZE-RING. From the practice of forming the crowd into a RING around the combatants or outside the racecourse.

ROUNDABOUTS: large swings of four compartments, each the size, and very much the shape, of the body of a cart, capable of seating six or eight boys and girls, erected in a high frame, and turned round by men at a windlass. Fairs and merry-makings generally abound with them. The frames take to pieces, and are carried in vans by miserable horses, from fair to fair, &c.

SLAP-BANG SHOPS: Low eating houses, where you have to pay down the ready money with a SLAP-BANG.—*Grose.*

SPELLKEN or **SPEELKEN:** a playhouse. *German,* SPIELEN.—*See* KEN *page 269.*—*Don Juan.*

TWOPENNY-HOPS: low dancing rooms, the price of admission to which was formerly—and not infrequently now—two pence. The clog hornpipe, the pipe dance, flash jigs, and hornpipes in fetters, *a la* Jack Sheppard, are the favourite movements, all entered into with great spirit and "joyous laborious capering."—*Mayhew.*

 # GENERAL PLACES

DAVY'S LOCKER or **DAVY JONES' LOCKER:** the sea, the common receptacle for all things thrown overboard—a nautical phrase for death, the other world.

GAMMY-VIAL: (Ville) a town where the police will not let persons hawk.

HERRING POND: the sea; "to be sent across the HERRING POND," to be transported.

HUEY: a town or village.

MAIN-TOBY: the highway or the main road.

MONKERY: the country or rural districts. *Old* word for a quiet or monastic life.—*Hall.*

PAD: the highway; a tramp.—*Lincolnshire.*

PITCH: a fixed locality where a patterer can hold forth to a gaping multitude for at least some few minutes continuously; "to do a PITCH in the drag," to perform in the street.

ROOKERY: a low neighbourhood inhabited by dirty Irish and thieves — as ST. GILES' ROOKERY. — *Old.* In *Military slang* that part of the barracks occupied by subalterns, often by no mean a pattern of good order.

SKY PARLOUR: the garret.

STANDING: the position at a street corner or on the curb of a market street, regularly occupied by a costermonger or street seller.

START: "THE START," London, the great starting point for beggars and tramps.

TEAGUELAND: Ireland.

TOBY: a road; "high TOBY," the turnpike road. "High TOBY spice," robbery on horse-back. — *Don Juan,* canto xi., 19.

VILLAGE or **THE VILLAGE:** *i.e.,* London. — *Sporting.*

VILLE or **VILE:** a town or village. — pronounced *phial* or *vial.* — *French.*

WILD: a village. — *Tramps' term.* — *See* VILE *above.*

GOVERNMENT PLACES

BURDON'S HOTEL: Whitecross-street prison, of which the Governor is or was a Mr. Burdon.

CAGE: a minor kind of prison. — *Shakespere,* part ii. Of Henry IV., iv. 2.

CHATTS: dice — formerly the gallows; a bunch of seals.

DOWN'S: Tothill Fields' prison.

GOVERNMENT SIGNPOST: the gallows.

HORSE: contraction of Horsemonger-lane Gaol.

JUG: a prison or jail.

LOBSTER BOX: a barrack or military station.

QUOD: a prison or lock up; QUODDED, put in prison. A slang expression used by Mr. Hughes, in *Tom Brown's Schooldays* (Macmillan's Magazine, January, 1860), throws some light upon the origin of this now very common street term: — "Flogged or whipped in QUAD," says the delineator of student life, in allusion to chastisement inflicted within the *Quadrangle* of a college. Quadrangle is the term given to the prison enclosure within which culprits are allowed to walk, and where whippings were formerly inflicted. Quadrangle also represents a building of four sides; and to be "within FOUR WALLS," or prison, is the frequent slang lament of unlucky vagabonds.

SALT BOX: the condemned cell in Newgate.

SPUNGING-HOUSE: the sheriff's officer's house, where prisoners, when arrested for debt, are sometimes taken. As extortionate charges are made there for accommodation, the name is far from inappropriate.

STEEL: the house of corrections in London, formerly named the *Bastile*, but since shortened to STEEL.

STIR: a prison, a lock-up; "IN STIR," in jail. *Anglo Saxon*, STYR, correction, punishment.

STONE JUG: a prison.

STURABAN: a prison. *Gipsey*, DISTARABIN.

THEATRE: a police court.

 # LODGING

BAWDYKEN: a brothel. — *See* KEN *below.*

CASA or **CASE:** a house, respectable or otherwise. Probably from the *Italian*, CASA. — *Old Cant.* The *Dutch* use the word KAST in a vulgar sense for a house, *i.e.*, MOTTEKAST, a brothel. CASE sometimes means a water-closet.

CHUM: to occupy a joint lodging with another person.

CRIB: house, public or otherwise; lodgings, apartments.

CROSS-CRIB: a house frequented by thieves.

DIGGINGS: lodgings, apartments, residence; an expression probably imported from California or Australia, with reference to *the gold diggings*.

DOSS-KEN: a lodging house.

DOUBLE-UP: to pair off, or "chum," with another man; to beat severely.

DRIZ: lace. In a low lodging house, this singular autograph inscription appears over the mantelpiece, "Scotch Mary, with DRIZ (lace), bound to Dover and back, please God."

DRUM: a house, a lodging, a street; HAZARD-DRUM, a gambling house; FLASH-DRUM, a house of ill-fame.

FLOWERY: lodging or house entertainment; "square the omee for the FLOWERY," pay the master for the lodging.

FLY THE KITE: to evacuate from a window—term used in padding kens or low lodging houses.

HANG OUT: to reside—in allusion to the ancient custom of *hanging out* signs.

KEN: a house.—*Ancient Cant.* KHAN, *Gipsey* and *Oriental.*

> **All slang and *Cant* words which end in KEN, such as SPIELKEN, SPINIKEN, BAWDYKEN, or BOOZINGKEN, refer to *houses*, and are partly of *Gipsey* origin.

KEN-CRACKERS: housebreakers.

KIDDEN: a low lodging house for boys.

PADDING KENS or **CRIBS:** tramps' and boys' lodging houses.

PANNY: a house—public or otherwise; "flash PANNY," a public-house used by thieves; PANNY MEN, housebreakers.

PERCH or **ROOST:** a resting place; "I'm off to PERCH," I'm going to bed.

ROOKERY: a low neighbourhood inhabited by dirty Irish and thieves —as ST. GILES' ROOKERY.—*Old.* In *Military slang* that part of the barracks occupied by subalterns, often by no mean a pattern of good order.

ROUGH IT: to put up with chance entertainment, to take pot luck, and what accommodation "turns up," without sighing for better. "ROUGHING IT *in the Bush*" is the title of an interesting work on Backwoods life.

SKIPPER IT: to sleep in the open air or in a rough way.

SKIPPER-BIRDS or **KEYHOLE WHISTLERS:** persons who sleep in barns or outhouses in preference to lodging-houses.

SLUMS or **BACK SLUMS:** dark retreats, low neighbourhoods; "the Westminster SLUMS," favourite haunts for thieves.

STALL: to lodge or put up at a public house. Also, to act a part. — *Theatrical.*

PUBLIC HOUSES and BARS

BOOZE or **SUCK-CASA:** a public-house.

BOOZING-KEN: a beer- shop, a low public house. — *Ancient.*

BUSKER: a man who sings or performs in a public house. — *Scotch.*

BUSTER (BURSTER): a small new loaf; "twopenny BUSTER," a twopenny loaf. "A pennorth o' BEES WAX (cheese) and a penny BUSTER," a common snack at beershops.

CAT AND KITTEN SNEAKING: stealing pint and quart pots from public-houses.

CHAUNTER-CULLS: a singular body of men who used to haunt certain well-known public-houses, and write satirical or libellous ballads on any person or body of persons, for a consideration. 7s. 6d. was the usual fee, and in three hours the ballad might be heard in St. Paul's Churchyard or other public spot. There are two men in London at the present day who gain their living in this way.

CLINK-RIG: stealing tankards from public-houses, taverns, &c.

COLD BLOOD: a house licensed for the sale of beer "NOT to be drunk on the premises."

CRIB: house, public or otherwise; lodgings, apartments.

FLATTY-KEN: a public house, the landlord of which is ignorant of the practices of the thieves and tramps who frequent it.

FREE AND EASY: a club held at most public houses, the members of which meet in the taproom or parlour for the purpose of drinking, smoking, and hearing each other sing and "talk politics." The name indicates the character of the proceedings.

HUSH-SHOP or **CRIB:** a shop where beer or spirits is sold "on the quiet" — no license being paid.

JERRY: a beer house.

LUSH-CRIB: a public house.

MUTTONWALK: the saloon at Drury Lane Theatre.

NOSE-BAGS: visitors at watering places, and houses of refreshment, who carry their own victuals.—*Term applied by waiters.*

PANNY: a house—public or otherwise; "flash PANNY," a public-house used by thieves; PANNY MEN, housebreakers.

PIC.: the Piccadilly Saloon.

PIG AND TINDER-BOX: the vulgar rendering of the well-known tavern sign, *"Elephant and Castle."*

PUB or **PUBLIC:** a public-house.

PUT UP: to suggest, to incite, "he PUT me UP to it;" to have done with; PUT IT UP, is a vulgar answer often heard in the streets. PUT UP, to stop at an hotel or tavern for entertainment.

SCORE: "to run up a SCORE at a public house," to obtain credit there until pay day or a fixed time when the debt must be WIPED OFF.

SLUICERY: a gin shop or public house.

STALL: to lodge or put up at a public house. Also, to act a part. —*Theatrical.*

SUCK-CASA: a public-house.

WOBBLESHOP: where beer is sold without a license.

SPECIFIC PLACES and BUILDINGS

BOILERS: the slang name given to the New Kensington Museum and School of Art, in allusion to the peculiar form of the buildings, and the fact of their being mainly composed of, and covered with, sheet iron.—*See* PEPPER-BOXES *below.*

BURDON'S HOTEL: Whitecross-street prison, of which the Governor is or was a Mr. Burdon.

DOWN'S: Tothill Fields' prison.

HOLY LAND: Seven Dials—where the St. Giles' Greek is spoken.

MUTTONWALK: the saloon at Drury Lane Theatre.

PEPPER-BOXES: the buildings of the Royal Academy and National Gallery, in Trafalgar-square. The name was first given by a wag, in allusion to the cupolas erected by Wilkins, the architect, upon the roof, and which at a distance suggest to the stranger the fact of their being enlarged **PEPPER-BOXES**, from their form and awkward appearance. — *See* **BOILERS** *above.*

PIC.: the Piccadilly Saloon.

PIG AND TINDER-BOX: the vulgar rendering of the well-known tavern sign, *"Elephant and Castle."*

RECENT INCISION: the busy thoroughfare on the Surrey side of the Thames, known by sober people as the **NEW CUT**.

SALT BOX: the condemned cell in Newgate.

SCULL or **SKULL:** the head or master of a college. — *University,* but *nearly obsolete*; the gallery, however, in St. Mary's (the University church), where the "Heads of Houses" sit in solemn state, is still nicknamed the **GOLGOTHA** by the undergraduates.

START: "**THE START**," London, the great starting point for beggars and tramps.

STEEL: the house of corrections in London, formerly named the *Bastile*, but since shortened to **STEEL**.

STINKOMALEE: a name given to the then New London University by Theodore Hook. Some question about *Trincomalee* was agitated at the same time. It is still applied by the students of the old Universities, who regard it with disfavour from its admitting all denominations.

TEAGUELAND: Ireland.

VIC.: the Victoria Theatre, London — patronised principally by costermongers and low people; also the street abbreviation of the Christian name of her Majesty the Queen.

WATER CLOSETS & CHAMBER POTS

BOG or **BOG-HOUSE:** a water-closet. — *School term*. In the Inns of Court, I am informed, this term is very common.

COFFEE-SHOP: a water-closet or house of office.

CRAPPING CASE or **KEN:** a privy or water-closet.

DUNNY-KEN: a water-closet. — *See* **KEN** *page 269.*

FORAKERS: a water-closet or house of office.—Term used by the boys at *Winchester school.*

FOURTH or **FOURTH COURT:** the court appropriated to the water-closets at *Cambridge;* from its really being No. 4 at Trinity College. A man leaving his room to go to this **FOURTH COURT** writes on his door *"gone to the* **FOURTH,**" or, in algebraic notation, "**GONE 4**—the *Cambridge* slang phrase.

HOUSE OF COMMONS: a water-closet.

JERRY: a chamber utensil, abbreviation of **JEROBOAM.**—*Swift.* **JERRY-COME-TUMBLE,** a water-closet.

JORDAN: a chamber utensil.—*Saxon.*

MRS. JONES: the house of office, a water-closet.

MY AUNT: a water-closet or house of office.

PROS: a water-closet. Abbreviated form of προς τινα τυπον.—*Oxford University.*

SCRAPING CASTLE: a water-closet.

WEST CENTRAL: a water-closet, the initials being the same as those of the London Postal District. It is said that for this reason very delicate people refuse to obey Rowland Hill's instructions in this particular.

OTHER PLACES

BAZAAR: a shop or counter. *Gipsey* and *Hindoo*, a market.

BIG-HOUSE: the work-house.

BOS-KEN: farm-house. *Ancient.*—*See* **KEN** *page 269.*

BUZ-NAPPER'S ACADEMY: school in which young thieves are trained. Figures are dressed up, and experienced tutors stand in various difficult attitudes for the boys to practice upon. When clever enough they are sent on the streets. It is reported that a house of this nature is situated in a court near Hatton Garden. The system is well explained in *Dickens' Oliver Twist.*

CHEEK BY JOWL: side by side—said often of persons in such close confabulation as almost to have their faces touch.

CHOVEY: a shop.

COCK ROBIN SHOP: a small printer's office where low wages are paid to journeymen who have never served a regular apprenticeship.

DOLLY SHOP: an illegal pawnshop where goods or stolen property, not good enough for the pawnbroker, are received and charged at so much per day. If not redeemed the third day, the goods are forfeited. *Anglo Saxon*, DAEL, a part—to dole?—*See* NIX *page 371.* A correspondent thinks it may have been derived from the *black doll*, the usual sign of a rag shop.

FENCE or FENCER: a purchasher or reciever of stolen goods; FENCE, the shop or warehouse of a FENCER.—*Old Cant.*

KIDDLEYWINK: a small shop where they retail the commodities of a village store. Also, a loose woman.

LEAVING SHOP: an unlicensed house where goods are taken in to pawn at exorbitant rates of interest.—*Daily Telegraph*, 1st August, 1859.

LUG CHOVEY: a pawnbroker's shop.

MOP: a hiring place (or fair) for servants. Steps are being taken to put down these assemblies, which have been proved to be greatly detrimental to the morality of the poor.

PITCH: a fixed locality where a patterer can hold forth to a gaping multitude for at least some few minutes continuously; "to do a PITCH in the drag," to perform in the street.

RAG-SHOP: a bank.

SCHISM-SHOP: a dissenters' meeting-house.—*University.*

SKIPPER: a barn.—*Ancient Cant.*

SPINIKEN: a workhouse.

STANDING: the position at a street corner or on the curb of a market street, regularly occupied by a costermonger or street seller.

SWAG-SHOP: a warehouse where "Brummagem" and general wares are sold—fancy trinkets, plated goods, &c. Jews are the general proprietors, and the goods are excessively low priced, trashy, and showy. SWAG-SHOPS were formerly plunder depots.—*Old Cant.*

TOMMY SHOP: where wages are generally paid to mechanics or others, who are expected to "take out" a portion of the money in goods.

WOOL-HOLE: the workhouse.

HOME IS WHERE THE HEARTH IS

They have been at a great feast of languages, and stolen the scraps.

William Shakespere

Household Items

*T*he big surprise in this section is the "lower order's" obsession with handkerchiefs. According to John Camden Hotten; "With both sexes they are more valued than any other article of clothing. A coster's caste, or position, is at stake, he imagines, if his **Kingsman** is not of the most approved pattern."

People were surprisingly delicate when it came to discussing their underwear—their **unutterables, inexpressibles**, or **unwhisperables**. Toilet paper, as well as water closets, had just been invented in Europe, and were a rarity. People used whatever they had on hand—from wool to corncobs—in lieu of toilet paper. Bathing was also a less frequent occurrence. So, given the possible state of their **unwhisperables**, they were probably best left unmentioned.

Their terms for household objects and food range from utile (**feeder** for a spoon, or **sticky** for wax) to familiar (like **Tommy** for a bread roll or **Betty** for a key) to downright political (like **Glasgow Magistrates** for salt herrings.) I can't help but wonder what the magistrates did to deserve that one!

Editor's Faves:

KISS-ME-QUICK: the name given to the very small bonnets worn by females since 1850.

SNOTTINGER: a coarse word for a pocket-handkerchief. The *German* SCHNUPFTUCH is, however, nearly as plain. A handkerchief was also anciently called a MUCKINGER or MUCKENDER.

WOOLBIRD: a lamb; "wing of a WOOLBIRD," a shoulder of lamb.

IN THIS CHAPTER

LODGING

 ## FURNITURE and FIXTURES

BACK JUMP: a back window.

BED-POST: "in the twinkling of a BED-POST," in a moment or very quickly. Originally BED-STAFF, a stick placed vertically in the frame of a bed to keep the bedding in its place.—*Shadwell's Virtuoso*, 1676, act i., scene 1. This was used sometimes as a defensive weapon.

CHATTY: a filthy person, one whose clothes are not free from vermin; CHATTY DOSS, a lousy bed.

CRUMMY-DOSS: a lousy or filthy bed.

DAB: a bed.

DANCERS: stairs.—*Old Cant.*

DOSS: a bed.—*North.* Probably from DOZE. Mayhew thinks it is from the Norman, DOSSEL, a hanging or bed canopy.

FLY THE KITE: to evacuate from a window—term used in padding kens or low lodging houses.

GLAZE: glass—generally applied to windows.

GLIM: a light, a lamp; "dowse the GLIM," put the candle out.—*Sea, and Old Cant.*

JACOB: a ladder. *Grose* says from Jacob's dream.—*Old Cant.*

JIGGER: a door; "dub the JIGGER," shut the door. *Ancient Cant*, GYGER. In billiards the *bridge* on the table is often termed the JIGGER."

LETTY: a bed. *Italian*, LETTO.

PERCH or ROOST: a resting place; "I'm off to PERCH," *i.e.*, I am going to bed.

PLUNDER: a common word in the horse trade to express profit. Also an *American* term for baggage, luggage.

SHINER: a looking-glass.

SIR HARRY: a close stool.

SPORTING DOOR: the outer door of chambers, also called the **OAK**. —*See* **SPORT** *page 179.*—*University*.

STICKS: furniture or household chattels; "pick up your **STICKS** and cut!" summary advice to a person to take himself and furniture away. —*Cumberland*.

STRIKE THE JIGGER: to pick the lock or break open the door.

TEETH-DRAWING: wrenching off knockers.

TRAP: a "fast" term for a carriage of any kind. **TRAPS**, goods and chattels of any kind, but especially luggage and personal effects; in Australia, **SWAG**.

PLACES TO LIVE and STAY

CASA or **CASE:** a house, respectable or otherwise. Probably from the *Italian*, **CASA**.—*Old Cant*. The *Dutch* use the word **KAST** in a vulgar sense for a house, *i.e.*, **MOTTEKAST**, a brothel. **CASE** sometimes means a water-closet.

CHUM: to occupy a joint lodging with another person.

CRIB: house, public or otherwise; lodgings, apartments.

CROSS-CRIB: a house frequented by thieves.

DIGGINGS: lodgings, apartments, residence; an expression probably imported from California or Australia, with reference to *the gold diggings*.

DOSS-KEN: a lodging house.

DRIZ: lace. In a low lodging house, this singular autograph inscription appears over the mantelpiece, "Scotch Mary, with **DRIZ** (lace), bound to Dover and back, please God."

DRUM: a house, a lodging, a street; **HAZARD-DRUM**, a gambling house; **FLASH-DRUM**, a house of ill-fame.

FLOWERY: lodging or house entertainment; "square the omee for the **FLOWERY**," pay the master for the lodging.

HANG OUT: to reside—in allusion to the ancient custom of *hanging out* signs.

Household Items: Lodging- Places to Live and Stay

KEN: a house.—*Ancient Cant.* **KHAN,** *Gipsey* and *Oriental.*

> ****All** slang and *Cant* words which end in **KEN,** such as **SPIELKEN, SPINIKEN, BAWDYKEN,** or **BOOZINGKEN,** refer to *houses,* and are partly of *Gipsey* origin.

KEN-CRACKERS: housebreakers.

KIDDEN: a low lodging house for boys.

MONKEY WITH A LONG TAIL: a mortgage.—*Legal.*

NEEDY MIZZLER: a shabby person; a tramp who runs away without paying for his lodging.

PADDING KENS or **CRIBS:** tramps' and boys' lodging houses.

PANNY: a house—public or otherwise; "flash **PANNY,**" a public-house used by thieves; **PANNY MEN,** housebreakers.

PERCH or **ROOST:** a resting place; "I'm off to **PERCH,**" *i.e.,* I am going to bed.

ROOKERY: a low neighbourhood inhabited by dirty Irish and thieves —as **ST. GILES' ROOKERY.**—*Old.* In *Military slang* that part of the barracks occupied by subalterns, often by no mean a pattern of good order.

SKIPPER IT: to sleep in the open air or in a rough way.

SKIPPER-BIRDS or **KEYHOLE WHISTLERS:** persons who sleep in barns or outhouses in preference to lodging-houses.

SKY PARLOUR: the garret.

SLUMS or **BACK SLUMS:** dark retreats, low neighbourhoods; "the Westminster **SLUMS,**" favourite haunts for thieves.

STALL: to lodge or put up at a public house. Also, to act a part. —*Theatrical.*

WATER CLOSETS and CHAMBER POTS

BOG or **BOG-HOUSE:** a water-closet.—*School term.* In the Inns of Court, I am informed, this term is very common.

COFFEE-SHOP: a water-closet or house of office.

CRAPPING CASE or **KEN:** a privy or water-closet.

DUNNY-KEN: a water-closet. — *See* KEN *page 280.*

FORAKERS: a water-closet or house of office. — Term used by the boys at *Winchester school.*

FOURTH or **FOURTH COURT:** the court appropriated to the water-closets at *Cambridge*; from its really being No. 4 at Trinity College. A man leaving his room to go to this **FOURTH COURT** writes on his door *"gone to the* **FOURTH***,"* or, in algebraic notation, "GONE 4—the *Cambridge* slang phrase.

HOUSE OF COMMONS: a water-closet.

JERRY: a chamber utensil, abbreviation of JEROBOAM. — *Swift.* JERRY-COME-TUMBLE, a water-closet.

JORDAN: a chamber utensil. — *Saxon.*

MRS. JONES: the house of office, a water-closet.

MY AUNT: a water-closet or house of office.

PROS: a water-closet. Abbreviated form of προς τινα τοπον. — *Oxford University.*

SCRAPING CASTLE: a water-closet.

WEST CENTRAL: a water-closet, the initials being the same as those of the London Postal District. It is said that for this reason very delicate people refuse to obey Rowland Hill's instructions in this particular.

 # CLOTHING and ACCESSORIES

BUILD: applied in fashionable slang to the make and style of dress, &c.; "it's a tidy **BUILD**, who made it?"

CANT OF TOGS: a gift of clothes.

CLY: a pocket. — *Old Cant* for to steal. A correspondent derives this word from the *Old English*, CLEYES, claw; *Anglo Saxon*, CLEA. This pronunciation is still retained in Norfolk; thus, to CLY would mean to pounce upon, snatch. — *See* FRISK *page 139.*

DEATH: "to dress to DEATH," *i.e.*, to the very extreme of fashion, perhaps so as to be KILLING.

DISHABBILLY: the ridiculous corruption of the *French*, DESHABILLE, [Stripped] amongst fashionably affected, but ignorant "stuck-up" people.

DRAWERS: formerly the *Ancient Cant* name for very long stockings, now a hosier's term.

DUDDS: clothes or personal property. *Gaelic*, DUD; *Ancient Cant*; also *Dutch*.

DUNNAGE: baggage, clothes. Also, a *Sea* term for wood or loose faggots laid at the bottom of ships, upon which is placed the cargo.

FIG: "in full FIG," *i.e.*, full dress costume, "extensively got-up."

FIGURE: "to cut a good or bad FIGURE," to make a good or indifferent appearance; "what's the FIGURE?" how much is to pay? FIGURE-HEAD, a person's face. — *Sea term.*

GET-UP: a person's appearance or general arrangement. Probably derived from the decorations of a play.

> "There's so much GETTING UP to please the town.
> It takes a precious deal of coming down."
> > — *Planche's Mr. Buckstone's Ascent of Parnassus.*

HANDSEL or **HANDSALE:** the *lucky money*, or first money taken in the morning by a pedlar. — *Cocker's Dictionary*, 1724. "Legs of mutton (street term for sheep's trotters, or feet) two for a penny; who'll give me a HANSEL? Who'll give me a HANSEL," — *Cry at Cloth Fair at the present day.* Hence, earnest money, first fruits, &c. In Norfolk, HANSELLING a thing is using it for the first time, as wearing a new coat, taking seizin of it, as it were. — *Anglo Saxon. N. Bailey.*

KICK: a pocket.

LULLY PRIGGERS: rogues who steal wet clothes hung on lines to dry.

MAKE UP: personal appearance. — *Theatrical.*

MUFTI: the civilian dress of a naval or military officer when off duty. — *Anglo Indian.*

PEEL: to strip or disrobe. — *Pugilistic.*

RIGGED: "well-RIGGED," well-dressed. — *Old slang*, in use in 1736. — *See Bailey's Dictionary.* — *Sea.*

SHALLOWS: "to go on the SHALLOWS," to go half-naked.

SHODDY: old cloth worked up into new; also, a term of derision applied to workmen in woolen factories.—*Yorkshire.*

SLOP: cheap or ready made, as applied to clothing, is generally supposed to be a modern appropriation; but it was used in this sense in 1691 by *Maydman* in his *Naval Speculations*; and by *Chaucer* two centuries before that. **SLOPS** properly signify sailors' working clothes.

SLOUR'D: buttoned up; **SLOUR'D HOXTER,** an inside pocket buttoned up.

SPIFFY: spruce, well-dressed, *tout à la mode.*

SPORT: to exhibit, to wear, &c.; a word which is made to do duty in a variety of senses, especially at the University.—*See the Gradus ad Cantabrigiam.* "To **SPORT** a new title," "to **SPORT** an Ægrotat" (*i.e.,* a permission from the "Dons" to abstain from lectures, &c., on account of illness); "to **SPORT ONE'S OAK,**" to shut the outer door and exclude the public—especially *duns* and boring acquaintances. Common also in the Inns of Court.—*See Notes and Queries,* 2ⁿᵈ series, vol. viii. P. 492, and *Gentleman's Magazine,* December, 1794.

SPRINGER-UP: a tailor who sells low-priced, ready-made clothing, and gives starvation wages to the poor men and women who "make up" for him. The clothes are said to be **SPRUNG-UP** or "blown together."

TACKLE: clothes.—*Sea.*

TITIVATE: to put in order or dress up.

TOG: to dress or equip with an outfit; "**TOGGED** out to the nines," dressed in the first style.

TOGERY: clothes, harness, domestic paraphernalia of any kind.

TOGS: clothes; "Sunday **TOGS,**" best clothes. One of the oldest *Cant* words, in use in the time of Henry VIII.

TRANSLATOR: a man who deals in old shoes or clothes, and refits them for cheap wear.

TURN OUT: personal show or appearance; a man with a showy carriage and horses is said to have a good **TURN OUT.**

WALL-FLOWERS: left-off and "regenerated" clothes, exposed for sale in Monmouth-Street.

WELL: to pocket or place as in a well.

CLOTHING MAKERS and TERMS

BANDY or **CRIPPLE:** a sixpence, so called from this coin being generally bent or crooked; old term for flimsy or bad cloth, temp. Q. Elizabeth.

BRADS: money. Properly, a small kind of nails used by cobblers. —Compare HORSE NAILS page 194.

CABBAGE: pieces of cloth said to be purloined by tailors.

COUNTER JUMPER: a shopman, a draper's assistant.

DRIZ: lace. In a low lodging house, this singular autograph inscription appears over the mantelpiece, "Scotch Mary, with DRIZ (lace), bound to Dover and back, please God."

GOOSE: a tailor's pressing iron.—Originally a slang term, but now in most dictionaries.

KNIGHT: a common and ironical prefix to a man's calling—thus, "KNIGHT of the whip," a coachman; "KNIGHT of the thimble," a tailor.

PASTE-HORN: the nose. Shoemakers nickname any shopmate with a large nose "old PASTE-HORN," from the horn in which they keep their paste.

PEAKING: remnants of cloth.

POST-HORN: the nose.—*See* PASTE-HORN *above.*

ROLL OF SNOW: a piece of Irish linen.

SANK WORK: making soldiers' clothes. *Mayhew* says from the *Norman,* SANC, blood—in allusion either to the soldier's calling or the colour of his coat.

SHODDY: old cloth worked up into new; also, a term of derision applied to workmen in woolen factories.—*Yorkshire.*

SIXES AND SEVENS: articles in confusion are said to be all SIXES AND SEVENS. The Deity is mentioned in the Towneley Mysteries as He that "sett all on seven," *i.e.,* set or appointed everything in seven days. A similar phrase at this early date implies confusion and disorder, and from these, *Halliwell* thinks, has been derived the phrase "to be at SIXES AND SEVENS." A Scotch correspondent, however, states that the phrase probably came from the workshop, and that amongst needle makers when the points and eyes are "heads and tails" ("heeds and thraws") or in confusion, they are said to be SIXES AND SEVENS, because those numbers are the sizes most generally used, and in the course of manufacture have frequently to be distinguished.

SNIP: a tailor.

SNYDER: a tailor. *German*, SCHNEIDER.

SPIFFS: the percentage allowed by drapers to their young men when they effect a sale of old-fashioned or undesirable stock.

SPRINGER-UP: a tailor who sells low-priced, ready-made clothing, and gives starvation wages to the poor men and women who "make up" for him. The clothes are said to be SPRUNG-UP or "blown together."

SQUEEZE: silk.

STANGEY: a tailor; a person under petticoat government—derived from the custom of "*riding the* STANG," mentioned in Hudibras:

> "It is a custom used of course
> Where the grey mare is the better horse."

STEEL BAR DRIVERS or **FLINGERS:** journeymen tailors.

SUFFERER: a tailor.

TINGE: the percentage allowed by drapers and clothiers to their assistants, upon the sale of old-fashioned articles.—*See* SPIFFS.

TROTTER: a tailor's man who goes 'round for orders.—*University.*

WHIPPING THE CAT: when an operative works at a private house by the day. Term used amongst tailors and carpenters.

HANDKERCHIEFS and NECKERCHIEFS

BILLY: a silk pocket handkerchief.—*Scotch.*—*See* WIPE *page 287.*

*** A list of the slang terms descriptive of the various patterns of handkerchiefs, pocket and neck, is here subjoined:

BELCHER, close striped pattern, yellow silk, and intermixed with white and a little black; named from the pugilist, Jim Belcher.

BIRD'S EYE WIPE, diamond spots.

BLOOD RED FANCY, red.

> BLUE BILLY, blue ground with white spots.
>
> CREAM FANCY, any pattern on a white ground.
>
> GREEN KING'S MAN, any pattern on a green ground.
>
> RANDAL'S MAN, green, with white spots; named after Jack Randal, pugilist.
>
> WATER'S MAN, sky coloured.
>
> YELLOW FANCY, yellow, with white spots.
>
> YELLOW MAN, all yellow.

BLUE-BILLY: the handkerchief (blue ground with white spots) worn and used at prize fights. Before a SET TO, it is common to take it from the neck and tie it around the leg as a garter, or round the waist, to "keep in the wind." Also, the refuse ammoniacal lime from gas factories.

CATARACT: a black satin scarf arranged for the display of jewellery, much in vogue among "commercial gents."

CHOKER: a cravat, a neckerchief. WHITE-CHOKER, the white neckerchief worn by mutes at a funeral and waiters at a tavern. Clergymen are frequently termed WHITE-CHOKERS.

CLOUT or **RAG:** a cotton pocket handkerchief.—*Old Cant.*

FOGLE: a silk handkerchief—not a CLOUT, which is of *cotton*. It has been hinted that this may have come from the *German*, VOGEL, a bird, from the *bird's eye* spots on some handkerchiefs (*see* BIRD'S-EYE-WIPE, *under* BILLY *above*), but a more probable derivation is the *Italian* slang (*Fourbesque*) FOGLIA, a pocket or purse; or from the *French argot*, FOUILLE, also a pocket.

KENT RAG or **CLOUT:** a cotton handkerchief.

KIDMENT: a pocket-handkerchief fastened to the pocket and partially hung out to entrap thieves.

KINGSMAN: the favourite coloured neckerchief of the costermongers. The women wear them thrown over their shoulders. With both sexes they are more valued than any other article of clothing. A coster's *caste*, or position, is at stake, he imagines, if his KINGSMAN is not of the most approved pattern. When he fights, his KINGSMAN is tied either around his waist as a belt or as a garter around his leg. This very singular partiality for a peculiar coloured neckcloth was doubtless derived from the Gipseys, and probably refers to an Oriental taste or custom long forgotten by these vagabonds. A singular similarity of taste for certain colours exists amongst the Hindoos, Gipseys, and London costermongers. Red and yellow (or orange) are the great favourites, and in these hues the Hindoo selects his turban and his robe; the Gipsey his breeches, and his wife her shawl or gown; and the costermonger his plush waistcoat and favourite KINGSMAN. Amongst either class, when a fight takes place, the greatest regard is paid to the favourite coloured article of dress. The Hindoo lays aside his turban, the Gipsey folds up his scarlet breeches or coat, whilst the pugilistic costermonger of Covent Garden or Billingsgate, as we have just seen, removes his favourite neckerchief to a part of his body, by the rules of the "ring" comparatively out of danger. Amongst the various patterns of kerchiefs worn by the wandering tribes of London, red and yellow are the oldest and most in fashion. Blue, intermixed with spots, is a late importation, probably from the Navy, through sporting characters.

MUCKENDER or **MUCKENGER:** a pocket handkerchief.—*Old.*

SNEEZER: a snuff box; a pocket-handkerchief.

SNOTTER or **WIPE-HAULER:** a pickpocket who commits great depredations upon gentlemen's pocket handkerchiefs.—*North.*

SNOTTINGER: a coarse word for a pocket-handkerchief. The *German* SCHNUPFTUCH is, however, nearly as plain. A handkerchief was also anciently called a MUCKINGER or MUCKENDER.

STOOK: a pocket-handkerchief.

STOOK HAULER or **BUZZER:** a thief who takes pocket-handkerchiefs.

TYE or **TIE:** a neckerchief. Proper hosier's term now, but slang thirty years ago, and as early as 1718. Called also, SQUEEZE.

WATERMAN: a light blue silk handkerchief. The Oxford and *Cambridge* boats' crews always wear these—light blue for *Cambridge,* and a darker shade for Oxford.

WIPE: a pocket handkerchief.—*Old Cant.*

HATS

BEAVER: old street term for a hat; GOSS is the modern word, BEAVER, except in the country, having fallen into disuse.

BONNET: to strike a man's cap or hat over his eyes and nose.

CANISTER-CAP: a hat. — *Pugilistic.*

CASTOR: a hat. CASTOR was once the ancient word for a BEAVER; and strange to add, BEAVER was the slang for CASTOR, or hat, thirty years ago, before gossamer came into fashion.

CHUMMY: a chimney sweep; also a low-crowned felt hat.

FANTAIL: a dustman's hat.

FELT: a hat. — *Old term, in use in the sixteenth century.*

FOUR AND NINE or **FOUR AND NINEPENNY GOSS:** a cheap hat. So called from 4s. 9d., the price at which a noted advertising hat maker sold his hats:

> "Whene'er to slumber you incline,
> Take a *short* NAP at 4 and 9." — 1844.

GOLGOTHA: a hat, "place of a skull,"

GOSS: a hat — from the gossamer silk with which modern hats are made.

KISS-ME-QUICK: the name given to the very small bonnets worn by females since 1850.

MORTAR-BOARD: the term given by the vulgar to the square college caps.

NAP or **NAPPER:** a hat. From NAB, a hat, cap, or head. — *Old Cant.*

PANTILE: a hat. The term PANTILE is properly applied to the mould into which the sugar is poured which is afterwards known as "loaf sugar." Thus, PANTILE, from whence comes the phrase "a sugar loaf hat," originally signified a tall, conical hat, in shape similar to that usually represented as the head gear of a bandit. From PANTILE, the more modern slang term TILE has been derived. — *Halliwell* gives PANTILE SHOP, a meeting-house.

RINGING CASTORS: changing hats.

TILE: a hat; a covering for the head.

> "I'm a gent, I'm a gent,
> In the Regent-street style,—
> Examine my vest,
> And look at my Tile,"—*Popular Song.*

Sometimes used in another sense, "Having a TILE loose," *i.e.,* being slightly crazy.—*See* **PANTILE** *above.*

WIDE-AWAKE: a broad-brimmed felt or stuff hat—so called because it never had a *nap,* and never wants one.

 ## MEN'S COATS

BENJAMIN: a coat. Formerly termed a **JOSEPH**, in allusion, perhaps, to Joseph's coat of many colours.—*See* **UPPER BENJAMIN** *below.*

BENJY: a waistcoat.

BLUE BLANKET: a rough overcoat made of coarse pilot cloth.

FAN: a waistcoat.

GARRET: the fob pocket.

HIP INSIDE: inside coat pocket.

HIP OUTSIDE: outside coat pocket.

HOXTER: an inside pocket.—*Old English,* **OXTER.**

JARVEY: the driver of a hackney coach; **JARVEY'S UPPER BENJAMIN**, a coachman's over-coat.

M. B. COAT: *i.e., Mark of the Beast,* a name given to the long surtout worn by the clergy—a modern Puritan form of abuse, said to have been accidentally disclosed to a Tractarian customer by a tailor's orders to his foreman.

NOAH'S ARK: a long closely buttoned overcoat, recently in fashion. So named by *Punch* from the similarity which it exhibits to the figure of Noah and his sons in children's toy arks.

PATENT COAT: a coat with pockets inside the skirts—termed **PATENT** from the difficulty of picking them.

PIT: a breast pocket.

PYGOSTOLE: the least irreverent of names for the peculiar "M. B." coats worn by Tractarian curates.

> "It is true that the wicked make sport
> Of our **PYGOSTOLES**, as we go by;
> And one gownsman, in Trinity Court,
> Went so far as to call me a 'Guy,'"

ROCK A LOW: an overcoat. Corruption of the *French* **ROQUELAURE.**

SLASH: a pocket in an overcoat.

TAIL BUZZER: a thief who picks coat pockets.

TOG: a coat. *Latin,* **TOGA.** *—Ancient Cant.*

UPPER BENJAMIN: a great coat.

WELL: to pocket or place as in a well.

 ## MEN'S SHIRTS

ALL-ROUNDERS: the fashionable shirt collars of the present time worn meeting in front.

CAMESA: shirt or chemise.*—Spanish. Ancient Cant,* **COMMISSION.**

CHITTERLINGS: the shirt frills worn still by ancient beaux; properly, the *entrails of a pig,* to which they are supposed to bear some resemblance. *Belgian,* **SCHYTERLINGH.**

COMMISSION: a shirt.*—Ancient Cant. Italian,* **CAMICIA.**

DICKEY: formerly the *Cant* for a worn-out shirt, but means now-a-days a front or half-shirt. **DICKEY** was originally **TOMMY** (from the Greek, τομη, a section), a name which I understand was formerly used in Trinity College, Dublin. The students are said to have invented the term, and the **GYPS** change it to **DICKEY**, in which dress it is supposed to have been imported into England.

FLESH-BAG: a shirt.

GILLS: shirt collars.

MILL-TOG: a shirt—most likely the prison garment.

MISH: a shirt or chemise. From **COMMISSION**, the *Ancient Cant* for a shirt, afterwards shortened to **K'MISH** or **SMISH**, and then to **MISH**. *French*, **CHEMISE**; *Italian*, **CAMICIA**.

"With his snowy **CAMESH** and his shaggy capote," — *Byron*.

NARP: a shirt. — *Scotch*.

ROUNDS: shirt collars — apparently a mere shortening of "All Rounds," or "All Rounders," names of fashionable collars.

SHAKER: a shirt.

SIDE BOARDS or **STICK-UPS:** shirt collars.

SMISH: a shirt or chemise. Corruption of the *Spanish*. — *See* **MISH** *above*.

STICK-UPS or **GILLS:** shirt collars.

TOMMY: — *See* **DICKEY** *above*.

 ## MEN'S TROUSERS

BAGS: trousers. Trousers of an extensive pattern or exaggerated fashionable cut, have lately been termed **HOWLING BAGS**, but only when the style has been very "*loud*." The word is probably an abbreviation for b-mbags. "To have the **BAGS** off," to be of age and one's own master, to have plenty of money.

BREEKS: breeches. — *Scotch*, now common.

BUM: the part on which we sit. — *Shakespere*. **BUMBAGS**, trousers.

INEXPRESSIBLES, UNUTTERABLES, UNWHISPERABLES, or **SIT-UPONS:** trousers, the nether garments.

KICKSIES: trousers.

PEG-TOPS: the loose trousers now in fashion, small at the ankle and swelling upwards, in imitation of the Zouave costume.

SIT-UPONS: trousers. — *See* **INEXPRESSIBLES** *above*.

TRUCKS: trousers.

UNUTTERABLES: trousers. — *See* **INEXPRESSIBLES** *above*.

UN-WHISPERABLES: trousers.

SHOES and STOCKINGS

BATS: a pair of bad boots.

BEATER-CASES: boots.—*Nearly obsolete.*

BOWLES: shoes.

CARTS: a pair of shoes. In Norfolk the carapace of a crab is called a *crab cart*, hence CARTS would be synonymous with CRABSHELLS.

CRABSHELLS or TROTTING CASES: shoes.—*See* CARTS *above.*

GADDING THE HOOF: going without shoes. GADDING, roaming about, although used in an old translation of the Bible, is now only heard amongst the lower orders.

HIGH-LOWS: laced boots reaching a trifle higher than anclejacks.

STAMPERS: shoes.—*Ancient Cant.*

TRANSLATORS: second hand boots mended and polished, and sold at a low price. Monmouth-street, Seven Dials, is a great market for TRANSLATORS.

TROTTER CASES: shoes.

VAMPS: old stockings. From VAMP, to piece.

WATCHES and JEWELRY

CHRISTENING: erasing the name of the maker from a stolen watch, and inserting a fictitious one in its place.

CHURCH A YACK: (or watch), to take the works of a watch from its original case and put them into another one, to avoid detection.—*See* CHRISTENING *above.*

FAWNEY: a finger ring.

FAWNEY or FAWNEY RIG: ring dropping. A few years ago, this practice or RIG, was very common. A fellow purposely dropped a ring or a pocket book with some little articles of jewellery, &c., in it, and when he saw any person pick it up, ran to claim half. The ring found, the questions of how the booty was to be divided had then to be decided. The *Fawney* says, "if you will give me eight or nine shilling for my share the things are yours." This the FLAT thinks very fair. The ring of course is valueless, and the swallower of the bait discovers the trick too late.

FAWNEY BOUNCING: selling rings for a wager. This practice is founded upon the old tale of a gentleman laying a wager that if he was to offer "real gold sovereigns" at a penny a piece at the foot of London Bridge, the English public would be too incredulous to buy. The story states that the gentleman stationed himself with sovereigns in a tea tray, and sold only two within the hour—winning the bet. This tale the FAWNEY BOUNCERS tell the public, only offering brass, double gilt rings, instead of sovereigns.

JARK: a seal or watch ornament.—*Ancient Cant.*

PROP: a gold scarf pin.

PROP-NAILER: a man who steals, or rather snatches, pins from gentlemen's scarfs.

RING DROPPING:—*See* FAWNEY *above.*

SLANG: a watch chain.

SUIT: a watch and seals.

SUPER: a watch; SUPER-SCREWING, stealing watches.

TATLER: a watch; "nimming a TATLER," stealing a watch.

THIMBLE or **YACK:** a watch.

THIMBLE TWISTERS: thieves who rob persons of their watches.

TICKER: a watch.

WATCHMAKER: a pickpocket or stealer of watches.

WHITE PROP: a diamond pin.

YACK: a watch, to "*church* a YACK," to take it out of its case to avoid detection.

WEAPONS and TOOLS

BARKING IRONS: pistols.

BILBO: a sword; abbrev. of BILBOA blade. Spanish swords were anciently very celebrated, especially those of Toledo, Bilboa, &c.

BROWN BESS: the old Government regulation musket.

CHIVE: a knife, a sharp tool of any kind.—*Old Cant*. This term is particularly applied to the tin knives used in goals.

FIDDLE: a whip.

FLOGGER: a whip.—*Obsolete.*

JEMMY: a crowbar.

JILT: a crowbar or housebreaking implement.

POPS: pocket pistols.

STICKS: pistols.—*Nearly obsolete.*

TOASTING FORK: derisive term for a sword.

WOMEN'S CLOTHING

CARDINAL: a lady's cloak. This, I am assured, is the *Seven Dials Cant* term for a lady's garment, but curiously enough the same name is given to the most fashionable patterns of the article by Regent-street drapers. A cloak with this name was in fashion in the year 1760. It received its title from its similarity in shape to one of the vestments of a cardinal.

CAT: a lady's muff; "to free a CAT," *i.e.*, steal a muff.

DOWD: a woman's nightcap.—*Devonshire*; also an *American* term; possibly from DOWDY, a slatternly woman.

DRAWERS: formerly the *Ancient Cant* name for very long stockings, now a hosier's term.

FLAG: an apron.

KISS-ME-QUICK: the name given to the very small bonnets worn by females since 1850.

MIDGE NET: a lady's veil.

MOLLSACK: a reticule or market basket.

SPREAD: a lady's shawl. SPREAD, at the *East* end of London, a feast, or a TIGHTENER; at the *West* end a fashionable reunion, an entertainment, display of good things.

WIRE: a thief with long fingers, expert at picking ladies' pockets.

 OTHER ACCESSORIES

BARNACLES: a pair of spectacles; corruption of **BINOCULI?**

CATCH EM ALIVE: a trap, also a small-toothed comb.

DEE: a pocket book, term used by tramps. — *Gipsey*.

DIGGERS: spurs; also the spades on cards.

DUMMY: a pocket book.

FLAG: an apron.

GIGLAMPS: spectacles. In my first edition I stated this to be a *University* term. *Mr. Cuthbert Bede*, however, in a communication to *Notes and Queries*, of which I have availed myself in the present edition, says: "If the compiler has taken this epithet from *Verdant Green*, I can only say that I consider the word not to be a 'University' word in general, but as only due to the inventive genius of Mr. Bouncer in particular." The term, however, has been adopted, and is now in general use.

GURRELL: a fob.

HADDOCK: a purse. — *See* **BEANS** *page 193*.

JAZEY: a wig. A corruption of **JERSEY**, the name for flax prepared in a peculiar manner, and of which common wigs were formerly made.

LOUSE-TRAP: a small-toothed comb. — *Old Cant.* — *See* **CATCH 'EM ALIVE**.

MOLLSACK: a reticule or market basket.

PERSUADERS: spurs.

READER: a pocket-book; "give it him for his **READER**," *i.e.*, rob him of his pocket-book. — *Old Cant*.

SKIN: a purse.

SLAP: paint for the face, rouge.

SLICK A DEE: a pocket book.

SNEEZER: a snuff box; a pocket-handkerchief.

SOOT BAG: a reticule.

FOOD

EATING AND HUNGER

ATTACK: to carve or commence operations on; "ATTACK that beef, and oblige!"

BANDED: hungry.

BANYAN-DAY: a day on which no meat is served out for rations; probably derived from the BANIANS, a Hindoo caste, who abstain from animal food. — *Sea.*

BOLT: to swallow without chewing.

BOX-HARRY: a term with bagmen or commercial travellers, implying dinner and tea at one meal; also dining with Humphrey, *i.e.*, going without. — *Lincolnshire.*

BROSIER: a bankrupt. — *Cheshire.* **BROSIER-MY-DAME,** school term, implying a clearing of the housekeeper's larder of provisions, in revenge for stinginess. — *Eton.*

CRUMBS: "to pick up one's CRUMBS," to begin to have an appetite after an illness; to improve in health, circumstances, &c., after a loss thereof.

DUTCH FEAST: where the host gets drunk before his guest.

FLYING-MESS: "to be in FLYING MESS" is a soldier's phrase for being hungry and having to mess where he can. — *Military.*

FOXY: rank, tainted. — *Lincolnshire.*

GILLS: the lower part of the face. — *Bacon.* "To grease one's GILLS," "to have a good feed," or make a hearty meal.

MUFFIN-WORRY: an old ladies' tea party.

NECK: to swallow. **NECK-OIL,** drink of any kind.

OFF ONE'S FEED: real or pretended want of appetite. — *Stable slang.*

PANNAM-BOUND: stopping the prison food or rations to a prisoner. **PANNAM-STRUCK,** very hungry.

PECKISH: hungry. *Old Cant,* **PECKIDGE,** meat.

ROUGH IT: to put up with chance entertainment, to take pot luck, and what accommodation "turns up," without sighing for better. "ROUGHING IT *in the Bush*" is the title of an interesting work on Backwoods life.

SAM: to "stand SAM," to pay for refreshment or drink, to stand paymaster for anything. An *Americanism* originating in the letter U.S. on the knapsacks of the United States soldiers, which letters were jocularly said to be the initials of *Uncle Sam* (the Government), who pays for all. In use in this country as early as 1827.

SHORT COMMONS: short allowance of food.—*See* COMMONS *p. 297.*

SLUSHY: a ship's cook.

STODGE: to surfeit, gorge, or clog with food.

TUCK: a schoolboy's term for fruit, pastry, &c. TUCK IN or TUCK OUT, a good meal.

TWIST: appetite; "Will's got a capital TWIST."

FOOD IN GENERAL

BATTLES: the students' term at Oxford for rations. At *Cambridge,* COMMONS.

BELLY-TIMBER: food or "grub."

BLOW OUT or TUCK IN: a feast.

CAG-MAG: bad food, scraps, odds and ends; or that which no one could relish. *Grose* gives CAGG MAGGS, old and tough Lincolnshire geese, sent to London to feast the poor cockneys.

CHUCK: a schoolboy's treat.—*Westminster school.* Food, provisions for an entertainment.—*Norwich.*

COMMONS: rations, because eaten *in common.*—*University.* SHORT COMMONS (derived from the University slang term), a scanty meal, a scarcity.

CRUG: food.—*Household Words*, No. 183.

GOLOPSHUS: splendid, delicious, luscious.—*Norwhich.*

GRUB: meat or food, of any kind—GRUB signifying food, and BUB, drink.

INSIDE LININGS: dinner, &c.

MUNGARLY: bread, food. **MUNG** is an *old word* for mixed food, but **MUNGARLY** is doubtless derived from the *Lingua Franca*, **MANGIAR**, to eat.—*See* **MUNGARLY CASA** *page 304.*

PANNAM: food, bread.—*Lingua Franca*, **PANNEN**; *Latin*, **PANIS**; *Ancient Cant*, **YANNAM**.

PECK: food; "**PECK** and booze," meat and drink.—*Lincolnshire. Ancient Cant*, **PEK**, meat.

POT-LUCK: just as it comes; to take **POT-LUCK**, *i.e.*, one's chance of a dinner—a hearty term used to signify whatever the pot contains you are welcome to.

SCRAN: pieces of meat, broken victuals. Formerly the reckoning at a public-house. **SCRANNING**, begging for broken victuals. Also, an *Irish* malediction of a mild sort, "Bad **SCRAN** to yer!"

SIZE: to order extras over and above the usual commons at the dinner in college halls. Soup, pastry, &c. are **SIZINGS**, and are paid for at a certain specified rate *per* **SIZE**, or portion, to the college cook.—*Peculiar to Cambridge. Minsheu* says, "**SIZE**, a farthing which schollers in *Cambridge* have at the buttery, noted with the letter *s*."

SNACK: booty or share. Also, a light repast.—*Old Cant* and *Gipsey* term.

SPREAD: a lady's shawl. **SPREAD**, at the *East* end of London, a feast, or a **TIGHTENER**; at the *West* end a fashionable reunion, an entertainment, display of good things.

TIGHTNER: a dinner or hearty meal.

TUCK: a schoolboy's term for fruit, pastry, &c. **TUCK IN** or **TUCK OUT**, a good meal.

VINNIED: mildewed or sour.—*Devonshire.*

BREAD and DAIRY

BEESWAX: poor soft cheese.

BUSTER (BURSTER): a small new loaf; "twopenny **BUSTER**," a twopenny loaf. "A pennorth o' **BEES WAX** (cheese) and a penny **BUSTER**," a common snack at beershops.

CASSAM: cheese—not CAFFAN, which Egan, in his edition of *Grose*, has ridiculously inserted.—*Ancient Cant. Latin,* CASEUS.

COW'S GREASE: butter.

DUFF: pudding; vulgar pronunciation of DOUGH.—*Sea.*

OINTMENT: medical student slang for butter.

PANNAM: food, bread.—*Lingua Franca,* PANNEN; *Latin,* PANIS; *Ancient Cant,* YANNAM.

SCRAPE: cheap butter; "bread and SCRAPE," the bread and butter issued to school-boys—so called from the butter being laid on, and then *scraped* off again, for economy's sake.

SOFT TACK: Bread.—*Sea.*

SPREAD: butter.

TOKE: dry bread.

TOMMY: bread—generally a penny roll.

TUCK: a schoolboy's term for fruit, pastry, &c. TUCK IN or TUCK OUT, a good meal.

DESSERTS

BOWLAS: round tarts made of sugar, apple, and bread, sold in the streets.

CAKEY-PANNUM-FENCER: a man who sells street pastry.

CLAGGUM: boiled treacle in a hardened state. *Hardbake.*—*See* CLIGGY.

DUFF: pudding; vulgar pronunciation of DOUGH.—*Sea.*

TUCK: a schoolboy's term for fruit, pastry, &c. TUCK IN or TUCK OUT, a good meal.

DRINKS (non-alcoholic)

ADAM'S ALE: water.—*English.* The *Scotch* term is ADAM'S WINE.

BITCH: tea, "a BITCH party," a tea-drinking.—*University.*

BUB: drink of any kind.—*See* GRUB *below. Middleton, the dramatist,* mentions BUBBER, a great drinker.

GRUB: meat, or food of any kind—GRUB signifying food, and BUB, drink.

LUG: to pull or slake thirst.—*Old.*

MUFFIN-WORRY: an old ladies' tea party.

NECK: to swallow. NECK-OIL, drink of any kind.

OLD GOWN: smuggled tea.

SALOOP, SALEP, or **SALOP:** a greasy-looking beverage, formerly sold on stalls at early morning, prepared from a powder made of the root of the *Orchis mascula*, or Red-handed Orchis. Within a few years coffee stands have superseded SALOOP stalls, but Charles Lamb, in one of his papers, has left some account of this drinkable, which he says was of all preparations the most grateful to the stomachs of young chimney sweeps.

SKY-BLUE: London milk much diluted with water or from which the cream has been too closely skimmed.

> "Hence, Suffolk dairy wives run mad for cream,
> And leave their milk with nothing but the name;
> Its name derision and reproach pursue,
> And strangers tell of three times skimmed—SKY-BLUE."
> —*Bloomfield's Farmer's Boy.*

Sky-blue formerly meant gin.

SLOPS: chests or packages of tea; "he shook a slum of SLOPS," *i.e.,* stole a chest of tea.

WATER-BEWITCHED: very weak tea, the third brew (or the first at some houses), grog much diluted.

FRUITS and VEGGIES

CRAB or **GRAB:** a disagreeable old person. *Name of a wild and sour fruit.* "To catch a CRAB," to fall backwards by missing a stroke in rowing.

GAWFS: cheap red-skinned apples, a favourite fruit with costermongers, who rub them well with a piece of cloth, and find ready purchasers.

MURPHY: a potato. Probably from the Irish national liking for potatoes, MURPHY being a common surname amongst the Irish.—*See* MIKE *page 171.* MURPHIES(*edible*) are sometimes called DUNNAMANS.

ROSE: an orange.

SPECKS: damaged oranges.

SPUDDY: a seller of bad potatoes. In *Scotland,* a SPUD is a raw potato; and roasted SPUDS are those cooked in the cinders with their jackets on.

TALLY: five dozen bunches of turnips.

TUCK: a schoolboy's term for fruit, pastry, &c. TUCK IN or TUCK OUT, a good meal.

◆ MEATS

ALDERMAN: a turkey.

ALDERMAN IN CHAINS: a turkey hung with sausages.

BALL: prison allowance, viz., six ounces of meat.

BLOCK ORNAMENTS: the small dark coloured pieces of meat exposed on the cheap butchers' blocks or counters—debatable points to all the sharp-visaged, argumentative old women in low neighbourhoods.

BLOODY-JEMMY: a sheep's head.—*See* SANGUINARY JAMES *below.*

BULL: term amongst prisoners for meat served to them in jail.

CHITTERLINGS: the shirt frills worn still by ancient beaux; properly, the *entrails of a pig,* to which they are supposed to bear some resemblance. *Belgian,* SCHYTERLINGH.

CHONKEYS: a kind of mince meat baked in a crust and sold in the streets.

DAB: street term for a flat fish of any kind.—*Old.*

FIELD-LANE-DUCK: a baked sheep's head. *Field-lane* is a low London thoroughfare, leading from the foot of Holbornhill to the purlieus of

Clerkenwell. It was formerly the market for stolen pocket handkerchiefs.

FINDER: one who FINDS bacon and meat at the market before they are lost, *i.e.,* steals them.

GALENY: *Old Cant* term for a fowl of any kind; now a respectable word in the West of England, signifying a Guinea fowl.—*Vide Grose. Latin,* GALLINA.

GLASGOW MAGISTRATES: salt herrings.—*Scotch.*

GOUROCK HAM: salt herrings. Gourock, on the Clyde, about twenty-five miles from Glasgow, was formerly a great fishing village. —*Scotch.*

GRUB: meat, or food of any kind—GRUB signifying food, and BUB, drink.

HUMBLE PIE: to "eat HUMBLE PIE," to knock under, be submissive. The UMBLES, or entails of a deer, were anciently made into a dish for servants, while their masters feasted off the haunch.

JEMMY: a sheep's head.—*See* SANGUINARY JAMES *below.*

JUNK: salt beef.—*See* OLD HORSE *below.*

LEGS OF MUTTON: inflated street term for sheeps' trotters, or feet.

MOKO: a name given by sportsmen to pheasant killed by mistake in partridge shooting during September, before the pheasant shooting comes in. They pull out their tails, and roundly assert they are no pheasants at all, but MOKOS.

MOUNTAIN PECKER: a sheep's head.—*See* JEMMY *above.*

OLD HORSE: salt junk or beef.—*Sea.*

PECKISH: hungry. *Old Cant,* PECKIDGE, meat.

PETER: a partridge.—*Poacher's term.*

PLUCK: the heart, liver, and lungs of an animal—all that is PLUCKED away in connection with the windpipe, from the chest of a sheep or hog; among low persons, courage, valour, and a stout heart.—*See* MOLLYGRUBS *page 78.*

POLONY: a *Bologna* sausage.

PROG: meat, food, &c. *Johnson* calls it "a low word."

SALT JUNK: navy salt beef.—*See* OLD HORSE *above.*

SANGUINARY JAMES: a sheep's head. —*See* **BLOODY JEMMY** *above.*

SAVELOY: a sausage of chopped beef smoked, a minor kind of **POLONY.**

SAWNEY: bacon. **SAWNEY HUNTER,** one who steals bacon.

SCRAN: pieces of meat, broken victuals. Formerly the reckoning at a public-house. **SCRANNING,** begging for broken victuals. Also, an *Irish* malediction of a mild sort, "Bad **SCRAN** to yer!"

SHARP'S-ALLEY BLOOD WORMS: beef sausages and black puddings. Sharp's-alley was very recently a noted slaughtering place near Smithfield.

SNAGGLING: angling for geese with a hook and line, the bait being a worm or snail. The goose swallows the bait, and is quietly landed and bagged.

SNOTS: small bream, a slimy kind of flat fish. —*Norwich.*

SOLDIER: a red herring.

SOW'S BABY: a pig; sixpence.

STAGGERING BOB: an animal to whom the knife only just anticipates death from natural disease or accident —said of meat on that account unfit for human food.

STICKINGS: bruised or damaged meat sold to sausage makers and penny pie shops. —*North.*

TOSS: a measure of sprats.

TROTTERS: feet. Sheep's **TROTTERS,** boiled sheep's feet, a favourite street delicacy.

TURKEY-MERCHANTS: dealers in plundered or contraband silk. Poulterers are sometimes termed **TURKEY MERCHANTS,** in memory of Horne Tooke's answer to the boys at Eton, who wished in an aristocratic way to know who *his* father was—a **TURKEY MERCHANT,** replied Tooke. His father was a poulterer. **TURKEY MERCHANT,** also, was formerly slang for a driver of turkeys or geese to market.

WATCH AND SEALS: a sheep's head and pluck.

WOOLBIRD: a lamb; "wing of a **WOOLBIRD,**" a shoulder of lamb.

WORMING: removing the beard of an oyster or muscle.

YARMOUTH CAPON: a bloater, or red herring. —*Old—Ray's Proverbs.*

OTHER FOOD

CLAGGUM: boiled treacle in a hardened state. *Hardbake. — See* **CLIGGY.**

KICKSHAWS: trifles; made, or French dishes — not English, or substantial. Corruption of the *French,* **QUELQUES CHOSES.**

LOBLOLLY: gruel. — *Old:* used by *Markham* as a sea term for grit gruel or hasty pudding.

SKILIGOLEE: prison gruel, also sailors' soup of many ingredients.

SKILLY: broth served on board the hulks to convicts. — *Line.*

SMIGGINS: soup served to convicts on board the hulks.

STUNNED ON SKILLY: to be sent to prison and compelled to eat **SKILLY** or **SKILLIGOLEE.**

TIFFIN: a breakfast, *dejeuner a la fourchette. — Anglo Indian slang.*

PLACES TO EAT and DRINK

BOOZE or **SUCK-CASA:** a public-house.

BOOZING-KEN: a beer- shop, a low public house. — *Ancient.*

COLD BLOOD: a house licensed for the sale of beer "NOT to be drunk on the premises."

CRIB: house, public or otherwise; lodgings, apartments.

FLATTY-KEN: a public house, the landlord of which is ignorant of the practices of the thieves and tramps who frequent it.

GRUBBING-KEN or **SPINIKIN:** a workhouse; a cook-shop.

HUSH-SHOP or **CRIB:** a shop where beer or spirits is sold "on the quiet" — no license being paid.

JERRY: a beer house.

LUSH-CRIB: a public house.

MUNGARLY CASA: a baker's shop; evidently a corruption of some *Lingua Franca* phrase for an eating house. The well-known "Nix mangiare" stairs at Malta derive their name from the endless beggars who lie there and shout **NIX MANGIARE,** *i.e.,* "nothing to eat," to excite the compassion of the English who land there—an expression which exhibits remarkably the mongrel composition of the *Lingua Franca*, MANGIARE being *Italian*, and *Nix* an evident importation from Trieste or other Austrian seaport.

MUTTONWALK: the saloon at Drury Lane Theatre.

NOSE-BAGS: visitors at watering places, and houses of refreshment, who carry their own victuals.—*Term applied by waiters.*

PANNY: a house—public or otherwise; "flash PANNY," a public-house used by thieves; PANNY MEN, housebreakers.

PIC.: the Piccadilly Saloon.

PIG AND TINDER-BOX: the vulgar rendering of the well-known tavern sign, *"Elephant and Castle."*

PUB or **PUBLIC:** a public-house.

SLUICERY: a gin shop or public house.

STALL: to lodge or put up at a public house. Also, to act a part. —*Theatrical.*

SUCK-CASA: a public-house.

WOBBLESHOP: where beer is sold without a license.

POSSESSIONS

BAUBLES and KNICKKNACKS

GIMCRACK: a bijou, a slim piece of mechanism. *Old slang* for "a spruce wench."—*N. Bailey.*

GINGUMBOB: a bauble.

JEW'S EYE: a popular simile for anything valuable. Probably a corruption of the *Italian*, GIOJE; *French*, JOUAILLE, a jewel. In ancient times, when a king was short of cash, he generally issued orders for so many *Jew's eyes* or equivalent sums of money. The Jews preferred paying the ransom, although often very heavy. We thus realize the popularly believed origin of JEW'S EYE. Used by *Shakespere.*

NICK-KNACK: a trifle.—Originally *Cant.*

CLOTH and RAGS

BANDY or **CRIPPLE:** a sixpence, so called from this coin being generally bent or crooked; old term for flimsy or bad cloth, temp. Q. Elizabeth.

CABBAGE: pieces of cloth said to be purloined by tailors.

DRIZ: lace. In a low lodging house, this singular autograph inscription appears over the mantelpiece, "Scotch Mary, with DRIZ (lace), bound to Dover and back, please God."

MILKY ONES: white linen rags.

PEAKING: remnants of cloth.

ROLL OF SNOW: a piece of Irish linen.

SHODDY: old cloth worked up into new; also, a term of derision applied to workmen in woolen factories. — *Yorkshire.*

SNOW: wet linen.

SNOW GATHERERS or **SNOW-DROPPERS:** rogues who steal linen from hedges and drying grounds.

SQUEEZE: silk.

TATS: old rags; MILKY TATS, white rags.

TATTING: gathering old rags.

CONTAINERS

CANNIKEN: a small can, similar to PANNIKIN. — *Shakespere.*

KYPSEY: a basket.

MOLLSACK: a reticule or market basket.

PETER: a bundle or valise. — *Bulwer's Paul Clifford.*

PIPKIN: the stomach — properly, an earthen round-bottomed pot. — *Norwich.*

POKE: a bag or sack; "to buy a pig in a POKE," to purchase anything without seeing it. — *Saxon.*

SHALLOW: a flat basket used by costers.

SLUM: a chest or package.—*See* **SLOPS** *page 300.*

YOKUFF: a chest or large box.

KITCHEN SUPPLIES

CHATTRY-FEEDER: a spoon.

FEEDER: a spoon.—*Old Cant.*

HEN AND CHICKENS: large and small pewter pots.

LATCHPAN: the lower lip—properly a dripping pan; "to hang one's LATCHPAN," to pout, be sulky.—*Norfolk.*

LIGHT-FEEDERS: silver spoons.

PANNIKIN: a small pan.

PEWTER: money, like **TIN**, used generally to signify silver; also, a pewter-pot.

SMASHFEEDER: a Britannia metal spoon—the best imitation shillings are made from this metal.

SMUT: a copper boiler. Also, the "blacks" from a furnace.

SNIPES: "a pair of **SNIPES**," a pair of scissors. They are occasionally made in the form of that bird.

WEDGE-FEEDER: silver spoon.

SMOKING ACCOUTREMENT

BLOW A CLOUD: to smoke a cigar or pipe—a phrase in use two centuries ago.

CHURCHWARDEN: a long pipe, "A YARD OF CLAY."

CUTTY PIPE: a short clay pipe. *Scotch*, **CUTTY**, short. *Cutty-sark*, a scantily draped lady is so called by *Burns*.

FOGUS: tobacco.—*Old Cant.* **FOGO**, *old word for stench.*

MUNDUNGUS: trashy tobacco. *Spanish*, **MONDONGO**, black pudding.

NINE CORNS: a pipeful of tobacco.

NOSE EM or FOGUS: tobacco.

QUID: a small piece of tobacco—one mouthful. *Quid est hoc?* asked one, tapping the swelled cheek of another; *hoc est quid*, promptly replied the other, exhibiting at the same time "a chaw" of the weed. Probably a corruption of CUD.

SCREW: a small packet of tobacco.

SPUNKS: Lucifer matches.—*Herefordshire; Scotland*. SPUNK, says Urry, in his MS. notes to Ray, "is the excrescency of some tree, of which they make a sort of tinder to light their pipes with."

WEED: a cigar; *the* WEED, tobacco generally.

YARD OF CLAY: a long, old-fashioned tobacco pipe, also called a *churchwarden*.

OTHER HOUSEHOLD ITEMS

BETTY: a skeleton key or picklock.—*Old Cant.*

CATCH EM ALIVE: a trap, also a small-toothed comb.

CRACK: dry firewood.—*Modern Gipsey.*

DUBS: a bunch of keys.—*Nearly obsolete.*

GRIFFIN: in India, a newly arrived cadet; general for an inexperienced youngster. "Fast" young men in London frequently term an umbrella a GRIFFIN.

JARK: a seal or watch ornament.—*Ancient Cant.*

MONKEY: a padlock.

MUSH: an umbrella. Contraction of *mushroom.*

PROPS: crutches.

RAIN NAPPER: umbrella.

SCREEVE: a letter, a begging petition.

SCREW: a key—skeleton or otherwise.

SLOUR: to lock or fasten.

SLUM: a letter.

STICKY: wax.

STIFF: paper, a bill of acceptance, &c.; "how did you get it, STIFF or hard?" *i.e.*, did he pay you cash or give a bill?

STROMMEL: straw.—*Ancient Cant*. Halliwell says that in Norfolk STRUMMEL is a name for hair.

UNBETTY: to unlock.—*See* BETTY *above*.

QUALITIES OF HOUSEHOLD ITEMS

ALL TO SMASH, or **GONE TO PIECES:** bankrupt or smashed to pieces.—*Somersetshire*.

CLIGGY or **CLIDGY:** sticky. —*Anglo Saxon*, CLÆG, clay. —*See* CLAGGUM.

CRACK: first-rate, excellent; "a CRACK HAND," an adept; a "CRACK article," a good one.—*Old*.

CRANKY: foolish, idiotic, ricketty, capricious, not confined to persons. *Ancient Cant*, CRANKE, simulated sickness. *German*, KRANK, sickly.

FOXY: rank, tainted.—*Lincolnshire*.

GRUBBY: musty or old-fashioned.—*Devonshire*.

HASH: a mess, confusion; "a pretty HASH he made of it," to HASH UP, to jumble together without order or regularity.

IT'S GOOD ON THE STAR: it's easy to open.

OUT AND OUT: prime, excellent, of the first quality. OUT AND OUTER, "one who is of an OUT AND OUT description," UP to anything. An ancient MS. has this couplet, which shows the antiquity of the phrase—

> "The Kyng was good alle aboute,
> And she was wycked *oute and oute*."

PLUMMY: round, sleek, jolly, or fat; excellent, very good, first-rate.

POKY: confined or cramped; "that corner is POKY and narrow." —*Times* article, 21ˢᵗ July, 1859.

REAM: good or genuine. From the *Old Cant*, RUM.

RUGGY: fusty, frowsy.

SHACKLY: loose, rickety.—*Devonshire*.

SIXES AND SEVENS: articles in confusion are said to be all SIXES AND SEVENS. The Deity is mentioned in the Towneley Mysteries as He that "sett all on seven," *i.e.*, set or appointed everything in seven days. A similar phrase at this early date implies confusion and disorder, and from these, *Halliwell* thinks, has been derived the phrase "to be at SIXES AND SEVENS." A Scotch correspondent, however, states that the phrase probably came from the workshop, and that amongst needle makers when the points and eyes are "heads and tails" ("heeds and thraws") or in confusion, they are said to be SIXES AND SEVENS, because those numbers are the sizes most generally used, and in the course of manufacture have frequently to be distinguished.

SLANTINGDICULAR: oblique, awry—as opposed to PERPENDICULAR.

SMITHERS or **SMITHEREENS:** "all to SMITHEREENS," all to smash. SMITHER, is a *Lincolnshire* word for a fragment.

SPLENDIFEROUS: sumptuous, first-rate.

TANNY or **TEENY:** little. *Gipsey*, TAWNO, little.

TIP-TOP: first-rate, of the best kind.

TWO-HANDED: awkward.

VINNIED: mildewed or sour.—*Devonshire*.

MOVE ALONG, FOLKS

Own only what you can carry with you; know language, know countries, know people. Let your memory be your travel bag.

Alexander Solzhenitsyn

G **iven** that the first shock absorbers weren't invented until the 1900s, travel back in the day had to be uncomfortable, to say the least. No wonder cabs, coaches, carts, and trains were all referred to as **rattlers**.

Although the first horseless carriages were invented in the late 1700s, by Hotten's day, they were still an oddity around town. Foot power—be that man or beast—was the way to go. And a man who was a good driver, or **jarvey,** might do well.

The **jarveys** seem to have been a competitive lot. Not only did they try to upset each other's vehicles, and edge out competing omnibuses, according to John Camden Hotten, "the old **jarveys**, to show their skill, used to drive against things so close as absolutely to touch, yet without injury. This they called **Toucher**, or **Touch and Go**, which was hence applied to anything which was within an ace of ruin." Not sure I'd want to be a passenger for that.

Editor's Faves:

DAISY-CUTTER: a horse which trots or gallops without lifting its feet much from the ground.

HUNTING THE SQUIRREL: when hackney and stage coachmen try to upset each other's vehicles on the public roads.—*Nearly obsolete.*

QUICK STICKS: in a hurry, rapidly; "to cut QUICK STICKS," to be in a great hurry.

IN THIS CHAPTER

DRIVERS and TERMS

BONE-PICKER: a footman.

BROTHER-CHIP: fellow carpenter. Also, BROTHER-WHIP, a fellow coachman; and BROTHER-BLADE, of the same occupation or calling —originally a fellow soldier.

CABBY: the driver of a cab.

CAD: an onminbus conductor.

CHARIOT-BUZZING: picking pockets in an omnibus.

CULLING or **CULING:** stealing from the carriages on racecourses.

DAISY-KICKERS: the name hostlers at large inns used to give each other, now *nearly obsolete*. DAISY-KICKER or GROGHAM was likewise the *Cant* term for a horse. The DAISY-KICKERS were sad rogues in the old posting days; frequently the landlords rented the stables to them, as the only plan to make them return a profit.

DRAG: a cart of any kind, a coach; gentlemen drive to the races in DRAGS.

DRAGGING: robbing carts, &c.

DRAGSMEN: fellows who cut trunks from the backs of carriages. They sometimes have a light cart, and "drop behind" the plundered vehicle, and then drive off in an opposite direction with the booty.

FIDDLE: a whip.

FLOGGER: a whip.—*Obsolete.*

HORSE'S NIGHTCAP: a halter; "to die in the HORSE'S NIGHTCAP," to be hung.

HUNTING THE SQUIRREL: when hackney and stage coachmen try to upset each other's vehicles on the public roads.—*Nearly obsolete.*

JARVEY: the driver of a hackney coach; JARVEY'S UPPER BENJAMIN, a coachman's over-coat.

JEHU: old slang term for a coachman or one fond of driving.

KNIGHT: a common and ironical prefix to a man's calling—thus, "KNIGHT of the whip," a coachman; "KNIGHT of the thimble," a tailor.

NURSE: a curious term lately applied to competition in omnibuses. Two omnibuses are placed on the road to NURSE, or oppose, each opposition "buss," one before, the other behind. Of course, the central or NURSED buss has very little chance, unless it happens to be a favourite with the public. NURSE, to cheat or swindle; trustees are said to NURSE property, *i.e.*, gradually eat it up themselves.

PEG: "to PEG away," to strike, run, or drive away; "PEG a hack," to drive a cab; "take down a PEG or two," to check an arrogant or conceited person.

PETERER or **PETERMAN:** one who follows hackney and stage coaches, and cuts off the portmanteaus and trunks from behind.—*Nearly obsolete. Ancient* term for a fisherman, still used at Gravesend.

RIBBONS: the reins.—*Middlesex.*

SPILT: thrown from a horse or chaise.—*See* PURL *page 133.*

TOOL: to drive a mail coach.

TOUCHER: "as near as a TOUCHER," as near as possible without actually touching.—*Coaching term.* The old jarveys, to show their skill, used to drive against things so close as absolutely to *touch*, yet without injury. This they called a TOUCHER, or, TOUCH AND GO, which was hence applied to anything which was within an ace of ruin.

TURN OUT: personal show or appearance; a man with a showy carriage and horses is said to have a good TURN OUT.

UNICORN: a style of driving with two wheelers abreast, and one leader, termed in the *United States*, a SPIKE TEAM. TANDEM is one wheeler and one leader. RANDOM, three horses in line.

HORSES and DONKEYS

BUFFER: a familiar expression for a jolly acquaintance, probably from the *French*, BOUFFARD, a fool or clown; a "jolly old BUFFER," said of a good-humoured or liberal old man. In 1737, a BUFFER was a "rogue that killed good sound horses for the sake of their skins, by running a long wire into them." — *Bacchus and Venus*. The term was once applied to those who took false oaths for a consideration.

COPER: properly HORSE-COUPER, a Scotch horse dealer—used to denote a dishonest one.

CRIB BITER: an inveterate grumbler; properly said of a horse which has the habit, a sign of its bad digestion.

DAISY-CUTTER: a horse which trots or gallops without lifting its feet much from the ground.

DAISY-KICKERS: the name hostlers at large inns used to give each other, now *nearly obsolete*. DAISY-KICKER or GROGHAM was likewise the *Cant* term for a horse. The DAISY-KICKERS were sad rogues in the old posting days; frequently the landlords rented the stables to them, as the only plan to make them return a profit.

DARK: "keep it DARK," *i.e.*, secret. DARK HORSE, in racing phraseology a horse whose chance of success is unknown, and whose capabilities have not been made the subject of comment.

DEVOTIONAL HABITS: horses weak in the knees and apt to stumble and fall are said to have these. — *Stable*.

DICKEY: a donkey.

DIGGERS: spurs; also the spades on cards.

FIDDLE: a whip.

FIG: "to FIG a horse," to play improper tricks with one in order to make him lively.

FLOGGER: a whip.—*Obsolete.*

FOALED: "thrown from a horse."—*Hunting term.*—*See* PURL *page 133, and* SPILT *page 131.*

FREE: to steal; generally applied to horses.

GIB-FACE: properly the lower lip of a horse; "TO HANG ONE'S GIB," to pout the lower lip, be angry or sullen.

GINGER: a showy, fast horse—as if he had been FIGGED with GINGER under his tail.

GROGGY: tipsy; when a prize-fighter becomes "weak on his pins," and nearly beaten, he is said to be GROGGY.—*Pugilistic.* The same term is applied to horses in a similar condition. *Old English,* AGGROGGYD, weighed down, oppressed.—*Prompt. Parvulorum.*

HORSE CHAUNTER: a dealer who takes worthless horses to country fairs and disposes of them by artifice. He is flexible in his ethics, and will put in a glass-eye or perform other tricks.—*See* COPER *page 131.*

HORSE'S NIGHTCAP: a halter; "to die in the HORSE'S NIGHTCAP," to be hung.

JERUSALEM PONY: a donkey.

JIB or **JIBBER:** a horse that starts or shrinks. *Shakespere* uses it in the sense of a worn-out horse.

KNACKER: an old horse; a horse slaughterer.—*Gloucestershire.*

LEG IT: to run; LEG BAIL, to run off, "to give a LEG," to assist, as when one mounts a horse; "making a LEG," a countryman's bow, —projecting the leg from behind as a balance to the head bent forward.—*Shakespere.*

MOKE: a donkey.—*Gipsey.*

NEDDY: a donkey.

OFF ONE'S FEED: real or pretended want of appetite.—*Stable slang.*

OUT-SIDER: a person who does not habitually bet or is not admitted to the "Ring." Also, a horse whose name does not appear among the "favourites."

PEACOCK HORSE: amongst undertakers, is one with a showy tail and mane, and holds its head up well.—*che va favor-reggiando, &c., Italian.*

PERSUADERS: spurs.

PLUNDER: a common word in the horse trade to express profit. Also an *American* term for baggage, luggage.

PRAD: a horse.

PRAD NAPPING: horse stealing.

PRANCER: a horse.—*Ancient Cant.*

PURL: hunting term for a fall, synonymous with FOALED, or SPILT; "he'll get PURLED at the rails."

RACKS: the bones of a dead horse. Term used by horse slaughterers.

RANDOM: three horses driven in line, a very appropriate term.—*See* UNICORN *below.*

RIBBONS: the reins.—*Middlesex.*

ROARER: a broken-winded horse.

RUCK: the undistinguished crowd; "to come in with the RUCK," to arrive at the winning post among the non-winning horses.—*Racing term.*

SCRATCH: to strike a horse's name out of the list of runners in a particular race. "Tomboy was SCRATCHED for the Derby, at 10, a.m., on Wednesday," from which period all bets made in reference to him (with one exception) are void.—*See* P.P.—*Turf.*

SCREW: an unsound or broken-down horse, that requires both whip and spur to get him along.

SICK AS A HORSE: popular simile—curious, because a horse never vomits.

SNAFFLED: arrested, "pulled up;" so termed from a kind of horse's bit, called a SNAFFLE. In *East Anglia*, to SNAFFLE is to talk foolishly.

SPANK: to move along quickly; hence a fast horse or vessel is said to be "a SPANKER to go."

SPILT: thrown from a horse or chaise.—*See* PURL *page 133.*

STALE: to evacuate urine.—*Stable term.*

TIT: favourite name for a horse.

TOOTH: "he has cut his eye TOOTH," *i.e.*, he is sharp enough or old enough, to be so; "up in the TOOTH," far advanced in age—said often of old maids. *Stable term* for aged horses which have lost the distinguishing mark in their teeth.

UNICORN: a style of driving with two wheelers abreast, and one leader, termed in the *United States*, a SPIKE TEAM. TANDEM is one wheeler and one leader. RANDOM, three horses in line.

WALK OVER: a re-election without opposition.—*Parliamentary*, but derived from the *Turf*, where a horse—which has no rivals entered —WALKS OVER the course, and wins without exertion.

ROADS, RAILWAYS, and TOWNS

BUFFER: a dog. Their skins were formerly in great request—hence the term, BUFF meaning in *Old English* to skin. It is still used in the ring, BUFFED meaning stripped to the skin. In *Irish Cant*, BUFFER is a *boxer*. The BUFFER of a railway carriage doubtless received its very appropriate name from the old pugilistic application of this term.

DRAG: a street or road; BACK-DRAG, back-street.

GAMMY-VIAL: (Ville) a town where the police will not let persons hawk.

HUEY: a town or village.

KNAPPING-JIGGER: a turnpike-gate; "to dub at the KNAPPING-JIGGER," to pay money at the turnpike.

MAIN-TOBY: the highway or the main road.

MONKERY: the country or rural districts. *Old* word for a quiet or monastic life.—*Hall*.

PAD: the highway; a tramp.—*Lincolnshire*.

PIKE: a turnpike: "to bilk a PIKE," to cheat the keeper of the toll-gate.

RATTLERS: a railway; "on the RATTLERS to the stretchers," *i.e.*, going to the races by railway.

RECENT INCISION: the busy thoroughfare on the Surrey side of the Thames, known by sober people as the NEW CUT.

SHUNT: to throw or turn aside.—*Railway term*.

TOBY: a road; "high **TOBY**," the turnpike road. "High **TOBY** spice," robbery on horse-back.—*Don Juan,* canto xi., 19.

TOBY CONSARN: a highway expedition.

VILLE or **VILE:** a town or village.—pronounced *phial* or *vial.*—*French.*

WILD: a village.—*Tramps' term.*—*See* **VILE** *above.*

VEHICLES

BIRD-CAGE: a four-wheeled cab.

BOUNDER: a four-wheeled cab. *Lucus a non lucendo?*

BUGGY: a gig or light chaise. Common term in America and in Ireland.

BUSS: an abbreviation of "omnibus," a public carriage. Also, a kiss.

CAB: in statutory language, "a hackney carriage drawn by one horse." Abbreviated from **CABRIOLET,** *French;* originally meaning "a light low chaise." The wags of Paris playing upon the word (quasi *cabri* au lait) used to call a superior turn-out of the kind a *cabri au creme.* Our abbreviation, which certainly smacks of slang, has been stamped with the authority of "George, *Ranger.*" See the notices affixed to the carriage entrances of St. James' Park.

CASK: fashionable slang for a brougham or other private carriage. —*Household Words,* No. 183.

DRAG: a cart of any kind, a coach; gentlemen drive to the races in **DRAGS.**

HUM-DRUM: tedious, tiresome, boring; "a society of gentleman who used to meet near the Charter house or at the King's Head, St. John's Street. They were characterised by less mystery and more pleasantry than the Freemasons."—*Bacchus and Venus,* 1737. In the *West,* a low cart.

KNIFE-BOARD: the seat running along the roof of an omnibus.

MAB: a cab or hackney coach.

RATTLER: a cab, coach, or cart.—*Old Cant.*

SHOWFULL or **SCHOFELL:** a Hansom cab—said to have been from the name of the inventor.—*Led de hor qu.*

SULKY: a one-horse chaise, having only room for one person.

TRAP: a "fast" term for a carriage of any kind. **TRAPS,** goods and chattels of any kind, but especially luggage and personal effects; in Australia, **SWAG.**

TROLLY or **TROLLY-CARTS:** term given by costermongers to a species of narrow cart, which can either be drawn by a donkey or driven by hand.

TURN OUT: personal show or appearance; a man with a showy carriage and horses is said to have a good **TURN OUT.**

VARDO: to look; "**VARDO** the cassey," look at the house. **VARDO** formerly was *Old Cant* for a wagon.

WHITECHAPEL or **WESTMINSTER BROUGHAM:** a costermonger's donkey-barrow.

 # SAILORS and SEA TERMS

A 1: first-rate, the very best; "she's a prime girl she is; she is **A 1.**" *— Sam Slick.* The highest classification of ships at Lloyd's; common term in the United States, also at Liverpool and other English seaports. Another even more intensive form, is "first-class, letter A, No. 1."

AVAST: a sailor's phrase for stop, shut up, go away — apparently connected with the *Old Cant,* **BYNGE A WASTE.**

BANYAN-DAY: a day on which no meat is served out for rations; probably derived from the **BANIANS,** a Hindoo caste, who abstain from animal food. *— Sea.*

BOOM: "to tip one's **BOOM** off," to be off or start in a certain direction. *— Sea.*

BULL-THE-CASK: to pour hot water into an empty rum puncheon, and let it stand until it extracts the spirit from the wood. The result is drunk by sailors in default of something stronger. *— Sea.*

BUM-BOATS: shore boats which supply ships with provisions, and serve as means of communication between the sailors and the shore.

CHALKS: "to walk one's **CHALKS,**" to move off or run away. An ordeal for drunkenness used on board ship, to see whether the suspected person can walk on a chalked line without overstepping it on either side.

CRAB or **GRAB:** a disagreeable old person. *Name of a wild and sour fruit.* "To catch a CRAB," to fall backwards by missing a stroke in rowing.

DAVY'S LOCKER or **DAVY JONES' LOCKER:** the sea, the common receptacle for all things thrown overboard—a nautical phrase for death, the other world.

DOLDRUMS: difficulties, low spirits, dumps.—*Sea.*

DOUSE: to put out; "DOUSE that glim," put out that candle.—*Sea.*

DUDDERS or **DUDSMEN:** persons who formerly travelled the country as pedlars, selling gown-pieces, silk waistcoats, &c., to countrymen. In selling a waistcoat-piece for thirty shillings or two pounds, which cost them perhaps five shillings, they would show great fear of the revenue officer, and beg of the purchasing clodhopper *to kneel down in a puddle of water, crook his arm, and swear that it might never become straight if he told an exciseman, or even his own wife.* The term and practice are *nearly obsolete.* In Liverpool, however, and at the east end of London, men dressed up as sailors with pretended silk handkerchiefs and cigars "only just smuggled from the Indies," are still to be plentifully found.

DUFF: pudding; vulgar pronunciation of **DOUGH**.—*Sea.*

DUNNAGE: baggage, clothes. Also, a *Sea* term for wood or loose faggots laid at the bottom of ships, upon which is placed the cargo.

FIGURE: "to cut a good or bad FIGURE," to make a good or indifferent appearance; "what's the FIGURE?" how much is to pay? **FIGURE-HEAD**, a person's face.—*Sea term.*

FIN: a hand; "come, tip us your FIN," viz., let us shake hands.—*Sea.*

FLIPPER: the hand; "give us your FLIPPER," give me your hand.—*Sea.* Metaphor taken from the flipper or paddle of a turtle.

GLIM: a light, a lamp; "dowse the GLIM," put the candle out.—*Sea, and Old Cant.*

GRAPPLING IRONS: fingers.—*Sea.*

HALF SEAS OVER: reeling drunk.—*Sea.* Used by *Swift.*

HARD UP: in distress, poverty-stricken.—*Sea.*

HAWSE HOLES: the apertures in a ship's bows through which the cables pass; "he has crept in through the **HAWSE HOLES**," said of an officer who has risen from the grade of an ordinary seaman. — *Navy*.

HORSE MARINE: an awkward person. In ancient times the "**JOLLIES**" or Royal Marines, were the butts of the sailors, from their ignorance of seamanship. "Tell that to the **MARINES**, the blue jackets won't believe it!" was a common rejoinder to a "stiff yarn." Now-a-days they are deservedly appreciated as the finest regiment in the service. A **HORSE MARINE** (an impossibility) was used to denote one more awkward still.

JACK TAR: a sailor.

JIB: the face or a person's expression; "the cut of his **JIB**," *i.e.*, his peculiar appearance. The sail of a ship, which in position and shape corresponds to the nose on a person's face. — *See* **GIB-FACE** *page 316*.

JUNK: salt beef. — *See* **OLD HORSE** *page 158*.

KEEL-HAULING: a good thrashing or mauling, rough treatment, — from the old nautical custom of punishing offenders by throwing them overboard with a rope attached and hauling them up from under the ship's keel.

LAGGER: a sailor.

LAND LUBBER: sea term for a landsman. — *See* **LOAFER** *below*.

LAND-SHARK: sailor's definition of a lawyer.

LARK: fun, a joke; "let's have a jolly good **LARK**," let us have a piece of fun. *Mayhew* calls it "a convenient word covering much mischief." — *Anglo Saxon*, **LAC**, sport; but more probably from the nautical term **SKYLARKING**, *i.e.*, mounting to the highest yards and sliding down the ropes for amusement, which is allowed on certain occasions.

LOAFER: a lazy vagabond. Generally considered an *Americanism*. **LOPER** or **LOAFER**, however, was in general use as a *Cant* term in the early part of the last century. **LANDLOPER** was a vagabond who begged in the attire of a sailor; and the sea phrase, **LAND LUBBER**, was doubtless synonymous. — *See the Times*, 3rd November, 1859, for a reference to **LOAFER**.

LOBLOLLY: gruel. — *Old*: used by *Markham* as a sea term for grit gruel or hasty pudding.

LOBLOLLY BOY: a derisive term for a surgeon's mate in the navy.

LUBBER'S HOLE: an aperture in the maintop of a ship, by which a timid climber may avoid the difficulties of the "futtock shrouds" —hence, a sea term for a cowardly way of evading duty.

LUMPER: a contractor. On the river, more especially a person who contracts to deliver a ship laden with timber.

LUMPERS: low thieves who haunt wharves and docks, and rob vessels; persons who sell old goods for new.

MARINE or MARINE RECRUIT: an empty bottle. This expression having once been used in the presence of an officer of marines, he was at first inclined to take it as an insult, until someone adroitly appeased his wrath by remarking that no offence could be meant, as all that it could possibly imply was, "one who had done his duty, and was ready to do it again." —*See* HORSE MARINE *page 55.*—*Naval.*

MATE: the term a coster or low person applies to a friend, partner, or companion; "me and my MATE did so and so," is a common phrase with a low Londoner.—Originally a *Sea term.*

MIDDY: abbreviation of MIDSHIPMAN.—*Naval.*

MUFTI: the civilian dress of a naval or military officer when off duty. —*Anglo Indian.*

NEDDY: a life preserver.—Contraction of KENNEDY, the name of the first man, it is said in St. Giles', who had his head broken by a poker. —*Vide Mornings at Bow Street.*

OLD HORSE: salt junk or beef.—*Sea.*

PAY: to beat a person or "serve them out." Originally a nautical term, meaning to stop the seams of a vessel with pitch (*French,* POIX); "here's the devil to PAY and no pitch hot," said when any catastrophe occurs which there is no means of averting; "to PAY over face and eyes, as the cat did the monkey;" "to PAY through the nose," to give a ridiculous price—whence the origin? *Shakespere* uses PAY in the sense of to beat or thrash.

PIPE: to shed tears or bewail; "PIPE one's eye." —*Sea term.*

> "He first began to eye his pipe,
> and then to PIPE HIS EYE."
> —*Old Song.*

Metaphor from the boatswain's pipe, which calls to duty.

PUMP SHIP: to evacuate urine. — *Sea.*

RIGGED: "well-RIGGED," well-dressed. *Old slang,* in use in 1736. — *See Bailey's Dictionary.* — *Sea.*

SALT JUNK: navy salt beef. — *See* OLD HORSE *page 158.*

SHAVER: a sharp fellow; "a young" or "old SHAVER," a boy or man. — *Sea.*

SHIP-SHAPE: proper, in good order; sometimes the phrase is varied to "SHIP-SHAPE and *Bristol* fashion." — *Sea.*

SING OUT: to call aloud. — *Sea.*

SKATES LURK: a begging impostor dressed as a sailor.

SKILIGOLEE: prison gruel, also sailors' soup of many ingredients.

SKIPPER: the master of a vessel. *Dutch,* SCHIFFER, from *schiff* a ship; sometimes used synonymous with "Governor."

SKY-LARK: — *See* LARK *page 157.*

SKY-SCRAPER: a tall man; "are you cold up there, old SKY-SCRAPER?" Properly a sea term; the light sails which some adventurous skippers set above the royals in calm latitudes are termed SKY-SCRAPERS and MOON-RAKERS.

SLEWED: drunk or intoxicated. — *Sea term.* When a vessel changes the tack she, as it were, staggers, the sails flap, she gradually heels over and, the wind catching the waiting canvas, she glides off at another angle. The course pursued by an intoxicated, or SLEWED man, is supposed to be analogous to that of the ship.

SLIP: "to give the **Slip**," to run away or elude pursuit. *Shakespere* has "you *gave me the counterfeit,*" in Romeo and Juliet. GIVING THE SLIP, however, is a *Sea phrase,* and refers to fastening an anchor and chain cable to a floating buoy or water cask, until such a time arrives that is convenient to return and take them on board. In fastening the cable, the home end is *slipped* through the hawse pipe. Weighing anchor is a noisy task, so that giving it the SLIP infers to leave it in quietness.

SLOP: cheap or ready made, as applied to clothing, is generally supposed to be a modern appropriation; but it was used in this sense in 1691 by *Maydman* in his *Naval Speculations*; and by *Chaucer* two centuries before that. SLOPS properly signify sailors' working clothes.

SLUSHY: a ship's cook.

SNAGGLE TEETH: uneven and unpleasant looking dental operators.
—*West.* **SNAGS** (*Americanism*) ends of sunken drift-wood sticking out of the water, on which river steamers are often wrecked.

SOFT TACK: Bread.—*Sea.*

SPANK: to move along quickly; hence a fast horse or vessel is said to be "a **SPANKER** to go."

SPLICE: to marry, "and the two shall become one flesh." —*Sea.*

SPLICE THE MAIN BRACE: to take a drink.—*Sea.*

SQUARE-RIGGED: well-dressed.—*Sea.*

SWIPES: sour or small beer. **SWIPE**, to drink.—Sea.

TACKLE: clothes.—*Sea.*

THREE SHEETS IN THE WIND: unsteady from drink.—*Sea.*

TIP: a douceur; also to give, lend, or hand over anything to another person; "come, **TIP** up the tin," *i.e.*, hand up the money; "**TIP** the wink," to inform by winking; "**TIP** us your fin," *i.e.*, give me your hand; "**TIP** one's boom off," to make off, depart.—*Sea.* "To miss one's **TIP**," to fail in a scheme.—*Old Cant.*

TOSHERS: men who steal copper from ships' bottoms in the Thames.

TRUCK-GUTTED: pot-bellied, corpulent.—*Sea.*

TURNPIKE-SAILORS: beggars who go about dressed as sailors.

WHIP: To "**WHIP** anything *up*," to take it up quickly; from the method of hoisting heavy goods or horses on board ship by a **WHIP**, or running tackle, from the yard-arm. Generally used to express anything dishonestly taken.—*L' Estrange* and *Johnson.*

WHIP JACK: a sham shipwrecked sailor, called also a **TURNPIKE SAILOR**.

WHISTLE: "as clean as a **WHISTLE**," neatly or "**SLICKLY** done," as an American would say; "to **WET ONE'S WHISTLE**," to take a drink. This is a very old term. *Chaucer* says of the Miller of Trumpington's wife (*Canterbury Tales*, 4153)—

"So was hir joly **WHISTAL** well **Y-WET**;"

"to **WHISTLE FOR ANYTHING**," to stand small chance of getting it, from the nautical custom of *whistling* for a wind in a calm, which of course comes none the sooner for it.

YARN: a long story or tale; "a tough YARN," a tale hard to be believed; "spin a YARN," tell a tale. — *Sea.*

YOUNKER: in street language, a lad or a boy. Term in general use amongst costermongers, cabmen, and old-fashioned people. *Barnefield's Affectionate Shepherd,* 1594, has the phrase, "a seemelie YOUNKER." *Danish* and *Friesic,* JONKER. In the *Navy,* a naval cadet is usually termed a YOUNKER.

WALKING

BOOM: "to tip one's BOOM off," to be off or start in a certain direction. — *Sea.*

GADDING THE HOOF: going without shoes. GADDING, roaming about, although used in an old translation of the Bible, is now only heard amongst the lower orders.

GRIND: "to take a GRIND," *i.e.,* a walk or constitutional. — *University.*

JOG-TROT: a slow but regular trot or pace.

NIGGLING: trifling or idling; talking short steps in walking. — *North.*

PAD THE HOOF: to walk not ride; "PADDING THE HOOF on the high toby," tramping or walking on the high road.

> "Trudge, plod away o' the hoof."
> — *Merry Wives,* i., 3.

QUICK STICKS: in a hurry, rapidly; "to cut QUICK STICKS," to be in a great hurry.

SCAMANDER: to wander about without a settled purpose; — possibly in allusion to the winding course of the Homeric river of that name.

SHANKS' NAG: "to ride SHANKS' NAG," to go on foot.

SHOOL: to saunter idly, become a vagabond, beg rather than work. — *Smollett's Roderick Random,* vol. i., p.262.

SPANK: to move along quickly; hence a fast horse or vessel is said to be "a SPANKER to go."

STUMP: to go on foot.

TODDLE: to walk as a child.

TRAPESING: gadding or gossiping about in a slatternly way.—*North.*

TROLLING: sauntering or idling.

JUST FOR THE FUN OF IT

Blessed are we who can laugh at ourselves, for we shall never cease to be amused.   Unknown

*T*he purveyors of slang had twenty-six different words for gin. That might seem like a lot, until you consider the quality of the drinking water in London at the time. Drinking water often came straight from the Thames, which was, for the most part, an open sewer. Distilled spirits might kill you, but not as quickly as drinking the water —which may explain why there were fifty-two words for being drunk.

Drunk or sober, they were a playful and rowdy lot. There are thirty terms for larks and pranks, and eleven words for a disturbance.

Some men combined their love of drinking in pubs, musical talent, and their sense of humor to make a living. The **chaunter-culls** would write satirical ballads about any person, or body of persons, for a fee. In three hours the ballads would be all over town. I imagine the songs were extremely entertaining—as long as they weren't about you. In 1859, the year the dictionary was published, there were two men in London making a living as chaunter-culls. I wonder how they would do today.

Editor's Faves:

BELLY-VENGEANCE: small sour beer, apt to cause gastralgia.

FLIP-FLAPS: a peculiar rollicking dance indulged in by costermongers when merry or excited—better described, perhaps, as the DOUBLE SHUFFLE, danced with an air of extreme *abandon*.

LAP THE GUTTER: to get drunk.

IN THIS CHAPTER

ALCOHOL

DRINK IN GENERAL

BOOZE: drink. *Ancient Cant,* **BOWSE.**

BREAKY-LEG: strong drink; "he's been to Bungay fair, and **BROKE BOTH HIS LEGS,**" *i.e.,* got drunk. In the ancient Egyptian language the 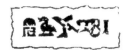 determinative character in the hieroglyphic verb "to be drunk," has the significant form of the leg of a man being amputated.

BUB: drink of any kind.—*See* **GRUB** *page 298. Middleton,* the dramatist, mentions **BUBBER,** a great drinker.

CAT-LAP: a contemptuous expression for weak drink.

COMMON SEWER: a **DRAIN,** or drink.

DODGER: a dram. In *Kent,* a **DODGER** signifies a nightcap; which name is often given to the last dram at night.

DRAIN: a drink; "to do a **DRAIN,**" to take a friendly drink—"do a wet;" sometime called a **COMMON SEWER.**

JIGGER: a secret still, illicit spirits.—*Scotch.*

LUSH: intoxicating drinks of all kinds, but generally used for beer. The *Globe,* 8th September, 1859, says "**LUSH** and its derivatives claim *Lushington,* the brewer, as sponsor."

NECK: to swallow. **NECK-OIL,** drink of any kind.

SWIG: a hearty drink.

SWIZZLE: small beer, drink.

TITLEY: drink.

WET QUAKER: a drunkard of that sect; a man who pretends to be religious, and is a dram drinker on the sly.

WET: a drink, a "drain."

BEER

BEERY: intoxicated or fuddled with beer.

BELLY-VENGEANCE: small sour beer, apt to cause gastralgia.

BIVVY or **GATTER:** beer; "shant of BIVVY," a pot, or quart of beer. In Suffolk, the afternoon refreshment of reapers is called BEVER. It is also an *Old English* term.

> "He is none of those same ordinary eaters, that will devour three breakfasts, and as many dinners, without any prejudice to their BEVERS, drinkings, or suppers."
> —*Beaumont and Fletcher's Woman Hater* 1—3.

Both words are probably from the *Italian,* BEVERE, *bere. Latin,* BIBERE. *English,* BEVERAGE.

BOOZING-KEN: a beer- shop, a low public house.—*Ancient.*

BUNKER: beer.

BUSTER (BURSTER): a small new loaf; "twopenny BUSTER," a twopenny loaf. "A pennorth o' BEES WAX (cheese) and a penny BUSTER," a common snack at beershops.

COLD BLOOD: a house licensed for the sale of beer "NOT to be drunk on the premises."

COOPER: stout half-and-half, *i.e.,* half stout and half porter.

DOGSNOSE: gin and beer, so called from the mixture being *cold,* like a dog's nose.

FLANNEL or **HOT FLANNEL:** the old term for gin and beer, drank hot, with nutmeg, sugar, &c. Also called FLIP. There is an anecdote told of Goldsmith helping to drink a quart of FLANNEL in a night house, in company with George Parker, Ned Shuter, and a demure grave looking gentleman, who continually introduced the words CRAP, STRETCH, SCRAG, and SWING. Upon the Doctor's asking who this strange person might be, and being told his profession, he rushed from the place in a frenzy, exclaiming, "Good God! and have I been sitting all this while with a hangman?"

GATTER: beer; "shant of **GATTER**," a pot of beer. A curious street melody, brimful and running over with slang, known in the Seven Dials as *Bet, the Coaley's Daughter*, thus mentions the word in a favourite verse:

> "But when I strove my flame to tell
> Says she, '*Come, stow that patter*,'
> If you're a cove wot likes a gal
> Vy don't you *stand* some **GATTER**?
> *In course* I instantly complied—
> Two brimming quarts of porter,
> With four *goes* of gin beside,
> Drained Bet the Coaley's daughter."

HALF AND HALF: a mixture of ale and porter, much affected by medical students; occasionally *Latinized* into **DIMIDIUM DIMIDIUMQUE**. —*See* **COOPER** page 332.

HEAVY WET: porter or beer—because the more a man drinks of it, the heavier he becomes.

JERRY: a beer house.

KNOCK DOWN or **KNOCK ME DOWN:** strong ale.

LUSH: intoxicating drinks of all kinds, but generally used for beer. The *Globe*, 8th September, 1859, says "**LUSH** and its derivatives claim *Lushington*, the brewer, as sponsor."

ROT GUT: bad small beer—in *America*, cheap whisky.

SHANDY-GAFF: ale and ginger beer; perhaps **SANG DE GOFF**, the favourite mixture of one Goff, a blacksmith.

SWANKEY: cheap beer.—*West.*

SWIPES: sour or small beer. **SWIPE**, to drink.—*Sea.*

SWIZZLE: small beer, drink.

WOBBLESHOP: where beer is sold without a license.

GIN

BLUE RUIN: gin.

CAT'S WATER: old Tom, or Gin.

CREAM OF THE VALLEY: gin.

DIDDLE: *Old Cant* word for geneva, or gin.

DOGSNOSE: gin and beer, so called from the mixture being *cold*, like a dog's nose.

DUKE: gin.—*Household Words*, No. 183.

EYE WATER: gin.

FLANNEL or **HOT FLANNEL:** the old term for gin and beer, drank hot, with nutmeg, sugar, &c. Also called FLIP. There is an anecdote told of Goldsmith helping to drink a quart of FLANNEL in a night house, in company with George Parker, Ned Shuter, and a demure grave looking gentleman, who continually introduced the words CRAP, STRETCH, SCRAG, and SWING. Upon the Doctor's asking who this strange person might be, and being told his profession, he rushed from the place in a frenzy, exclaiming, "Good God! and have I been sitting all this while with a hangman?"

GO: a GO of gin, a quartern of that liquor; GO is also synonymous with circumstance or occurrence; "a rummy GO," and "a great GO," signify curious and remarkable occurrences; "no GO," no good; "here's a pretty GO!" here's a trouble! "to GO the jump," to enter a house by the window; "all the GO," in fashion.—*See* LITTLE GO *page 177.*

> "Gemmen (says he), you all well know
> The joy there is whene'er we meet;
> It's what I call the primest GO,
> And rightly named, 'tis—'quite a treat,'"
> —*Jack Randall's Diary*, 1820

JACKEY: gin.

JUNIPER: gin.—*Household Words*, No. 183.

LIGHTNING: gin; "FLASH O' LIGHTNING," a glass of gin.

MAX: gin; MAX-UPON TICK, gin obtained upon credit.

MOONLIGHT or **MOONSHINE:** smuggled gin.

OLD TOM: gin.

SENSATION: a quartern of gin.

SKY-BLUE: London milk much diluted with water or from which the cream has been too closely skimmed.

> "Hence, Suffolk dairy wives run mad for cream,
> And leave their milk with nothing but the name;
> Its name derision and reproach pursue,
> And strangers tell of three times skimmed—SKY-BLUE."
> —*Bloomfield's Farmer's Boy.*

SKY-BLUE formerly meant gin.

SLUICERY: a gin shop or public house.

STAFF NAKED: gin.

STARK-NAKED: (originally STRIP-ME-NAKED, *vide Randall's Diary*, 1820), raw gin.—*Bulwer's Paul Clifford.*

TAPE: gin—term with female servants.

TWIST: brandy and gin mixed.

WATER OF LIFE: gin.

WHITE SATIN: gin—term amongst women.

WHITE TAPE: gin—term used principally by female servants.

WHITE WINE: the fashionable term for gin.

> "Jack Randall then impatient rose,
>   And said, 'Tom's speech were just as fine
> If he would call that first of GO'S
>   By that genteeler name—WHITE WINE.'"
> —*Randall's Diary*, 1820.

WEAK DRINKS and LEFT OVERS

ALLS: tap-droppings refuse spirits sold at a cheap rate in gin-palaces. —*See* LOVAGE *below.*

BULL-THE-CASK: to pour hot water into an empty rum puncheon, and let it stand until it extracts the spirit from the wood. The result is drunk by sailors in default of something stronger.—*Sea.*

CAT-LAP: a contemptuous expression for weak drink.

HEEL-TAPS: small quantities of wine or other beverage left in the bottom of glasses, considered as a sign that the liquor is not liked, and therefore unfriendly and unsocial to the host and the company.

LOVEAGE: tap droppings, a mixture of spirits, sweetened and sold to habitual dram-drinkers, principally females. Called also ALLS.

WATER-BEWITCHED: very weak tea, the third brew (or the first at some houses), grog much diluted.

WINE, MIXED DRINKS, and OTHER SPIRITS

BLACK-STRAP: port wine.

COPUS: a *Cambridge* drink consisting of ale combined with spices and varied by spirits, wines, &c. Corruption of HIPPOCRAS.

DOGSNOSE: gin and beer, so called from the mixture being *cold*, like a dog's nose.

FLANNEL or **HOT FLANNEL:** the old term for gin and beer, drank hot, with nutmeg, sugar, &c. Also called FLIP. There is an anecdote told of Goldsmith helping to drink a quart of FLANNEL in a night house, in company with George Parker, Ned Shuter, and a demure grave looking gentleman, who continually introduced the words CRAP, STRETCH, SCRAG, and SWING. Upon the Doctor's asking who this strange person might be, and being told his profession, he rushed from the place in a frenzy, exclaiming, "Good God! and have I been sitting all this while with a hangman?"

FLESH AND BLOOD: brandy and port in equal quantities.

FRENCH CREAM: brandy.

FRIZZLE: champagne.

HOT TIGER: an Oxford mixture of hot-spiced ale and sherry.

LOVEAGE: tap droppings, a mixture of spirits, sweetened and sold to habitual dram-drinkers, principally females. Called also ALLS.

MOUNTAIN-DEW: whisky, advertised as from the Highlands.

PARNEY: rain; "dowry of PARNEY," a quantity of rain. *Anglo-Indian* slang from the *Hindoo*, PANI, water; *Gipsey*, PANE. Old Indian officers always call brandy and water **BRANDY PAWNEE.**

PEG: brandy and soda water.

PURL: a mixture of hot ale and sugar, with wormwood infused in it, a favourite morning drink to produce an appetite, sometimes with gin and spice added:

> "Two penn'orth o' **PURL** —
> Good 'early **PURL**,'
> 'Gin all the world
> To put your hair into a curl,
> When you feel yourself queer of a mornin'."

TWIST: brandy and gin mixed.

 # DRINKING

BATTER: "on the **BATTER**," literally "on the streets," or given up to roistering and debauchery.

BEMUSE: to fuddle one's self with drink, "**BEMUSING** himself with beer," &c. — *Sala's Gas-light and Day-light*, p. 308.

BOOZE: to drink, or more properly, to use another slang term, to "**LUSH**," viz, to drink continually, until drunk, or nearly so. The term is an old one. Harman, in Queen Elizabeth's days, speaks of "**BOUSING** (or boozing) and belly-cheere." The term was good *English* in the fourteenth century, and comes from the *Dutch*, **BUYZEN**, to tipple.

BOOZING-KEN: a beer- shop, a low public house. — *Ancient.*

BROWN: "to do **BROWN**," to do well or completely (in allusion to roasting); "doing it **BROWN**," prolonging the frolic or exceeding sober bounds; "**DONE BROWN**," taken in, deceived or surprised.

BULL-THE-CASK: to pour hot water into an empty rum puncheon, and let it stand until it extracts the spirit from the wood. The result is drunk by sailors in default of something stronger. — *Sea.*

BUZ: to share equally the last of a bottle of wine, when there is not enough for a full glass for each of the party.

CRACK A BOTTLE: to drink. *Shakespere* uses CRUSH in the same slang sense.

DEAD MEN: the term for wine bottles after they are emptied of their contents.—*Old.*—*See* MARINE *below.*

DOCTOR: to adulterate or drug liquor; also to falsify accounts.—*See* COOK *page 188.*

DRAIN: a drink; "to do a DRAIN," to take a friendly drink—"do a wet;" sometime called a COMMON SEWER.

DUTCH FEAST: where the host gets drunk before his guest.

FOOTING: "to pay FOOTING."—*See* SHOE *below.*

FREEMAN'S QUAY: "drinking at FREEMAN'S QUAY," *i.e.*, at another's cost. This quay was formerly a celebrated wharf near London Bridge, and the saying arose from the beer which was given gratis to porters and carmen who went there on business.

GREEKS: the low Irish. ST. GILES' GREEK, slang or *Cant* language. *Cotgrave* gives MERIE GREEK as a definition for a roystering fellow, a drunkard.—*Shakespere.*—*See* MEDICAL GREEK *page 141.*

HUSH-SHOP or **CRIB:** a shop where beer or spirits is sold "on the quiet"—no license being paid.

IVORIES: teeth; "a box" or "cage of IVORIES," a set of teeth, the mouth; "wash your IVORIES," *i.e.*, "drink." The word is also used to denote DICE.

KEEP IT UP: to prolong a debauch or the occasion of a rejoicing—a metaphor drawn from the game of shuttlecock.—*Grose.*

KNOCK ABOUT THE BUB: to hand or pass about the drink.

LAP THE GUTTER: to get drunk.

LIQUOR or **LIQUOR UP:** to drink drams.—*Americanism.* IN LIQUOR, tipsy or drunk.

LUG: to pull or slake thirst.—*Old.*

LUSH: to drink or get drunk.

LUSHINGTON: a drunkard or one who continually soaks himself with drams, and pints of beer. Some year since there was a "Lushington Club" in Bow-street, Covent Garden.

MARINE or **MARINE RECRUIT:** an empty bottle. This expression having once been used in the presence of an officer of marines, he was at first inclined to take it as an insult, until someone adroitly appeased his wrath by remarking that no offence could be meant, as all that it could possibly imply was, "one who had done his duty, and was ready to do it again." — *See* **HORSE MARINE** *page 55.* — *Naval.*

MOP UP: to drink or empty a glass. — *Old.*

MUG: "to MUG oneself," to get tipsy.

ON THE LOOSE: obtaining a living by prostitution, in reality, on the streets. The term is applied to females only, excepting in the case of SPREES, when men carousing are sometimes said to be ON THE LOOSE.

ON THE TILES: out all night "on the SPREE," or carousing — in allusion to the London cats on their amatory excursions.

OUT: a dram glass. The *habitue* of a gin-shop, desirous of treating a brace of friends, calls for a quartern of gin and three OUTS, by which he means three glasses which will exactly contain the quartern.

PIN: "to put in the PIN," to refrain from drinking. From the ancient peg tankard, which was furnished with a row of PINS or pegs, to regulate the amount which each person was to drink. A MERRY PIN, a roisterer.

PULL: to drink; "come, take a PULL at it," *i.e.*, drink up.

PUT UP: to suggest, to incite, "he PUT me UP to it;" to have done with; PUT IT UP, is a vulgar answer often heard in the streets. PUT UP, to stop at an hotel or tavern for entertainment.

SAM: to "stand SAM," to pay for refreshment or drink, to stand paymaster for anything. An *Americanism*, originating in the letter U.S. on the knapsacks of the United States soldiers, which letters were jocularly said to be the initials of *Uncle Sam* (the Government), who pays for all. In use in this country as early as 1827.

SHANT: a pot or quart; "SHANT of bivvy," a quart of beer.

SHOE: to free, or initiate a person a practice common in most trades to a newcomer. The SHOEING consists in paying for beer or other drink, which is drunk by the older hands. The cans emptied, and the bill paid, the stranger is considered properly SHOD.

SHORT: when spirit is drunk without any admixture of water, it is said to be taken "short;" "summat SHORT," a dram. A similar phrase is used at the counters of banks: upon presenting a cheque, the clerk asks, "how will you take it?" *i.e.*, in gold or in notes? Should it be desired to receive it in as small a compass as possible, the answer is, "**SHORT.**"

SPLICE THE MAIN BRACE: to take a drink.—*Sea.*

STASH: to cease doing anything, to refrain, be quiet, leave off; "**STASH IT**, there, you sir!" *i.e.*, be quiet, sir; to give over a lewd or intemperate course of life is termed **STASHING IT**.

SUCK THE MONKEY: to rob a cask of liquor by inserting a straw through a gimlet hole, and sucking a portion of the contents.

SWIG: to drink. *Saxon*, **SWIGAN**.

SWIPES: sour or small beer. **SWIPE**, to drink.—*Sea.*

TEETOTALLER: a total abstainer from alcoholic drinks.

WET: to drink. Low people generally ask an acquaintance to **WET** any recently purchased article, *i.e.*, to stand treat on the occasion. "**WET** your whistle," *i.e.*, take a drink; "**WET** the other eye," *i.e.*, take another glass.

WHISTLE: "as clean as a **WHISTLE**," neatly or "**SLICKLY** done," as an American would say; "to **WET ONE'S WHISTLE**," to take a drink. This is a very old term. *Chaucer* says of the Miller of Trumpington's wife (*Canterbury Tales*, 4153)—

"So was hir joly **WHISTAL** well **Y-WET**;"

"to **WHISTLE FOR ANYTHING**," to stand small chance of getting it, from the nautical custom of *whistling* for a wind in a calm, which of course comes none the sooner for it.

 # HANGOVERS

BLUE DEVILS: the apparitions supposed to be seen by habitual drunkards.

HORRORS: the low spirits, or "blue devils," which follow intoxication.

HOT COPPERS: the feverish sensations experienced next morning by those who have been drunk over night.

HYPS or **HYPO:** the blue devils. *From hypochondriasis.*—*Swift.*

TO BE DRUNK

ATTIC: the head; "queer in the ATTIC," intoxicated.—*Pugilistic.*

BEARGERED: to be drunk.

BEERY: intoxicated or fuddled with beer.

BEMUSE: to fuddle one's self with drink, "BEMUSING himself with beer," &c.—*Sala's Gas-light and Day-light*, p. 308.

BLUED or **BLEWED:** tipsey or drunk.

BOOZY: intoxicated or fuddled.

BOSKY: inebriated.—*Household Words*, No. 183.

BUFFY: intoxicated.—*Household Words*, No. 183.

BUG-HUNTERS: low wretches who plunder drunken men.

CORNED: drunk or intoxicated. Possibly from soaking or pickling oneself like CORNED beef.

COXY-LOXY: good-tempered, drunk.—*Norfolk.*

CUT: tipsey.—*Household Words*, No. 183.

DAVID'S SOW: "as drunk as DAVID'S SOW," *i.e.*, beastly drunk.—*See* origin of the phrase in *Grose's Dictionary.*

DISGUISED: intoxicated.—*Household Words*, No 183.

DUTCH COURAGE: false courage, generally excited by drink—*pot-valour.*

FOGGY: tipsy.

FOU: slightly intoxicated.—*Scotch.*

FRESH: said of a person slightly intoxicated.

GRAVEL-RASH: a scratched face—telling its tale of a drunken fall.

GROGGY: tipsy; when a prize-fighter becomes "weak on his pins," and nearly beaten, he is said to be GROGGY.—*Pugilistic.* The same term is applied to horses in a similar condition. *Old English*, AGGROGGYD, weighed down, oppressed.—*Prompt. Parvulorum.*

HALF SEAS OVER: reeling drunk.—*Sea.* Used by *Swift.*

HAZY: intoxicated.—*Household Words*, No. 183.

KISKY: drunk, fuddled.

LADDER: "can't see a hole in a LADDER," said of anyone who is intoxicated.

LAP THE GUTTER: to get drunk.

LIQUOR or LIQUOR UP: to drink drams.—*Americanism.* **IN LIQUOR,** tipsy or drunk.

LORD: "drunk as a LORD," a common saying, probably referring to the facilities a man of fortune has for such a gratification; perhaps a sly sarcasm at the supposed habits of the "haristocracy."

LUMPY: intoxicated.

LUSHY: intoxicated. Johnson says "opposite to pale," so red with drink.

MOONEY: intoxicated.—*Household Words*, No. 183.

MOPS AND BROOMS: intoxicated.—*Household Words*, No. 183.

MUGGY: drunk.

MUZZY: intoxicated.—*Household Words*, No. 183

NUT: to be "off one's NUT," to be in liquor, or "ALL MOPS AND BROOMS."

OBFUSCATED: intoxicated.

ON: "to be ON," in public-house or vulgar parlance, is synonymous with getting "tight," or tipsy; "It's *Saint Monday* with him, I see he's ON again," *i.e.,* drunk as usual or ON *the road* to it.

PLOUGHED: drunk.—*Household Words*, No. 183. Also a *University* term equivalent to PLUCKED.

PODGY: drunk; dumpy, short and fat.

PRIMED: said of a person in that state of incipient intoxication that if he takes more drink it will become evident.

RAN-TAN: "on the RAN-TAN," drunk.—*Household Words*, No. 183

RE-RAW: "on the RE-RAW." tipsy or drunk.—*Household Words*, No. 183

SCAMMERED: drunk.

SCREWED: intoxicated or drunk.

SEWED-UP: done up, used-up, intoxicated. *Dutch,* SEEUWT, sick.

SLEWED: drunk or intoxicated.—*Sea term.* When a vessel changes the tack she, as it were, staggers, the sails flap, she gradually heels over and, the wind catching the waiting canvas, she glides off at another angle. The course pursued by an intoxicated, or **SLEWED** man, is supposed to be analogous to that of the ship.

SNUFF: "up to **SNUFF**," knowing and sharp; "to take **SNUFF**," to be offended. *Shakespere* uses **SNUFF** in the sense of anger or passion. **SNUFFY**, tipsy.

SPIFFED: slightly intoxicated.—*Scotch slang.*

SUN IN THE EYES: to have too much to drink.—*Dickens.*

SWIPEY: (from **SWIPES**) intoxicated.

THREE SHEETS IN THE WIND: unsteady from drink.—*Sea.*

TIGHT: close, stingy; hard up, short of cash; **TIGHT**, spruce, strong, active; "a **TIGHT** lad," a smart, active young fellow; **TIGHT**, drunk or nearly so; "**TIGHT**-laced," puritanical, over-precise. Money is said to be **TIGHT** when the public, from want of confidence in the aspect of affairs, are not inclined to speculate.

TOPHEAVY: drunk.

TOUCHED: slightly intoxicated.

WINEY: intoxicated.

 # BOXERS and BOXING TERMS

ATTIC: the head; "queer in the **ATTIC**," intoxicated.—*Pugilistic.*

BELCHER: a kind of handkerchief.—*See* **BLUE BILLY** *below.*

BLUE-BILLY: the handkerchief (blue ground with white spots) worn and used at prize fights. Before a **SET TO**, it is common to take it from the neck and tie it around the leg as a garter, or round the waist, to "keep in the wind." Also, the refuse ammoniacal lime from gas factories.

BODMINTON: blood.—*Pugilistic.*

BOTTLE-HOLDER: an assistant to a "Second,"—*Pugilistic*; an abettor; also, the bridegroom's man at a wedding.

BRUISER: a fighting man, a pugilist.—*Pugilistic. Shakespere* uses the word **BRUISING** in a similar sense.

BUCKHORSE: a smart blow or box on the ear; derived from the name of a celebrated "bruiser" of that name.

BUFFER: a dog. Their skins were formerly in great request—hence the term, BUFF meaning in *Old English* to skin. It is still used in the ring, BUFFED meaning stripped to the skin. In *Irish Cant*, BUFFER is a *boxer*. The BUFFER of a railway carriage doubtless received its very appropriate name from the old pugilistic application of this term.

BUNG: to give, pass, hand over, drink, or indeed to perform any action; BUNG UP, to close up.—*Pugilistic*; "BUNG over the rag," hand over the money—*Old*, used by *Beaumont and Fletcher*, and *Shakespere*. Also, to deceive one by a lie, to CRAM.—*See page 176.*

CANISTER: the head.—*Pugilistic.*

CANISTER-CAP: a hat.—*Pugilistic.*

CLARET: blood.—*Pugilistic.*

CORINTHIANISM: a term derived from the classics, much in vogue some years ago, implying pugilism, high life, SPREES, roistering, &c. —*Shakespere*. The immorality of *Corinth* was proverbial in Greece. To Κορινθιαζ εσθαι, *Corinthianise*, indulge in the company of courtesans, was a *Greek* slang expression. Hence the proverb:

$$\text{Οὐ παντὸς ἀνδρὸς εἰς Κόρινθον ἔσθ' ὁ πλοῦς,}$$

and *Horace*, Epist. Lib. 1, xvii. 36:

Non cuivis homini contingit adire Corinthum,

In allusion to the spoliation practiced by the "hetæræ" on those who visited them.

CORK: "to draw a CORK," to give a bloody nose.—*Pugilistic.*

DO: this useful and industrious verb has for many years done service as a slang term. To DO a person is to cheat him. Sometimes another tense is employed, such as "I DONE him," meaning I cheated or "paid him out;" DONE BROWN, cheated thoroughly, befooled; DONE OVER, upset, cheated, knocked down, ruined; DONE UP, used-up, finished, or quieted. DONE also means convicted or sentenced; so does DONE FOR. To DO a person in pugilism is to excel him in fisticuffs. Humphreys, who fought Mendoza, a Jew, wrote this laconic note to his supporter: "Sir, I have DONE the Jew, and am in good health. Rich. Humphries." Tourists use the expression "I have DONE France and Italy," meaning I have completely explored those countries.

FANCY: the favourite sports, pets, or pastime of a person, *the tan of low life*. Pugilists are sometime termed THE FANCY. *Shakespere* uses the word in the sense of a favourite or pet; and the paramour of a prostitute is still called her FANCY-MAN.

FLOOR: to knock down.—*Pugilistic.*

GROGGY: tipsy; when a prize-fighter becomes "weak on his pins," and nearly beaten, he is said to be GROGGY.—*Pugilistic.* The same term is applied to horses in a similar condition. *Old English,* AGGROGGYD, weighed down, oppressed.—*Prompt. Parvulorum.*

HANDER: a second or assistant, in a prize fight.

HANDLE: a nose; the title appended to a person's name; also a term in boxing, "HANDLING one's fists."

KNOWLEDGE BOX: the head.—*Pugilistic.*

LOBB: the head.—*Pugilistic.*

LOLLY: the head.—*See* LOBB *above.—Pugilistic.*

MAULEY: a fist, that with which one strikes as with a MALL.—*Pugilistic.*

MITTENS: fists.—*Pugilistic.*

MUGGING: a thrashing. Synonymous with SLOGGING, both terms of the "ring," and frequently used by fighting men.

NOB: the head.—*Pugilistic;* "BOB A NOB," a shilling a head. *Ancient Cant,* NEB. NOB is an early *English* word, and is used in the Romance of Kynge Alisaunder (thirteenth century) for a head; originally, no doubt, the same as *Knob.*

NOSER: a bloody or contused nose.—*Pugilistic.*

PEEL: to strip or disrobe.—*Pugilistic.*

PEPPER: to thrash or strike.—*Pugilistic,* but used by *Shakespere.—East.*

POLISH OFF: to finish off anything quickly—a dinner for instance; also to finish off an adversary.—*Pugilistic.*

RING: a generic term given to horse racing and pugilism. The latter is sometimes termed the PRIZE-RING. From the practice of forming the crowd into a RING around the combatants or outside the racecourse.

RUMBUMPTIOUS: haughty, pugilistic.

SCRATCH: a fight, contest, point of dispute; "coming up to the SCRATCH," going or preparing to fight—in reality, approaching the line usually chalked on the ground to divide the ring.—*Pugilistic.*

SET TO: a sparring match, a fight; "a dead set," a determined stand, in argument or in movement.

SLASHER: a powerful roisterer, a pugilist; "the TIPTON SLASHER."

SPONGE: "to throw up the SPONGE," to submit, give over the struggle —from the practice of throwing up the SPONGE used to cleanse the combatants' faces, at a prize fight, as a signal that the "mill" is concluded.

STICK: to cheat; "he got STUCK," he was taken in; STICK, to forget one's part in a performance.—*Theatrical.* **STICK ON,** to overcharge or defraud; **STICK UP FOR,** to defend a person, especially when slandered in his absence; **STICK UP TO,** to preserver in courting or attacking, whether in fisticuffs or argument; "to STICK in one's gizzard," to rankle in one's heart; "to STICK TO a person," to adhere to one, be his friend through adverse circumstances.

WHITECHAPEL: the "upper-cut," or strike.—*Pugilistic.*

 # ENTERTAINMENT TERMS

BREAK-DOWN: a jovial, social gathering, a FLARE UP; in Ireland, a wedding.

CHOUT: an entertainment.

DONKEY: "three more and up goes the DONKEY," a vulgar street phrase for extracting as much money as possible before performing any task. The phrase had its origin with a travelling showman, the *finale* of whose performance was the hoisting of a DONKEY on a pole or ladder; but this consummation was never arrived at unless the required number of "browns" was first paid up, and "three more" was generally the unfortunate deficit.

FAD: a hobby, a favourite pursuit.

FANCY: the favourite sports, pets, or pastime of a person, *the tan of low life.* Pugilists are sometime termed THE FANCY. *Shakespere* uses the word in the sense of a favourite or pet; and the paramour of a prostitute is still called her FANCY-MAN.

FAT: rich, abundant, &c.; "a FAT lot;" "to cut it FAT," to exaggerate, to show off in an extensive or grand manner, to assume undue importance; "CUT UP FAT." — *See under* CUT *page 479.* As a *Theatrical* term, a part with plenty of FAT in it, is one which affords the actor an opportunity of effective display.

GAFF: a fair or penny-playhouse. — *See* PENNY GAFF *page 152.*

HOCUS POCUS: *Gipsey* words of magic, similar to the modern "Presto fly." The Gipseys pronounce *"Habeas Corpus"* HAWCUS PACCUS (*see Crabb's Gipsey's Advocate*, p.18); can this have anything to do with the origin of HOCUS POCUS? *Turner* gives OCHUS BOCHUS, an old demon. Pegge, however, states that it is a burlesque rendering of the words of the unreformed church service at the delivery of the host, HOC EST CORPUS, which the early Protestants considered as a species of conjuring, and ridiculed accordingly.

To **JOE BLAKE THE BARTLEMY:** to visit a low woman.

LARK: fun, a joke; "let's have a jolly good LARK," let us have a piece of fun. *Mayhew* calls it "a convenient word covering much mischief." — *Anglo Saxon*, LAC, sport; but more probably from the nautical term SKYLARKING, *i.e.,* mounting to the highest yards and sliding down the ropes for amusement, which is allowed on certain occasions.

LOOSE: — *See* ON THE LOOSE *below.*

ON THE LOOSE: obtaining a living by prostitution, in reality, on the streets. The term is applied to females only, excepting in the case of SPREES, when men carousing are sometimes said to be ON THE LOOSE.

POT-HUNTER: a sportsman who shoots anything he comes across, having more regard to filling his bag than to the rules which regulate the sport.

RIG: a trick, SPREE, or performance; "run a RIG," to play a trick — *Gipsey*; "RIG the market." In reality to play tricks with it — a mercantile slang phrase often used in the newspapers.

ROUGH IT: to put up with chance entertainment, to take pot luck, and what accommodation "turns up," without sighing for better. "ROUGHING IT *in the Bush*" is the title of an interesting work on Backwoods life.

SCHWASSLE BOX: the street performance of Punch and Judy. —*Household Words*, No. 183.

SCORE: "to run up a SCORE at a public house," to obtain credit there until pay day or a fixed time when the debt must be WIPED OFF.

SHOPPING: purchasing at shops. Termed by *Todd* a slang word, but used by *Cowper* and *Byron*.

SKIT: a joke, a squib.

SKY-LARK:—*See* LARK *page 157.*

SPREAD: a lady's shawl. SPREAD, at the *East* end of London, a feast, or a TIGHTENER; at the *West* end a fashionable reunion, an entertainment, display of good things.

STALL: to lodge or put up at a public house. Also, to act a part. —*Theatrical.*

STAND: "to STAND treat," to pay for a friend's entertainment; to bear expense; to put up with treatment, good or ill; "this house STOOD me in £1,000," *i.e.*, cost that sum; "to STAND PAD," to beg on the curb with a small piece of paper pinned on the breast, inscribed "*I'm starving.*"

SUP: abbreviation of *supernumerary.*—*Theatrical.*

 # GAMBLING and GAMBLERS

BAR or **BARRING:** excepting; in common use in the betting ring; "I bet against the field BAR two." The Irish use of BARRIN' is very similar.

BESTER: a low betting cheat.

BLACK-LEG: a rascal, swindler, or card cheat.

BONNET: a gambling cheat. "A man who sits at a gaming table, and appears to be playing against the table; when a stranger enters, the BONNET generally wins."—*Times*, Nov. 17, 1856. Also, a pretense or make-believe, a sham bidder at auctions.

BONNETTER: one who induces another to gamble.

BROWN PAPERMEN: low gamblers.

BUTTONER: a man who entices another to play.—*See* BONNETTER *above.*

CHARLEY-PITCHERS: low, cheating gamblers.

DRUM: a house, a lodging, a street; **HAZARD-DRUM,** a gambling house; **FLASH-DRUM,** a house of ill-fame.

FIDDLING: doing any odd jobs in the street, holding horses, carrying parcels, &c. for a living. Among the middle classes, **FIDDLING** means idling away time or trifling; and amongst sharpers, it means gambling.

FLUE FAKERS: chimney sweeps; also low sporting characters, who are so termed from their chiefly betting on the *Great Sweeps.*

HELL: a fashionable gambling house. In printing offices, the term is generally applied to the old tin box in which is thrown the broken or spoilt type, purchased by the founders for re-casting. *Nearly obsolete.*

LEGS or **BLACKLEGS:** disreputable sporting characters and racecourse *habitues.*

LEVANTER: a card sharper or defaulting gambler. A correspondent states that it was formerly the custom to give out to the creditors, when a person was in pecuniary difficulties, and it was convenient for him to keep away, that he was gone to the *East,* or the **LEVANT;** hence, when one loses a bet and decamps without settling, he is said to **LEVANT.**

MUCK OUT: to clean out. Often applied to one utterly ruining an adversary in gambling. From the *Provincial* **MUCK,** dirt.

MUCK-SNIPE: one who had been "**MUCKED OUT**" or beggared, at gambling.

OFFICE: "to give the **OFFICE,**" to give a hint dishonestly to a confederate, thereby enabling him to win a game or bet, the profits being shared.

OUT-SIDER: a person who does not habitually bet or is not admitted to the "Ring." Also, a horse whose name does not appear among the "favourites."

PONY: twenty-five pounds. — *Sporting.*

ROOK: a cheat or tricky gambler; the opposite of **PIGEON.** — *Old.*

ROULEAU: a packet of sovereigns. — *Gaming.*

SCHOOLING: a low gambling party.

SHINEY RAG: "to win the **SHINEY RAG,**" to be ruined — said in gambling, when anyone continues betting after "luck has set in against him."

CARD GAMES and PLAYING CARDS

BLACK-LEG: a rascal, swindler, or card cheat.

BLIND-HOOKEY: a gambling game at cards.

BONNET: a gambling cheat. "A man who sits at a gaming table, and appears to be playing against the table; when a stranger enters, the BONNET generally wins." —*Times*, Nov. 17, 1856. Also, a pretense or make-believe, a sham bidder at auctions.

BRAD-FAKING: playing at cards.

BROADS: cards. BROADSMAN, a card sharper.

CURSE OF SCOTLAND: the Nine of Diamonds. Various hypotheses have been set up as to the appellation—that it was the card on which the "Butcher Duke" wrote a cruel order with respect to the rebels after the battle of Culloden; that the diamonds are the nine lozenges in the arms of Dalrymple, Earl of Stair, detested for his share in the Massacre of Glencoe; that it is a corruption of *Cross of Scotland*, the nine diamonds being arranged somewhat after the fashion of the St. Andrew's Cross; but the most probable explanation is, that in the game of Pope Joan the nine of diamonds is the Pope, of whom the Scotch have an especial horror.

DECK: a pack of cards.—*Old*. Used by Bulwer as a *Cant* term. General in the *United States*.

DEUCE: twopence; DEUCE at cards or dice, one with two pips or holes.

DIGGERS: spurs; also the spades on cards.

DUMMY: in three-handed whist the person who holds two hands plays DUMMY.

EARL OF CORK: the ace of diamonds.—*Hibernicism*.

> "What do you mean by the Earl of Cork?" asked Mr. Squander. "The ace of diamonds, your honour. It's the worst ace, and the poorest card in the pack, and is called the Earl of Cork, because he's the poorest nobleman in Ireland." —*Carleton's Traits and Stories of the Irish Peasantry*.

ELBOW: "to shake one's ELBOW," to play at cards.

GRACE-CARD: the ace of hearts.

JACKS, HALF JACKS: card counters, resembling in size and appearance sovereigns and half-sovereigns for which they are occasionally passed to simple persons. In large gambling establishments the "heaps of gold" are frequently composed mainly of JACKS.

JOGUL: to play up, at cards or other game. *Spanish*, JUGAR.

KNOCK-IN: the game of *loo*.

LEVANTER: a card sharper or defaulting gambler. A correspondent states that it was formerly the custom to give out to the creditors, when a person was in pecuniary difficulties, and it was convenient for him to keep away, that he was gone to the *East*, or the LEVANT; hence, when one loses a bet and decamps without settling, he is said to LEVANT.

NED STOKES: the four of spades. —*North Hampshire.* —*See Gentleman's Magazine* for 1791, p.141.

PAM: the knave of clubs; or, in street phraseology, Lord Palmerston.

PUT: a game at cards.

QUEEN BESS: the Queen of Clubs—perhaps because that queen, history says, was of a swarthy complexion. —*North Hampshire.* —*See Gentleman's Magazine* for 1791, p. 141.

RUBBER: a term at whist, &c., two games out of three. —*Old*, 1677.

HORSE RACING and OTHER RACING

BOOK: an arrangement of bets for and against, chronicled in a pocket-book made for that purpose; "making a BOOK upon it," common phrase to denote the general arrangement of a person's bets on a race. "That does not suit my BOOK," *i.e.*, does not accord with my other arrangements. *Shakespere* uses BOOK in the sense of "a paper of conditions."

BROAD-FENCER: card seller at races.

CART: a racecourse.

CULLING or **CULING:** stealing from the carriages on racecourses.

DARK: "keep it DARK," *i.e.*, secret. **DARK HORSE**, in racing phraseology a horse whose chance of success is unknown, and whose capabilities have not been made the subject of comment.

DRAG: a cart of any kind, a coach; gentlemen drive to the races in DRAGS.

HEDGE: to secure a doubtful bet by making others. — *Turf.*

LEGS or **BLACKLEGS:** disreputable sporting characters and racecourse *habitues.*

NECK OR NOTHING: desperate. — *Racing phrase.*

OUT-SIDER: a person who does not habitually bet or is not admitted to the "Ring." Also, a horse whose name does not appear among the "favourites."

PUT THE POT ON: to bet too much upon one horse. — *Sporting.*

RING: a generic term given to horse racing and pugilism. The latter is sometimes termed the PRIZE-RING. From the practice of forming the crowd into a RING around the combatants or outside the racecourse.

RUCK: the undistinguished crowd; "to come in with the RUCK," to arrive at the winning post among the non-winning horses. — *Racing term.*

SCRATCH: to strike a horse's name out of the list of runners in a particular race. "Tomboy was SCRATCHED for the Derby, at 10, a.m., on Wednesday," from which period all bets made in reference to him (with one exception) are void. — *See* P.P. — *Turf.*

SCRATCH-RACE: (on the *Turf*), a race where any horse, aged, winner, or loser, can run with any weights; in fact, a race without restrictions. At *Cambridge* a boat-race, where the crews are drawn by lot.

SLOGGERS: *i.e.*, SLOW-GOERS, the second division of race-boats at *Cambridge.* At *Oxford* they are called TORPIDS. — *University.*

TAKE: "to TAKE THE FIELD," when said of a General, to commence operations against the enemy; when a racing man TAKES THE FIELD he stakes his money against the favourite. — *See* TAKE *in the Index for more meanings on page 504.*

TORPIDS: the second-class race-boats at Oxford, answering to the *Cambridge* SLOGGERS.

TURF: horse racing and betting thereon; "on the TURF," one who occupies himself with racecourse business; said also of a streetwalker, nymph of the pavé.

WALK OVER: a re-election without opposition.—*Parliamentary*, but derived from the *Turf*, where a horse—which has no rivals entered—WALKS OVER the course, and wins without exertion.

TOSSING DICE and COINS

BONES: dice; also called ST. HUGH'S BONES.

CHATTS: dice—formerly the gallows; a bunch of seals.

COG: to cheat at dice.—*Shakespere*. Also, to agree with, as one cog-wheel does with another.

COVER-DOWN: a tossing coin with a false cover, enabling either head or tail to be shown, according as the cover is left on or taken off.

DESPATCHES: false "dice with two sides, double four, double five, and double six."—*Times*, 27th November, 1856.

DEUCE: twopence; DEUCE at cards or dice, one with two pips or holes.

DEVIL'S TEETH: dice.

DIBBS: money; so called from the buckle bones of sheep, which have been used from the earliest times for gambling purposes, being thrown up five at a time and caught on the back of the hand like halfpence.

FULLAMS: false dice, which always turn up high.—*Shakespere*.

GAFFING: tossing halfpence or counters.—*North*, where it means tossing up three pennies.

GRAYS: halfpennies, with either two "heads" or two "tails," —both sides alike. *Low gamblers* use GRAYS, and they cost from 2d. to 6d. each.

IVORIES: teeth; "a box" or "cage of IVORIES," a set of teeth, the mouth; "wash your IVORIES," *i.e.*, "drink." The word is also used to denote **Dice.**

NEWMARKET: in tossing halfpence, when it is agreed that the first toss shall be decisive, the play is said to be NEWMARKET.

ODD MAN: a street or public-house game at tossing. The number of players is three. Each tosses up a coin, and if two come down head, and one tail or *vice versa*, the last is **ODD MAN**, and loses or wins as may have been agreed upon. Frequently used to victimise a "flat." If all three be alike, then the toss goes for nothing, and the coppers are again "*skied*."

PLANT: a dodge, a preconcerted swindle; a position in the street to sell from. **PLANT**, a swindle, may be thus described: a coster will join a party of gaming costers that he never saw before, and commence tossing. When sufficient time has elapsed to remove all suspicions of companionship, his mate will come up and commence betting on each of his **PAL'S** throws with those standing around. By a curious quickness of hand, a coster can make the toss tell favourably for his wagering friend, who meets him in the evening after the play is over and shares the spoil.

SHOVE-HALFPENNY: a gambling street game.

SICES or **SIZES:** a throw of sixes at dice.

SINKS: a throw of fives at dice. *French,* **CINQS.**

SKIE: to throw upwards, to toss "coppers." — *See* **ODD MAN** *above.*

TAT BOX: a dice box.

TATS: dice.

THREE-UP: a gambling game played by costers. Three halfpennies are thrown up, and when they fall all "heads," or all "tails," it is a mark; and the man who gets the greatest number of marks out of a given amount—three, five, or more—wins. The costers are very quick and skillful at this game, and play fairly at it amongst themselves; but should a stranger join in they invariably unite to cheat him.

TOY, OTHER GAMES, and FAIR RIDES

AUNT SALLY: A favourite game on racecourses and at fairs, consisting of a wooden head mounted on a stick, firmly fixed in the ground; in the nose of which, or rather in that part of the facial arrangement of **AUNT SALLY** which is generally considered incomplete without a nasal projection, a tobacco pipe is inserted. The fun consists on standing at a distance and demolishing **AUNT SALLY'S** pipe-clay projection with short bludgeons, very similar to the half of a broom handle. The Duke of Beaufort is a "crack hand" at smashing pipe noses, and his performances two years ago on Brighton racecourse are yet fresh in remembrance. The noble Duke, in the summer months, frequently drives the old London and Brighton four-horse mail coach, "Age"—a whim singular enough now, but common forty years ago.

BOWL-OUT: to put out of the game, to remove out of one's way, to detect.—*Cricketing term.*

COCKSHY: a game at fairs and races, where trinkets are set upon sticks, and for one penny three throws at them are accorded, the thrower keeping whatever he knocks off. From the ancient game of throwing or "shying" at live cocks.

DOWN THE DOLLY: a favourite gambling contrivance, often seen in the tap rooms of public houses, at racecourses, and fairs, consisting of a round board and the figure of an old man or "doll," down which is a spiral hole. A marble is dropped "down the doll," and stops in one of the small holes or pits (numbered) on the board. The bet is decided according as the marble stops on a high or low figure.

FID FAD: a game similar to chequers or drafts, played in the West of England.

FLUKE: at billiards, playing for one thing and getting another. Hence, generally what one gets accidentally, an unexpected advantage, "more by luck than wit."

HIGH FLYERS: large swings, in frames, at fairs and races.

HUNTER PITCHING: cockshies or three throws a penny.—*See* **COCKSHY** *above.*

JIGGER: a door; "dub the **JIGGER**," shut the door. *Ancient Cant*, **GYGER**. In billiards the *bridge* on the table is often termed the **JIGGER**."

JOGUL: to play up, at cards or other game. *Spanish*, **JUGAR**.

LOVE: at billiards, "five to none" would be "five **LOVE**,"—a **LOVE** being the same as when one player does not score at all.

POT: to finish; "don't **POT** me," term used at billiards. This word was much used by our soldiers in the Crimea, for firing at the enemy from a hole or ambush. These were called **POT-SHOTS**.

PRICK THE GARTER or **PITCH THE NOB:** a gambling and cheating game common at fairs, and generally practiced by thimble riggers. It consists of a "garter" or a piece of list doubled, and then folded up tight. The bet is made upon your asserting that you can, with a pin, "prick" the point at which the garter is doubled. The garter is then unfolded, and nine times out of ten you will find that you have been deceived, and that you pricked one of the false folds. The owner of the garter, I should state, holds the ends tightly with one hand. This was, doubtless, originally a Gipsey game, and we are informed by *Brand* that it was much practiced by the Gipseys in the time of *Shakespere*. In those days, it was termed PRICKING AT THE BELT or FAST AND LOOSE.

QUOCKERWODGER: a wooden toy figure, which, when pulled by a string, jerks its limbs about. The term is used in a slang sense to signify a pseudo-politician, one whose strings of action are pulled by somebody else.—*West*.

ROUNDABOUTS: large swings of four compartments, each the size, and very much the shape, of the body of a cart, capable of seating six or eight boys and girls, erected in a high frame, and turned round by men at a windlass. Fairs and merry-makings generally abound with them. The frames take to pieces, and are carried in vans by miserable horses, from fair to fair, &c.

SHY: to fling; COCKSHY, a game at fairs, consisting of throwing short sticks at trinkets set upon other sticks—both name and practice derives from the old game of throwing or SHYING at live cocks.

SKITTLES: a game similar to Ten Pins, which, when interdicted by the Government was altered to Nine Pins, or SKITTLES. They are set up in an alley and are *thrown at* (not bowled) with a round piece of hard wood, shaped like a small flat cheese. The costers consider themselves the best players in London.

SMUGGINGS: snatching or purloining—shouted out by boys, when snatching the tops or small play property, of other lads, and then running off at full speed.

> "Tops are in; spin 'em agin.
> Tops are out; SMUGGING about."

SPIN-EM ROUNDS: a street game consisting of a piece of brass, wood, or iron, balanced on a pin, and turned quickly around on a board, when the point, arrow-shaped, stops at a number and decides the bet one way or the other. The contrivance very much resembles a sea compass, and was formerly the gambling accompaniment of London piemen. The apparatus then was erected on the tin lids of their pie cans, and the bets were ostensibly for pies, but more frequently for "coppers," when no policeman frowned upon the scene, and when two or three apprentices or porters happened to meet.

STUMPED: bowled out, done for, bankrupt, poverty-stricken.
—*Cricketing term.*

TAW: a large or principal marble; "I'll be one on your TAW," I will pay you out or be even with you—a simile taken from boys aiming always at winning the TAW when playing at marbles.

THIMBLE-RIG: a noted cheating game played at fairs and places of great public thronging, consisting of two or three thimbles rapidly and dexterously placed over a pea, when the THIMBLE-RIGGER, suddenly ceasing, asks you under which thimble the pea is found. If you are not a practised hand you will lose nine times out of ten any bet you may happen to make with him. The pea is sometimes concealed under his nail.

TIBBING OUT: going out of bounds.—*Charterhouse.*

TIN-POT: "he plays a TIN-POT game," *i.e.*, a low or shabby one.
—*Billiards.*

 LARKING and PRANKS

BARNEY: a LARK, SPREE, rough enjoyment; "get up a BARNEY," to have a "lark."

BATTER: "on the BATTER," literally "on the streets," or given up to roistering and debauchery.

BREAK-DOWN: a jovial, social gathering, a FLARE UP; in Ireland, a wedding.

BROWN: "to do BROWN," to do well or completely (in allusion to roasting); "doing it BROWN," prolonging the frolic or exceeding sober bounds; "DONE BROWN," taken in, deceived, or surprised.

CARRY-ON: to joke a person to excess, to carry on a SPREE too far, "how we CARRIED ON, to be sure!" *i.e.*, what fun we had.

CHAFF: to gammon, joke, quiz, or praise ironically. **CHAFF**-bone, the jaw-bone.—*Yorkshire.* **CHAFF**, jesting. In *Anglo Saxon*, **Ceaf** is chaff; and **CEAFL**, bill, beak, or jaw. In the "Ancien Riwle," A.D. 1221, *ceafle* is used in the sense of idle discourse.

CHESHIRE CAT: "to grin like a **CHESHIRE CAT**," to display the teeth and gums when laughing. Formerly the phrase was "to grin like a **CHESHIRE CAT** *eating* **CHEESE**." *A hardly satisfactory* explanation has been give of this phrase—that Cheshire is a county palatine, and the cats, when they think of it, are so tickled with the notion that they can't help grinning.

CORINTHIANISM: a term derived from the classics, much in vogue some years ago, implying pugilism, high life, **SPREES**, roistering, &c.—*Shakespere.* The immorality of *Corinth* was proverbial in Greece. To Κοριυθίαζ εσθαι, *Corinthianise*, indulge in the company of courtesans, was a *Greek* slang expression. Hence the proverb:

$$\text{Οὐ παντὸς ἀνδρὸς εἰς Κόρινθον ἐσθ' ὁ πλοῦς,}$$

and *Horace*, Epist. Lib. 1, xvii. 36:

> Non cuivis homini contingit adire Corinthum,

In allusion to the spoliation practiced by the "hetæræ" on those who visited them.

CUT: to **CUT DIDOES**, synonymous with to **CUT CAPERS**; **CUT A DASH**, make a show; **CUT A CAPER**, to dance or show off in a strange manner; **CUT UP SHINES**, to play tricks; **CUT IT FAT**, to exaggerate or show off in an extensive manner. **CUT OUT**, to excel, thus in affairs of gallantry one Adonis is said to *"cut the other out"* in the affections of the wished for lady.—*Cambridge. Old* **CUTTE**, to say.—*See* **CUT** *in the Index for more meanings on page 479.*

DAGS: feat or performance; "I'll do your **DAGS**," *i.e.*, I will do something that you cannot do.

DIDOES: pranks or capers; "to cut up **DIDOES**," to make pranks.

FLARE UP: a jovial social gathering, a "break down," a "row."

GAMMON: to hoax, to deceive merrily, to laugh at a person, to tell an untrue but plausible story, to make game of, or in the provincial dialect, to make **GAME ON**; "who's thou makin' thy **GAM' ON**?" *i.e.*, who are you making a fool of?—*Yorkshire.*

GIG: fun, frolic, a **SPREE**.

> "In search of *lark*, or some delicious **GIG**,
> The mind delights on, when 'tis in *prime twig.*"
> —*Randall's Diary*, 1820.

KEEP IT UP: to prolong a debauch or the occasion of a rejoicing—a metaphor drawn from the game of shuttlecock.—*Grose.*

KIDDYISH: frolicsome, jovial.

> "Think on the **KIDDYISH** spree we had on such a day."
> —*Randall's Diary*, 1820.

LARK: fun, a joke; "let's have a jolly good **LARK**," let us have a piece of fun. *Mayhew* calls it "a convenient word covering much mischief." —*Anglo Saxon*, **LAC**, sport; but more probably from the nautical term **SKYLARKING**, *i.e.*, mounting to the highest yards and sliding down the ropes for amusement, which is allowed on certain occasions.

MOLROWING: "out on the **SPREE**" in company with so-called gay women. In allusion to the amatory serenading of the London cats.

ON THE TILES: out all night "on the **SPREE**," or carousing—in allusion to the London cats on their amatory excursions.

OUT ON THE LOOSE: "on the **SPREE**," in search of adventures.

OUT ON THE PICKAROON: **PICARONE** is *Spanish* for a thief, but this phrase does not necessarily mean anything dishonest, but ready for anything in the way of excitement to turn up; also to be in search of anything profitable.

POKE: "come, none of your **POKING** fun at me," *i.e.*, you must not laugh at me.

QUEER: "to **QUEER** a flat," to puzzle or confound a "gull" or silly fellow.

> Who in a *row* like Tom could lead the van,
> *Booze* in the *ken*, or at the *spellken* hustle?
> Who **QUEER** a flat, &c.
> —*Don Juan*, canto xi., 19.

QUIZ: to pry or joke.

RACKET: a dodge, maneuver, exhibition; a disturbance.

RIG: a trick, SPREE, or performance; "run a RIG," to play a trick—*Gipsey*; "RIG the market." In reality to play tricks with it—a mercantile slang phrase often used in the newspapers.

ROAST: to expose a person to a running fire of jokes at his expense from a whole company, in his presence. QUIZZING is done by a single person only.

SELL: to deceive, swindle, or play a practical joke upon a person. A sham is a SELL in street parlance. "SOLD again, and got the money," a costermonger cries after having successfully deceived somebody. *Shakespere* uses SELLING in a similar sense, viz., blinding or deceiving.

SHAPES: "to cut up" or "show SHAPES," to exhibit pranks or flightiness.

SKY WANNOCKING: unsteady, frolicking.—*Norfolk.*

SKY-LARK:—*See* LARK *page 157.*

SNOOKS: an imaginary personage often brought forward as the answer to an idle question or as the perpetrator of a senseless joke.

SPREE: a boisterous piece of merriment; "going on the SPREE," starting out with intent to have a frolic. *French*, ESPRIT. In the *Dutch* language, SPREEUW is a jester.

TANTREMS: pranks, capers, or frolicking; from the *Tarantula* dance? See account of the involuntary phrensy and motions caused by the bite of the tarantula in Italy.—*Penny Cyclopœdia.*

WILD OATS: youthful pranks.

 MUSIC and DANCING TERMS

BELL: a song.

BOSH: a fiddle.

BOSH-FAKER: a violin player.

CATGUT-SCRAPER: a fiddler.

DOUBLE-SHUFFLE: a low, shuffling, noisy dance, common amongst costermongers.—*See* FLIP-FLAPS *below.*

DUTCH CONCERT: where each performer plays a different tune.

FIDDLER: a sixpence.—*Household Words*, No. 183.

FIDDLERS' MONEY: a lot of sixpences; 6d. was the remuneration to fiddlers from each of the company in old times.

FLIP-FLAPS: a peculiar rollicking dance indulged in by costermongers when merry or excited—better described, perhaps, as the DOUBLE SHUFFLE, danced with an air of extreme *abandon*.

HA'PURTH OF LIVELINESS: the music at a low concert or theatre.

HOP: a dance.—*Fashionable slang*.

HOP-MERCHANT: a dancing-master.

HURDY-GURDY: a droning musical instrument shaped like a large fiddle and turned by a crank, used by Savoyards and itinerant foreign musicians in England, now nearly superseded by the hand-organ. A correspondent suggests that the name is derived from being *girded* on the HARDIES, loins or buttocks.—*Scotch; Tam o'Shanter*. In *Italy* the instrument is called VIOLA.

MENAGERY: the orchestra of a theatre.—*Theatrical*.

PENNY GAFFS: shops turned into temporary theatres (admission one penny), where dancing and singing take place every night. Rude pictures of the performers are arranged outside to give the front a gaudy and attractive look, and at nighttime coloured lamps and transparencies are displayed to draw an audience.

TANTREMS: pranks, capers, or frolicking; from the *Tarantula* dance? See account of the involuntary phrensy and motions caused by the bite of the tarantula in Italy.—*Penny Cyclopædia*.

TOM-TOM: a street instrument, a small kind of drum beaten with the fingers, somewhat like the ancient tabor; a performer on this instrument. It was imported, doubtless, with the *Negro* melodies, —TOM-TOMS being a favourite instrument with the darkies.

TWOPENNY-HOPS: low dancing rooms, the price of admission to which was formerly—and not infrequently now—two pence. The clog hornpipe, the pipe dance, flash jigs, and hornpipes in fetters, *a la* Jack Sheppard, are the favourite movements, all entered into with great spirit and "joyous laborious capering."—*Mayhew*.

PERFORMERS & THEATRICAL TERMS

BARKER: a man employed to cry at the doors of "gaffs," shows, and puffing shops, to entice people inside.

BARN-STORMERS: theatrical performers who travel the country and act in barns, selecting short and frantic pieces to suit the rustic taste. —*Theatrical*.

BEN: a benefit.—*Theatrical*.

BILLY–BARLOW: a street clown; sometimes termed a JIM CROW or SALTIMBANCO—so called from the hero of a slang song.—*Bulwer's Paul Clifford*.

BOSH-FAKER: a violin player.

BUSKER: a man who sings or performs in a public house.—*Scotch*.

CATGUT-SCRAPER: a fiddler.

CHAUNTER-CULLS: a singular body of men who used to haunt certain well-known public-houses, and write satirical or libellous ballads on any person or body of persons, for a consideration. 7s. 6d. was the usual fee, and in three hours the ballad might be heard in St. Paul's Churchyard or other public spot. There are two men in London at the present day who gain their living in this way.

CHERUBS or **CHERUBIMS:** the chorister boys who chaunt in the services at the abbeys.

CLAP-TRAP: high-sounding nonsense. An *Ancient Theatrical* term for a "TRAP to catch a CLAP by way of applause from the spectators at a play." —*Bailey's Dictionary*.

CORPSE: to confuse or put out the actors by making a mistake. —*Theatrical*.

CUT: in theatrical language, means to strike out portions of a dramatic piece, so as to render it shorter for representation. A late treasurer of one of the so-called *Patent Theatres*, when asked his opinion of a new play, always gave utterance to the brief, but safe piece of criticism "*wants* CUTTING."

FAT: rich, abundant, &c.; "a FAT lot;" "to cut it FAT," to exaggerate, to show off in an extensive or grand manner, to assume undue importance; "CUT UP FAT." — *See under* CUT *page 479.* As a *Theatrical* term, a part with plenty of FAT in it, is one which affords the actor an opportunity of effective display.

GAFF: a fair or penny-playhouse. — *See* PENNY GAFF *page 152.*

GHOST: "the GHOST doesn't walk," *i.e.*, the manager is too poor to pay salaries as yet. — *Theatrical; — Household Words, No.*183.

GODS: the people in the upper gallery of a theatre; "up amongst the GODS," a seat amongst the low persons in the gallery — so named from the high position of the gallery, and the blue sky generally painted on the ceiling of the theatre; termed by the *French,* PARADIS.

GOOSE: to ruin or spoil. Also, to hiss a play. — *Theatrical.*

HA'PURTH OF LIVELINESS: the music at a low concert or theatre.

LENGTH: forty-two lines of a dramatic composition. — *Theatrical.*

MAKE UP: personal appearance. — *Theatrical.*

MENAGERY: the orchestra of a theatre. — *Theatrical.*

MUG-UP: to paint one's face. — *Theatrical.* To "cram" for an examination. — *Army.*

MUMMER: a performer at a travelling theatre. — *Ancient.* Rustic performers at Christmas in the West of England.

OUT OF COLLAR: out of place — in allusion to servants. When in place, the term is COLLARED UP. — *Theatrical* and *general.*

PARADIS: *French slang* for the gallery of a theatre, "up amongst the Gods." — *See above.*

PENNY GAFFS: shops turned into temporary theatres (admission one penny), where dancing and singing take place every night. Rude pictures of the performers are arranged outside to give the front a gaudy and attractive look, and at nighttime coloured lamps and transparencies are displayed to draw an audience.

PITCH: a fixed locality where a patterer can hold forth to a gaping multitude for at least some few minutes continuously; "to do a PITCH in the drag," to perform in the street.

PRO: a professional. — *Theatrical.*

PROSS: breaking in or instructing a stage-infatuated youth. — *Theatrical.*

RUN: (good or bad), the success of a performance. — *Theatrical.*

SADDLE: an additional charge made by the manager to a performer upon his benefit night. — *Theatrical.*

SAL: a salary. — *Theatrical.*

SALAMANDERS: street acrobats and jugglers who eat fire.

SCHWASSLE BOX: the street performance of Punch and Judy. — *Household Words*, No. 183.

SCREAMING: first-rate, splendid. Believed to have been first used in the *Adelphi* play-bills; "a SCREAMING farce," one calculated to make the audience scream with laughter. Now a general expression.

SLAP: paint for the face, rouge.

STALL: to lodge or put up at a public house. Also, to act a part. — *Theatrical.*

STAR IT: to perform as the centre of attraction, with inferior subordinates to set off one's abilities. — *Theatrical.*

SURF: an actor who frequently pursues another calling. — *Theatrical.*

TAKE: to succeed or be patronised; "do you think the new opera will TAKE?" "No, because the same company TOOK so badly under the old management." — *See* TAKE *in the Alphabetical Index for more meanings on page 504.*

 # PLACES FOR ENTERTAINMENT

BAWDYKEN: a brothel. — *See* KEN *page 269.*

BOOZE or **SUCK-CASA:** a public-house.

BOOZING-KEN: a beer- shop, a low public house. — *Ancient.*

CART: a racecourse.

CATCH-PENNY: any temporary contrivance to obtain money from the public, penny shows, or cheap exhibitions.

COLD BLOOD: a house licensed for the sale of beer "NOT to be drunk on the premises."

CRIB: house, public or otherwise; lodgings, apartments.

DRUM: a house, a lodging, a street; HAZARD-DRUM, a gambling house; FLASH-DRUM, a house of ill-fame.

FLATTY-KEN: a public house, the landlord of which is ignorant of the practices of the thieves and tramps who frequent it.

FREE AND EASY: a club held at most public houses, the members of which meet in the taproom or parlour for the purpose of drinking, smoking, and hearing each other sing and "talk politics." The name indicates the character of the proceedings.

GAFF: a fair or penny-playhouse. — *See* PENNY GAFF *page 152.*

GRUBBING-KEN or **SPINIKIN:** a workhouse; a cook-shop.

HELL: a fashionable gambling house. In printing offices, the term is generally applied to the old tin box in which is thrown the broken or spoilt type, purchased by the founders for re-casting. *Nearly obsolete.*

HUSH-SHOP or **CRIB:** a shop where beer or spirits is sold "on the quiet" —no license being paid.

JERRY: a beer house.

KNOCKING-SHOP: a brothel or disreputable house frequented by prostitutes.

LUSH-CRIB: a public house.

MUNGARLY CASA: a baker's shop; evidently a corruption of some *Lingua Franca* phrase for an eating house. The well-known "Nix mangiare" stairs at Malta derive their name from the endless beggars who lie there and shout NIX MANGIARE, *i.e.*, "nothing to eat," to excite the compassion of the English who land there—an expression which exhibits remarkably the mongrel composition of the *Lingua Franca*, MANGIARE being *Italian*, and *Nix* an evident importation from Trieste or other Austrian seaport.

MUTTONWALK: the saloon at Drury Lane Theatre.

NANNY-SHOP: a disreputable house.

NOSE-BAGS: visitors at watering places, and houses of refreshment, who carry their own victuals. — *Term applied by waiters.*

PANNY: a house—public or otherwise; "flash PANNY," a public-house used by thieves; PANNY MEN, housebreakers.

PARADIS: *French slang* for the gallery of a theatre, "up amongst the GODS." — *See page 363.*

PENNY GAFFS: shops turned into temporary theatres (admission one penny), where dancing and singing take place every night. Rude pictures of the performers are arranged outside to give the front a gaudy and attractive look, and at nighttime coloured lamps and transparencies are displayed to draw an audience.

PIC.: the Piccadilly Saloon.

PIG AND TINDER-BOX: the vulgar rendering of the well-known tavern sign, "*Elephant and Castle.*"

PUB or **PUBLIC:** a public-house.

PUT UP: to suggest, to incite, "he PUT me UP to it;" to have done with; PUT IT UP, is a vulgar answer often heard in the streets. PUT UP, to stop at an hotel or tavern for entertainment.

RING: a generic term given to horse racing and pugilism. The latter is sometimes termed the PRIZE-RING. From the practice of forming the crowd into a RING around the combatants or outside the racecourse.

SLANG: a travelling show.

SLUICERY: a gin shop or public house.

SPELLKEN or **SPEELKEN:** a playhouse. *German*, SPIELEN. — *See* KEN *page 269.* — *Don Juan.*

STALL: to lodge or put up at a public house. Also, to act a part. — *Theatrical.*

SUCK-CASA: a public-house.

TWOPENNY-HOPS: low dancing rooms, the price of admission to which was formerly — and not infrequently now — two pence. The clog hornpipe, the pipe dance, flash jigs, and hornpipes in fetters, *a la* Jack Sheppard, are the favourite movements, all entered into with great spirit and "joyous laborious capering." — *Mayhew.*

VIC.: the Victoria Theatre, London — patronised principally by costermongers and low people; also the street abbreviation of the Christian name of her Majesty the Queen.

WOBBLESHOP: where beer is sold without a license.

ROWS and DISTURBANCES

DUST: a disturbance or noise, "to raise a **DUST**," to make a row.

KICK UP: "to **KICK UP** a *row*," to create a tumult.

KICK-UP: a noise or disturbance.

PIN: "to put in the **PIN**," to refrain from drinking. From the ancient peg tankard, which was furnished with a row of **PINS**, or pegs, to regulate the amount which each person was to drink. A **MERRY PIN**, a roisterer.

RACKET: a dodge, maneuver, exhibition; a disturbance.

RACKETY: wild or noisy.

RANTIPOLE: a wild, noisy fellow.

ROW: a noisy disturbance, tumult, or trouble. Originally *Cambridge*, now universal. Seventy years ago it was written **ROUE**, which would indicate a *French* origin from *roue*, a profligate or disturber of the peace.—*Vide George Parker's Life's Painter*, 1789, p. 122.

ROWDY: money. In *America*, a ruffian, a brawler, "rough."

RUMPUS: a noise, disturbance, a "row."

SCRIMMAGE or **SCRUMMAGE:** a disturbance or row.—*Ancient*. Corruption of *skirmish*?

SHINDY: a row or noise.

SHINE: a row or disturbance.

SLASHER: a powerful roisterer, a pugilist; "the **TIPTON SLASHER**."

TO-DO: (pronounced quickly, and as one word) a disturbance, trouble; "here's a pretty **TO-DO**," here is an unpleasant difficulty. This exactly tallies with the *French* word **AFFAIRE** (*a faire*).—*See Forby's Vocabulary of East Anglia*.

TURN UP: a street fight; a sudden leaving or making off.

TUSSLE: a pull, struggle, fight, or argument. *Johnson* and *Webster* call it a vulgar word.

TUSSLE: to struggle or argue.

AU NATURALE

Language exerts hidden power, like a moon on the tides.

Rita Mae Brown

*T*he "lower orders" had a strange penchant for giving things names generally reserved for people, and this penchant is shown off in this section. The moon is called **Oliver**, a fog is termed **Jerry,** and a pheasant is **Peter.**

Mr. Hotten gives us no explanation as to why. Was it that people just felt friendly toward these things? It seems unlikely. But perhaps the nature of a *cant* language gives us some clues. The purpose of a *cant* language is to let those in the know speak freely in front of those who are not. What better way to disguise the real subject of discussion than by giving it a name that might easily apply to a person?

After all, *when* **Jerry** *was around* was probably a great time to commit a crime. Hunting pheasant out of season was illegal, but *nabbing* **Peter** sounds innocent enough, as does planning an outing *when* **Oliver** *shows his face.*

Editor's Faves:

B. FLATS: bugs.

DEVOTIONAL HABITS: horses weak in the knees and apt to stumble and fall are said to have these. — *Stable.*

POLICEMAN: a fly.

IN THIS CHAPTER

AMOUNTS, NUMBERS, & DISTANCES

BETTER: more; "how far is it to town?" "Oh, **BETTER** 'n a mile." — *Saxon* and *Old English,* now a vulgarism.

CHEEK BY JOWL: side by side — said often of persons in such close confabulation as almost to have their faces touch.

CHUNK: a thick or dumpy piece of any substance. — *Kentish.*

DOLLOP: a lump or portion. — *Norfolk. Anglo Saxon,* **DAEL,** *dole.*

DOWRY: a lot, a great deal; "**DOWRY** of parny," a lot of rain or water. — *See* **PARNY** *page 379.* Probably from the *Gipsey.*

FIGURE: "to cut a good or bad **FIGURE,**" to make a good or indifferent appearance; "what's the **FIGURE**?" how much is to pay? **FIGURE-HEAD,** a person's face. — *Sea term.*

GOB: a portion.

MADZA: half. *Italian,* **MEZZA.** This word enters into combination with various *Cant* phrases, mainly taken from the *Lingua Franca,* as **MADZA CAROON,** half-a-crown, two-and-sixpence; **MADZA SALTEE,** a halfpenny (*see* **SALTEE** *page 199*); **MADZA POONA,** half-a-sovereign; **MADZA ROUND THE BULL,** half a pound of steak, &c.

NANTEE: not any or "I have none." *Italian*, **NIENTE**, nothing.—*See* **DINARLY** *page 194.*

NIL: half; half profits, &c.

NIX: nothing, "**NIX** my doll," synonymous with **NIX**. *German*, **NICHTS**, nothing.—*See* **MUNGARLY** *page 298.*

NOBBA: nine. *Italian*, **NOVE**; *Spanish*, **NOVA**—the *b* and *v* being interchangeable, as Se*b*astópol and Se*v*astópol.

POWER: a large quantity.—Formerly *Irish*, but now general; "a **POWER** of money."

ROUND: "**ROUND** dealing," honest trading; "**ROUND** sum," a large sum. Synonymous also in a *slang* sense with **SQUARE**.—*See* **SQUARE** *p. 117.*

SCOT: a quantity of anything, a lot, a share.—*Anglo Saxon*, **SCEAT**, pronounced **SHOT**.

SLANG: counterfeit or short weights and measures. A **SLANG** quart is a pint and a half. **SLANG** measures are lent out at 2d. per day. The term is used principally by costermongers.

SUP: abbreviation of *supernumerary*.—*Theatrical.*

SWAG: a lot or plenty of anything, a portion or division of property. In Australia the term is used for the luggage carried by diggers: in India the word **LOOT** is used. *Scotch*, **SWEG** or **SWACK**; *German*, **SWEIG**, a flock. *Old Cant* for a shop.

TIT FOR TAT: an equivalent.

ANIMALS

HORSES and DONKEYS

BACK OUT: to retreat from a difficulty; the reverse of **GO AHEAD**. Metaphor borrowed from the stables.

BUFFER: a familiar expression for a jolly acquaintance, probably from the *French*, **BOUFFARD**, a fool or clown; a "jolly old **BUFFER**," said of a good-humoured or liberal old man. In 1737, a **BUFFER** was a "rogue that killed good sound horses for the sake of their skins, by running a long wire into them." —*Bacchus and Venus*. The term was once applied to those who took false oaths for a consideration.

COPER: properly **HORSE-COUPER**, a Scotch horse dealer—used to denote a dishonest one.

CRIB BITER: an inveterate grumbler; properly said of a horse which has the habit, a sign of its bad digestion.

DAISY-CUTTER: a horse which trots or gallops without lifting its feet much from the ground.

DAISY-KICKERS: the name hostlers at large inns used to give each other, now *nearly obsolete*. **DAISY-KICKER** or **GROGHAM**, was likewise the *Cant* term for a horse. The **DAISY-KICKERS** were sad rogues in the old posting days; frequently the landlords rented the stables to them, as the only plan to make them return a profit.

DARK: "keep it **DARK**," *i.e.*, secret. **DARK HORSE**, in racing phraseology a horse whose chance of success is unknown, and whose capabilities have not been made the subject of comment.

DEVOTIONAL HABITS: horses weak in the knees and apt to stumble and fall are said to have these. —*Stable*.

DICKEY: a donkey.

DIGGERS: spurs; also the spades on cards.

FIDDLE: a whip.

FIG: "to **FIG** a horse," to play improper tricks with one in order to make him lively.

FLOGGER: a whip. —*Obsolete*.

FOALED: "thrown from a horse." —*Hunting term.* —*See* **PURL** *page 133, and* **SPILT** *page 131.*

FREE: to steal; generally applied to horses.

GIB-FACE: properly the lower lip of a horse; "**TO HANG ONE'S GIB**," to pout the lower lip, be angry or sullen.

GINGER: a showy, fast horse—as if he had been **FIGGED** with **GINGER** under his tail.

GROGGY: tipsy; when a prize-fighter becomes "weak on his pins," and nearly beaten, he is said to be **GROGGY**. —*Pugilistic*. The same term is applied to horses in a similar condition. *Old English,* **AGGROGGYD**, weighed down, oppressed. —*Prompt. Parvulorum*.

HORSE CHAUNTER: a dealer who takes worthless horses to country fairs and disposes of them by artifice. He is flexible in his ethics, and will put in a glass-eye or perform other tricks.—*See* **COPER** *page 131.*

HORSE'S NIGHTCAP: a halter; "to die in the **HORSE'S NIGHTCAP**," to be hung.

JERUSALEM PONY: a donkey.

JIB or **JIBBER:** a horse that starts or shrinks. *Shakespere* uses it in the sense of a worn-out horse.

KNACKER: an old horse; a horse slaughterer.—*Gloucestershire.*

LEG IT: to run; **LEG BAIL**, to run off, "to give a **LEG**," to assist, as when one mounts a horse; "making a **LEG**," a countryman's bow, —projecting the leg from behind as a balance to the head bent forward.—*Shakespere.*

MOKE: a donkey.—*Gipsey.*

NEDDY: a donkey.

OFF ONE'S FEED: real or pretended want of appetite.—*Stable slang.*

OUT-SIDER: a person who does not habitually bet or is not admitted to the "Ring." Also, a horse whose name does not appear among the "favourites."

PEACOCK HORSE: amongst undertakers, is one with a showy tail and mane, and holds its head up well.—*che va favor-reggiando, &c., Italian.*

PERSUADERS: spurs.

PLUNDER: a common word in the horse trade to express profit. Also an *American* term for baggage, luggage.

PRAD: a horse.

PRAD NAPPING: horse stealing.

PRANCER: a horse.—*Ancient Cant.*

PURL: hunting term for a fall, synonymous with **FOALED** or **SPILT**; "he'll get **PURLED** at the rails."

RACKS: the bones of a dead horse. Term used by horse slaughterers.

RANDOM: three horses driven in line, a very appropriate term.—*See* **UNICORN** *below.*

RIBBONS: the reins.—*Middlesex.*

ROARER: a broken-winded horse.

RUCK: the undistinguished crowd; "to come in with the RUCK," to arrive at the winning post among the non-winning horses. — *Racing term.*

SCRATCH: to strike a horse's name out of the list of runners in a particular race. "Tomboy was SCRATCHED for the Derby, at 10, a.m., on Wednesday," from which period all bets made in reference to him (with one exception) are void. — *See* P.P. — *Turf.*

SCREW: an unsound or broken-down horse, that requires both whip and spur to get him along.

SICK AS A HORSE: popular simile — curious, because a horse never vomits.

SNAFFLED: arrested, "pulled up;" so termed from a kind of horse's bit, called a SNAFFLE. In *East Anglia,* to SNAFFLE is to talk foolishly.

SPANK: to move along quickly; hence a fast horse or vessel is said to be "a SPANKER to go."

SPILT: thrown from a horse or chaise. — *See* PURL *page 133.*

STALE: to evacuate urine. — *Stable term.*

TIT: favourite name for a horse.

TOGERY: clothes, harness, domestic paraphernalia of any kind.

TOOTH: "he has cut his eye TOOTH," *i.e.,* he is sharp enough or old enough, to be so; "up in the TOOTH," far advanced in age — said often of old maids. *Stable term* for aged horses which have lost the distinguishing mark in their teeth.

UNICORN: a style of driving with two wheelers abreast, and one leader, termed in the *United States,* a SPIKE TEAM. TANDEM is one wheeler and one leader. RANDOM, three horses in line.

WALK OVER: a re-election without opposition. — *Parliamentary,* but derived from the *Turf,* where a horse — which has no rivals entered — WALKS OVER the course, and wins without exertion.

WHITECHAPEL or **WESTMINSTER BROUGHAM:** a costermonger's donkey-barrow.

VERMIN

B. FLATS: bugs.

CHATTS: lice or body vermin.

CHATTY: a filthy person, one whose clothes are not free from vermin; **CHATTY DOSS**, a lousy bed.

CRUMMY-DOSS: a lousy or filthy bed.

GRAYS or **SCOTCH GRAYS:** lice. — *Scotch.*

LIVE-STOCK: vermin of the *insect* kind.

POLICEMAN: a fly.

SCOTCH GRAYS: lice. Our northern neighbours are calumniously reported, from their living on oatmeal, to be peculiarly liable to cutaneous eruptions and parasites.

OTHER ANIMALS

ALDERMAN: a turkey.

BEAKER-HUNTER: a stealer of poultry.

BLOODY-JEMMY: a sheep's head. — *See* **SANGUINARY JAMES** *page 303.*

BODY-SNATCHERS: cat stealers.

BUFFER: a dog. Their skins were formerly in great request — hence the term, **BUFF** meaning in *Old English* to skin. It is still used in the ring, **BUFFED** meaning stripped to the skin. In *Irish Cant*, **BUFFER** is a *boxer*. The **BUFFER** of a railway carriage doubtless received its very appropriate name from the old pugilistic application of this term.

CHITTERLINGS: the shirt frills worn still by ancient beaux; properly, the *entrails of a pig*, to which they are supposed to bear some resemblance. *Belgian*, **SCHYTERLINGH.**

COCKYOLY BIRDS: little birds, frequently called "dickey birds." — *Kingsley's Two Years Ago.*

DAB: street term for a flat fish of any kind. — *Old.*

DUNAKER: a stealer of cows or calves. — *Nearly obsolete.*

GALENY: *Old Cant* term for a fowl of any kind; now a respectable word in the West of England, signifying a Guinea fowl. — *Vide Grose. Latin,* GALLINA.

GLASGOW MAGISTRATES: salt herrings. — *Scotch.*

GOUROCK HAM: salt herrings. Gourock, on the Clyde, about twenty-five miles from Glasgow, was formerly a great fishing village. — *Scotch.*

HACKLE: "to show HACKLE," to be willing to fight. HACKLES are the long feathers on the back of a cock's neck, which he erects when angry — hence the metaphor.

JEMMY: a sheep's head. — *See* SANGUINARY JAMES *page 303.*

MOKO: a name given by sportsmen to pheasant killed by mistake in partridge shooting during September, before the pheasant shooting comes in. They pull out their tails, and roundly assert they are no pheasants at all, but MOKOS.

MURKARKER: a monkey — vulgar cockney pronunciation of MACAUCO, a species of monkey. *Jackey Macauco* was the name of a famous fighting monkey, which used about thirty years ago to display his prowess at the Westminster pit, where, after having killed many dogs, he was at last "chawed up" by a bull terrier.

PETER: a partridge. — *Poacher's term.*

PLUCK: the heart, liver, and lungs of an animal — all that is PLUCKED away in connection with the windpipe, from the chest of a sheep or hog; among low persons, courage, valour, and a stout heart. — *See* MOLLYGRUBS *page 78.*

PURE FINDERS: street collectors of dogs' dung.

SNAGGLING: angling for geese with a hook and line, the bait being a worm or snail. The goose swallows the bait, and is quietly landed and bagged.

SNOTS: small bream, a slimy kind of flat fish. — *Norwich.*

SOLDIER: a red herring.

SOW'S BABY: a pig; sixpence.

STAGGERING BOB: an animal to whom the knife only just anticipates death from natural disease or accident — said of meat on that account unfit for human food.

TIKE or **BUFFER LURKING:** dog stealing.

TOSS: a measure of sprats.

TURKEY-MERCHANTS: dealers in plundered or contraband silk. Poulterers are sometimes termed TURKEY MERCHANTS, in memory of Horne Tooke's answer to the boys at Eton, who wished in an aristocratic way to know who *his* father was—a TURKEY MERCHANT, replied Tooke. His father was a poulterer. TURKEY MERCHANT, also, was formerly slang for a driver of turkeys or geese to market.

WOOLBIRD: a lamb; "wing of a WOOLBIRD," a shoulder of lamb.

WORMING: removing the beard of an oyster or muscle.

YARMOUTH CAPON: a bloater, or red herring.—*Old—Ray's Proverbs.*

 # METALS

BILLY-HUNTING: buying old metal.

BLUE-PIGEON FLYERS: journeymen plumbers, glaziers, and others, who, under the plea of repairing houses, strip off the lead, and make way with it. Sometimes they get off with it by wrapping it round their bodies.

BLUEY: lead. *German,* BLEI.

GEN: a shilling. Also, GENT, silver. Abbreviation of the *French,* ARGENT.

GENT: silver. From the *French,* ARGENT.

PEWTER: money, like TIN, used generally to signify silver; also, a pewter-pot.

PIG: a mass of metal; so called from its being poured in a fluid state from a SOW.—*See* SOW *below.—Workmen's term.*

PIGEON or **BLUEY CRACKING:** breaking into empty houses and stealing lead.

REDGE: gold.

SOW: the receptacle into which the liquid iron is poured in a gun-foundry. The melted metal poured from it is termed PIG.—*Workmen's terms.*

TIN: money—generally applied to silver.

TOSHERS: men who steal copper from ships' bottoms in the Thames.

WEDGE: silver.—*Old Cant.*

NATURE

BASH: to beat or thrash; "BASHING a donna," beating a woman; originally a provincial word, and chiefly applied to the practice of beating walnut trees, when in bud, with long poles, to increase their productiveness. Hence the West country proverb:

> "A woman, a whelp, and a walnut tree,
> The more you BASH 'em, the better they be."

BLOWEN: a showy or flaunting prostitute, a thief's paramour. In *Wilts*, a BLOWEN is a blossom. *Germ.* BLUHEN, to bloom.

> "O du *bulhende* Madchen viel schone Willkomm!"
> —*German Song.*

Possibly however, the street term, BLOWEN may mean one whose reputation has been BLOWN UPON, or damaged.

CRAB or **GRAB:** a disagreeable old person. *Name of a wild and sour fruit.* "To catch a CRAB," to fall backwards by missing a stroke in rowing.

FOGUS: tobacco.—*Old Cant.* FOGO, *old word for stench.*

JERRY: a fog.

MIZZLE: to run away or decamp; to disappear as in a mist. From MIZZLE, a drizzling rain; a Scotch mist.

> "And then one *mizzling* Michaelmas night
> The Count he MIZZLED too."—*Hood.*

MONKERY: the country or rural districts. *Old* word for a quiet or monastic life.—*Hall.*

NOSE EM or **FOGUS:** tobacco.

OLIVER: the moon; "OLIVER don't widdle," *i.e.,* the moon does not shine.—*Nearly obsolete.*—*Bulwer's Paul Clifford.*

PARISH LANTERN: the moon.

PARNEY: rain; "dowry of PARNEY," a quantity of rain. *Anglo-Indian* slang from the *Hindoo*, PANI, water; *Gipsey*, PANE. Old Indian officers always call brandy and water BRANDY PAWNEE.

SNAGGLE TEETH: uneven and unpleasant looking dental operators. —*West.* SNAGS (*Americanism*) ends of sunken drift-wood sticking out of the water, on which river steamers are often wrecked.

STROMMEL: straw.—*Ancient Cant.* Halliwell says that in Norfolk STRUMMEL is a name for hair.

WEED: a cigar; *the* WEED, tobacco generally.

WIDDLE: to shine.—*See* OLIVER *above.*

WINKS: periwinkles.

 # SPECIFIC DAYS and TIMES

ARY: corruption of ever a, e'er a; ARY ONE, e'er a one.

BANYAN-DAY: a day on which no meat is served out for rations; probably derived from the BANIANS, a Hindoo caste, who abstain from animal food.—*Sea.*

BED-POST: "in the twinkling of a BED-POST," in a moment or very quickly. Originally BED-STAFF, a stick placed vertically in the frame of a bed to keep the bedding in its place.—*Shadwell's Virtuoso*, 1676, act i., scene 1. This was used sometimes as a defensive weapon.

BLUE MOON: an unlimited period.

BRAGGADOCIO: three months' imprisonment as a reputed thief or old offender—sometimes termed a DOSE or a DOLLOP.—*Household Words*, vol. i., p. 579.

CRACK: "in a CRACK (of the finger and thumb)," in a moment.

DARKEY: twilight. DARKMANS, the night.

DOSE: three months' imprisonment as a known thief.—*See* BRAGGADOCIO *page 259.*

DRAG or THREE MOON: three months in prison.

GANDER MONTH: the period when the monthly nurse is in the ascendant, and the husband has to shift for himself.

HALF A STRETCH: six months in prison.

JIFFY: "in a JIFFY," in a moment.

KICK: a moment; "I'll be there in a KICK," *i.e.*, in a minute.

LENGTH: six months' imprisonment. — *See* STRETCH *below.*

MOON: a month — generally used to express the length of time a person has been sentenced by the magistrate; thus "ONE MOON" is one month. — *See* DRAG *above*. It is a curious fact that the Indians of America and the roaming vagabonds of England should both calculate time by the MOON.

PIG'S WHISPER: a low or inaudible whisper; also a short space of time, synonymous with COCKSTRIDE, *i.e., cock's tread.*

SAINT MONDAY: a holiday most religiously observed by journeymen shoemakers and other mechanics. An Irishman observed that this saint's anniversary happened every week. — *North*, where it is termed COBBLERS' MONDAY.

SHITTEN-SATURDAY: (corruption of SHUT-IN-SATURDAY), the Saturday between Good Friday and Easter Sunday, when our Lord's body was enclosed in the tomb.

STIR UP SUNDAY: the Sunday next before Advent, the collect for that day commencing with the words "Stir up." Schoolboys, growing excited at the prospect of the vacation, irreverently commemorate it by stirring up — pushing and poking each other. CRIB CRUST MONDAY and TUG BUTTON TUESDAY are distinguished by similar tricks; while on PAY-OFF WEDNESDAY they retaliate small grudges in a playful facetious way. Forby says, good housewives in Norfolk consider themselves reminded by the name to mix the ingredients for their Christmas mince pies.

STRETCH: twelve months — generally used to intimate the time anyone has been sentenced by the judge or magistrate. ONE STRETCH is to be imprisoned for twelve months, TWO STRETCH is two years, THREE STRETCH is three years, and so on.

YOU DON'T SAY

Think like a wise man, but communicate in the language of the people.

William Butler Yeats

*O*f this chapter, my favorite section is the interjections. From "**blow me tight**" to "**zounds**," the interjections are entertaining and fun. A few have stood the test of time, like "**by George**," (an appeal to England's patron saint.) But most have gone the way of "**od rabbit**" and "**s'elp my tater**."

I'm surprised there aren't more slang words for romance and sex. Some that are included are rather frightening, like this little rhyme about wife-beating:

> "A woman, a whelp, and a walnut tree,
> The more you **Bash** 'em, the better they be."

Apparently chivalry died early.

Honesty, too, takes a beating. There are thirty-four words for lies or exaggerations—more than any other category.

Editor's Faves:

BY THE HOLY POKER AND THE TUMBLING TOM!: an Irish oath.

To **JOE BLAKE THE BARTLEMY:** to visit a low woman.

MUFFIN-WORRY: an old-ladies' tea party.

IN THIS CHAPTER

CUSTOMS and MANNERS

COLD SHOULDER: "to show or give anyone the **COLD SHOULDER**," to assume a distant manner toward them, to evince a desire to cease acquaintanceship. Sometimes it is termed "cold shoulder of *mutton*."

HEEL-TAPS: small quantities of wine or other beverage left in the bottom of glasses, considered as a sign that the liquor is not liked, and therefore unfriendly and unsocial to the host and the company.

HULK: to hang about in hopes of an invitation. — *See* **MOOCH** *below.*

INVITE: an invitation—a corruption used by stuck-up people of mushroom origin.

LED CAPTAIN: a fashionable spunger, a swell who, by artifice ingratiates himself into the good graces of the master of the house, and lives at his table.

LEG IT: to run; **LEG BAIL**, to run off, "to give a **LEG**," to assist, as when one mounts a horse; "making a **LEG**," a countryman's bow, —projecting the leg from behind as a balance to the head bent forward. — *Shakespere.*

MOOCH: to sponge; to obtrude yourself upon friends just when they are about to sit down to dinner or other lucky time—of course quite accidentally.—Compare **HULK**. To slink away, and allow your friends to pay for the entertainment. *In Wiltshire*, on the **MOUTCH** is to shuffle.

MUFFIN-WORRY: an old ladies' tea party.

OAK: the outer door of college rooms; to "sport one's **OAK**," to be "not at home" to visitors. — *See* **SPORT** *below.* — *University.*

P'S AND Q'S: particular points, precise behaviour; "mind your **P'S AND Q'S**," be very careful. Originating, according to some, from the similarity of p's and q's in the hornbook alphabet, and therefore the warning of an old dame to her pupils; or, according to others, of a French dancing master to his pupils, to mind their *pieds* (feet) and *queues* (wigs) when making a bow.

SHOE: to free, or initiate a person a practice common in most trades to a newcomer. The **SHOEING** consists in paying for beer or other drink, which is drunk by the older hands. The cans emptied, and the bill paid, the stranger is considered properly **SHOD**.

SPORT: to exhibit, to wear, &c.; a word which is made to do duty in a variety of senses, especially at the University. — *See the Gradus ad Cantabrigiam.* "To **SPORT** a new title," "to **SPORT** an Ægrotat" (*i.e.,* a permission from the "Dons" to abstain from lectures, &c., on account of illness); "to **SPORT ONE'S OAK**," to shut the outer door and exclude the public—especially *duns* and boring acquaintances. Common also in the Inns of Court. — *See Notes and Queries,* 2nd series, vol. viii. P. 492, and *Gentleman's Magazine,* December, 1794.

SPORTING DOOR: the outer door of chambers, also called the **OAK**. — *See* under **SPORT** *page 179.* — *University.*

WET: to drink. Low people generally ask an acquaintance to **WET** any recently purchased article, *i.e.,* to stand treat on the occasion. "**WET** your whistle," *i.e.,* take a drink; "**WET** the other eye," *i.e.,* take another glass.

FRIENDSHIP

CHUM: an acquaintance. A recognised term, but in such frequent use with the lower orders that it demanded a place in this glossary.

COLD SHOULDER: "to show or give anyone the **COLD SHOULDER**," to assume a distant manner toward them, to evince a desire to cease acquaintanceship. Sometimes it is termed "cold shoulder of *mutton.*"

COTTON: to like, adhere to, or agree with any person; "to **COTTON** on to a man," to attach yourself to him or fancy him, literally, to stick to him as cotton would. *Vide Bartlett,* who claims it as an Americanism; and *Halliwell,* who terms it an Archaism; also *Bacchus and Venus,* 1737.

COVENTRY: "to send a man to **COVENTRY**," not to speak to or notice him. Coventry was one of those town in which the privilege of practicing most trades was anciently confined to certain privileged persons, as the freemen, &c. Hence a stranger stood little chance of custom or countenance, and "to send a man to **COVENTRY**," came to be equivalent to putting him out of the pale of society.

CRONY: a termagant or malicious old woman; an intimate friend. *Johnson* calls it *Cant.*

CUT: CUT AN ACQUAINTANCE, to cease friendly intercourse with them.
—*Cambridge. Old* CUTTE, to say.—*See* CUT *in the Index for more
meanings on page 479.*

DOUBLE-UP: to pair off or "chum," with another man; to beat severely.

FORK OUT: bring out one's money, to pay the bill, to STAND FOR or
treat a friend; to hand over what does not belong to you.—*Old Cant*
term for picking pockets, and very curious it is to trace its origin. In
the early part of the last century, a little book on purloining was
published, and of course it had to give the latest modes. FORKING was
the newest method, and it consisted in thrusting the fingers stiff and
open into the pocket, and then quickly closing them and extracting
any article.

FREE AND EASY: a club held at most public houses, the members of
which meet in the taproom or parlour for the purpose of drinking,
smoking, and hearing each other sing and "talk politics." The name
indicates the character of the proceedings.

GEE: to agree with or be congenial to a person.

MATE: the term a coster or low person applies to a friend, partner, or
companion; "me and my MATE did so and so," is a common phrase
with a low Londoner.—*Originally a Sea term.*

MOBS: companions; MOBSMEN, dressy swindlers.

MOOCH: to sponge; to obtrude yourself upon friends just when they are
about to sit down to dinner or other lucky time—of course quite
accidentally.—Compare HULK. To slink away, and allow your friends
to pay for the entertainment. *In Wiltshire*, on the MOUTCH is to shuffle.

NUTS: to be NUTS upon anything or person is to be pleased with or fond
of it; a self-satisfied man is said to be NUTS upon himself. NUTTED,
taken in by a man who professed to be NUTS upon you.

OUT: a dram glass. The *habitue* of a gin-shop, desirous of treating a brace
of friends, calls for a quartern of gin and three OUTS, by which he
means three glasses which will exactly contain the quartern.

PAL: a partner, acquaintance, friend, an accomplice. *Gipsey*, a brother.

SAM: to "stand SAM," to pay for refreshment or drink, to stand
paymaster for anything. An *Americanism*, originating in the letter U.S.
on the knapsacks of the United States soldiers, which letters were

jocularly said to be the initials of *Uncle Sam* (the Government), who pays for all. In use in this country as early as 1827.

SCREW LOOSE: when friends become cold and distant towards each other, it is said there is a SCREW LOOSE betwixt them; said also when anything goes wrong with a person's credit or reputation.

SHY: "to fight SHY of a person," to avoid his society either from dislike, fear, or any other reason. SHY has also the sense of flighty, unsteady, untrustworthy.

SPLIT: to inform against one's companions, to tell tales. "To SPLIT with a person," to cease acquaintanceship, to quarrel.

STAND: "to STAND treat," to pay for a friend's entertainment; to bear expense; to put up with treatment, good or ill; "this house STOOD me in £1,000," *i.e.,* cost that sum; "to STAND PAD," to beg on the curb with a small piece of paper pinned on the breast, inscribed *"I'm starving."*

STICK: to cheat; "he got STUCK," he was taken in; STICK, to forget one's part in a performance.—*Theatrical.* STICK ON, to overcharge or defraud; STICK UP FOR, to defend a person, especially when slandered in his absence; STICK UP TO, to preservere in courting or attacking, whether in fisticuffs or argument; "to STICK in one's gizzard," to rankle in one's heart; "to STICK TO a person," to adhere to one, be his friend through adverse circumstances.

TAKE: to "TAKE UP for anyone," to protect or defend a person; "to TAKE OFF," to mimic.—*See* TAKE *in the Alphabetical Index for more meanings on page 504.*

THICK: intimate, familiar. *Scotch,* CHIEF; "the two are very CHIEF now," *i.e.,* friendly.

 # LOVE, SEX, and ROMANCE

BASH: to beat or thrash; "BASHING a donna," beating a woman; originally a provincial word, and chiefly applied to the practice of beating walnut trees, when in bud, with long poles, to increase their productiveness. Hence the West country proverb:

> "A woman, a whelp, and a walnut tree,
> The more you BASH 'em, the better they be."

BOTTLE-HOLDER: an assistant to a "Second," —*Pugilistic*; an abettor; also, the bridegroom's man at a wedding.

BOW- CATCHERS or **KISS CURLS:** small curls twisted on the cheeks or temples of young—and often old—girls, adhering to the face as if gummed or pasted. Evidently a corruption of **BEAU-CATCHERS**. In old times these were called *lovelocks*, when they were the marks at which all the puritan and ranting preachers levelled their pulpit pop-guns, loaded with sharp and virulent abuse. Hall and Pryune looked upon all women as strumpets who dared to let the hair depart from a straight line upon their cheeks. The French prettily term them *accroche-cœurs*, whilst in the United States they are plainly and unpleasantly called **SPIT-CURLS**. Bartlett says: "**SPIT CURL**, a detached lock of hair curled upon the temple; probably from having been first filastered into shape by the saliva. It is now understood that the mucilage of quince seed is used by the ladies for this purpose."

> "You may prate of your lips, and your teeth of pearl,
>   And your eyes so brightly flashing;
> My song shall be of that SALIVA CURL
>   Which threatens my heart to smash in."
> —*Boston Transcript*, October 30, 1858.

When men twist the hair on each side of their faces into ropes they are sometime called **BELL-ROPES**, as being wherewith to *draw the belles*. Whether **BELL-ROPES** or **BOW-CATCHER**, it is singular they should form part of the prisoner's paraphernalia, and that a jaunty little kiss-me quick curl should, of all things in the world, ornament a gaol dock; yet such was formerly the case. Hunt, the murderer of Weare, on his trial, we are informed by the *Athenæum*, appeared at the bar with a highly pomatumed love-lock sticking tight to his forehead. Young ladies, think of this!

BREAK-DOWN: a jovial, social gathering, a **FLARE UP**; in Ireland, a wedding.

BREECHES: "to wear the **BREECHES**," said of a wife who usurps the husband's prerogative.

BUB: a teat, woman's breast.

BUCK: a gay or smart man, cuckold.

BURYING A MOLL: running away from a mistress.

BUSS: an abbreviation of "omnibus," a public carriage. Also, a kiss.

CASE: a few years ago the term CASE was applied to persons and things; "what a CASE he is," *i.e.,* what a curious person; "a rum CASE that," or "you are a CASE," both synonymous with the phrase "odd fish," common half a century ago. Among young ladies at boarding schools a CASE means a love affair.

CAVAULTING: coition. *Lingua Franca,* CAVOLTA.

CHIVARLY: coition. Probably a corruption from the *Lingua Franca.*

COTTON: to like, adhere to, or agree with any person; "to COTTON on to a man," to attach yourself to him or fancy him, literally, to stick to him as cotton would. *Vide Bartlett,* who claims it as an Americanism; and *Halliwell,* who terms it an Archaism; also *Bacchus and Venus,* 1737.

CROOKY: to hang on to, to lead, walk arm-in-arm; to court or pay addresses to a girl.

CUT: CUT A FIGURE, to make either a good or bad appearance; CUT OUT, to excel, thus in affairs of gallantry one Adonis is said to *"cut the other out"* in the affections of the wished for lady.—*Cambridge.* Old CUTTE, to say.—*See* CUT *in the Index for more meanings on page 479.*

DEATH: "to dress to DEATH," *i.e.,* to the very extreme of fashion, perhaps so as to be KILLING.

DILLY DALLY: to trifle.

FLAME: a sweetheart.

FROW: a girl or wife. *German,* FRAU; *Dutch,* VROUW.

GALLAVANT: to wait upon the ladies.—*Old.*

GANDER MONTH: the period when the monthly nurse is in the ascendant, and the husband has to shift for himself.

GAY: loose, dissipated; "GAY woman," a kept mistress or prostitute.

GRASS-WIDOW: an unmarried mother; a deserted mistress. In the United States, during the gold fever in California, it was common for an adventurer to put both his GRASS-WIDOW and his children to *school* during his absence.

HEN-PECKED: said of one whose wife "wears the breeches."

<u>Communication:</u> Love, Sex, and Romance

INTERESTING: "to be in an INTERESTING situation," applied to females when *enceinte*. [pregnant]

To **JOE BLAKE THE BARTLEMY:** to visit a low woman.

JOMER: a sweetheart or favourite girl. — *See* **BLOWER** *page 35.*

KERTEVER-CARTZO: the venereal disease. From the *Lingua Franca*, CATTIVO, bad, and CAZZO, the male generative organ.

KILLING: bewitching, fascinating. The term is akin to the phrase "dressing to DEATH."

KNOCKED-UP: tired, jaded, used-up, done for. In the United States, amongst females, the phrase is equivalent to being *enceinte*, so that Englishmen often unconsciously commit themselves when amongst our Yankee cousins.

MARRIAGE LINES: a marriage certificate. — *Provincial.*

MOLL'D: followed or accompanied by a woman.

MOLROWING: "out on the SPREE" in company with so-called gay women. In allusion to the amatory serenading of the London cats.

MOOE: the mouth; the female generative organ. — *Gipsey* and *Hindoo.* *Shakespere* has **MOE**, to make mouths.

MUFF: a silly or weak-minded person; MUFF has been defined to be "a soft thing that holds a lady's hand without squeezing it."

MY TULIP: a term of endearment used by the lower orders to persons and animals; "kim up, MY TULIP," as the coster said to his donkey when thrashing him with an ash stick.

NINCOMPOOP: a fool, a hen-pecked husband, a "Jerry Sneak." Corruption of *non compos mentis.*

NUB: a husband.

NUTS: to be NUTS upon anything or person is to be pleased with or fond of it; a self-satisfied man is said to be NUTS upon himself. **NUTTED,** taken in by a man who professed to be NUTS upon you.

NUTTY: amorous.

OGLE: to look or reconnoitre.

ON THE FLY: getting one's living by thieving or other illegitimate means; the phrase is applied to men the same as ON THE LOOSE is to women.

ON THE SHELF: to be transported. With old maids it has another and very different meaning.

PLUM: £100,000, usually applied to the dowry of a rich heiress or a legacy.

POLL: a prostitute. **POLLED UP**, living with a woman without being married to her.

PUCKERING: talking privately.

RACLAN: a married woman.—*Gipsey*.

RANDY: rampant, violent, warm, amorous. *North*, **RANDY-BEGGAR**, a Gipsey tinker.

RIB: a wife.—*North*.

RUMY: a good woman or girl.—*Gipsey slang*. In the regular *Gipsey* language, **ROMI**, a woman, a wife, is the feminine of **RO**, a man; and in the *Robber's Language* of Spain (partly *Gipsey*,) **RUMI** signifies a harlot.

SHEEP'S EYES: "to make **SHEEP'S EYES** at a person," to cast amorous glances towards one on the sly:

> "But he, the beast, was casting **SHEEP'S EYES** at her,
> Out of his bullock head."
>
> —*Colman, Broad Grins*, p.57.

SHELF: "on the **SHELF**," not yet disposed of; young ladies are said to be so situated when they cannot meet with a husband; "on the **SHELF**," pawned.

SLAP: paint for the face, rouge.

SPLICE: to marry, "and the two shall become one flesh." —*Sea*.

SPOON: synonymous with **SPOONEY**. A **SPOON** has been defined to be "a thing that touches a lady's lips without kissing them."

SPOONEY: a weak-minded and foolish person, effeminate or fond, "to be **SPOONEY** on a girl," to be foolishly attached to one.

SPOONS: "when I was **SPOONS** with you," *i.e.*, when young, and in our courting days before marriage.—*Charles Mathews*, in the farce of *Everybody's Friend*.

STANGEY: a tailor; a person under petticoat government, — derived from the custom of "*riding the* STANG," mentioned in Hudibras:

> "It is a custom used of course
> Where the grey mare is the better horse."

STRAW: married ladies are said to be "in THE STRAW" at their *accouchements*. The phrase is a coarse allusion to farm-yard animals in a similar condition.

SWEET: loving or fond; "how SWEET he was upon the moll," *i.e.*, what marked attention he paid the girl.

SWISHED: married.

THICK: intimate, familiar. *Scotch,* CHIEF; "the two are very CHIEF now," *i.e.*, friendly.

TIED UP: given over, finished; also married, in allusion to the Hymenial knot, unless a jocose allusion be intended to the *halter* (altar).

TITIVATE: to put in order or dress up.

TOG: to dress or equip with an outfit; "TOGGED out to the nines," dressed in the first style.

TOOTH: "he has cut his eye TOOTH," *i.e.*, he is sharp enough or old enough, to be so; "up in the TOOTH," far advanced in age — said often of old maids. *Stable term* for aged horses which have lost the distinguishing mark in their teeth.

USED-UP: broken-hearted, bankrupt, fatigued.

WALK-THE BARBER: to lead a girl astray.

THINGS SPOKEN

AGREEING, DISAGREEING, and ARGUING

CARPET: "upon the CARPET," any subject or matter that is uppermost for discussion or conversation. Frequently quoted as *sur le tapis,* but it does not seem to be a correct Parisian phrase.

CAUCUS: a private meeting held for the purpose of concerting measures, agreeing upon candidates for office before an election, &c.—*See Pickering's Vocabulary.*

CLINCHER: that which rivets or confirms an argument, an incontrovertible position. Metaphor from the workshop.

COG: to cheat at dice.—*Shakespere.* Also, to agree with, as one cog-wheel does with another.

COTTON: to like, adhere to, or agree with any person; "to COTTON on to a man," to attach yourself to him or fancy him, literally, to stick to him as cotton would. *Vide Bartlett,* who claims it as an Americanism; and *Halliwell,* who terms it an Archaism; also *Bacchus and Venus,* 1737.

CROW: "I have a CROW to pick with you," *i.e.,* an explanation to demand, a disagreeable matter to settle; "to COCK-CROW over a person," to exalt over his abasement or misfortune.

DRIVE-AT: to aim at; "what is he DRIVING AT?" what does he intend to imply? A phrase often used when a circuitous line of argument is adopted by a barrister, or a strange set of questions asked, the purpose of which in not very evident.

EGG or EGG ON: to excite, stimulate, or provoke one person to quarrel with another, &c. *Corruption of edge or edge on.—Ancient.*

GEE: to agree with or be congenial to a person.

HUM AND HAW: to hesitate, raise objections.—*Old English.*

IPSAL DIXAL: Cockney corruption of *ipse dixit*—said of one's simple uncorroborated assertion.

KID-ON: to entice or incite a person on to the perpetration of an act.

NAP ONE'S BIB: to cry, shed tears, or carry one's point.

NICK: to hit the mark; "he's NICKED it," *i.e.,* won his point.

PUT UP: to suggest, to incite, "he PUT me UP to it;" to have done with; PUT IT UP, is a vulgar answer often heard in the streets. PUT UP, to stop at an hotel or tavern for entertainment.

RIDER: in a University examination, a problem or question appended to another, as directly arising from or dependent on it;—beginning to be generally used for any corollary or position which naturally arises from any previous statement or evidence.

RUB: a quarrel or impediment: "there's the **RUB**," *i.e.*, that is the difficulty. — *Shakespere and L'Estrange.*

SCRATCH: a fight, contest, point of dispute; "coming up to the **SCRATCH**," going or preparing to fight — in reality, approaching the line usually chalked on the ground to divide the ring. — *Pugilistic.*

SET TO: a sparring match, a fight; "a dead set," a determined stand, in argument or in movement.

SPLIT: to inform against one's companions, to tell tales. "To **SPLIT** with a person," to cease acquaintanceship, to quarrel.

STICK: to cheat; "he got **STUCK**," he was taken in; **STICK**, to forget one's part in a performance. — *Theatrical.* **STICK ON**, to overcharge or defraud; **STICK UP FOR**, to defend a person, especially when slandered in his absence; **STICK UP TO**, to preserver in courting or attacking, whether in fisticuffs or argument; "to **STICK** in one's gizzard," to rankle in one's heart; "to **STICK TO** a person," to adhere to one, be his friend through adverse circumstances.

TONGUED: talkative; "to **TONGUE** a person," *i.e.*, talk him down.

TUSSLE: a pull, struggle, fight, or argument. *Johnson* and *Webster* call it a vulgar word.

TUSSLE: to struggle or argue.

 BEGGING

BLOB: (from **BLAB**), to talk. Beggars are of two kinds — those who **SCREEVE** (introduce themselves with a **FAKEMENT**, or false document), and those who **BLOB**, or state their case in their own truly "unvarnished" language.

CAD or **CADGER** (from which it is shortened): a mean or vulgar fellow; a beggar; one who would rather live on other people than work for himself; a man trying to worm something out of another, either money or information. *Johnson* uses the word, and gives *huckster* as the meaning, but I never heard it used in this sense. **CAGER** or **GAGER**, the *Old Cant* term for a man. The exclusives in the Universities apply the term **CAD** to all non-members.

CADGE: to beg in an artful or wheedling manner. — *North.*

CADGING: begging of the lowest degree.

MACE: to spunge, swindle, or beg, in a polite way; "give it him (a shopkeeper) on the MACE," *i.e.*, obtain goods on credit and never pay for them; also termed "striking the MACE."

MAUND: to beg; "MAUNDERING on the fly," begging of people in the streets.—*Old Cant.* MAUNG, to beg, is a term in use amongst the Gipseys, and may also be found in the *Hindoo* vocabulary. MAUND, however, is pure *Anglo Saxon*, from MAND, a basket. Compare "beg," which is derived from BAG, a curious parallel.

MUNGING or **MOUNGING:** whining, begging, muttering.—*North.*

STAG: to demand money, to "cadge."

WHEEDLE: to entice by soft words. "This word cannot be found to derive itself from any other, and therefore is looked upon as wholly invented by the CANTERS." —*Triumph of Wit*, 1705.

FLATTERY and INSULTS

BLARNEY: flattery, exaggeration.—*Hibernicism.*

BUTTER or **BATTER:** praise or flattery. To BUTTER, to flatter, cajole.

CHAFF: to gammon, joke, quiz, or praise ironically. CHAFF-bone, the jaw-bone.—*Yorkshire.* CHAFF, jesting. In *Anglo Saxon*, CEAF is chaff; and CEAFL, bill, beak, or jaw. In the "Ancien Riwle,"A.D. 1221, *ceafle* is used in the sense of idle discourse.

CHI-IKE: a hurrah, a good word or hearty praise.

CRAB: to offend or insult; to expose or defeat a robbery, to inform against.

CRACK-UP: to boast or praise.—*Ancient English.*

FILLIBRUSH: to flatter, praise ironically.

FLUMMERY: flattery, gammon, genteel nonsense.

FRUMP: to mock or insult. —*Beaumont and Fletcher.*

HOAX: to deceive or ridicule—*Grose* says was originally a *University Cant* word. Corruption of HOCUS, to cheat.

Communication: **Things Spoken-** Flattery and Insults

JOLLY: a word of praise or favourable notice; "chuck Harry a JOLLY, Bill!" *i.e.*, go and praise up his goods or buy of him, and speak well of the article, that the crowd standing around his stall may think it a good opportunity to lay out their money. "Chuck a JOLLY," literally translated, is to throw a shout or a good word.

KIBOSH: nonsense, stuff, humbug; "it's all KIBOSH," *i.e.*, palaver or nonsense; "to put on the KIBOSH," to run down, slander, degrade, &c. —*See* **BOSH** *page 399.*

KOTOOING: misapplied flattery. —*Illustrated London News,* 7th January, 1860.

PUFF: to blow up, swell with praise, was declared by a writer in the Weekly Register, as far back as 1732, to be illegitimate.

> "PUFF has become a *Cant* word, signifying the applause set forth by writers, &c. to increase the reputation and sale of a book, and is an excellent stratagem to excite the curiosity of gentle readers."

Lord Bacon, however, used the word in a similar sense a century before.

SALVE: praise, flattery, chaff.

SIGHT: "to take a SIGHT at a person," a vulgar action employed by street boys to denote incredulity or contempt for authority, by placing the thumb against the nose and closing all the fingers except the little one, which is agitated in token of derision. —*See* **WALKER** *page 400.*

SLANG: to cheat, to abuse in foul language.

SOAP: flattery. —*See* **SOFT-SOAP** *below.*

SOFT-SOAP or **SOFT-SAWDER:** flattery, ironical praise.

STUFF: to make false but plausible statements, to praise ironically, to make game of a person—literally, to STUFF or CRAM him with gammon or falsehood.

WIPE: to strike; "he fetcht me a WIPE over the knuckles," he struck me on the knuckles; "to WIPE a person down," to flatter or pacify a person; to WIPE off a score, to pay one's debts, in allusion to the slate or chalk methods of account keeping; "to WIPE a person's eye," to shoot game which he has missed—*Sporting term*; hence to gain an advantage by superior activity.

INFORMING and IMPEACHING

BLEW or **BLOW:** to inform or peach.

BLOW: to expose or inform; "**BLOW** the gaff," to inform against a person. In *America*, to **BLOW** is slang for to taunt.

BUDGE: to move, to inform, to **SPLIT**, or tell tales.

BUFF: to swear to or accuse; to **SPLIT**, or peach upon. *Old* word for boasting, 1582.

BUST or **BURST:** to tell tales, to **SPLIT**, to inform. **BUSTING**, informing against accomplices when in custody.

CAT-IN-THE-PAN: a traitor, a turn-coat—derived by some from the *Greek*, Καraπav, altogether; or from *cake in pan*, a pan cake, which is frequently turned from side to side.

CHEEK: impudence, assurance; **CHEEKY**, saucy or forward. *Lincolnshire*, **CHEEK**, to accuse.

COME: a slang verb used in many phrases; "A'nt he **COMING IT**," *i.e.*, is he not proceeding at a great rate? "Don't **COME TRICKS** here," "don't **COME THE OLD SOLDIER** over me," *i.e.*, we are aware of your practices, and "twig" your manoeuver. **COMING IT STRONG**, exaggerating, going a-head, the opposite of "*drawing it mild*." **COMING IT** also means informing or disclosing.

CRAB: to offend or insult; to expose or defeat a robbery, to inform against.

MOUNTER: a false swearer. Derived from the borrowed clothes men used to **MOUNT**, or dress in, when going to swear for a consideration.

NARK: a person in the pay of the police; a common informer; one who gets his living by laying traps for publicans, &c.

NOSE: a thief who turns informer or Queen's evidence; a spy or watch; "on the **NOSE**," on the look out.

PEACH: to inform against or betray. *Webster* states that *impeach* is now the modification mostly used, and that **PEACH** is confined principally to the conversation of thieves and the lower orders.

RAT: a sneak, an informer, a turn-coat, one who changes his party for interest. The late Sir Robert Peel was called the **RAT**, or the

TAMWORTH RATCATCHER, for altering his views on the Roman Catholic question. From rats deserting vessels about to sink.

ROUND: to tell tales, to "SPLIT,"(*see below*); "to ROUND on a man," to swear to him as being the person, &c. Synonymous with "BUFF." —*See* BUFF *above. Shakespere* has ROUNDING, whispering.

SNITCHERS: persons who turn queen's evidence or who tell tales. In *Scotland*, SNITCHERS signify handcuffs.

SPLIT: to inform against one's companions, to tell tales. "To SPLIT with a person," to cease acquaintanceship, to quarrel.

WHIDDLE: to enter into parley or hesitate with many words, &c.; to inform or discover.

INTERJECTIONS and SAYINGS

ENCOURAGEMENT and AGREEMENT

ALL-SERENE: an ejaculation of acquiescence.

GO IT: a term of encouragement, implying "keep it up!" Sometimes amplified to GO IT, YE CRIPPLES; said to have been a facetious rendering of the last line of *Virgil's Eclogues*:

"Ite domum Saturæ, Venit Hesperus, *ite capillae;*"

or, "GO IT, YE CRIPPLES, crutches are cheap."

NINEPENCE: "right as NINEPENCE," all right, right to a nicety.

PECKER: "keep your PECKER up," *i.e.,* don't get down-hearted, —literally, keep your beak or head well up, "never say die!"

RATHER!: a ridiculous street exclamation synonymous with yes; "do you like fried chickens?" "RATHER!" "are you going out of town?" "RATHER!"

SIMON PURE: "the real SIMON PURE," the genuine article. Those who have witnessed Mr. C. Mathews' performance in Mrs. Centlivre's admirable comedy of *A Bold Stroke for a Wife*, and the laughable coolness with which he, the *false* SIMON PURE, assuming the quaker dress and character of the REAL ONE, elbowed that worthy out of his expected entertainment, will at once perceive the origin of this phrase.—*See* act v., scene 1.

STRIKE ME LUCKY!: an expression used by the lower orders when making a bargain, derived from the old custom of striking hands together, leaving in that of the seller a LUCK PENNY as an earnest that the bargain is concluded. In Ireland, at cattle markets, &c., a penny or other small coin, is always given by the buyer to the seller to ratify the bargain.—*Hudibras*. Anciently this was called a GOD'S PENNY.

"With that he cast him a God's Peny." —*Heir of Linne.*

The origin of the phrase being lost sight of, like that of many others, it is often corrupted now-a-days into STRIKE ME SILLY.

TICKET: "that's the TICKET," *i.e.,* what was wanted or what is best. Corruption of "that is not *etiquette*," by adding, in vulgar pronunciation, *th* to the first *e* of etiquette; or, perhaps from TICKET, a bill or invoice. This phrase is sometimes extended into "that's the TICKET FOR SOUP," in allusion to the card given to beggars for immediate relief at soup kitchens.—*See* TICK *page 185.*

DISAPPOINTMENT and DISBELIEF

ALL MY EYE: answer of astonishment to improbable story; ALL MY EYE AND BETTY MARTIN, a vulgar phrase with similar meaning, said to be the commencement of a Popish prayer to St. Martin, "Oh mihi, beate Martine," and fallen into discredit at the Reformation.

BOSH: nonsense, stupidity.—*Gipsey* and *Persian*. Also pure *Turkish*, BOSH LAKERDI, empty talk. A person, in the *Saturday Reivew*, has stated that BOSH is coeval with Morier's novel, *Hadji Babi*, which was published in 1828; but this is a blunder. The term was used in this country as early as 1760, and may be found in the *Student*, vol. ii., P. 217.

BOTHERATION!: trouble, annoyance; "BOTHERATION to it," confound it or deuce take it, an exclamation when irritated.

FIDDLE STICKS!: nonsense.

HOOKEY WALKER!: ejaculation of incredulity, usually shortened to WALKER!—*See below.* A correspondent thinks HOOKEY WALKER may have been a certain *Hugh K. Walker.*

OVER! or **OVER THE LEFT:** *i.e.,* the left shoulder—a common exclamation of disbelief in what is being narrated—implying that the results of a proposed plan will be "over the left," *i.e.,* in the wrong direction, loss instead of gain.

PICKLES!: gammon.

SOLD: "SOLD again! and the money taken," gulled, deceived.—*Vide* SELL.

TENPENCE TO THE SHILLING: a vulgar phrase denoting a deficiency in intellect.

WALKER! or **HOOKEY WALKER!:** an ejaculation of incredulity, said when a person is telling a story which you know to be all gammon, or false. The *Saturday Reviewer's* explanation of the phrase is this: —"Years ago, there was a person named *Walker*, an aquiline-nosed Jew, who exhibited an orrery which he called by the erudite name of *Eidouranion.* He was also a popular lecturer on astronomy, and often invited his pupils, telescope in hand, to *take a sight* at the moon and stars. The lecturer's phrase struck his school-boy auditory, who frequently "took a sight" with that gesture of outstretched arm, and adjustment to nose and eye, which was the first garnish of the popular saying. The next step was to assume phrase and gesture as the outward and visible mode of knowingness in general." A correspondent, however, denies this, and states that HOOKEY WALKER was a magistrate of dreaded acuteness and incredulity, whose hooked nose gave the title of BEAK to all his successors; and, moreover, that the gesture of applying the thumb to the nose and agitating the little finger, as an expression of "Don't you wish you may get it?" is considerably older than the story in the *Saturday Review* would seem to indicate. There is a third explanation of HOOKEY WALKER in *Notes and Queries*, iv., 425

WHISKER: there is a curious slang phrase connected with this word. When an improbable story is told, the remark is, "the mother of that was a WHISKER," meaning it is a lie.

OATHS and SWEARING

BE-BLOWED: a windy exclamation equivalent to an oath. — *See* **BLOW-ME** *below.*

BENDER: the arm; "over the **BENDER**, "synonymous with "over the left," — *See* **OVER** *page 400.* Also an ironical exclamation similar to **WALKER**.

BILLINGSGATE: (when applied to speech), foul and coarse language. Not many years since, one of the London notorieties was to hear the fishwomen at Billingsgate abuse each other. The anecdote of Dr. Johnson and the Billingsgate virago is well known.

BLAST: to curse.

BLEST: a vow; "**BLEST** if I'll do it," *i.e.*, I am determined not to do it; euphemism for **CURST**.

BLOW ME or **BLOW ME TIGHT:** a vow, a ridiculous and unmeaning ejaculation, inferring an appeal to the ejaculator; "I'm **BLOWED** if you will" is a common expression among the lower orders; "**BLOW ME UP**" was the term a century ago. — *See Parker's Adventures*, 1781.

BOB: "s'help my **BOB**," a street oath, equivalent to "so help me God." Other words are used in street language for a similarly evasive purpose, *i.e.*, **CAT**, **GREENS**, **TATUR**, &c., all equally profane and disgusting.

BY GEORGE: an exclamation similar to **BY JOVE**. The term is older than is frequently imagined; vide *Bacchus and Venus* (p. 117), 1737. "Fore (or by) **GEORGE**, I'd knock him down." A street compliment to Saint George, the patron Saint of England, or possibly to the House of Hanover.

BY GOLLY: an ejaculation or oath; a compromise for "by God." In the United States, small boys are permitted by their guardians to say **GOL DARN** anything, but they are on no account allowed to commit the profanity of G—d d—ing anything. An effective ejaculation and moral waste pipe for interior passion or wrath is seen in the exclamation: **BY THE EVER-LIVING-JUMPING-MOSES**—a harmless phrase, that from its length expends a considerable quantity of fiery anger.

CRIKEY: profane exclamation of astonishment; "Oh, CRIKEY, you don't say so!" corruption of *"Oh Christ."*

DARN: vulgar corruption of d   n. —*American.*

DAVY: "on my DAVY," on my affidavit, of which it is a vulgar corruption. Latterly DAVY has become synonymous in street language with the name of the Deity; "so help me DAVY," slang rendering of the conclusion of the oath usually exacted of witnesses.

DICKENS: synonymous with devil; "what the DICKENS are you after?" what the d—l are you doing? Used by *Shakespere* in the *Merry Wives of Windsor.*

DOG-ON-IT: a form of mild swearing used by boys. It is just worthy of mention that DOGONE, in *Anglo-Norman,* is equivalent to a term of contempt. *Friesic,* **DOGENIET.**

GAR: euphuistic corruption of the title of the Deity; "be GAR, you don't say so!" —*Franco-English.*

GORMED: a Norfolk corruption of a profane oath. So used by Mr. Peggotty, one of Dickens' characters.

JIGGER: "I'm JIGGERED if you will," a common form of mild swearing. —*See* SNIGGER *below.*

JINGO: "by JINGO," a common form of oath, said to be a corruption of St. Gingoulph. —*Vide Halliwell.*

LA!: a euphuistic rendering of LORD, common amongst females and very precise persons; imagined by many to be a corruption of LOOK! but this is a mistake. Sometimes pronounced LAW or LAWKS.

NEVER-TRUST-ME: an ordinary phrase with low Londoners, and common in Shakespere's time, *vide Twelfth Night.* It is generally used instead of an oath, calling vengeance on the asseverator, if such and such does not come to pass.

OD DRAT IT, OD RABBIT (*Coleman's broad grins*), **OD'S BLOOD:** and all other exclamations commencing with OD, are nothing but softened or suppressed oaths. OD is a corruption of GOD, and DRAT of ROT. —*Shakespere.*

POKER: "by the holy POKER and the tumbling Tom!" an Irish oath.

SCRAN: pieces of meat, broken victuals. Formerly the reckoning at a public-house. SCRANNING, begging for broken victuals. Also, an *Irish* malediction of a mild sort, "Bad SCRAN to yer!"

SHOT: "I wish I may be **SHOT**, if," &c., a common form of mild swearing.

SIVVY: "'pon my **SIVVY**," *i.e.*, upon my soul or honour. Corruption of *asseveration*, like **DAVY**, which is an abridgment of *affidavit*.

SNIGGER: "I'm **SNIGGERED** if you will," a mild form of swearing. Another form of this is **JIGGERED**.

TATER: "s'elp my **TATER**," another street evasion of a profane oath, sometimes varied by "s'elp my **GREENS**."

ZOUNDS!: a sudden exclamation—abbreviation of *God's wounds*.

"STOP" and "GO AWAY"

AVAST: a sailor's phrase for stop, shut up, go away—apparently connected with the *Old Cant*, **BYNGE A WASTE**.

CHEESE or **CHEESE IT:** (evidently a corruption of *cease*), leave off or have done; "**CHEESE** your barrikin," hold your noise.

CHUFF IT: be off or take it away, in answer to a street seller who is importuning you to purchase. *Halliwell* mentions **CHUFF** as a "term of reproach," surly, &c.

CUT: CUT THAT! be quiet or stop.—*Cambridge. Old* **CUTTE**, *to say.—See* **CUT** *in the Index for more meanings on page 479.*

FLUFF IT: a term of disapprobation, implying "take it away, I don't want it."

GRASS: "gone to **GRASS**," dead—a coarse allusion to *burial*; absconded or disappeared suddenly; "oh, go to **GRASS**," a common answer to a troublesome or inquisitive person—possibly a corruption of "go to **GRACE**," meaning, of course, a directly opposite fate.

HOOK IT: "get out of the way," or "be off about your business," "**TO HOOK IT**," to run away, to decamp; "on one's own **HOOK**," dependant upon one's own exertions.—*See* **HOOK OR BY CROOK** *page 240.*

KNIFE IT: "cut it," cease, stop, don't proceed.

NIX!: the signal word of school boys to each other that the master or other person in authority, is approaching.

NOMMUS: be off.—*See* **NAMUS** *page 73.*

POT: "to GO TO POT," to die; from the classic custom of putting the ashes of the dead in an urn; also, to be ruined or broken up—often applied to tradesmen who fail in business. GO TO POT! *i.e.,* go and hang yourself, shut up and be quiet. *L 'Estrange,* to PUT THE POT ON, to overcharge or exaggerate.

SAW YOUR TIMBER: "be off!" equivalent to *cut your stick.—See* CUT.

SHOE LEATHER!: a thief's warning cry, when he hears footsteps. This exclamation is used in the same spirit as Bruce's friend, who, when he suspected treachery towards him at King Edward's court, in 1306, sent him a purse and a pair of spurs, as a sign that he should use them in making his escape.

STALL YOUR MUG: go away; spoken sharply by anyone who wishes to be rid of a troublesome or inconvenient person.

STASH: to cease doing anything, to refrain, be quiet, leave off; "STASH IT, there, you sir!" *i.e.,* be quiet, sir; to give over a lewd or intemperate course of life is termed STASHING IT.

STOW FAKING!: leave off there, be quiet! FAKING implying anything that may be going on.

WALK YOUR CHALKS!: be off or run away—spoken sharply by anyone who wished to get rid of you.—*See* CHALKS *page 435.*

◆ OTHER INTERJECTIONS

ALL OF A HUGH!: all on one side or with a thump; the word HUGH being pronounced with a grunt.—*Suffolk.*

ALL TO PIECES: utterly excessively; "he beat him ALL TO PIECES," *i.e.,* excelled or surpassed him exceedingly.

AWFUL: (or, with the Cockneys, ORFUL), a senseless expletive, used to intensify a description of anything good or bad; "what an AWFUL fine woman!" *i.e.,* how handsome or showy!

BLUE MURDER: a desperate or alarming cry. *French,* MORT BLEU.

BROWN SALVE: a token of surprise at what is heard, and at the same time means "I understand you."

COCK: or more frequently now a days, **COCK-E-E**, a vulgar street salutation—corruption of **COCK-EYE**. The latter is frequently heard as a shout or street cry after a man or boy.

HOCUS POCUS: *Gipsey* words of magic, similar to the modern "Presto fly." The Gipseys pronounce "*Habeas Corpus*" **HAWCUS PACCUS** (*see Crabb's Gipsey's Advocate*, p.18); can this have anything to do with the origin of **HOCUS POCUS**? *Turner* gives **OCHUS BOCHUS**, an old demon. Pegge, however, states that it is a burlesque rendering of the words of the unreformed church service at the delivery of the host, **HOC EST CORPUS**, which the early Protestants considered as a species of conjuring, and ridiculed accordingly.

MY TULIP: a term of endearment used by the lower orders to persons and animals; "kim up, **MY TULIP**," as the coster said to his donkey when thrashing him with an ash stick.

SHUT UP!: be quiet, don't make a noise; to stop short, to make cease in a summary manner, to silence effectually. "Only the other day we heard of a preacher who, speaking of the scene with the doctors in the Temple, remarked that the Divine disputant completely **SHUT THEM UP!**" —*Athen.* 30th July, 1859. **SHUT UP**, utterly exhausted, done for.

SICK AS A HORSE: popular simile—curious, because a horse never vomits.

JOKES and TEASING

BAMBOOZLE: to deceive, make fun of, or cheat a person; abbreviated to **BAM**, which is used also as a substantive, a deception, a sham, a "sell." *Swift* says **BAMBOOZLE** was invented by a nobleman in the reign of Charles II. But this I conceive to be an error. The probability is that a nobleman first *used* it in polite society. The term is derived from the Gipseys.

BLOW: to expose or inform; "**BLOW** the gaff," to inform against a person. In *America*, to **BLOW** is slang for to taunt.

BOTHER: to tease, to annoy.

CARRY-ON: to joke a person to excess, to carry on a **SPREE** too far, "how we **CARRIED ON**, to be sure!" *i.e.*, what fun we had.

CHAFF: to gammon, joke, quiz, or praise ironically. **CHAFF-**bone, the jaw-bone.—*Yorkshire.* **CHAFF**, jesting. In *Anglo Saxon*, **CEAF** is chaff; and **CEAFL**, bill, beak, or jaw. In the "Ancien Riwle,"A.D. 1221, *ceafle* is used in the sense of idle discourse.

GAMMON: to hoax, to deceive merrily, to laugh at a person, to tell an untrue but plausible story, to make game of, or in the provincial dialect, to make **GAME ON**; "who's thou makin' thy **GAM' ON?**" *i.e.,* who are you making a fool of?—*Yorkshire.*

KID: to joke, to quiz, to hoax anybody.

LARK: fun, a joke; "let's have a jolly good **LARK,**" let us have a piece of fun. *Mayhew* calls it "a convenient word covering much mischief." —*Anglo Saxon*, **LAC**, sport; but more probably from the nautical term **SKYLARKING,** *i.e.,* mounting to the highest yards and sliding down the ropes for amusement, which is allowed on certain occasions.

POKE: "come, none of your **POKING** fun at me," *i.e.,* you must not laugh at me.

QUIZ: to pry or joke.

ROAST: to expose a person to a running fire of jokes at his expense from a whole company, in his presence. **QUIZZING** is done by a single person only.

SELL: to deceive, swindle, or play a practical joke upon a person. A sham is a **SELL** in street parlance. "**SOLD** again, and got the money," a costermonger cries after having successfully deceived somebody. *Shakespere* uses **SELLING** in a similar sense, viz., blinding or deceiving.

SKIT: a joke, a squib.

SNOOKS: an imaginary personage often brought forward as the answer to an idle question or as the perpetrator of a senseless joke.

STUFF: to make false but plausible statements, to praise ironically, to make game of a person—literally, to **STUFF** or **CRAM** him with gammon or falsehood.

WILD OATS: youthful pranks.

❧ LANGUAGE and SPEECH

ARGOT: a term used amongst London thieves for their secret or *Cant* language. *French* term for slang.

BARRIKIN: jargon, speech, or discourse; "we can't tumble to that BARRIKIN," *i.e.*, we don't understand what he says. *Miege* calls it "a sort of stuff."

BILLINGSGATE: (when applied to speech), foul and coarse language. Not many years since, one of the London notorieties was to hear the fishwomen at Billingsgate abuse each other. The anecdote of Dr. Johnson and the Billingsgate virago is well known.

DOG-LATIN: barbarous *Latin*, such as was formerly used by lawyers in their pleadings.

DOUBLE DUTCH: gibberish or any foreign tongue.

FLASH: showy, smart, knowing; a word with various meanings. A person is said to be dressed FLASH when his garb is showy, and after a fashion, but without taste. A person is said to be FLASH when he apes the appearance or manners of his betters, or when he is trying to be superior to his friends and relations. FLASH also means "fast," roguish, and sometimes infers counterfeit or deceptive—and this, perhaps, is its general signification. "FLASH, my young friend, or slang, as others call it, is the classical language of the Holy Land; in other words, St. Giles' Greek."—*Tom and Jerry, by Moncreiff.* Vulgar language was first termed FLASH in the year 1718, by Hitchin, author of "*The Regulator of Thieves, &c., with account of FLASH words.*"

GIBBERISH: unmeaning jargon; the language of the Gipseys, synonymous with SLANG, another *Gipsey* word. Somner says, "*French,* GABBER; *Dutch,* GABBEREN; and our own GAB, GABBER; hence also, I take it, our GIBBERISH, a kind of canting language used by a sort of rogues we vulgarly call Gipseys, a *gibble gabble* understood only among themselves."—*Gipsey.*

GREEKS: the low Irish. ST. GILES' GREEK, slang or *Cant* language. *Cotgrave* gives MERIE GREEK as a definition for a roystering fellow, a drunkard.—*Shakespere.—See* MEDICAL GREEK *page 141.*

JAW-BREAKERS: hard or many-syllabled words.

LINGO: talk or language. Slang is termed LINGO amongst the lower orders. *Italian,* LINGUA.

LOBS: words.—*Gipsey.*

MARROWSKYING:—*See* MEDICAL GREEK *page 141.*

MEDICAL GREEK: the slang used by medical students at the hospitals. At the London University they have a way of disguising *English,* described by Albert Smith as the *Gowerstreet Dialect,* which consists in transposing the initials of words, *e.g., "poke a smipe"* —smoke a pipe, *"flutter-by"* —butterfly, &c. This disagreeable nonsense is often termed MORROWSKYING.—*See* GREEK, St. Giles' Greek, or the *"Ægidiac"* dialect, Language of ZIPH *page 141,* &c.

PATTER: a speech or discourse, a pompous street oration, a judge's summing up, a trial. *Ancient* word for muttering. Probably from the *Latin,* PATER NOSTER, or Lord's Prayer. This was said, before the Reformation, in a *low voice* by the priest, until he came to, "and lead us not into temptation," to which the choir responded, "but deliver us from evil." In our reformed Prayer Book this was altered, and the Lord's Prayer directed to be said "with a *loud voice."*—*Dr. Pusey* takes this view of the derivation in his *Letter to the Bishop of London,* p. 78, 1851. *Scott* uses the word twice in *Ivanhoe* and the *Bride of Lammermoor.*

ROMANY: a Gipsey or the *Gipsey* language; the speech of the Roma or Zincali.—*Spanish Gipsey.*

SLANG: low, vulgar, unwritten, or unauthorized language. *Gipsey,* SLANG, the secret language of the Gipseys, synonymous with GIBBERISH, another *Gipsey* word. This word is only to be found in the Dictionaries of *Webster* and *Ogilvie.* It was, perhaps, first recorded by *Grose,* in his Dictionary of the Vulgar Tongue, 1785. SLANG, since it has been adopted as an *English* word, generally implies vulgar language not known or recognized as CANT; and latterly, when applied to speech, has superseded the word FLASH.

SMUTTY: obscene—vulgar as applied to conversation.

VOKER: to talk; "can you VOKER Romany?" can you speak the canting language.—*Latin,* VOCARE; *Spanish,* VOCEAR.

WHIDS: words.—*Old Gipsey Cant.*

ZIPH: "**LANGUAGE OF**," a way of disguising *English* in use among the students at *Winchester College*. Compare **MEDICAL GREEK** above.

LIES and EXAGGERATIONS

ABRAM-SHAM or **SHAM-ABRAHAM:** to feign sickness or distress. From **ABRAM MAN**, the *Ancient Cant* term for a begging impostor or one who pretended to have been mad. — *Burton's Anatomy of Melancholy*, part i., sec. 2, vol. i., p. 360. When Abraham Newland was Cashier of the Bank of England, and signed their notes, it was sung:

> "I have heard people say
> That **SHAM ABRAHAM** you may,
> But you mustn't **SHAM ABRAHAM** Newland."

BAMBOOZLE: to deceive, make fun of, or cheat a person; abbreviated to **BAM**, which is used also as a substantive, a deception, a sham, a "sell." *Swift* says **BAMBOOZLE** was invented by a nobleman in the reign of Charles II. But this I conceive to be an error. The probability is that a nobleman first *used* it in polite society. The term is derived from the Gipseys.

BIG: "to look **BIG**," to assume an inflated dress or manner, "to talk **BIG**," *i.e.*, boastingly or with an "extensive" air.

BLARNEY: flattery, exaggeration. — *Hibernicism*.

BLIND: a pretense or make-believe.

BLUFF: an excuse.

BOUNCER: a person who steals whilst bargaining with a tradesmen; a lie.

BUFF: to swear to or accuse; to **SPLIT**, or peach upon. *Old* word for boasting, 1582.

BUNG: to give, pass, hand over, drink, or indeed to perform any action; **BUNG UP**, to close up. — *Pugilistic*; "**BUNG** over the rag," hand over the money — *Old*, used by *Beaumont and Fletcher*, and *Shakespere*. Also, to deceive one by a lie, to **CRAM**. — *See below*.

COME: a slang verb used in many phrases; "A'nt he **COMING IT**," *i.e.*, is he not proceeding at a great rate? "Don't **COME TRICKS** here," "don't

COME THE OLD SOLDIER over me," *i.e.*, we are aware of your practices, and "twig" your manoeuver. COMING IT STRONG, exaggerating, going a-head, the opposite of *"drawing it mild."* COMING IT also means informing or disclosing.

CRACK-UP: to boast or praise.—*Ancient English.*

CRAM: to lie or deceive, implying to fill up or CRAM a person with false stories; to acquire learning quickly, to *"grind"* or prepare for an examination.

CRAMMER: a lie; or a person who commits a falsehood.

CUT: CUT IT FAT, to exaggerate or show off in an extensive manner. —*Cambridge.* Old CUTTE, to say.—*See* CUT *in the Index for more meanings on page 479.*

DRAW: "come, DRAW it mild!" *i.e.*, don't exaggerate; opposite of "come it strong." From the phraseology of the bar (of a PUBLIC), where customers desire the beer to be DRAWN mild.

EXTENSIVE: frequently applied in a slang sense to a person's appearance or talk; "rather EXTENSIVE that!" intimating that the person alluded to is showing off or "cutting it fat."

FIMBLE-FAMBLE: a lame prevaricating excuse.—*Scand.*

FLAM: nonsense, blarney, a lie.—*Kentish; Anglo Saxon.*

GAMMON: to hoax, to deceive merrily, to laugh at a person, to tell an untrue but plausible story, to make game of, or in the provincial dialect, to make GAME ON; "who's thou makin' thy GAM' ON?" *i.e.*, who are you making a fool of?—*Yorkshire.*

GAMMON: deceit, humbug, a false and ridiculous story. *Anglo Saxon*, GAMEN, game, sport.

HATCHET: "to throw the HATCHET," to tell lies.

HOAX: to deceive or ridicule—*Grose* says was originally a *University Cant* word. Corruption of HOCUS, to cheat.

LET ON: to give an intimation of having some knowledge of a subject. *Ramsay* employs the phrase in the *Gentle Shepherd*. Common in Scotland.

LONG-BOW: "to draw," or "shoot with the LONGBOW," to exaggerate.

MARE'S NEST: a Cockney discovery of marvels, which turn out no marvels at all. An old preacher in Cornwall, up to very lately employed a different version, viz.: "a cow calving up in a tree."

MEALY-MOUTHED: plausible, deceitful.

MOONSHINE: palaver, deception, humbug.

NUTS: to be NUTS upon anything or person is to be pleased with or fond of it; a self-satisfied man is said to be NUTS upon himself. NUTTED, taken in by a man who professed to be NUTS upon you.

PITCH THE FORK: to tell a pitiful tale.

POT: "to GO TO POT," to die; from the classic custom of putting the ashes of the dead in an urn; also, to be ruined or broken up—often applied to tradesmen who fail in business. GO TO POT! *i.e.,* go and hang yourself, shut up and be quiet. *L 'Estrange,* to PUT THE POT ON, to overcharge or exaggerate.

PUT UPON: cheated, deluded, oppressed.

SELL: a deception, disappointment; also a lying joke.

SELL: to deceive, swindle, or play a practical joke upon a person. A sham is a SELL in street parlance. "SOLD again, and got the money," a costermonger cries after having successfully deceived somebody. *Shakespere* uses SELLING in a similar sense, viz., blinding or deceiving.

SHAM ABRAHAM: to feign sickness.—*See* ABRAHAM *page 85.*

SHOOT WITH THE LONG BOW: to tell lies, to exaggerate. Synonymous with THROWING THE HATCHET.

SING SMALL: to lessen one's boasting, and turn arrogance into humility.

SOLD: "SOLD again! and the money taken," gulled, deceived. —*Vide* **Sell.**

STALL or **STALL OFF:** a dodge, a blind, or an excuse. STALL is *Ancient Cant.*

STORY: a falsehood—the soft synonyme for a *lie,* allowed in family circles and boarding-schools. A Puritanism that came in fashion with the tirade against romances, all novels and stories being considered as dangerous and false.

STRETCHER: a falsehood.

STUFF: to make false but plausible statements, to praise ironically, to make game of a person—literally, to STUFF or CRAM him with gammon or falsehood.

WALKER! or **HOOKEY WALKER!:** an ejaculation of incredulity, said when a person is telling a story which you know to be all gammon, or false. The *Saturday Reviewer's* explanation of the phrase is this: "Years ago, there was a person named *Walker*, an aquiline-nosed Jew, who exhibited an orrery which he called by the erudite name of *Eidouranion*. He was also a popular lecturer on astronomy, and often invited his pupils, telescope in hand, to *take a sight* at the moon and stars. The lecturer's phrase struck his school-boy auditory, who frequently "took a sight" with that gesture of outstretched arm, and adjustment to nose and eye, which was the first garnish of the popular saying. The next step was to assume phrase and gesture as the outward and visible mode of knowingness in general." A correspondent, however, denies this, and states that HOOKEY WALKER was a magistrate of dreaded acuteness and incredulity, whose hooked nose gave the title of BEAK to all his successors; and, moreover, that the gesture of applying the thumb to the nose and agitating the little finger, as an expression of "Don't you wish you may get it?" is considerably older than the story in the *Saturday Review* would seem to indicate. There is a third explanation of HOOKEY WALKER in *Notes and Queries*, iv., 425.

WASH: "it won't WASH," *i.e.*, will not stand investigation, is not genuine, can't be believed.

WHALE: "very like a WHALE in a teacup," said of anything that is very improbable; taken from a speech of Polonius in *Hamlet*.

WHISKER: there is a curious slang phrase connected with this word. When an improbable story is told, the remark is, "the mother of that was a WHISKER," meaning it is a lie.

WHITE LIE: a harmless lie, one told to reconcile people at variance; "mistress is not at home, sir," is a WHITE LIE often told by servants.

WHOPPER: a big one, a lie.

NONSENSE

BOSH: nonsense, stupidity.—*Gipsey* and *Persian*. Also pure *Turkish*, **BOSH LAKERDI,** empty talk. A person, in the *Saturday Reivew*, has stated that **BOSH** is coeval with Morier's novel, *Hadji Babi*, which was published in 1828; but this is a blunder. The term was used in this country as early as 1760, and may be found in the *Student*, vol. ii., P. 217.

CARNEY: soft talk, nonsense, gammon.—*Hibernicism.*

CLAP-TRAP: high-sounding nonsense. An *ancient Theatrical* term for a "**TRAP** to catch a **CLAP** by way of applause from the spectators at a play."—*Bailey's Dictionary.*

FIDDLE FADDLE: twaddle or trifling discourse.—*Old Cant.*

FIDDLE STICKS!: nonsense.

FLAM: nonsense, blarney, a lie.—*Kentish; Anglo Saxon.*

FLUMMERY: flattery, gammon, genteel nonsense.

FUDGE: nonsense, stupidity. *Todd and Richardson* only trace the word to *Goldsmith. Disraeli*, however, gives the origin to a Captain Fudge, a great fibber, who told monstrous stories, which made his crew say in answer to any improbability, "you **FUDGE** it!"—*See Remarks on the Navy*, 1700.

GIFFLE-GAFFLE: nonsense.—*See* **CHAFF** *page 406. Icelandic,* **GAFLA.**

KIBOSH: nonsense, stuff, humbug; "it's all **KIBOSH,**" *i.e.*, palaver or nonsense; "to put on the **KIBOSH,**" to run down, slander, degrade, &c.—*See* **BOSH** *page 399.*

MOONSHINE: palaver, deception, humbug.

PICKLES!: gammon.

ROT: nonsense; anything bad, disagreeable, or useless.

SLUM: gammon; "up to **SLUM,**" wide-awake, knowing.

> "And this, without more **SLUM**, began,
> Over a flowing Pot-house can,
> To settle, without botheration,
> The rigs of this here tip-top nation"—*Jack Randall's Diary*, 1820

SNAFFLED: arrested, "pulled up;" so termed from a kind of horse's bit, called a **SNAFFLE**. In *East Anglia*, to **SNAFFLE** is to talk foolishly.

WALKER! or **HOOKEY WALKER!:** an ejaculation of incredulity, said when a person is telling a story which you know to be all gammon, or false. The *Saturday Reviewer's* explanation of the phrase is this: — "Years ago, there was a person named *Walker*, an aquiline-nosed Jew, who exhibited an orrery which he called by the erudite name of *Eidouranion*. He was also a popular lecturer on astronomy, and often invited his pupils, telescope in hand, to *take a sight* at the moon and stars. The lecturer's phrase struck his school-boy auditory, who frequently "took a sight" with that gesture of outstretched arm, and adjustment to nose and eye, which was the first garnish of the popular saying. The next step was to assume phrase and gesture as the outward and visible mode of knowingness in general." A correspondent, however, denies this, and states that **HOOKEY WALKER** was a magistrate of dreaded acuteness and incredulity, whose hooked nose gave the title of **BEAK** to all his successors; and, moreover, that the gesture of applying the thumb to the nose and agitating the little finger, as an expression of "Don't you wish you may get it?" is considerably older than the story in the *Saturday Review* would seem to indicate. There is a third explanation of **HOOKEY WALKER** in *Notes and Queries*, iv., 425.

WHIM-WAM: an alliterative term, synonymous with *fiddle-faddle, riff-raff*, &c. denoting nonsense, rubbish, &c.

OFFENDING, IRRITATING, and CONFUSING

BOTHER: to tease, to annoy.

CHEEK: to irritate by impudence.

CRAB: to offend, or insult; to expose or defeat a robbery, to inform against.

DUMB-FOUND: to perplex, to beat soundly till not able to speak. Originally a *Cant* word. *Johnson* cites the *Spectator* for the earliest use. *Scotch*, **DUMFOUNDER**.

FLUMMUX: to perplex, hinder; **FLUMMUXED**, stopped, used-up.

GRAVEL: to confound, to bother; "I'm GRAVELLED," *i.e.,* perplexed or confused.—*Old.*

HUFF: to vex or offend; a poor temper.

NAB: to catch, to seize; "NAB the rust," to take offence.—*Ancient, fourteenth century.*

QUEER: "to QUEER a flat," to puzzle or confound a "gull" or silly fellow.

> Who in a *row* like Tom could lead the van,
> *Booze* in the *ken*, or at the *spellken* hustle?
> Who QUEER a flat, &c.
> —*Don Juan*, canto xi., 19.

RILE: to offend, to render very cross, irritated or vexed. Properly, to render liquor turbid.—*Norfolk.*

RUST: "to nab the RUST," to take offense. RUSTY, cross, ill-tempered, morose, one who cannot go through life like a person of easy and *polished* manners.

SHIRTY: ill-tempered or cross. When one person makes another in an ill humour he is said to have "got his SHIRT out."

SNUFF: "up to SNUFF," knowing and sharp; "to take SNUFF," to be offended. *Shakespere* uses SNUFF in the sense of anger or passion. SNUFFY, tipsy.

SPIFLICATE: to confound, silence, or thrash.

STREAKY: irritated, ill-tempered.

STUNNERS: feelings of great astonishment "it put the STUNNERS on me," it confounded me.

WHERRET or **WORRIT:** to scold, trouble, or annoy.—*Old English.*

WILD: vexed, cross, passionate. In the United States the word *mad* is supplemented with a vulgar meaning similar to our Cockneyism, WILD; and to make a man MAD on the other side of the Atlantic is to vex him or "rile" his temper - not to render him a raving maniac or a fit subject for Bedlam.

SCOLDING

BALLYRAG: to scold vehemently, to swindle one out of his money by intimidation and sheer abuse, as alleged in a late cab case (*Evans* v. *Robinson*).

BLOW UP: to make a noise or scold; formerly a *Cant* expression used amongst thieves, now a recognized and respectable phrase. BLOWING UP, a jobation, a scolding.

COALS: "to call (or pull) over the COALS," to take to task, to scold.

DROP: "to DROP INTO a person," to give him a thrashing.—*See* SLIP and WALK. "To DROP ON to a man," to accuse or rebuke him suddenly.

EARWIGGING: a rebuke in private; a WIGGING is more public.

GAS: "to give a person GAS," to scold him or give him a good beating. Synonymous with "to give him JESSIE."

GIVE: to strike or scold; "I'll GIVE it to you," I will thrash you. Formerly, *to rob*.

LICK: to excel or overcome; "if you aint sharp he'll LICK you," *i.e.*, be finished first. Signifies, also, to whip, chastise, or conquer. *Ancient Cant*, LYCKE.

MUG: to fight or chastise.

RUN: "to get the RUN upon any person," to have the upper hand or be able to laugh at them. RUN DOWN, to abuse or backbite anyone.

SLANG: to cheat, to abuse in foul language.

SLATE: to pelt with abuse, to beat, to "LICK;" or, in the language of the reviewers, to "cut up."

TAKE: "to TAKE UP," to reprove.—*See* TAKE *in the Index for more meanings on page 504.*

WALK INTO: to overcome, to demolish; "I'll WALK INTO his affections" *i.e.*, I will scold or thrash him. The word DRIVE (*see page 450*) is used in an equally curious sense in slang speech.

WHERRET or **WORRIT:** to scold, trouble, or annoy.—*Old English.*

WIGGING: a rebuke *before comrades*. If the head of a firm calls a clerk into the parlour, and rebukes him, it is an *earwigging;* if done before the other clerks, it is a **WIGGING.**

TALES and ANECDOTES

COCK AND A BULL STORY: a long, rambling anecdote.—*See Notes and Queries*, vol. iv., p. 313.

CROAKS: last dying speeches and murderers' confessions.

DIES: last dying speeches and criminal trials.

FLIM FLAMS: idle stories.—*Beaumont and Fletcher.*

GAMMON: to hoax, to deceive merrily, to laugh at a person, to tell an untrue but plausible story, to make game of, or in the provincial dialect, to make **GAME ON**; "who's thou makin' thy **GAM' ON?**" *i.e.,* who are you making a fool of?—*Yorkshire.*

PITCH THE FORK: to tell a pitiful tale.

RIGMAROLE: a prolix story.

TELL-ON: to tell about.

TOPS: dying speeches and gallows broadsides.

WHALE: "very like a **WHALE** in a teacup," said of anything that is very improbable; taken from a speech of Polonius in *Hamlet.*

WHISKER: there is a curious slang phrase connected with this word. When an improbable story is told, the remark is, "the mother of that was a **WHISKER,**" meaning it is a lie.

YARN: a long story or tale; "a tough **YARN,**" a tale hard to be believed; "spin a **YARN,**" tell a tale.—*Sea.*

TALKING and CONVERSING

AXE: to ask.—*Saxon,* **ACSIAN.**

BLOB: (from **BLAB**), to talk. Beggars are of two kinds—those who **SCREEVE** (introduce themselves with a **FAKEMENT,** or false document), and those who **BLOB**, or state their case in their own truly "unvarnished" language.

BLURT OUT: to speak from impulse, and without reflection. —*Shakespere.*

CHATTER-BOX: an incessant talker or chatterer.

CHEEK BY JOWL: side by side—said often of persons in such close confabulation as almost to have their faces touch.

COVENTRY: "to send a man to **COVENTRY**," not to speak to or notice him. Coventry was one of those town in which the privilege of practicing most trades was anciently confined to certain privileged persons, as the freemen, &c. Hence a stranger stood little chance of custom or countenance, and "to send a man to **COVENTRY**," came to be equivalent to putting him out of the pale of society.

GAB, GABBER, GABBLE: talk; "gift of the **GAB**," loquacity or natural talent for speech-making.—*Anglo Norman.*

GOB: the mouth; mucus or saliva.—*North.* Sometimes used for **GAB**, talk:

> "There was a man called *Job,*
> Dwelt in the land of Uz;
> He had a good gift of the **GOB**;
> The same case happen us."
> —*Zach. Boyd.*

JABBER: to talk or chatter. A *Cant* word in *Swift's* time.

JAW: speech or talk; "hold your **JAW**," don't speak any more; "what are you **JAWING** about?" *i.e.*, what are you making a noise about.

LINGO: talk or language. Slang is termed **LINGO** amongst the lower orders. *Italian,* **LINGUA**.

LOBS: words.—*Gipsey.*

MAG: to talk. A corruption of **NAG**.—*Old*; hence **MAGPIE**.

MANG: to talk.—*Scotch.*

NANTEE PALAVER: no conversation, *i.e.*, hold your tongue.—*Lingua Franca.*—See **PALAVER** *below.*

PALAVER: to ask or talk—not deceitfully, as the term usually signifies; "PALAVER to the nibs for a shant of bivvy," ask the master for a quart of beer. In this sense used by *tramps.*—Derived from *French,* PARLER.

PATTER: to talk. PATTER FLASH, to speak the language of thieves, talk *Cant.*

PUCKERING: talking privately.

SLANGY: flashy, vulgar; loud in dress, manner, and conversation.

SMUTTY: obscene—vulgar as applied to conversation.

SOUND: to pump or draw information from a person in an artful manner.

SUCK: to pump or draw information from a person.

TONGUED: talkative; "to TONGUE a person," *i.e.,* talk him down.

VOKER: to talk; "can you VOKER Romany?" can you speak the canting language.—*Latin,* VOCARE; *Spanish,* VOCEAR.

WHIDDLE: to enter into parley or hesitate with many words, &c.; to inform or discover.

WHIDS: words.—*Old Gipsey Cant.*

WHISPERING and YELLING
(INCLUDING STREET SELLING)

BLAST: to curse.

BLUE MURDER: a desperate or alarming cry. *French,* MORT BLEU.

CHAUNT: to sing the contents of any paper in the streets. CANT, as applied to vulgar language, was derived from CHAUNT.

CHIVE or CHIVEY: a shout; a halloo or cheer, loud tongued. From CHEVY-CHASE, a boy's game, in which the word CHEVY is bawled aloud; or from the *Gipsey?*

CHUCKING A JOLLY: when a costermonger praises the inferior article his mate or partner is trying to sell.

COCKS: fictitious narratives, in verse or prose, of murders, fires, and terrible accidents, sold in the streets as true accounts. The man who hawks them, a patterer, often changes the scene of the awful event to suit the taste of the neighbourhood he is trying to delude. Possibly a corruption of *cook*, a cooked statement, or, as a correspondent suggests, the COCK LANE Ghost may have given rise to the term. This had a great run, and was a rich harvest to the running stationers.

CROAKS: last dying speeches and murderers' confessions.

DIES: last dying speeches and criminal trials.

MUNGING or **MOUNGING:** whining, begging, muttering.—*North.*

PIG'S WHISPER: a low or inaudible whisper; also a short space of time, synonymous with **COCKSTRIDE**, *i.e., cock's tread.*

RAP: to utter; "he RAPPED out a volley of oaths."

ROUND: to tell tales, to "SPLIT,"(*see page 374*); "to ROUND on a man," to swear to him as being the person, &c. Synonymous with "BUFF." —*See* BUFF *above. Shakespere* has ROUNDING, whispering.

SING OUT: to call aloud.—*Sea.*

TOPS: dying speeches and gallows broadsides.

OTHER SPOKEN THINGS

BLUFF: to turn aside, stop, or excuse.

BOUNCE: to boast, cheat, or bully.—*Old Cant.*

EARWIG: a clergyman, also one who prompts another maliciously.

EGG or **EGG ON:** to excite, stimulate, or provoke one person to quarrel with another, &c. *Corruption of edge or edge on.*—*Ancient.*

FLABERGAST or **FLABBERGHAST:** to astonish or strike with wonder. —*Old.*

FLASH IT: "show it;" said when any bargain is offered.

HANDLE: a nose; the title appended to a person's name; also a term in boxing, "HANDLING one's fists."

HOCUS POCUS: *Gipsey* words of magic, similar to the modern "Presto fly." The Gipseys pronounce "*Habeas Corpus*" HAWCUS PACCUS (*see Crabb's Gipsey's Advocate*, p. 18); can this have anything to do with the origin of HOCUS POCUS? *Turner* gives OCHUS BOCHUS, an old demon. Pegge, however, states that it is a burlesque rendering of the words of the unreformed church service at the delivery of the host, HOC EST

CORPUS, which the early Protestants considered as a species of conjuring, and ridiculed accordingly.

JAPAN: to ordain.—*University.*

NANTEE PALAVER: no conversation, *i.e.*, hold your tongue.—*Lingua Franca.*—*See* **PALAVER** *page 419.*

QUIZ: to pry or joke.

SING SMALL: to lessen one's boasting, and turn arrogance into humility.

SNIGGERING: laughing to oneself.—*East.*

SPOUT: to preach or make speeches; **SPOUTER**, a preacher or lecturer.

STALL or **STALL OFF:** a dodge, a blind, or an excuse. **STALL** is *Ancient Cant.*

STUN: to astonish.

SUCK: to pump or draw information from a person.

SUCK-UP: "to **SUCK UP** to a person," to insinuate oneself into his good graces.

TELL-ON: to tell about.

TRAPESING: gadding or gossiping about in a slatternly way.—*North.*

THINGS WRITTEN

BALAAM: printers' slang for matter kept in type about monsterous productions of nature, &c., to fill up spaces in newspapers that would otherwise be vacant. The term **BALAAM-BOX** has long been used in *Blackwood* as the name of the depository for rejected articles.

BLACK AND WHITE: handwriting.

BOOK: an arrangement of bets for and against, chronicled in a pocket-book made for that purpose; "making a **BOOK** upon it," common phrase to denote the general arrangement of a person's bets on a race. "That does not suit my **BOOK**," *i.e.*, does not accord with my other arrangements. *Shakespere* uses **BOOK** in the sense of "a paper of conditions."

CHALK-OUT or **CHALK DOWN:** mark out a line of conduct or action; to make a rule, order. Phrase derived from the *Workshop*.

COCKS: fictitious narratives, in verse or prose, of murders, fires, and terrible accidents, sold in the streets as true accounts. The man who hawks them, a patterer, often changes the scene of the awful event to suit the taste of the neighbourhood he is trying to delude. Possibly a corruption of *cook*, a cooked statement, or, as a correspondent suggests, the **COCK LANE** Ghost may have given rise to the term. This had a great run, and was a rich harvest to the running stationers.

CRIB: a literal translation of a classic author. — *University.*

CROAKS: last dying speeches and murderers' confessions.

CUT: in theatrical language, means to strike out portions of a dramatic piece, so as to render it shorter for representation. A late treasurer of one of the so called *Patent Theatres*, when asked his opinion of a new play, always gave utterance to the brief, but safe piece of criticism *"wants* **CUTTING."**

DIES: last dying speeches and criminal trials.

FLIMSY: the thin, prepared copying paper used by newspaper reporters and "penny-a-liners" for making several copies at once, thus enabling them to supply different papers with the same article without loss of time. — *Printers' term.*

GIN AND GOSPEL GAZETTE: the *Morning Advertiser*, so called from its being the organ of the dissenting party, and of the Licensed Victuallers' Association. Sometimes termed the **TAP TUB**, or the **'TIZER.**

HANDLE: a nose; the title appended to a person's name; also a term in boxing, "**HANDLING** one's fists."

JEAMES: (a generic for "flunkies,") the *Morning Post* newspaper — the organ of Belgravia and the "Haristocracy."

LENGTH: forty-two lines of a dramatic composition. — *Theatrical.*

LOBS: words. — *Gipsey.*

MRS. HARRIS and **MRS. GAMP:** nicknames of the *Morning Herald* and *Standard* newspapers, while united under the proprietorship of Mr. Baldwin. **MRS. GAMP**, a monthly nurse, was a character in Mr. Charles Dickens' popular novel of *Martin Chuzzlewit*, who continually quoted an imaginary *Mrs. Harris* in attestation of the superiority of her qualifications, and the infallibility of her opinions; and thus afforded a parallel to the two newspapers, who appealed to each other as independent authorities, being all the while the production of the same editorial staff.

PAD: "to stand PAD," to beg with a small piece of paper pinned on the breast, inscribed "I'm starving."

SCREEVE: a letter, a begging petition.

SCREEVE: to write or devise; "to SCREEVE a fakement," to concoct or write, a begging letter, or other impostor's document. From the *Dutch,* SCHRYVEN; *German,* SCHRIEBEN; *French,* ECRIVANT (old form), to write.

SLUM: a letter.

SNIPE: a long bill; also a term for attorneys, a race remarkable for their propensity to long bills.

STAND: "to STAND treat," to pay for a friend's entertainment; to bear expense; to put up with treatment, good or ill; "this house STOOD me in £1,000," *i.e.,* cost that sum; "to STAND PAD," to beg on the curb with a small piece of paper pinned on the breast, inscribed "*I'm starving.*"

STIFF: paper, a bill of acceptance, &c.; "how did you get it, STIFF or *hard?*" *i.e.,* did he pay you cash or give a bill?

STIFF FENCER: a street seller of writing paper.

TAP TUB: the *Morning Advertiser.*

THUNDERER: the *Times* newspaper.

'TIZER: the *Morning Advertiser.*

TOPS: dying speeches and gallows broadsides.

LEGAL DOCUMENTS

COOPER: to forge or imitate in writing; "COOPER a moniker," to forge a signature.

MARRIAGE LINES: a marriage certificate. — *Provincial.*

MAULEY: a signature, from MAULEY, a fist; "put your FIST to it," is sometimes said by a low tradesman when desiring a fellow trader to put his signature to a bill or note.

MONEKEER: a person's name or signature.

MONKEY WITH A LONG TAIL: a mortgage.—*Legal.*

ROUND ROBIN: a petition or paper of remonstrance, with the signatures written in a circle—to prevent the first signer, or ringleader, from being discovered.

STIFF: paper, a bill of acceptance, &c.; "how did you get it, STIFF or *hard?" i.e.,* did he pay you cash or give a bill.

DO OR DO NOT. THERE IS NO TRY.

It is in vain to say human beings ought to be satisfied with tranquillity: they must have action; and they will make it if they cannot find it.

Charlotte Bronte

*T*here's no getting around it! If their language is any indication, violence was a part of everyday life. There are eighty-eight words for striking or beating someone or something —starting with **anointing**, and ending with **wipe**. That's more than any other category in the book. Plus there's another thirty-two words for getting the better of someone. It's easy to see what was on people's minds.

Some of the terms are quite specific. There are three terms for hitting someone in the nose, a **buckhorse** is a blow to the ear, and to **bonnet** a man is to strike his cap or hat over his eyes and nose.

Of course, not everyone was up for a fight. There are forty-seven words for escaping or running away. Given the prevalence of violence, you can't fault a man for wanting to **mizzle**, or disappear as in a mist. Personally, I'd **take beef** as well.

When the "lower orders" did escape, they seem to have gone on foot. There are few words for horseback riding, (though a couple for being thrown from a horse) and twelve terms for **riding shank's nag** —going on foot.

Editor's Faves:

COCK ONE'S TOES: to die.

FERRICADOUZER: a knock-down blow, a good thrashing. Probably derived through the *Lingua Franca* from the *Italian*, FAR' CADER' MORTO, to knock down dead.

GADDING THE HOOF: going without shoes. GADDING, roaming about, although used in an old translation of the Bible, is now only heard amongst the lower orders.

IN THIS CHAPTER

MENTAL ACTIVITIES

A MIND THAT'S ELSEWHERE

BLIND: a pretense or make-believe.

BONNET: a gambling cheat. "A man who sits at a gaming table, and appears to be playing against the table; when a stranger enters, the **BONNET** generally wins." —*Times*, Nov. 17, 1856. Also, a pretense or make-believe, a sham bidder at auctions.

BROWN-STUDY: a reverie. Very common even in educated society, but hardly admissible in writing, and therefore must be considered a vulgarism. It is derived, by a writer in *Notes and Queries*, from **BROW** study, from the old *German* **BRAUN** or **AUG-BRAUN**, an eye-brow. —*Ben Johnson.*

MAGGOTTY: fanciful, fidgetty. Whims and fancies were formerly termed **MAGGOTS**, from the popular belief that a maggot in the brain was the cause of any odd notion or caprice a person might exhibit.

SNOBBISH: stuck up, proud, make-believe.

WOOL-GATHERING: said of any person's wits when they are wandering or in a reverie. – *Florio.*

KNOWING or UNDERSTANDING

AWAKE or FLY: knowing, thoroughly understanding, not ignorant of. The phrase **WIDE-AWAKE** carries the same meaning in ordinary conversation.

BROWN-TO: to understand, to comprehend. —*American.*

BUCKLE: to bend; "I can't **BUCKLE** to that," I don't understand it; to yield or give in to a person. *Shakespere* uses the word in the latter sense, Henry IV., i. 1; and *Halliwell* says that "the commentators do not supply another example." How strange that in our own streets the term should be used every day! Stop the first costermonger, and he will soon inform you the various meanings of **BUCKLE**. — *See Notes and Queries*, vols. vii., viii., and ix.

CLOCK: "to know what's **O'CLOCK**," a definition of knowingness in general. — *See* **TIME O'DAY** *page 221.*

COCKSURE: certain.

COME: a slang verb used in many phrases; "A'nt he **COMING IT**," *i.e.*, is he not proceeding at a great rate? "Don't **COME TRICKS** here," "don't **COME THE OLD SOLDIER** over me," *i.e.*, we are aware of your practices, and "twig" your manoeuver. **COMING IT STRONG**, exaggerating, going a-head, the opposite of *"drawing it mild."* **COMING IT** also means informing or disclosing.

DOWN: to be aware of or awake to, any move — in this meaning, synonymous with **UP**; "**DOWN** upon one's luck," unfortunate; "**DOWN** in the mouth," disconsolate; "to be **DOWN** on one," to treat him harshly or suspiciously, to pounce upon him or detect his tricks.

ELEPHANT: "to have seen the **ELEPHANT**," to be *"up* to the latest move," or *"down* to the last new trick;" to be knowing, and not "green," &c. Possibly a metaphor taken from the travelling menageries, where the **ELEPHANT** is the *finale* of the exhibition. — Originally an *Americanism. Bartlett* gives conflicting examples. *General* now, however.

FLY: knowing, wide-awake, fully understanding another's meaning.

GRANNY: to know or recognise; "de ye **GRANNY** the bloke?" do you know the man?

GUMPTION or **RUMGUMPTION:** comprehension, capacity. From **GUAM**, to comprehend; "I canna **GAUGE** it, and I canna **GUAM** it," as a Yorkshire exciseman said of a hedgehog.

KNOWING: a slang term for sharpness, "**KNOWING** codger," or "a **KNOWING** blade," one who can take you in or cheat you, in any transaction you may have with him. It implies also deep cunning and foresight, and generally signifies dishonesty.

> "Who, on a spree with black-eyed Sal, his blowen,
> So swell, so prime, so nutty and so **KNOWING**."
> —*Don Juan*

NOUSE: comprehension, perception. — *Old*, apparently from the *Greek*, νους

O'CLOCK or **A'CLOCK:** "like ONE O'CLOCK," a favourite comparison with the lower orders, implying briskness; "to know what O'CLOCK it is," to be wide-awake, sharp, and experienced.

RUMGUMPTION or **GUMPTION:** knowledge, capacity, capability, —hence, RUMGUMPTIOUS, knowing, wide-awake, forward, positive, pert, blunt.

RUN: to comprehend, &c.; "I don't RUN, to it," *i.e.*, I can't do it, or I don't understand, or I have not money enough.—*North.*

SAVEY: to know; "do you SAVEY that?"—*French*, SAVEZ VOUS CELA? In the negro and *Anglo Chinese patois*, this is SABBY, "me no SABBY." The Whampoa slang of this description is very extraordinary; from it we have got our word CASH!

SMOKE: to detect or penetrate an artifice.

SNUFF: "up to SNUFF," knowing and sharp; "to take SNUFF," to be offended. *Shakespere* uses SNUFF in the sense of anger or passion. SNUFFY, tipsy.

TRAP: "up to TRAP," knowing, wide-awake—synonymous with "up to SNUFF."

TUMBLE: to comprehend or understand. A coster was asked what he thought of *Macbeth*—"the witches and the fighting was all very well, but the other moves I couldn't TUMBLE to exactly; few on us can TUMBLE to the jaw-breakers; they licks us, they do."

TWIG: to understand, detect or observe.

UP: "to be UP to a thing or two," to be knowing or understanding; "to put a man UP to a move," to teach him a trick; "it's all UP with him," *i.e.*, it is all over with him, often pronounced U.P., naming the two letters separately; "UP a tree."—*See* TREE *page 110.* "UP to TRAP," "UP to SNUFF," wide-awake, acquainted with the last new move; "UP to one's GOSSIP," to be a match for one who is trying to take you in;—"UP to SLUM," proficient in roguery, capable of committing a theft successfully.

ꙮ PLANNING, DISCOVERING, and LEARNING

CRAM: to lie or deceive, implying to fill up or CRAM a person with false stories; to acquire learning quickly, to *"grind"* or prepare for an examination.

GRIND: to work up for an examination, to cram with a GRINDER, or private tutor.—*Medical.*

NOBBLE: to cheat, to overreach; to discover.

ORACLE: "to work the ORACLE," to plan, manoeuvre, to succeed by a wily stratagem.

PALL: to detect.

SCREEVE: to write or devise; "to SCREEVE a fakement," to concoct or write, a begging letter, or other impostor's document. From the *Dutch,* SCHRYVEN; *German,* SCHRIEBEN; *French,* ECRIVANT (old form), to write.

WHIDDLE: to enter into parley or hesitate with many words, &c.; to inform or discover.

WORK: to plan, or lay down and execute any course of action, to perform anything; "to WORK the BULLS," *i.e.,* to get rid of false crown pieces; "to WORK the ORACLE," to succeed by maneuvering, to concert a wily plan, to victimise—a possible reference to the stratagems and bribes used to corrupt the *Delphic oracle,* and cause it to deliver a favourable response. "To WORK a street or neighborhood," trying at each house to sell all one can, or so bawling that every housewife may know what you have to sell. The general plan is to drive a donkey barrow a short distance, and then stop and cry. The term implies thoroughness; To "WORK a street well" is a common saying with a coster.

WRINKLE: an idea or fancy; an additional piece of knowledge which is supposed to be made by a WRINKLE *a posteriori.*

OTHER MENTAL ACTIVITY

COCUM: advantage, luck, cunning, or sly, "to fight **COCUM**," to be wily and cautious.

FANCY: the favourite sports, pets, or pastime of a person, *the tan of low life*. Pugilists are sometime termed **THE FANCY**. *Shakespere* uses the word in the sense of a favourite or pet; and the paramour of a prostitute is still called her **FANCY-MAN**.

HEAP: "a **HEAP** of people," a crowd; "struck all of a **HEAP**," suddenly astonished.

NILLY-WILLY: *i.e., Nill ye, will ye,* whether you will or no, a familiar version of the *Latin*, **NOLENS VOLENS**.

OFF AND ON: vacillating; "an **OFF AND ON** kind of a chap," one who is always undecided.

SCONCE: the head, judgment, sense.—*Dutch.*

SHOT: from the modern sense of the word to **SHOOT**—a guess, a random conjecture; "to make a bad **SHOT**," to expose one's ignorance by making a wrong guess or random answer without knowing whether it is right or wrong.

SPELL: "to **SPELL** for a thing," hanker after it, intimate a desire to possess it.

MOVING and MOTION

LOITERING and IDLING

COLLAR: "out of **COLLAR**," *i.e.,* out of place, no work.

DAWDLE: to loiter or fritter away time.

FIDDLING: doing any odd jobs in the street, holding horses, carrying parcels, &c. for a living. Among the middle classes, **FIDDLING** means idling away time or trifling; and amongst sharpers, it means gambling.

HULK: to hang about in hopes of an invitation.—*See* **MOOCH** *page 441.*

LED CAPTAIN: a fashionable spunger, a swell who, by artifice ingratiates himself into the good graces of the master of the house, and lives at his table.

MIKE: to loiter; or, as a costermonger defined it, to "lazy about." The term probably originated at St. Giles', which used to be thronged with Irish labourers (Mike being so common a term with them as to become a generic appellation for Irishmen with the vulgar) who used to loiter about the Pound, and lean against the public-houses in the "Dials" waiting for hire.

NIGGLING: trifling or idling; talking short steps in walking.—*North.*

SHILLY SHALLY: to trifle or fritter away time; irresolute. Corruption of *Shall I, shall I?*

SHOOL: to saunter idly, become a vagabond, beg rather than work. —*Smollett's Roderick Random*, vol. i., p.262.

TROLLING: sauntering or idling.

 ## MOVING AN OBJECT

BUNG: to give, pass, hand over, drink, or indeed to perform any action; **BUNG UP**, to close up—*Pugilistic;* "**BUNG** over the rag," hand over the money—*Old*, used by *Beaumont and Fletcher*, and *Shakespere*. Also, to deceive one by a lie, to **CRAM**.—*See page 409.*

CANT: a blow or toss; "a **CANT** over the kisser," a blow on the mouth. —*Kentish.*

CHIVE: to cut, saw, or file.

CHIVEY: to chase around or hunt about.

CHUCK: to throw or pitch.

CLAP: to place; "do you think you can **CLAP** your hand on him?" *i.e.,* find him out.

CLICK: to snatch.

COLLAR: to seize, to lay hold of.

COP: to seize or lay hold of anything unpleasant; used in the similar sense to *catch* in the phrase "to cop (or catch) a beating," "to get COPT."

DING: to strike; to throw away, or get rid of anything; to pass to a confederate.

FLY: to lift, toss, or raise; "FLY the *mags*," *i.e.*, toss up the halfpence; "to FLY a window," *i.e.*, to lift one for the purpose of stealing.

GRABB: to clutch or seize.

GRABBED: caught, apprehended.

HUNCH: to shove or jostle.

KNAP: to receive, to take, to steal.

LUG: to pull or slake thirst.—*Old.*

NAB: to catch, to seize; "NAB the rust," to take offence.—*Ancient,* fourteenth century.

NAP or NAB: to take, steal, or receive; "You'll NAP it," *i.e.*, you will catch a beating!—*North;* also *Old Cant.*—*Bulwer's Paul Clifford.*

NICK: to hit the mark; "he's NICKED it," *i.e.*, won his point.

NIP: to steal, to take up quickly.

PEG: "to PEG away," to strike, run, or drive away; "PEG a hack," to drive a cab; "take down a PEG or two," to check an arrogant or conceited person.

PLANT: to mark a person out for plunder or robbery, to conceal or place. —*Old Cant.*

SCROUGE: to crowd or squeeze.—*Wiltshire.*

SHUNT: to throw or turn aside.—*Railway term.*

SHY: a throw.

SHY: to fling; COCKSHY, a game at fairs, consisting of throwing short sticks at trinkets set upon other sticks—both name and practice derives from the old game of throwing or SHYING at live cocks.

SKIE: to throw upwards, to toss "coppers."—*See* ODD MAN *page 227.*

SKROUGE: to push or squeeze.—*North.*

SLING: to pass from one person to another.

SMUDGE: to smear, obliterate, daub. Corruption of **SMUTCH.** —*Times,* 10th August, 1859.

TIP: a douceur; also to give, lend, or hand over anything to another person; "come, **TIP** up the tin," *i.e.,* hand up the money; "**TIP** the wink," to inform by winking; "**TIP** us your fin," *i.e.,* give me your hand; "**TIP** one's boom off," to make off, depart. —*Sea.* "To miss one's **TIP**," to fail in a scheme. —*Old Cant.*

TRINE: to hang. —*Ancient Cant.*

TUSSLE: a pull, struggle, fight, or argument. *Johnson* and *Webster* call it a vulgar word.

WABBLE: to move from side to side, to roll about. *Johnson* terms it a "low, barbarous word."

WHIP: To "**WHIP** anything *up,*" to take it up quickly; from the method of hoisting heavy goods or horses on board ship by a **WHIP**, or running tackle, from the yard-arm. Generally used to express anything dishonestly taken. —*L' Estrange* and *Johnson.*

RUNNING AWAY and ESCAPING

ABSQUATULATE: to run away or abscond; a hybrid *American* expression, from the *Latin* **AB**, and **SQUAT**, to settle.

BACK OUT: to retreat from a difficulty; the reverse of **GO AHEAD**. Metaphor borrowed from the stables.

BACK SLANG IT: to go out the back way.

BACON: "to save one's **BACON**," to escape.

BOLT: to run away, decamp, or abscond.

BOOM: "to tip one's **BOOM** off," to be off or start in a certain direction. —*Sea.*

BRUSH or BRUSH-OFF: to run away or move on. —*Old Cant.*

BUNDLE: "to **BUNDLE** a person off," *i.e.,* to pack him off, send him flying.

BURYING A MOLL: running away from a mistress.

CHALKS: "to walk one's **CHALKS**," to move off or run away. An ordeal for drunkenness used on board ship, to see whether the suspected person can walk on a chalked line without overstepping it on either side.

CUT: to run away, move off quickly; to cease doing anything; CUT AND RUN, to quit work or occupation and start off at once; CUT ONE'S STICK, to be off quickly, *i.e.*, be in readiness for a journey, further elaborated into AMPUTATE YOUR MAHOGANY (*see* STICK *below*); CUT YOUR LUCKY, to run off.—*Cambridge. Old* CUTTE, to say.—*See* CUT *in the Index for more meanings on page 479.*

DOUBLE: "to tip (or give) the DOUBLE," to run away from any person; to double back, turn short round upon one's pursuers and so escape, as a hare does.—*Sporting.*

DUBLIN PACKET: to turn a corner; to "take the DUBLIN PACKET," viz., run round the corner.

EVAPORATE: to go or run away.

FLY THE KITE: to evacuate from a window—term used in padding kens or low lodging houses.

FRENCH LEAVE: to leave or depart slyly, without saying anything.

GRASS: "gone to GRASS," dead—a coarse allusion to *burial*; absconded or disappeared suddenly; "oh, go to GRASS," a common answer to a troublesome or inquisitive person—possibly a corruption of "go to GRACE," meaning, of course, a directly opposite fate.

HOOK IT: "get out of the way," or "be off about your business," "TO HOOK IT," to run away, to decamp; "on one's own HOOK," depending upon one's own exertions.—*See* HOOK OR BY CROOK *page 240.*

HOP THE TWIG: to run away or BOLT.—*See above.*—*Old.*

LEG IT: to run; LEG BAIL, to run off, "to give a LEG," to assist, as when one mounts a horse; "making a LEG," a countryman's bow—projecting the leg from behind as a balance to the head bent forward. —*Shakespere.*

LUCKY: "to cut one's LUCKY," to go away quickly.

MAHOGANY: "to have one's feet under another man's MAHOGANY," to sit at his table, be supported on other than one's own resources; "amputate your MAHOGANY," *i.e.*, go away or "cut your stick."

MIZZLE: to run away or decamp; to disappear as in a mist. From MIZZLE, a drizzling rain; a Scotch mist.

> "And then one *mizzling* Michaelmas night
> The Count he MIZZLED too." —*Hood.*

MORRIS: to decamp, be off. Probably from the ancient MORESCO, or MORRIS DANCE.

PACK: to go away; "now, then, PACK off there," *i.e.,* be off, don't stop here any longer. *Old, "Make speede to flee, be PACKING and awaie."* —*Baret's Alvearie,* 1580.

PADDLE: to go or run away. —*Household Words,* No. 183.

PEG: "to PEG away," to strike, run, or drive away; "PEG a hack," to drive a cab; "take down a PEG or two," to check an arrogant or conceited person.

PIKE: to run away.

RUM MIZZLERS: persons who are clever at making their escape or getting out of a difficulty.

RUSH: "doing it on the RUSH," running away or making off.

SCARPER: to run away. —*Spanish,* ESCAPAR, to escape, make off; *Italian,* SCAPPARE. "SCARPER with the feele of the donna of the cassey," to run away with the daughter of the landlady of the house; almost pure Italian, "*scappare colla figlia della donna della casa.*"

SHAVE: a narrow escape. At *Cambridge,* "just SHAVING through," or "making a SHAVE," is just escaping a "pluck" by coming out at the bottom of the list.

> "My terms are anything but dear,
> Then read with me, and never fear;
> The examiners we're sure to queer,
> And get through, if you make a SHAVE on't."
> —*The Private Tutor.*

SHY: "to fight SHY of a person," to avoid his society either from dislike, fear, or any other reason. SHY has also the sense of flighty, unsteady, untrustworthy.

SLIP: "to give the SLIP," to run away or elude pursuit. *Shakespere* has "you *gave me the counterfeit,*" in Romeo and Juliet. GIVING THE SLIP, however, is a *Sea phrase,* and refers to fastening an anchor and chain cable to a floating buoy or water cask, until such a time arrives that is convenient to return and take them on board. In fastening the cable, the home end is *slipped* through the hawse pipe. Weighing anchor is a noisy task, so that giving it the SLIP infers to leave it in quietness.

SLOPE: to decamp, to run, or rather *slip* away. Originally from LOPE, to make off; the *s* probably became affixed as a portion of the preceding word, as in the case of *"let's lope,"* let us run.—*Americanism.*

SMUG: to snatch another's property and run.

SMUGGINGS: snatching or purloining—shouted out by boys, when snatching the tops or small play property, of other lads, and then running off at full speed.

> "Tops are in; spin 'em agin.
> Tops are out; SMUGGING about."

SPEEL: to run away, make off; "SPEEL the drum," to go off with stolen property.—*North.*

STEP IT: to run away or make off.

STICK: "cut your STICK," be off or go away; either simply equivalent to a recommendation to prepare a walking staff in readiness for a journey—in allusion to the Eastern custom of cutting a stick before setting out—or from the ancient mode of reckoning by notches or tallies on a stick. In Cornwall the peasantry tally sheaves of corn by cuts in a stick, reckoning by the score. CUT YOUR STICK in this sense may mean to make your mark and pass on—and so realise the meaning of the phrase "IN THE NICK (or notch) OF TIME." Sir J. Emerson Tennent, in *Notes and Queries* (December, 1859), considers the phrase equivalent to "cutting the connection," and suggest a possible origin in the prophets breaking the staves of "Beauty" and "Bands," —*vide* Zech., xi., 10,14.

STREAK: to decamp, run away.—*Saxon.* In *America* the phrase is "to make STREAKS," or "make TRACKS."

TAKE BEEF: to run away.

TIP THE DOUBLE: to "bolt," or run away from a creditor or officer. Sometimes TIP THE DOUBLE TO SHERRY, *i.e.*, to the sheriff.

TRACKS: "to make TRACKS," to run away.—*See STREAK above.*

TURN UP: a street fight; a sudden leaving or making off.

TURN UP: to quit, change, abscond, or abandon; "Ned has **TURNED UP**," *i.e.*, run away; "I intend **TURNING IT UP**," *i.e.*, leaving my present abode or altering my course of life. Also to happen; let's wait, and see what will **TURN UP**.

TWIG: "to hop the **TWIG**," to decamp, "cut one's stick," to die.

VAMOS or **VAMOUS:** to go or be off. *Spanish*, **VAMOS**, "let us go!" Probably **NAMUS** or **NAMOUS** the costermonger's word, was from this, although it is generally considered back slang.

WALK YOUR CHALKS!: be off or run away—spoken sharply by anyone who wished to get rid of you.—*See* **CHALKS** *page 435.*

 # STOPPING

AVAST: a sailor's phrase for stop, shut up, go away—apparently connected with the *Old Cant*, **BYNGE A WASTE**.

CHEESE or **CHEESE IT:** (evidently a corruption of *cease*), leave off or have done; "**CHEESE** your barrikin," hold your noise.

CHOKE OFF: to get rid of. Bull dogs can only be made to lose their hold by choking them.

COVENTRY: "to send a man to **COVENTRY**," not to speak to or notice him. Coventry was one of those town in which the privilege of practicing most trades was anciently confined to certain privileged persons, as the freemen, &c. Hence a stranger stood little chance of custom or countenance, and "to send a man to **COVENTRY**," came to be equivalent to putting him out of the pale of society.

CURTAIL: to cut off. *Originally a Cant word, vide Hudibras, and Bacchus and Venus*, 1737.

CUT: in theatrical language, means to strike out portions of a dramatic piece, so as to render it shorter for representation. A late treasurer of one of the so-called *Patent Theatres*, when asked his opinion of a new play, always gave utterance to the brief, but safe piece of criticism "*wants* **CUTTING**."

CUT: to run away, move off quickly; to cease doing anything; **CUT AND RUN**, to quit work or occupation and start off at once; **CUT THAT!** be quiet or stop; **CUT ONE'S STICK**, to be off quickly, *i.e.*, be in readiness for a journey, further elaborated into AMPUTATE YOUR MAHOGANY (*see* **Stick** *page 438*); CUT AN ACQUAINTANCE, to cease friendly intercourse with them.—*Cambridge. Old* CUTTE, to say.—*See* CUT *in the Index for more meanings on page 479.*

DISH: to stop, to do away with, to suppress; DISHED, done for, floored, beaten, or silenced. A correspondent suggests that meat is usually DONE BROWN before being DISHED, and conceives that the latter term may have arisen as the natural sequence of the former.

DOUSE: to put out; "DOUSE that glim," put out that candle.—*Sea.*

DROP: to quit, go off, or turn aside; "DROP the main Toby," go off the main road.

KNIFE IT: "cut it," cease, stop, don't proceed.

KNOCK OFF: to give over or abandon. A saying used by workmen about dinner or other meal times, for upwards of two centuries.

NANTEE PALAVER: no conversation, *i.e.*, hold your tongue.—*Lingua Franca.*—*See* PALAVER *page 419.*

NIX: nothing, "NIX my doll," synonymous with NIX. *German,* NICHTS, nothing.—*See* MUNGARLY *page 298.*

PETER: to run short or give out.

POLISH OFF: to finish off anything quickly—a dinner for instance; also to finish off an adversary.—*Pugilistic.*

SHUT UP!: be quiet, don't make a noise; to stop short, to make cease in a summary manner, to silence effectually. "Only the other day we heard of a preacher who, speaking of the scene with the doctors in the Temple, remarked that the Divine disputant completely SHUT THEM UP!"—*Athen.* 30th July, 1859. SHUT UP, utterly exhausted, done for.

SHY: "to fight SHY of a person," to avoid his society either from dislike, fear, or any other reason. SHY has also the sense of flighty, unsteady, untrustworthy.

SPLIT: to inform against one's companions, to tell tales. "To SPLIT with a person," to cease acquaintanceship, to quarrel.

SPONGE: "to throw up the SPONGE," to submit, give over the struggle —from the practice of throwing up the SPONGE used to cleanse the combatants' faces, at a prize fight, as a signal that the "mill" is concluded.

STASH: to cease doing anything, to refrain, be quiet, leave off; "STASH IT, there, you sir!" *i.e.*, be quiet, sir; to give over a lewd or intemperate course of life is termed **STASHING IT.**

STOW: to leave off or have done; "STOW it, the gorger's leary," leave off, the person is looking.—*See* **STASH** *above*, with which it is synonymous. —*Ancient Cant.*

STOW FAKING!: leave off there, be quiet! **FAKING** implying anything that may be going on.

TAPER: to gradually give over, to run short.

TURN UP: to quit, change, abscond, or abandon; "Ned has **TURNED UP**," *i.e.*, run away; "I intend **TURNING IT UP**," *i.e.*, leaving my present abode or altering my course of life. Also to happen; let's wait, and see what will **TURN UP.**

 WALKING

GADDING THE HOOF: going without shoes. **GADDING**, roaming about, although used in an old translation of the Bible, is now only heard amongst the lower orders.

GRIND: "to take a **GRIND**," *i.e.*, a walk or constitutional.—*University.*

JOG-TROT: a slow but regular trot or pace.

MOOCH: to sponge; to obtrude yourself upon friends just when they are about to sit down to dinner or other lucky time—of course quite accidentally.—Compare **HULK.** To slink away, and allow your friends to pay for the entertainment. *In Wiltshire,* on the **MOUTCH** is to shuffle.

NIGGLING: trifling or idling; talking short steps in walking.—*North.*

PAD THE HOOF: to walk not ride; "**PADDING THE HOOF** on the high toby," tramping or walking on the high road.

> "Trudge, plod away o' the hoof."
> —*Merry Wives*, i., 3.

QUICK STICKS: in a hurry, rapidly; "to cut **QUICK STICKS**," to be in a great hurry.

SCAMANDER: to wander about without a settled purpose;—possibly in allusion to the winding course of the Homeric river of that name.

SHANKS' NAG: "to ride SHANKS' NAG," to go on foot.

SHOOL: to saunter idly, become a vagabond, beg rather than work. —*Smollett's Roderick Random,* vol. i., p.262.

STUMP: to go on foot.

TODDLE: to walk as a child.

TRAPESING: gadding or gossiping about in a slatternly way.—*North.*

TROLLING: sauntering or idling.

WORKING and PUTTING IN EFFORT

BONES: "he made no BONES of it," he did not hesitate, *i.e.,* undertook and finished work without difficulty, "found no BONES in the jelly." —*Ancient, vide Cotgrave.*

BROWN: "to do BROWN," to do well or completely (in allusion to roasting); "doing it BROWN," prolonging the frolic or exceeding sober bounds; "DONE BROWN," taken in, deceived, or surprised.

BUCKLE-TO: to bend to one's work, to begin at once and with great energy.

DEAD HORSE: "to draw the DEAD HORSE," DEAD-HORSE work, —working for wages already paid; also any thankless or unassisted service.

ELBOW GREASE: labour or industry.

GRAFT: to work; "where are you GRAFTING?" *i.e.,* where do you live or work?

LICK: a blow. LICKING, a beating; "to put in big LICKS," a curious and common phrase meaning that great exertions are being made. —*Dryden; North.*

POLISH OFF: to finish off anything quickly—a dinner for instance; also to finish off an adversary.—*Pugilistic.*

SPIRT or SPURT: "to put on a SPIRT," to make an increased exertion for a brief space, to attain one's end; a nervous effort.

WORK: to plan, or lay down and execute any course of action, to perform anything; "to **WORK** the **BULLS**," *i.e.*, to get rid of false crown pieces; "to **WORK** the **ORACLE**," to succeed by maneuvering, to concert a wily plan, to victimise—a possible reference to the stratagems and bribes used to corrupt the *Delphic oracle*, and cause it to deliver a favourable response. "To **WORK** a street or neighborhood," trying at each house to sell all one can, or so bawling that every housewife may know what you have to sell. The general plan is to drive a donkey barrow a short distance, and then stop and cry. The term implies thoroughness; To "**WORK** a street well" is a common saying with a coster.

 ## OTHER MOVEMENTS

BUCKLE: to bend; "I can't **BUCKLE** to that," I don't understand it; to yield or give in to a person. *Shakespere* uses the word in the latter sense, Henry IV., i. 1; and *Halliwell* says that "the commentators do not supply another example." How strange that in our own streets the term should be used every day! Stop the first costermonger, and he will soon inform you the various meanings of **BUCKLE**.—*See Notes and Queries*, vols. vii., viii., and ix.

CAB: to stick together, to muck or tumble up.—*Devonshire.*

CHOP: to change.—*Old.*

COCK: "to **COCK** your eye," to shut or wink one eye.

DAGS: feat or performance; "I'll do your **DAGS**," *i.e.*, I will do something that you cannot do.

DOG: to follow in one's footsteps on the sly, to track.

DROP: to quit, go off, or turn aside; "**DROP** the main Toby," go off the main road.

FAKE: to cheat or swindle; to do anything; to go on or continue; to make or construct; to steal or rob—a verb variously used. **FAKED**, done or done for; "**FAKE AWAY**, there's no down," go on, there is nobody looking. *Mayhew* says it is from the *Latin*, **FACIMENTUM**.

FOXING: to pretend to be asleep like a fox, which is said to take its rest with one eye open.

FRISK: to search; FRISKED, searched by a constable or other officer.

GOOSE: to ruin or spoil. Also, to hiss a play.—*Theatrical*.

LOPE: This old form of *leap* is often heard in the streets.

MULL: "to make a MULL of it," to spoil anything or make a fool of oneself.—*Gipsey*.

NARK: to watch or look after, "NARK the titter;" watch the girl.

OGLE: to look or reconnoitre.

PINK: to stab or pierce.

RENCH: vulgar pronunciation of RINSE. "*Wrench* your mouth out," said a fashionable dentist one day.—*North*.

SPORT: to exhibit, to wear, &c.; a word which is made to do duty in a variety of senses, especially at the University.—*See the Gradus ad Cantabrigiam*. "To SPORT a new title," "to SPORT an Ægrotat" (*i.e.*, a permission from the "Dons" to abstain from lectures, &c., on account of illness); "to SPORT ONE'S OAK," to shut the outer door and exclude the public—especially *duns* and boring acquaintances. Common also in the Inns of Court.—*See Notes and Queries*, 2nd series, vol. viii. P. 492, and *Gentleman's Magazine*, December, 1794.

STAG: to see, discover, or watch—like a STAG at gaze; "STAG the push," look at the crowd. Also, to dun, or demand payment.

T: "to suit to a **T**," to fit to a nicety.—*Old*. Perhaps from the T-square of carpenters, by which the accuracy of work is tested.

TITIVATE: to put in order or dress up.

TRANSMOGRIPHY: to alter or change.

TWIG: to understand, detect, or observe.

VARDO: to look; "VARDO the cassey," look at the house. VARDO formerly was *Old Cant* for a wagon.

WELL: to pocket or place as in a well.

WIDDLE: to shine.—*See* OLIVER *page 378*.

TO SURPASS or EXCEL (Nonviolent)

ALL TO PIECES: utterly excessively; "he beat him **ALL TO PIECES**," *i.e.*, excelled or surpassed him exceedingly.

BANG: to excel or surpass; **BANGING**, great or thumping.

BEAT or **BEAT-HOLLOW:** to surpass or excel.

BESTING: excelling, cheating. **BESTED**, taken in or defrauded.

HOLLOW: "to beat **HOLLOW**," to excel.

IN: "to be **IN** with a person," to be even with or **UP** to him.

LICK: to excel or overcome; "if you aint sharp he'll **LICK** you," *i.e.*, be finished first. Signifies, also, to whip, chastise, or conquer. *Ancient Cant*, **LYCKE**.

MUCK: to beat or excel; "it's no use, luck's set in him; he'd **MUCK** a thousand," —*Mayhew*, vol, i, p. 18. **TO RUN A MUCK** or **GO A MUCKER**, to rush headlong into certain ruin. From a certain religious phrenzy, which is common among the Malays, causing one of them, kreese in hand, to dash into a crowd and devote every one to death he meets with, until he is himself killed or falls from exhaustion.—*Malay*, **AMOK**, slaughter.

ONE-ER: that which stands for **ONE**, a blow that requires no more. In *Dickens'* amusing work, the "Marchioness" tells Dick Swiveller that "her missus is a **ONE-ER** at cards."

PIPE: "to put one's **PIPE** out," to traverse his plans, "take a rise" out of him.

PULL: an advantage or hold upon another; "I've the **PULL** over you," *i.e.*, you are in my power—perhaps an oblique allusion to the judicial sense.—*See* **PULL** *page 140.*

RIGHTS: "to have one to **RIGHTS**," to be even with him, to serve him out.

RISE: "to take a **RISE** out of a person," to mortify, outwit, or cheat him, by superior cunning.

RUN: "to get the **RUN** upon any person," to have the upper hand or be able to laugh at them. **RUN DOWN**, to abuse or backbite anyone.

SHINE: "to take the **SHINE** out of a person," to surpass or excel him.

START: a proceeding of any kind; "a rum START," an odd circumstance; "to get the START of a person," to anticipate him, overreach him.

TAW: a large or principal marble; "I'll be one on your TAW," I will pay you out or be even with you—a simile taken from boys aiming always at winning the TAW when playing at marbles.

VIOLENCE

DYING and KILLING

BURKE: to kill, to murder, by pitch plaster or other foul means. From Burke, the notorious Whitechapel murderer, who with others used to waylay people, kill them, and sell their bodies for dissection at the hospitals.

CHOKER or **WIND-STOPPER:** a garrotter.

COCK ONE'S TOES: to die.

COLD MEAT: a corpse.

COOK ONE'S GOOSE: to kill or ruin any person.—*North.*

CROAK: to die—from the gurgling sound a person makes when the breath of life is departing.—*Oxfordshire.*

CROAKER: a corpse or dying person beyond hope.

CUT: to CUT UP FAT, to die, leaving a large property.—*Cambridge. Old* CUTTE, to say.—*See* CUT *in the Alphabetical Index for more meanings on page 479.*

DAVY'S LOCKER or **DAVY JONES' LOCKER:** the sea, the common receptacle for all things thrown overboard—a nautical phrase for death, the other world.

FRUMMAGEMMED: annihilated, strangled, garotted, or spoilt.—*Old Cant.*

GRASS: "gone to GRASS," dead—a coarse allusion to *burial*; absconded or disappeared suddenly; "oh, go to GRASS," a common answer to a troublesome or inquisitive person—possibly a corruption of "go to GRACE," meaning, of course, a directly opposite fate.

HOOKS: "dropped off the **HOOKS**," said of a deceased person. Derived from the ancient practice of suspending on hooks the quarters of a traitor or felon sentenced by the old law to be hung, drawn, and quartered, and which dropped off the hooks as they decayed.

KENNEDY: to strike or kill with a poker. A St. Giles' term, so given from a man of that name being killed by a poker. Frequently shortened to **NEDDY**.

KICK THE BUCKET: to die.—*Norfolk*. According to Forby, a metaphor taken from the descent of a well or mine, which is of course absurd. The Rev. E. S. Taylor supplies me with a following note from his MS. additions to the work of the East–Anglian lexicographer:

> "The allusion is to the way in which a slaughtered pig is hung up, viz., by passing the ends of a bent piece of wood behind the tendons of the hind legs, and so suspending it to a hook in a beam above. This piece of wood is locally termed a *bucket*, and so by a coarse metaphor the phrase came to signify to die. Compare the Norfolk phrase "as wrong as a bucket."

The natives of the West Indies have converted the expression into **KICKERABOO**.

KNIFE: "to **KNIFE** a person," to stab, an un-English but now-a-days a very common expression.

NAIL: to steal or capture; "paid on the **NAIL**," *i.e.*, ready money; **NAILED**, taken up or caught—probably in allusion to the practice of **NAILING** bad money to the counter. We say "as dead as a **DOORNAIL**;"—why? *Shakespere* has the expression in Henry IV:

> "*Falstaff*. What! Is the old king dead?
> *Pistol*. As nail in door."

A correspondent thinks the expression is only alliterative humour, and compares as "*Flat as a flounder*," "straight as a soldier," &c.

POT: "to **GO TO POT**," to die; from the classic custom of putting the ashes of the dead in an urn; also, to be ruined or broken up—often applied to tradesmen who fail in business. **GO TO POT!** *i.e.*, go and hang yourself, shut up and be quiet. *L 'Estrange,* to **PUT THE POT ON,** to overcharge or exaggerate.

POTTED or **POTTED OUT:** cabined, confined; "the patriotic member of Parliament **POTTED OUT** in a dusty little lodging somewhere about Bury-street." — *Times* article, 21st July, 1859. Also applied to burial.

SETTLE: to kill, ruin, or effectually quiet a person.

SHOES: "to die in one's **SHOES,**" to be hung.

STIFF 'UN: a corpse. — *Term used by undertakers.*

STRETCH: abbreviation of "**STRETCH** one's neck." to hang, be executed as a malefactor. — *Bulwer's Paul Clifford.*

SWING: to be hanged.

TWIG: "to hop the **TWIG,**" to decamp, "cut one's stick," to die.

WIND: "to raise the **WIND,**" to procure money; "to slip one's **WIND,**" coarse expression meaning to die.

GETTING THE BETTER OF SOMEONE

APPLE CART: "down with his **APPLE CART,**" *i.e.,* upset him. — *North.*

BESTING: excelling, cheating. **BESTED,** taken in or defrauded.

BLEED: to victimise or extract money from a person, to spunge on, to make suffer vindictively.

BOUNCE: to boast, cheat, or bully. — *Old Cant.*

BREECHES: "to wear the **BREECHES,**" said of a wife who usurps the husband's prerogative.

BUCKLE: to bend; "I can't **BUCKLE** to that," I don't understand it; to yield or give in to a person. *Shakespere* uses the word in the latter sense, Henry IV., i. 1; and *Halliwell* says that "the commentators do not supply another example." How strange that in our own streets the term should be used every day! Stop the first costermonger, and he will soon inform you the various meanings of **BUCKLE.** — *See Notes and Queries*, vols. vii., viii., and ix.

CAVE or **CAVE IN:** to submit, shut up. — *American.* Metaphor taken from the sinking of an abandoned mining shaft.

CLEAN OUT: to thrash or beat; to ruin or bankrupt anyone; to take all they have got, by purchase or force. *De Quincey*, in his article on "Richard Bentley," speaking of the lawsuit between that great scholar and Dr. Colbatch, remarks that the latter "must have been pretty well CLEANED OUT."

COOK ONE'S GOOSE: to kill or ruin any person. — *North.*

COOPER: to destroy, spoil, settle, or finish. COOPER'D, spoilt, "done up," synonymous with the Americanism, CAVED IN, fallen in and ruined. The vagabonds' hieroglyphic ▽, chalked by them on gate posts and houses, signifies that the place has been spoilt by too many tramps calling there.

CROW: "I have a CROW to pick with you," *i.e.*, an explanation to demand, a disagreeable matter to settle; "to COCK-CROW over a person," to exalt over his abasement or misfortune.

CUT: CUT OUT, to excel, thus in affairs of gallantry one Adonis is said to "*cut the other out*" in the affections of the wished for lady. CUT OUT OF, done out of; to CUT ONE'S COMB, to take down a conceited person, from the practice of cutting the combs of capons (*see* COMB-CUT); CUT UP, mortified, to criticize severely, or expose; CUT UP SHINES, to play tricks; CUT ONE'S CART, to expose their tricks; — *Cambridge.* Old CUTTE, to say. — *See* CUT *in the Index for more meanings on page 479.*

DAGS: feat or performance; "I'll do your DAGS," *i.e.*, I will do something that you cannot do.

DISH: to stop, to do away with, to suppress; DISHED, done for, floored, beaten, or silenced. A correspondent suggests that meat is usually DONE BROWN before being DISHED, and conceives that the latter term may have arisen as the natural sequence of the former.

DO: this useful and industrious verb has for many years done service as a slang term. To DO a person is to cheat him. Sometimes another tense is employed, such as "I DONE him," meaning I cheated or "paid him out;" DONE BROWN, cheated thoroughly, befooled; DONE OVER, upset, cheated, knocked down, ruined; DONE UP, used-up, finished, or quieted. DONE also means convicted or sentenced; so does DONE FOR. To DO a person in pugilism is to excel him in fisticuffs. Humphreys, who fought Mendoza, a Jew, wrote this laconic note to his supporter: "Sir, I have DONE the Jew, and am in good health. Rich. Humphries."

Tourists use the expression "I have DONE France and Italy," meaning I have completely explored those countries.

DOWN: to be aware of or awake to, any move—in this meaning, synonymous with UP; "DOWN upon one's luck," unfortunate; "DOWN in the mouth," disconsolate; "to be DOWN on one," to treat him harshly or suspiciously, to pounce upon him or detect his tricks.

DRIVE: a term used by tradesmen in speaking of business; "he's DRIVING a *roaring* trade," *i.e.*, a very good one; hence, to succeed in a bargain, "I DROVE a good bargain," *i.e.*, got the best end of it.

FAKE: to cheat or swindle; to do anything; to go on or continue; to make or construct; to steal or rob—a verb variously used. FAKED, done or done for; "FAKE AWAY, there's no down," go on, there is nobody looking. *Mayhew* says it is from the *Latin*, FACIMENTUM.

FIX: a predicament, dilemma; "an awful FIX," a terrible position; "to FIX one's flint for him," *i.e.*, to "settle his *hash*," "put a spoke in his wheel."

GOOSEBERRY: to "play up old GOOSEBERRY" with anyone, to defeat or silence a person in a quick or summary manner.

GREASE-SPOT: a minute remnant, the only distinguishable remains of an antagonist after a terrific contest.

HUMBLE PIE: to "eat HUMBLE PIE," to knock under, be submissive. The UMBLES, or entails of a deer, were anciently made into a dish for servants, while their masters feasted off the haunch.

IN: "to be IN with a person," to be even with or UP to him.

KIMBO or **A KIMBO:** holding the arms in a bent position from the body, and resting the hands upon the hips, in a bullying attitude. Said to be from **A SCHEMBO,** *Italian;* but more probably from KIMBAW, the *Old Cant* for beating or bullying.—*See Grose.*

KNUCKLE TO or **KNUCKLE UNDER:** to yield or submit.

LICK: to excel or overcome; "if you aint sharp he'll LICK you," *i.e.*, be finished first. Signifies, also, to whip, chastise, or conquer. *Ancient Cant,* LYCKE.

MUCK: to beat or excel; "it's no use, luck's set in him; he'd MUCK a thousand,"—*Mayhew*, vol, i, p. 18. TO RUN A MUCK or GO A MUCKER, to rush headlong into certain ruin. From a certain religious phrenzy, which is common among the Malays, causing one of them, kreese in hand, to dash into a crowd and devote every one to death he meets with, until he is himself killed or falls from exhaustion.—*Malay,* **AMOK,** slaughter.

MUCK OUT: to clean out. Often applied to one utterly ruining an adversary in gambling. From the *Provincial* **MUCK,** dirt.

PIPE: "to put one's **PIPE** out," to traverse his plans, "take a rise" out of him.

POT: to finish; "don't **POT** me," term used at billiards. This word was much used by our soldiers in the Crimea, for firing at the enemy from a hole or ambush. These were called **POT-SHOTS.**

PULL: an advantage or hold upon another; "I've the **PULL** over you," *i.e.,* you are in my power—perhaps an oblique allusion to the judicial sense.—*See* **PULL** *page 140.*

PUT UPON: cheated, deluded, oppressed.

RIGHTS: "to have one to **RIGHTS,**" to be even with him, to serve him out.

RISE: "to take a **RISE** out of a person," to mortify, outwit, or cheat him, by superior cunning.

SERVE OUT: to punish or be revenged on anyone.

SETTLE: to kill, ruin, or effectually quiet a person.

SLATE: to pelt with abuse, to beat, to "**LICK;**" or, in the language of the reviewers, to "cut up."

SPIFLICATE: to confound, silence, or thrash.

SQUARE: "to be **SQUARE** with a man," to be *even* with him or to be revenged; "to **SQUARE** up to a man," to offer to fight him. *Shakespere* uses **SQUARE** in the sense of to quarrel.

START: a proceeding of any kind; "a rum **START,**" an odd circumstance; "to get the **START** of a person," to anticipate him, overreach him.

TAKE: "to **TAKE** down a peg or two," to humiliate or tame; "to **TAKE UP,**" to reprove; "to **TAKE IN,**" to cheat or defraud, from the lodging-house keepers' advertisements, "single men **TAKEN IN AND DONE FOR;**" an engagement which is as frequently performed in a bad as a good sense.—*See* **TAKE** *in the Index for more meanings on page 504.*

TAKE IN: a cheating or swindling transaction—sometimes termed "a **DEAD TAKE IN.**" *Shakespere* has **TAKE IN** in the sense of conquering. To

BE HAD or TO BE SPOKE TO, were formerly synonymous phrases with TO BE TAKEN IN.

TAW: a large or principal marble; "I'll be one on your TAW," I will pay you out or be even with you—a simile taken from boys aiming always at winning the TAW when playing at marbles.

WALK INTO: to overcome, to demolish; "I'll WALK INTO his affections" *i.e.*, I will scold or thrash him. The word DRIVE (*see above*) is used in an equally curious sense in slang speech.

WIND: "I'll WIND your cotton," *i.e.*, I will give you some trouble. The Byzantine General, Narses, used the same kind of threat to the Greek Empress—"I will spin such a thread that they shall not be able to unravel."

WIPE: to strike; "he fetcht me a WIPE over the knuckles," he struck me on the knuckles; "to WIPE a person down," to flatter or pacify a person; to WIPE off a score, to pay one's debts, in allusion to the slate or chalk methods of account keeping; "to WIPE a person's eye," to shoot game which he has missed—*Sporting term*; hence to gain an advantage by superior activity.

STRIKING and BEATING

ANOINTING: a good beating.

BAKER'S DOZEN: this consists of thirteen or fourteen; the surplus number, called the *inbread*, being thrown in for fear of incurring the penalty for short weight. To "give a man a BAKER'S DOZEN," in a slang sense, means to give him an extra good beating or pummelling.

BASH: to beat or thrash; "BASHING a donna," beating a woman; originally a provincial word, and chiefly applied to the practice of beating walnut trees, when in bud, with long poles, to increase their productiveness. Hence the West country proverb:

> "A woman, a whelp, and a walnut tree,
> The more you BASH 'em, the better they be."

BOBBY: a policeman. Both **BOBBY** and **PEELER** were nicknames given to the new police, in allusion to the christian and surnames of the late *Sir Robert Peel*, who was the prime mover in effecting their introduction and improvement. The term **BOBBY** is, however, older than the *Saturday Reviewer*, in his childish and petulant remarks, imagines. The official square-keeper, who is always armed with a cane to drive away idle and disorderly urchins, has, time out of mind, been called by the said urchins, **BOBBY** *the Beadle*. **BOBBY** is also, I may remark, an *Old English* word for striking or hitting, a quality not unknown to policemen.—*See Halliwell's Dictionary.*

BONNET: to strike a man's cap or hat over his eyes and nose.

BUCKHORSE: a smart blow or box on the ear; derived from the name of a celebrated "bruiser" of that name.

BUNDLE: "to **BUNDLE** a person off," *i.e.*, to pack him off, send him flying.

CANT: a blow or toss; "a **CANT** over the kisser," a blow on the mouth. —*Kentish.*

CLEAN OUT: to thrash or beat; to ruin or bankrupt anyone; to take all they have got, by purchase or force. *De Quincey*, in his article on "Richard Bentley," speaking of the lawsuit between that great scholar and Dr. Colbatch, remarks that the latter "must have been pretty well **CLEANED OUT.**"

CLICK: knock or blow. **CLICK-HANDED**, left-handed.—*Cornish.*

CLOUT: a blow or intentional strike.—*Ancient.*

CLUMP: to strike.

CORK: "to draw a **CORK**," to give a bloody nose.—*Pugilistic.*

DEAD-SET: a pointed attack on a person.

DEWSKITCH: a good thrashing.

DIGS: hard blows.

DING: to strike; to throw away, or get rid of anything; to pass to a confederate.

DOUBLE-UP: to pair off, or "chum," with another man; to beat severely.

DROP: "to **DROP INTO** a person," to give him a thrashing.—*See* **SLIP** *and* **WALK.** "To **DROP ON** to a man," to accuse or rebuke him suddenly.

DUMB-FOUND: to perplex, to beat soundly till not able to speak. Originally a *Cant* word. *Johnson* cites the *Spectator* for the earliest use. *Scotch*, **DUMFOUNDER.**

FAG: to beat, also one boy working for another at school.

FERRICADOUZER: a knock-down blow, a good thrashing. Probably derived through the *Lingua Franca* from the *Italian,* **FAR' CADER' MORTO,** to knock down dead.

FIB: to beat or strike.—*Old Cant.*

FLICK or **FLIG:** to whip by striking, and drawing the lash back at the same time, which causes a stinging blow.

FLIP: corruption of **FILLIP,** a light blow.

FLOG: to whip. Cited both by *Grose* and the author of *Bacchus and Venus* as a *Cant* word. It would be curious to ascertain the earliest use; *Richardson* cites Lord Chesterfield.—*Latin.*

FLOOR: to knock down.—*Pugilistic.*

FLOORER: a blow sufficiently strong to knock a man down.

GAS: "to give a person **GAS,**" to scold him or give him a good beating. Synonymous with "to give him **JESSIE.**"

GIVE: to strike or scold; "I'll **GIVE** it to you," I will thrash you. Formerly, *to rob.*

GOOSER: a settler or finishing blow.

GREASE-SPOT: a minute remnant, the only distinguishable remains of an antagonist after a terrific contest.

HACKLE: "to show **HACKLE,**" to be willing to fight. **HACKLES** are the long feathers on the back of a cock's neck, which he erects when angry—hence the metaphor.

HANDLE: a nose; the title appended to a person's name; also a term in boxing, "**HANDLING** one's fists."

HIDING: a thrashing. *Webster* gives this word, but not its root, **HIDE,** to beat, flay by whipping.

INTO: "hold my hat, Jim, I'll be **INTO** him," *i.e.,* I will fight him. In this sense equivalent to **PITCH INTO** or **SLIP INTO.**

JACKETING: a thrashing.

JESSIE: "to give a person **JESSIE,**" to beat him soundly.—*See* **GAS** *above.*

JUMP: to seize or rob; "to JUMP a man," to pounce upon him, and either rob or maltreat him; "to JUMP a house," to rob it.—*See* **GO** *page 334.*

KEEL-HAULING: a good thrashing or mauling, rough treatment, —from the old nautical custom of punishing offenders by throwing them overboard with a rope attached and hauling them up from under the ship's keel.

KENNEDY: to strike or kill with a poker. A St. Giles' term, so given from a man of that name being killed by a poker. Frequently shortened to **NEDDY.**

KINGSMAN: the favourite coloured neckerchief of the costermongers. The women wear them thrown over their shoulders. With both sexes they are more valued than any other article of clothing. A coster's *caste*, or position, is at stake, he imagines, if his **KINGSMAN** is not of the most approved pattern. When he fights, his **KINGSMAN** is tied either around his waist as a belt, or as a garter around his leg. This very singular partiality for a peculiar coloured neckcloth was doubtless derived from the Gipseys, and probably refers to an Oriental taste or custom long forgotten by these vagabonds. A singular similarity of taste for certain colours exists amongst the Hindoos, Gipseys, and London costermongers. Red and yellow (or orange) are the great favourites, and in these hues the Hindoo selects his turban and his robe; the Gipsey his breeches, and his wife her shawl or gown; and the costermonger his plush waistcoat and favourite **KINGSMAN**. Amongst either class, when a fight takes place, the greatest regard is paid to the favourite coloured article of dress. The Hindoo lays aside his turban, the Gipsey folds up his scarlet breeches or coat, whilst the pugilistic costermonger of Covent Garden or Billingsgate, as we have just seen, removes his favourite neckerchief to a part of his body, by the rules of the "ring" comparatively out of danger. Amongst the various patterns of kerchiefs worn by the wandering tribes of London, red and yellow are the oldest and most in fashion. Blue, intermixed with spots, is a late importation, probably from the Navy, through sporting characters.

LACING: a beating. From the phrase "I'll LACE your jacket." —*L'Estrange.* Perhaps to give a beating with a *lace* or *lash.*

LAMMING: a beating.—*Old English*, LAM; used by *Beaumont and Fletcher.*

LARRUP: to beat or thrash.

LARRUPING: a good beating or "hiding." —*Irish.*

LEATHER: to beat or thrash. From the leather belt worn by soldiers and policemen, often used as a weapon in street rows.

LET DRIVE: to strike or attack with vigour.

LICK: a blow. LICKING, a beating; "to put in big LICKS," a curious and common phrase meaning that great exertions are being made. —*Dryden; North.*

MAULEY: a fist, that with which one strikes as with a MALL. —*Pugilistic.*

MILL: a fight or SET TO. *Ancient Cant*, MYLL, to rob.

MILL: to fight or beat.

MITTENS: fists. —*Pugilistic.*

MONKEY'S ALLOWANCE: to get blows instead of alms, more kicks than half-pence.

MUCK: to beat or excel; "it's no use, luck's set in him; he'd MUCK a thousand," —*Mayhew*, vol, i, p. 18. TO RUN A MUCK or GO A MUCKER, to rush headlong into certain ruin. From a certain religious phrenzy, which is common among the Malays, causing one of them, kreese in hand, to dash into a crowd and devote every one to death he meets with, until he is himself killed or falls from exhaustion. —*Malay,* AMOK, slaughter.

MUG: to fight or chastise.

MUGGING: a thrashing. Synonymous with SLOGGING, both terms of the "ring," and frequently used by fighting men.

MUZZLE: to fight or thrash.

NOSER: a bloody or contused nose. —*Pugilistic.*

ONE-ER: that which stands for ONE, a blow that requires no more. In *Dickens'* amusing work, the "Marchioness" tells Dick Swiveller that "her missus is a ONE-ER at cards."

PASH: to strike; now corrupted to BASH. —*See page 451.* —*Shakespere.*

PAY: to beat a person or "serve them out." Originally a nautical term, meaning to stop the seams of a vessel with pitch (*French,* POIX); "here's the devil to PAY and no pitch hot," said when any catastrophe occurs which there is no means of averting; "to PAY over face and eyes, as the cat did the monkey;" "to PAY through the nose," to give a ridiculous price—whence the origin? *Shakespere* uses **PAY** in the sense of to beat or thrash.

PEG: "to **PEG** away," to strike, run, or drive away; "**PEG** a hack," to drive a cab; "take down a **PEG** or two," to check an arrogant or conceited person.

PEPPER: to thrash or strike.—*Pugilistic*, but used by *Shakespere*.—*East.*

PICK: "to **PICK** oneself up," to recover after a beating or illness; "to **PICK** a man up," "to do," or cheat him.

PINK: to stab or pierce.

PITCH INTO: to fight; "**PITCH INTO** him, Bill," *i.e.*, give him a thrashing.

PUMMEL: to thrash—from **POMMEL**.

QUILT: to thrash or beat.

RAMSHACKLE: to shatter as with a battering ram: **RAMSHACKLED**, knocked about, as standing corn is after a high wind. Corrupted from *ram-shatter*, or possibly from *ransack*.

RIBROAST: to beat till the ribs are sore.—*Old*; but still in use:

> "And he departs, not meanly boasting
> Of his magnificent **RIBROASTING**." –*Hudibras.*

SCRATCH: a fight, contest, point of dispute; "coming up to the **SCRATCH**," going or preparing to fight—in reality, approaching the line usually chalked on the ground to divide the ring.—*Pugilistic.*

SCRUFF: the back part of the neck seized by the adversary in an encounter.

SET TO: a sparring match, a fight; "a dead set," a determined stand, in argument or in movement.

SISERARA: a hard blow.—*Suffolk.* Moor derives it from the story of Sisera in the Old Testament, but it is more probably a corruption of **CERTIORARI**, a Chancery writ reciting a complaint of hard usage.

SLATE: to pelt with abuse, to beat, to "**LICK**;" or, in the language of the reviewers, to "cut up."

SLIP, or LET SLIP: "to **SLIP** into a man," to give him a sound beating; "to **LET SLIP** at a cove," to rush violently upon him, and assault with vigour.

SLOG or **SLOGGER** (its original form): to beat, baste, or wallop. *German*, SCHLAGEN; or, perhaps a vulgar corruption of SLAUGHTER. The pretended *Greek* derivation from σλογω, which *Punch* puts in the mouth of the schoolboy, in his impression of 4th May, 1859, is of course only intended to mystify grandmamma, there being no such word in the language.

SLOGGING: a good beating.

SMELLER: a blow on the nose, or a NOSER.

SPANK: a smack or hard slap.

SPIFLICATE: to confound, silence, or thrash.

SQUARE: "to be SQUARE with a man," to be *even* with him or to be revenged; "to SQUARE up to a man," to offer to fight him. *Shakespere* uses SQUARE in the sense of to quarrel.

STOCKDOLAGER: a heavy blow, a "finisher." *Italian*, STOCCADO, a fencing term.

STOTOR: a heavy blow, a SETTLER.—*Old Cant.*

TAN: to beat or thrash; I'll TAN your hide, *i.e.*, give you a good beating.

TOWEL: to beat or whip. In *Warwickshire* an oaken stick is termed a **Towel**—whence, perhaps, the vulgar verb.

TOWELLING: a rubbing down with an *oaken* TOWEL, a beating.

TURN UP: a street fight; a sudden leaving or making off.

TUSSLE: a pull, struggle, fight, or argument. *Johnson* and *Webster* call it a vulgar word.

TUSSLE: to struggle or argue.

WALK INTO: to overcome, to demolish; "I'll WALK INTO his affections" *i.e.*, I will scold or thrash him. The word DRIVE (*see page 450*) is used in an equally curious sense in slang speech.

WALLOP: to beat or thrash. Mr. John Gough Nichols derives this word from an ancestor of the Earl of Portsmouth one Sir John Wallop, Knight of the Garter, who, in King Henry VIII's time, distinguished himself by WALLOPING the French; but it is more probably connected with WEAL, a livid swelling in the skin, after a blow.—*See* POT WALLOPERS *page 155*.

WALLOPING: a beating or thrashing; sometimes in an adjective sense, as big or very large.

WARM: to thrash or beat; "I'll **WARM** your jacket."

WHACK: to beat; **WHACK** or **WHACKING,** a blow or thrashing.

WHITECHAPEL: the "upper-cut," or strike. — *Pugilistic.*

WHOP: to beat or hide. Corruption of **WHIP**; sometimes spelled **WAP.**

WIPE: a blow.

WIPE: to strike; "he fetcht me a **WIPE** over the knuckles," he struck me on the knuckles; "to **WIPE** a person down," to flatter or pacify a person; to **WIPE** off a score, to pay one's debts, in allusion to the slate or chalk methods of account keeping; "to **WIPE** a person's eye," to shoot game which he has missed — *Sporting term*; hence to gain an advantage by superior activity.

OTHER VIOLENCE

CHOKE OFF: to get rid of. Bull dogs can only be made to lose their hold by choking them.

COOPER: to destroy, spoil, settle, or finish. **COOPER'D,** spoilt, "done up," synonymous with the Americanism, **CAVED IN,** fallen in and ruined. The vagabonds' hieroglyphic ▽ chalked by them on gate posts and houses, signifies that the place has been spoilt by too many tramps calling there.

CRUNCH: to crush. *Corruption*; or, perhaps from the sound of teeth grinding against each other.

HUMP: to botch or spoil.

APPENDIX

IN THIS CHAPTER

 ## WORDS I DON'T UNDERSTAND

BAT: "on his own **BAT**," on his own account.—*See* **HOOK** *page 241.*

FUNK: to smoke out.—*North.*

NESTS: varieties.—*Old.*

SHACK: a "chevalier d'industrie."

 ## BACK SLANG

Back slang was invented and principally used by the costermongers, or street sellers, of London. The purpose was secrecy. They could speak in front of customers and policemen without being understood.

When John Camden Hotten wrote his book, street sellers numbered between thirty and forty thousand people in London alone. That's a lot of speaking backwards! Words were not always exact reversals, sometimes letters were changed to make them more pronounceable.

BIRK: a "crib," —house.

COOL: to look.

COOL HIM: look at him. A phrase frequently used when one costermonger warns another of the approach of a policeman.

DAB: bad.

DABHENO: one bad or a bad market.—*See* **DOOGHENO** *below.*

DAB TROS: a bad sort.

DA-ERB: bread.

DEB or **DAB**: a bed; "I'm on to the **DEB**," I'm going to bed.

DILLO-NAMO: an old woman.

DLOG: gold.

DOOG: good.

DOOGHENO: literally "one-good," or "good-one," but implying generally a good market.

DOOGHENO HIT: one good hit. A coster remarks to a "mate," *Jack made a* **DOOGHENO HIT** *this morning,"* implying that he did well at market or sold out with good profit.

DUNOP: a pound.

ERTH: three.

EARTH* GENS: three shillings.

EARTH SITH-NOMS: three months.

EARTH YANNOPS or **YENEPS:** threepence.

EDGABAC: cabbage.

EDGENARO: an orange.

E-FINK: knife.

EKAME: a "make," or swindle.

EKOM: a "moke," or donkey.

Appendix: Back Slang

ELRIG: a girl.

ENIF: fine.

ENIN GENS: nine shillings.

ENIN YENEP: ninepence.

ENO: one.

ERIF: fire.

ERTH GENS: three shillings.

ERTH-PU: three-up, a street game.

ERTH SITH-NOMS: three months—a term of imprisonment unfortunately very familiar to the lower orders.

ERTH-YENEPS: threepence.

ESCLOP: the police.

ES-ROPH or **ES-ROCH:** a horse.

EVIF-YENEPS: five pence.

EVLENET-GENS: twelve shillings.

ELVENET SITH-NOMS: twelve months.

EWIF-YENEPS: fivepence.

EXIS GENS: six shillings.

*My informant preferred EARTH to ERTH—for the reason, he said, "that it looked more sensible!"

EXIS-EWIF-GENS: six times five shillings, *i.e., 30s*. All moneys may be reckoned in this manner, either with YENEPS or GENS.

EXIS-EVIF YENEPS: elevenpence—literally, "sixpence and fivepence = elevenpence." This mode of reckoning, distinct from the preceeding, is also common amongst those who use the back slang.

EXIS SITH-NOMS: six months.

EXIS-YENEPS: sixpence.

FI-HEATH: a thief.

FLATCH: a half, or halfpenny.

FLATCH KEN-NURD: half drunk.

FLATCH YENEP: a halfpenny.

FLATCH-YENORK: half a-crown.

GEN: twelvepence or one shilling. Possibly an abbreviation of **ARGENT**, *Cant* term for silver—*See following.*

GENERALIZE: a shilling, generally shortened to **GEN**.

GEN-NET or **NET GENS:** ten shillings.

HEL-BAT: a table.

HELPA: an apple.

KENNETSEENO: stinking.

KENNURD: drunk.

KEW: a week.

KEWS or **SKEW:** weeks.

KRIB: a brick.

KOOL: to look.

LAWT: tall.

LEVEN: in back slang, is sometimes allowed to stand for *eleven*, for the reason that it is a number which seldom occurs. An article is either 10d. or 1s.

LUR-AC-HAM: mackerel.

MOTTAB: bottom.

MUR: rum.

NALE or **NAEL:** lean.

NAM: man.

NAMESCLOP: a policeman.

NAMOW: a woman; **DILLO NAMOW**, an old woman.

NEERGS: greens.

NETENIN GENS: nineteen shillings.

NEETEWIF GENS: fifteen shillings.

NEETEXIS or **NETEXIS GENS:** sixteen shillings.

NETNEVIS GENS: seventeen shillings.

NET-THEG GENS: eighteen shillings.

NEETRITH GENS: thirteen shillings.

NEETROUF GENS: fourteen shillings.

NET-GEN: ten shillings or half a sovereign.

NET-YENEPS: tenpence.

NEVELE GENS: eleven shillings.

NEVELE YENEPS: elevenpence—generally LEVEN YENEPS.

NEVIS GENS: seven shillings.

NEVIS STRETCH: seven years' transportation or imprisonment—*See* STRETCH *page 260.*

NEVIS YENEPS: sevenpence.

NIRE: rain.

NIG: gin.

NI-OG OT TAKRAM: going to market.

NITRAPH: a farthing.

NOL: long.

NOOM: the moon.

NOS-RAP: a parson.

OCCABOT: tobacco; "tib of OCCABOT," a bit of tobacco.

ON: no.

ON DOOG: no good.

OWT GENS: two shillings.

OWT YENEPS: twopence.

PAC: a cap.

PINURT POTS: turnip tops.

POT: top.

RAPE: a pear.

REEB: beer.

REV-LIS: silver.

ROUF-EFIL: for life—sentence of punishment.

ROUF-GENS: four shillings.

ROUF-YENEPS: fourpence.

RUTAT or **RATTAT:** a "tatur," or potato.

SAY: yes.

SEE O: shoes.

SELOPAS: apples.

SHIF: fish.

SIR-ETCH: cherries.

SITH-NOM: a month.

SLAOC: coals.

SLOP: a policeman. — *See* **SLOP** *page 137*.

SNEERG: greens.

SOUSH: a house.

SPINSRAP: parsnips.

SRES WORT: trousers.

STARPS: sprats.

STOOB: boots.

STORRAC: carrots.

STUN: nuts

STUNLAWS: walnuts.

SWRET-SIO: oysters.

TACH: a hat.

TAF or **TAFFY:** fat.

THEG or **TEAICH GENS:** eight shillings.

TEAICH-GUY: eight shillings — a slight deviation from the numerical arrangements of **GENS.**

TENIP: a pint.

THEG YENEPS: eightpence.

TIB: a bit or piece.

TOAC or **TOG:** a coat. **TOG** is the *Old Cant* term. – *See* **TOG** *page 290.*

TOAC-TISAW: a waistcoat.

TOL: lot, stock, or share.

TOP O' REEB: a pot of beer.

TOP-YOB: a pot boy.

TORRAC: a carrot.

TRACK (OR TRAG): a quart.

TROSSENO: literally, "one sort," but the costermongers use it to imply anything that is bad.

WAR-RAB: a barrow.

WEDGE: a Jew.

YAD: a day; YADS, days.

YADNAB: brandy.

YENEP: a penny.

YENEP-A-TIME: penny each time—term in betting.

YENEP-FLATCH: three halfpence—all the halfpence and pennies continue in the same sequence.

YAP-POO: pay up.

YEKNOD or **JERK-NOD:** a donkey.

YENORK: a crown.

YOB: a boy.

ZEB: best.

RHYMING SLANG

According to John Camden Hotten, "There exists in London a tribe of men known as Chaunters and Patterers. Both classes are great talkers. The first sing or chaunt through the public thoroughfares ballads—political and humorous—carols, dying speeches, and the various other kinds of gallows and street literature. The second deliver street orations on grease-removing compounds, plating powders, high polishing blacking, and the thousand and one wonderful pennyworths that are retailed to gaping mobs from the London kerb stone.

They are quite a distinct tribe from the costermongers; indeed, amongst tramps, they term themselves the 'harristocrats of the streets,' and boast that they live by their intellect."

These were the creators and speakers of rhyming slang which has little to do with the slang of the costers, although occasionally slang words themselves were turned into rhyming slang. Their choice of rhymes says a lot about their colorful pronunciation of some words.

ABRAHAM'S WILLING: a shilling.

ALACOMPAIN: rain.

ALL AFLOAT: a coat.

ANY RACKET: a penny faggot.

APPLES AND PEARS: stairs.

ARTFUL DODGER: a lodger.

ARTICHOKE RIPE: smoke a pipe.

BABY PAPS: caps.

BARNET FAIR: hair.

BATTLE OF THE NILE: a tile—vulgar term for a hat.

BEN FLAKE: a steak.

BILLY BUTTON: mutton.

BIRCH BROOM: a room.

BIRD LIME: time.

BOB, MY PAL: a gal—vulgar pronunciation of *girl*.

BONNETS SO BLUE: Irish stew.

BOTTLE OF SPRUCE: a deuce—slang for twopence.

BOWL THE HOOP: soup.

BRIAN O'LINN: gin.

BROWN BESS: yes—the affirmative.

BROWN JOE: no—the negative.

BULL AND COW: a row.

BUSHY PARK: a lark.

BUTTER FLAP: a cap.

CAIN AND ABEL: a table.

CAMDEN TOWN: a brown—vulgar term for a halfpenny.

CASTLE RAG: a flag—slang term for fourpence.

CAT AND MOUSE: a house.

Appendix: Rhyming Slang

CHALK FARM: the arm.

CHARING CROSS: a horse.

CHARLEY LANCASTER: a handkercher—vulgar pronunciation of handkerchief.

CHARLEY PRESCOTT: waistcoat.

CHERRY RIPE: a pipe.

CHEVY CHASE: the face.

CHUMP (OR CHUNK) OF WOOD: no good.

COW AND CALF: to laugh.

COVENT GARDEN: a farden—Cockney pronunciation of farthing.

COWS AND KISSES: mistress or missus—referring to the ladies.

CURRANTS AND PLUMS: thrums—slang for threepence.

DAISY RECROOTS (so spelt by my informant of Seven Dials; he means, doubtless, *recruits*): a pair of boots.

DAN TUCKER: butter.

DING DONG: a song.

DRY LAND: you understand.

DUKE OF YORK: take a walk.

EAST AND SOUTH: a mouth.

EAT A FIG: to "crack a crib," to break into a house or commit a burglary.

EGYPTIAN HALL: a ball.

ELEPHANT'S TRUNK: drunk.

EPSOM RACES: a pair of braces.

EVERTON TOFFEE: coffee.

FANNY BLAIR: the hair.

FILLET OF VEAL: the treadwheel, house of correction.

FINGER AND THUMB: rum.

FLAG UNFURLED: a man of the world.

FLEA AND LOUSE: a bad house.

FLOUNDER AND DAB (two kinds of flat fish): a cab.

FLY MY KITE: a light.

FROG AND TOAD: the main road.

GARDEN GATE: a magistrate.

GERMAN FLUTES: a pair of boots.

GIRL AND BOY: a saveloy—a penny sausage.

GLORIOUS SINNER: a dinner.

GODDESS DIANA (pronounced DIANER): a tanner—sixpence.

GOOSEBERRY PUDDING (*vulgo* PUDDEN): a woman.

HANG BLUFF: snuff.

HOD OF MORTAR: a pot of porter.

HOUNSLOW HEATH: teeth.

I DESIRE: a fire.

I'M AFLOAT: a boat.

ISLE OF FRANCE: a dance.

ISABELLA (vulgar pronunciation, ISABELLER): an umbrella.

I SUPPOSE: the nose.

JACK DANDY: brandy.

JACK RANDALL (a noted pugilist): a candle.

JENNY LINDER: a winder—vulgar pronunciation of window.

JOE SAVAGE: a cabbage.

LATH AND PLASTER: a master.

LEAN AND LURCH: a church.

LEAN AND FAT: a hat.

LINENDRAPER: paper.

LIVE EELS: fields.

LOAD OF HAY: a day.

LONG ACRE: a baker.

LONG ACRE: a newspaper.—*See the proceding.*

LORD JOHN RUSSELL: a bustle.

LORD LOVEL: a shovel.

LUMP OF COKE: a bloak—slang term for a man.

LUMP OF LEAD: the head.

Appendix: Rhyming Slang

MACARONI: a pony.

MAIDS A DAWNING (I suppose my informant means *maids adorning*):
the morning.

MAIDSTONE JAILOR: a tailor.

MINCE PIES: the eyes.

MOTHER AND DAUGHTER: water.

MUFFIN BAKER: a Quaker.

NAVIGATORS: taturs—vulgar pronunciation of potatoes.

NAVIGATOR SCOT: baked potatoes all hot.

NEEDLE AND THREAD: bread.

NEVER FEAR: a pint of beer.

NIGHT AND DAY: go to the play.

NOSE AND CHIN: a winn—*Ancient Cant* for a penny.

NOSE-MY: backy—vulgar pronunciation of tobacco.

OATS AND BARLEY: Charley.

OATS AND CHAFF: a footpath.

ORINOKO (pronounced ORINOKER): a poker.

OVER THE STILE: sent for trial.

PADDY QUICK: thick; or, a stick.

PEN AND INK: a stink.

PITCH AND FILL: Bill—vulgar shortening for William.

PLATE OF MEAT: a street.

PLOUGH THE DEEP: to go to sleep.

PUDDINGS AND PIES: the eyes.

READ OF TRIPE (?): transported for life.

READ AND WRITE: to fight.

READ AND WRITE: flight. – *See preceding.*

RIVER LEA: tea.

ROGUE AND VILLAIN: a shillin—common pronunciation of shilling.

RORY O'MORE: the floor.

ROUND THE HOUSES: trouses—vulgar pronunciation of trousers.

SALMON TROUT: the mouth.

SCOTCH PEG: a leg.

SHIP IN FULL SAIL: a pot of ale.

SIR WALTER SCOTT: a pot—of beer.

SLOOP OF WAR: a whore.

SNAKE IN THE GRASS: a looking glass.

SORROWFUL TALE: three months in jail.

SPLIT ASUNDER: a costermonger.

SPLIT PEA: tea.

SPORT AND WIN: Jim.

STEAM PACKET: a jacket.

ST. MARTIN'S-LE-GRAND: the hand.

STOP THIEF: beef.

SUGAR AND HONEY: money.

SUGAR CANDY: brandy.

TAKE A FRIGHT: night.

THREE QUARTERS OF A PECK: the neck—in writing, expressed by the simple "$\frac{3}{4}$."

THROW ME IN THE DIRT: a shirt.

TOMMY O'RANN: scran—vulgar term for food.

TOM TRIPE: a pipe.

TOM RIGHT: night.

TOP JINT (vulgar pronunciation of joint): a pint—of beer.

TOP OF ROME: home.

TURTLE DOVES: a pair of gloves.

TWO FOOT RULE: a fool.

WIND DO TWIRL: a fine girl.

ALPHABETICAL INDEX

CUT: to run away, move off quickly; to cease doing anything; **Cut and run**, to quit work or occupation and start off at once; to **Cut didoes**, synonymous with to **Cut capers**; **Cut a dash**, make a show; **Cut a caper**, to dance or show off in a strange manner; **Cut a figure**, to make either a good or bad appearance; **Cut out**, to excel, thus in affairs of gallantry one Adonis is said to "*cut the other out*" in the affections of the wished for lady; **Cut that!** be quiet, or stop; **Cut out of**, done out of; **Cut one's Gib**, the expression or cast of his countenance (*see* **Gib**); **To Cut one's comb**, to take down a conceited person, from the practice of cutting the combs of capons (*see* **Comb-cut**); **Cut and come again**, plenty, if one cut does not suffice, plenty remains to "come again;" **Cut up**, mortified, to criticize severely, or expose; **Cut up shines**, to play tricks; **Cut one's stick**, to be off quickly, *i.e.*, be in readiness for a journey, further elaborated into **Amputate your mahogany** (*see* **Stick**); **Cut it fat**, to exaggerate or show off in an extensive manner; to **Cut up fat**, to die, leaving a large property; **Cut under**, to undersell; **Cut your lucky**, to run off; **Cut one's cart**, to expose their tricks; **Cut an acquaintance**, to cease friendly intercourse with them.—*Cambridge. Old* **Cutte**, to say.

D

E

F

G

I

J

K

M

S

T

TAKE: to succeed, or be patronised; "do you think the new opera will **Take**?" "No, because the same company **Took** so badly under the old management;" "to **Take On**," to grieve; *Shakespere* uses the word **Taking** in this sense. To "**Take up** for anyone," to protect or defend a person; "to **Take Off**," to mimic; "to **Take** heart," to have courage; "to **Take** down a peg or two," to humiliate, or tame; "to **Take Up**," to reprove; "to **Take After**," to resemble; "to **Take In,**" to cheat or defraud, from the lodging-house keepers' advertisements, "single men **Taken in and done for**," —an engagement which is as frequently performed in a bad as a good sense; "to **Take the Field**," when said of a *General*, to commence operations against the enemy; when a *racing man* **Takes the field** he stakes his money against the favourite.

U

Y

Z

 ABBREVIATIONS

Ancient, or *Ancient English*—Whenever these terms are employed, it is meant to signify that the words to which they are attached were in respectable use in or previous to the reign of Elizabeth.

Ancient Cant—In use as a *Cant* word in or previous to the reign of Elizabeth.

East.—Used in the Eastern Counties.

Old, or *Old English*—In general use as a respectable word in or previous to the reign of Charles the Second.

Old Cant—In use as a *Cant* word in or previous to the reign of Charles II.

West.—Used in the Western Counties.

BIBLIOGRAPHY

BACCHUS AND VENUS; or, a Select Collection of near 200 of the most Witty and Diverting Songs and Catches in Love and Gallantry, with Songs in the Canting Dialect, with a Dictionary, *explaining all Burlesque and Canting Terms.*   1738

BAILEY'S (Nath.) Etymolocial English Dictionary, 2 vols, 8 vo.
                                                    1737

BARTLETT'S Dictionary of Americanisms; a Glossary of Words and Phrases colloquially used in the United States, 8 vo.
                                                    New York, 1859

BEAUMONT and FLETCHER'S Comedy of *The Beggar's bush,* 4 to, 1661, or any edition.

BULWER'S (Sir Edward Lytton) Paul Clifford.   V. D.

CAMBRIDGE. Gradus ad Cantabrigiam; or a Dictionary of Terms, Academical and Colloquial, or Cant, which are used at the University, *with Illustrations,* 12 mo.   *Camb.,* 1803

CAREW, Life and Adventures of Bamfylde Moore Carew, the King of the Beggars, *with Canting Dictionary, portrait,* 8 vo. 1791

DECKER'S (Thomas) Gulls Hornbook, 4 to.   1609

DICTIONARY of all the Cant and Flash Languages, both Ancient and Modern, 18 mo.   *Bailey,* 1790

EGAN, Grose's Classical Dictionary of the Vulgar Tongue, with the
addition of numerous Slang Phrases, edited by Pierce Egan, 8 vo.
1823

GROSE'S (Francis, generally styled *Captain*) Classical Dictionary of the
Vulgar Tongue, 8 vo.   178

HALL'S (B. H.) Collection of College Words and Customs, 12 mo.
Cambridge (U.S.) 1856

HALLIWELL'S Archaic Dictionary, 2 vol, 8 vo.   1855

HENLEY'S (John, *better known as* Orator Henley) Various Sermons and
Orations.   1719-53

HOUSEHOLD WORDS, No. 183, September 24.

JOHNSON'S (Dr. Samuel) Dictionary (the earlier editions).   V. D.

JONSON'S (Ben.) Bartholomew Fair, ii., 6.

JONSON'S (Ben.) Masque of the Gipsies Metamorphosed, 4to.
16—

L'ESTRANGE'S (Sir Roger) Works (principally translations). V. D.

MAYHEW'S (Henry) London Labour and London Poor, 3 vol, 8 vo.
1851

MAYHEW'S (Henry) Great World of London, 8 vo. 1857

NOTES AND QUERIES. The invaluable Index to this most useful
periodical may be consulted with advantage by the seeker after
etymologies of slang and *Cant* words.

PARKER'S (Geo.) Life's Painter of Variegated Characters, with a
Dictionary of Cant Language and Flash Songs, to which is added a
Dissertation on Freemasonry, *portrait*, 8 vo. 1789

PEGGE'S (Samuel) Anecdotes of the English Language, chiefly regarding
the Local Dialect of London and Environs, 8 vo.
1803-41

PICKERING'S (F.) Vocabulary, or Collection of Words and Phrases
which have been supposed to be peculiar to te United States of
America, to which is prefixed an Essay on the present state of the

English Language in the United States, 8 vo.

Boston, 1816

RANDALL'S (Jack, *the pugilist*, formerly of the *"Hole in theWall,"* Chancery lane) Diary of Proceedings at the House of Call for Genius, edited by Mr. Breakwindow, to which are added several of Mr. B.'s minor pieces, 12 mo.   1820

SWIFT'S coarser pieces abound in vulgarities and slang expressions.

THE TRIUMPH OF WIT, or Ingenuity display'd in its Perfection, being the Newest and most Useful Academy, Songs, Art of Love, *and the Mystery and Art of Canting, with Poems, Songs, &c., in the Canting Language*, 16 mo.   *J.Clarke*, 1735

WEBSTER'S (Noah) Letter to the Hon. John Pickering, on the Subject of his Vocabulary, or Collection of Words and Phrases supposed to be peculiar to the United States, 8 vo, pp. 69.

Boston, 1817

ABOUT THE EDITOR

Originally from Appleton Wisconsin, Catherine Thrush wrote and illustrated a children's novel, Quest of the Faes at the age of 18. After studying Studio Art at the College of Saint Benedict in Minnesota she moved to California and became a glass artist. In 2012 she returned to her love of writing and will soon publish her young adult historical fiction novel, Lady Blade. She currently lives in San Jose, California with her wonderful husband and their naughty cat.

Special Thanks

To my husband Tom Thrush for all his help and support, and to my brave editors, Susan Rojo and Doug Stillinger.

THANK YOU TO OUR BACKERS

Nobs

A. Harley Karen N

Dan Donahue

Lucy Geever-Conroy
and Laurence Goodby

Meowhous

Nelson

Dons

David Gaba

Doug "Gutter Blood" Stillinger

Escanor

Harriet Culver

Lord and Lady Zintak of Campbell

Patricia

Rebecca Williams

Sean

Shannon J. Casey

Wendy Pfile

Willhameena power

Swells

Anthony Anglorus

Brandon Luke

Brian and Heather Strickland

Brian 'Shining Arrow"

Chris Nelson

Christy Watchous

Clyde Lee Graham

Darren Stalder

Deb Wunder

Donna B.

Erik W. Charles

Ernest Allred

Hillery Koontz

Jennifer Milligan

Joe Parrino

Joseph Vittorelli

Judith Laik

Judy Vujas

Jules M. Vanfau

K. Maves

K.M. Braithwaite

Kita Inoru

Lev Agranovich EA

Mark Franceschini

Matt Rollefson

Michael Brost

Morten Poulsen

Ownermental

Samantha N.

Tom B

Whitcraft

CPSIA information can be obtained
at www.ICGtesting.com
Printed in the USA
FFOW03n1359080218